The Lion and the Lamb

THE LION AND THE LAMB

JOHN P. NEWPORT

BROADMAN PRESS
Nashville, Tennessee

© Copyright 1986 • Broadman Press
4213-24
ISBN: 0-8054-1324-3
Dewey Decimal Classification: 228
Subject Heading: BIBLE. N.T. REVELATION
Library of Congress Catalog Card Number: 85-29887
Printed in the United States of America

Library of Congress Cataloging-in-Publication Data

Newport, John P., 1917-
  The lion and the lamb.

  Bibliography: p.
  Includes index.
  1. Bible. N.T. Revelation—Commentaries.
I. Title.
BS2825.3.N43   1986   228'.07   85-29887
ISBN 0-8054-1324-3

To
Nicholas, Calvin, Christopher, and Sarah
(and others yet unborn), beloved grandchildren,
with hope for their future, both earthly and eternal

Preface

Why would I want to write on the Book of Revelation? My interest in this book began in a small Missouri town. First, my devout mother was fascinated by Revelation—especially as it came alive to her through the notes of the "old" *Scofield Bible*. I now have her tattered and worn copy of this Bible.

My pastor taught in a dramatic and vivid way the dispensationalist premillennial view of Revelation. The pastor and visiting evangelists often used huge dispensational charts by Larkin. At least all of this brought those of us in a provincial town into the drama of world history. We heard of how Russia, the empire of Mussolini, and the menacing ambitions of Hitler fit into the teachings of Ezekiel, Daniel, and Revelation. Mussolini and his vision of a revived Roman Empire were seen as the ten-horned beast of Revelation.

In college days, I was drawn to the experiential side of Christianity. I was caught up in the youth revival movement. In reaction to the libertinism of the era, I saw moral and spiritual renewal as a priority. This led to a call to the ministry.

In my seminary days, I continued to pursue my interest in the Bible with doctoral study in the New Testament field. My doctoral thesis was on the apocalyptic background of the messianism of the New Testament. I was introduced to the importance of the historical and cultural background in understanding Revelation. During this period there was a reaction to some of the ways in which radical dispensationalists, such as Frank Norris, used and interpreted Revelation.

After a period in the pastorate, I enrolled for Ph.D. studies at the University of Edinburgh, with additional periods of study at the Universities of Basel and Zurich in Switzerland. At Edinburgh William Manson and James Stewart strongly emphasized the covenant approach to Revelation.

At Basel University I encountered the historical premillennial view of Oscar Cullmann and Karl Ludwig Schmidt. I saw in perspective that the people whom I knew back in the United States believed and loved the Bible. However, in some cases, they reacted to extreme views and often tried to make the Bible "reasonable." In contrast, Cullmann and Schmidt were not as concerned with such problems. Their agenda was to reflect what John said in Revelation, regardless of how "reasonable" it appeared to be. I began to see in their historical premillennial approach a view which made a great deal of sense to my seeking mind.

I continued my interest in principles of biblical interpretation by writing a thesis on the nature of biblical language with special emphasis on John Calvin's doctrine of accommodation. This was the beginning of my interest in the dramatic symbolism of Revelation. Later I was to write an M.A. thesis on the unique nature of biblical language in the light of language analysis criticism.

Upon my return to the United States, I had the privilege of teaching New Testament at Baylor University and New Orleans Baptist Theological Seminary. After moving to Southwestern Baptist Theological Seminary, I was introduced to the historical premillennial approach of George Ladd and George R. Beasley-Murray. In connection with a speaking engagement in Southern California, I had a long conference with Professor Ladd of Fuller Seminary. He shared with me the reasons for his shift from the dispensational view to the historical premillennial view. Shortly after this conference with Ladd, I spent a year in Boston where I was a member of the Tremont Temple Baptist Church. There I encountered again the dispensational view and began to see it in perspective.

Also in Boston, through Amos Wilder and John Wild, I came to appreciate the literary significance of Revelation. Amos Wilder helped me realize that the literary nature of Revelation is a very important factor in a proper understanding of the book. The dramatic symbolism of Revelation has tended to issue in either a wooden literalism or a highly imaginative subjectivism. For an evangelical interpreter, there is a more appropriate way which properly understands the reality behind the highly symbolic language.

Professor Wilder also emphasized that the dramatic language, the play of symbols, and the communication of John in Revelation are all anchored in and controlled by a personal and historical realism. John's empirical reality is identified with the actuality of the early

New Testament churches and their ordeal. In the original setting of Revelation, John urged the churches to carry on in spite of the terrors of martyrdom and the prevalence of heresy. To do this John marshaled his tremendous spectrum of language. His total constellation of language came out of a world orientation founded in faith and history. Thus Revelation is a dynamic "word" grounded in and wedded to actuality.

Wilder quoted with agreement a contemporary author who stated that Revelation is our best guide for viewing and understanding the contemporary human condition. Revelation gives us a large and flexible dramatic form that is grand enough to allow a full expression of our agonies and aspirations. It is responsive to the major cataclysms of twentieth-century life and death. The purveyors of florid extremism should not blind us to the healthy function of Revelation.

For Wilder, Revelation projected a universal view of history which included all people and all times. It took history with utter seriousness. It confronted the seemingly total disaster of the present and assigned meaning and hope to it in terms of the wider cosmic drama. The symbols, motifs, and styles, which might strike us as fantastic, spoke effectively to the consciousness and lives of the early Christians. Adela Yarbro Collins and Elisabeth Fiorenza have also been helpful in their extensive writings on Revelation from sociological, psychological, and literary perspectives.

A visit with Dan Fuller, professor at Fuller Theological Seminary, was very helpful. He told of his own personal pilgrimage from the dispensational view to historical premillennialism. This change came primarily as a result of his intensive study of Romans 9—11. My colleague, the respected New Testament scholar, Curtis Vaughn, alerted me to a similar change to historical premillennialism by Alan Johnson of Wheaton College. I have profited greatly from Johnson's writings.

My continuing interest in the debate over the Bible and eschatology led to my book *Why Christians Fight Over the Bible*. This, in turn, led to being invited to participate in a nationally televised dialogue with Hal Lindsey on "Biblical Prophecy Today." Hundreds of letters came to me as a result of this program. This alerted me again to the widespread interest in Revelation.

During my teaching tenure at Rice University in Houston, Texas, I continued to teach Revelation in churches of many denominations. I also conducted Doctor of Ministry seminars on Revelation for Southwestern Seminary. In Houston, I attended the lectures of R. B. Thieme and saw what for me were disturbing implications of his version of dispensationalism. During this period, I lectured on cruise ships in the Mediterranean where we conducted "prophecy conferences." The continuing interest of lay people in prophecy was quite evident on these cruises.

Returning to Southwestern Seminary, I continued my interest in Revelation in terms of teaching and study. I attended the National Conference on Inerrancy in San Diego, California. I noted with interest that it was clearly stated there that a person's view of the interpretation of Revelation was not to be seen as a test of orthodoxy.

However, as my study continued, I found myself more and more becoming sympathetic with the historical premillennial view. I felt that this view was more in keeping with a conservative view of the Bible properly interpreted. Because of this interest, I was asked by Broadman Press to write a book presenting the historical-premillennial view of Revelation in semipopular fashion. It was to be one of a series of three books elaborating different views of Revelation.

I seek to be very frank about my reasons for holding the historical-premillennial or covenant-premillennial view. This does not mean that I want in any way to disparage the dispensational view of my mother and other friends who sincerely hold this view. I also treasure the friendship of many friends and colleagues who hold the amillennial view. I have less appreciation for those who adopt a view for its apparent popular appeal as the "in" approach.

I realize that my ideas about what the Bible (including the Book of Revelation) teaches do not come entirely from my ability to objectively interpret the Bible. I affirm unreservedly the total authority of the Bible (including Revelation) for Christian faith and practice. I do not approach the Bible with prior humanistic assumptions. If this is true, why should my interpretation of Revelation be different from another equally devoted Christian (such as my mother). Obviously, each of us brings to the Bible conscious or subconscious preferences which influence the understanding of the Bible into a particular direction. We need to develop an awareness of how our approach to Revelation is affected by preunderstanding.

Very important in bringing my biases to the surface is my personal pilgrimage, including dominant influences in the past and the anxieties and challenges of the present. The same is true for most interpreters prominent on the Christian scene. Each forms his or her approach to the Bible with some reference to personal psychohistory. We need to seek a greater personal understanding of our own biases. Such an awareness is important to the proper interpretation of Revelation. We need to free ourselves of the bondage of wanting to please ourselves and others at the expense of truth.

As Christian believers, we do not walk alone in this task. The Spirit of truth lives within our lives. In this fellowship, we can progressively move beyond subjective distortions in interpretation and know the joy of being set free by God's truth.

I hope that this study will not separate Christians but rather will keep open the dialogue concerning the proper way to interpret Revelation. For many of us, the search for the best way to interpret and apply the Bible is central in our lives and ministries.

As for the nature of this book, it seeks to appeal to a broad variety of readers. It combines the historical, prophetic, theological, devotional, and practical approaches. I have also used some of the newer literary, psychological, and sociological approaches as aids to understanding this important book. I hope the book can be a springboard for personal and group study of Revelation, as well as a tool for teachers and pastors.

To acknowledge all who have helped in the preparation of this book would be impossible. New insights and much helpful material have come from doctoral seminars at Southwestern Seminary and Rice University and a masters level course at Southwestern Seminary at Houston.

The reception of popular presentations of the Book of Revelation at various churches, especially the Park Cities Baptist Church, Dallas; First Presbyterian Church, Houston; and St. John's Episcopal Church, Houston, have been very encouraging.

At Southwestern Seminary, I am indebted to Norma Haynes, my administrative associate, and Susan Ingouf, my research assistant. Bruce Corley, associate professor of New Testament, has read the manuscript carefully and made many valuable comments. And I am most indebted to my wife, Eddie Belle, without whose help and encouragement this book could not have been written.

Contents

2. You should understand the distinct and dominant literary types of forms used in Revelation which are apocalypse, prophecy, and letter.
3. You should know about the personal and social identity of the author of Revelation.
4. You should know about the date of the writing of Revelation.
5. You should know how Revelation became a part of the New Testament canon.
6. You should know about the purpose of Revelation.

1. Revelation is primarily for the encouragement of first-century Christians. This is called the preterist, historical background or contemporary-historical view.
2. Revelation portrays in a symbolic way truths for each age and for the end of history. This is known as the amillennial view.
3. Revelation is primarily a forecast of the development of history. This is called the historicist or continuous-historical view.
4. Revelation is a forecast of Christian triumph in history before the second coming of Christ. This method is known as postmillennialism.
5. Revelation is primarily a statement of eternal theological principles. This is also called the symbolical or idealist or spiritualist principles view.
6. Revelation is primarily a forecast of the very last days of history. This is known as the extreme futurist or dispensational premillennial view.
7. Revelation was written to encourage, inform, and challenge first-century Christians and Christians in every generation. Furthermore, it teaches eternal theological principles and por-

trays the last days of history and beyond. This view is known as the combination approach, the synthesis view, the prophetic-apocalyptic perspective, the moderate futurist view, and historical-premillennial approach. It is also called covenant-premillennialism.

1. Prologue and John's vision (chs. 1—2)

2. Letters to the seven churches (chs. 2—3)

3. Vision of heaven and the dominant theme (chs. 4—5)

4. The dynamics of history (ch. 6)

5. The first interlude—encouragement of the church (ch. 7)

6. The seven trumpet judgments (chs. 8—9)

7. The second interlude—call to witness (chs. 10—11)

8. The third interlude—Satan's defeat and activity (chs. 12—14)

9. The vengeance of Babylon (chs. 13—14)

10. The seven bowl judgments, the return of Christ, the millennium, and the final state (chs. 15—22)

1. A vivid sense of the majesty of God and the centrality of Jesus Christ who triumphed through His vicarious sacrifice

2. A realistic statement of the reality and power of evil

3. A strong implication that the Christian churches should take a stand against collective forces of evil

4. The truth of the doctrine of the Antichrist

5. Portrayal of the church as embattled

6. An emphasis on the fact that suffering in the world is the reverse side of fellowship with Christ in glory
7. Strong emphasis on worship
8. An emphasis on the fact that history is linear and not cyclical and is moving toward the divine destiny
9. A strong emphasis on judgment
10. An important emphasis on the separation of true from false belief
11. Implications for political perspective, Christian social action, and Christian humanization
12. Assurance of triumph
13. The emphasis on a Christian philosophy of the meaning of history

    1. God, Jesus Christ, the angel, and the source of the book (1:1)
    2. Nature of the contents of the book (1:2)
    3. The happiness of blessedness which results from understanding the nature of prophecy, the importance of obedience, and the foreshortened future (1:3)

Excursus on the Foreshortened Future

    1. The significance of the seven churches
    2. The blessing from the Trinity

    1. The present and future victory in Christ
    2. The present and future priesthood in Christ's kingdom (1:6)

    1. The nature of Christ's return
    2. The responsibility for the crucifixion of Christ
    3. The rapture or "catching up" of the church

Introduction

Why Is There a Continuing Interest
in the Book of Revelation?

Interest in Revelation has exploded in recent years for both biblical scholars and lay Bible readers. What is the attraction of this complex, often strange writing which seems so far removed from the modern world of science and technology? Why this interest?

1. Because Some People Claim that Revelation Speaks to the Sense of Cosmic Crisis in Our Culture

In the 1950s and 1960s, the well-known French writer Albert Camus portrayed man's life as absurd in such novels as *The Stranger, The Plague,* and *The Fall.* Samuel Beckett, the Nobel prize winning dramatist, wrote *Waiting for Godot.* This play states that there is no Easter after Good Friday. These literary artists raised the question "Does my personal life have any meaning?"

In the 1980s the futurists have come front stage. Nuclear power, environmental pollution, the population explosion, and the withering away of natural resources confront us with the possibility of the end of the world as we now know it. Movies such as *Apocalypse Now* and books such as *America's Decision: Who Will Survive?* cause us to talk about lifeboat ethics. The present cultural climate is "apocalyptic" or concerned with last things. For many, the destruction of all life seems to be near. There is a cosmic crisis. We have serious doubts about whether technological progress and the military-industrial complex can control the future. In his article on "Psychology and Armageddon," Harvard Professor Robert Coles described a vivid worldwide feeling that mankind is headed for its Armageddon.

This concern opened the door for the unprecedented sale of Hal Lindsey's *The Late Great Planet Earth, Countdown to Armageddon, The*

Terminal Generation, and *There's a New World Coming.* These and similar writings on Revelation claim to give people, in disarray about a world gone out of control, a handle on the future in the name of Christian prophecy.[1]

Evangelical churches should do more than criticize Hal Lindsey and his method of interpretation. They should note his ability to read the signs of the times. In a more responsible way, they should respond to the fears and hopes of ordinary people today. Authentic biblical teachings on last things should be presented clearly.[2]

2. Because Some People Claim that Revelation Provides a Forecast and Explanation for Certain Contemporary Developments

Judeo-Christian history has seen many periods of interest in predictive prophecy, usually in times of social upheaval. The present period seems to have more interest in "last things" than other periods have had. Hundreds of ministers and laypeople predict with confidence that contemporary events are an immediate prelude to the last days of history.

Jerry Falwell, Pat Robertson, Rex Humbard, Oral Roberts, Kenneth Copeland, and Jack Van Impe share these "last days" predictions with millions by television. The predictions are updated regularly in periodicals, such as *Bible in the News, Bible Prophecy Newsletter,* and the *Endtime Messenger.* Films, plays, hymns, gospel songs, and bumper stickers carry the message.

Hal Lindsey's successful prophecy books led the *New York Times* to name Lindsey as the best-selling author of the decade of the 1970s. In fact, Lindsey scored the most stunning literary success in American religious history. By 1981 he had sold 18 million copies of *The Late Great Planet Earth.* It is still selling at the rate of 20,000 a month. It has been translated into thirty-one languages and has been made into a commercial film. In the 1970s Lindsey wrote five other books. The combined sales of the author's prophetic interpretations during the decade reached some 30 million copies. He continues to publish and update his predictions. In the 1970s, I had a dialogue with Hal Lindsey on "Biblical Prophecy Today" on the ABC national television network.

A native of Houston, Lindsey received his biblical training at Dallas Theological Seminary. The influence of Dallas Seminary on Lindsey remains strong. His basic interpretative ideas can be found in a more scholarly and subdued form in the writings of J. Dwight Pentecost and John F. Walvoord. Basically Lindsey's writings are an application of dispensational premillennial teachings to current events.[3]

What are some of the developments or signs which dispensational premillennialists see forecast and explained in the Bible in general and in Revelation in particular?

a. A FIRST DEVELOPMENT IS THE RETURN OF ISRAEL

Two generations before Zionism emerged, dispensational premillennialists insisted that the one prologue to the very last days would be the return of the Jewish people to the Holy Land. The 1917 Balfour Declaration, which permitted the Jews to settle in Palestine, was widely seen as the fulfillment of Jeremiah 29:14: "I will bring you back to the place from which I sent you into exile." When Israel was founded in 1948, Hal Lindsey proclaimed that "the prophetic countdown began. We are living in the terminal generation."[4]

Israel is God's clock. Hal Lindsey will admit that we cannot know the day and the hour but that we can know the generation when the end will come. Matthew 24:34 teaches that "this generation" means the generation in which it first begins to be recognized that we are living in the last days. This is the generation which sees Israel (the fig tree of Matt. 24:32) back in the land of Palestine. This is the chief sign. The fig tree has been a historic symbol of national Israel. A biblical generation may be somewhere between sixty and eighty years. The state of Israel was established in 1948. Many world leaders, says Lindsey, are pointing to the 1980s as the end. For Lindsey, the "last days" of history must certainly take place before the year 2000.[5]

The return of Israel thus determines the generation when Christ will return to earth. First, He will rapture believers from the great tribulation. Seven years later He will judge unbelievers and establish the earthly messianic kingdom. Thus it is possible to claim that the next to final apocalyptic events mentioned in Matthew 24 will all occur within the generation following 1948. The return of Israel has been the most important catalyst of the current boom in prophecy studies.[6]

The chief problem was that Israel was supposed to be in control of Jerusalem as well. Israel's capture of Old Jerusalem in 1967 at the end of the "Six-Day War" was seen as crucially significant. Lindsey states that this event made theoretically possible the rebuilding of the Temple on its original site. This rebuilding is a long-established requirement of many dispensationalists. The Antichrist will make his headquarters there just before the last coming of Jesus.[7]

b. A SECOND DEVELOPMENT IS THE POSSIBILITY AND EVEN IMMI-NENCE OF WORLDWIDE DESTRUCTION

Scientists are stating that the discovery of nuclear fission could bring about the destruction of the civilized world. This is seen as forecast in Revelation 8:7-13.[8]

Dispensational writers see Revelation as predicting famines produced by population explosion, growing frequency of earthquakes (Rev. 16:18), and wars and rumors of wars. Other related signs foretold in Revelation include loss of respect for law and government and widespread terrorism. Widespread abortion, disposal of the newborn children in trash bags, putting children up for adoption, and continual child abuse are the results of the predicted breakup of the biblical family structure.[9]

c. A THIRD DEVELOPMENT IS THE RISE OF APOSTASY AND THE WORLD CHURCH MOVEMENT

The biblical prediction found in Revelation 17—18 is seen as being fulfilled in the establishment of councils of churches, interfaith movements, and religious eclecticism. These groups require either the dilution or "watering down" of orthodox biblical doctrine or its denial. Lindsey calls this development the appearance of "Scarlot O'Harlot."[10]

d. A FOURTH DEVELOPMENT IS THE RISE OF BIZARRE NEW RELIGIOUS SECTS AND LEADERS

There is a growth of interest in the occult and satanology. This is seen as predicted in Revelation 19 as a preparation for the appearance of the "false prophet" (v. 20) who will lead many into Satan's false religious system.[11]

e. A FIFTH DEVELOPMENT IS THE RISE OF WORLD GOVERNMENT

According to the dispensational view, Revelation 13 and 17 predict that in the last days a world ruler or beast will have economic and political control over the entire world (Rev. 13:11-18). For this to happen there must be the right developments.

A century ago, John Walvoord states, a world government would have been impossible. Now it is possible with rapid transportation. Furthermore, rapid communication enables a world leader to communicate with the entire world via satellite television. A bank of computers can control the financial transactions of the entire world.

The Satan-supported charismatic czar can thus institute and enforce a political and economic dictatorship. Buying or selling will be impossible without his authorization, symbolized by some form of 666 on the hand or forehead (Rev. 13:18). In a cashless and checkless society, economic transactions will require that each person be assigned a number consisting of three sets of six digits, to be invisibly tattooed on our hands or foreheads. The laser-read computer code (already used in supermarkets) makes possible a total control by the beast as explained in Revelation. [12]

Mary Relfe claims that Revelation explains the use of 666 in Israel as a prefix for Arab-owned vehicles, overseas telephone calls, and national lottery. This is part of an effort to educate, prepare, and condition the Jews to accept 666. It is the number of the false messiah (the Antichrist) and his world government system.[13]

John Walvoord contends that the oil resources of the Middle East will enable the ruler or beast to have sufficient power, wealth, and political control to set up a world government. With the formation of OPEC there was a flow of billions of dollars into the oil-producing areas. The fact that this power will run out in twenty-five or thirty years because of oil depletion shows that we are in the "last days."[14]

f. A SIXTH DEVELOPMENT IS THE RISE OF THE EUROPEAN COMMON MARKET AND A REVIVED ROMAN EMPIRE

Revelation 17:12-13,17 and the Book of Daniel predict that the Roman Empire will be restored in the time of the end, in a ten-kingdom form. This explains the rise of the European Common Market. When the tenth nation was admitted, it was possible for the first time since the collapse of the Holy Roman Empire to see the last days emerging.[15] This confederation will serve as the power base for the Antichrist of the last days. Already the giant computer complex of the Common Market is nicknamed "The Beast."[16]

In all fairness, we must say that some dispensational premillennial scholars deplore attempts to be overspecific on Revelation predictions. However, even if these overstatements are granted, dispensational leaders, such as John Walvoord, affirm that most of the graphic signs which have been listed are predicted and explained by Revelation. This means that the last days or end time and the rapture of the true church are near.[17]

3. Because of the Many References to Revelation in Contemporary Politics, Television, Literature, and Films

In the American elections of the 1980s John's apocalyptic vision of the "end times" emerged as a political issue. In national television presidential debates President Reagan was asked about Armageddon.[18]

Hal Lindsey's popularity is only the most visible example of the successful marketing of dispensational premillennialism in the 1970s and 1980s. Pat Robertson's "700 Club" television program and his newsletter are laced with references to the "last days." The "700 Club" has increasingly become a sophisticated news and interview program spiced with prophetic insights.[19]

Hal Lindsey is the most visible of the modern dispensational popularizers. However, there are thousands of others, each with his own version of the end-time scenario. Most members of fundamentalist churches are taught regularly by the local pastor on the intricacies of Revelation and dispensationalism. Almost any young person at a fundamentalist Christian school can talk knowledgeably about the rapture, pretribulationism, and Armageddon. Scores of books and tracts supporting particular interpretations of the signs of the times have sold millions of copies. Charles Anderson's "Rapture Painting" pictures autos colliding, planes crashing, and spirits ascending from graves. It is marketed by Independent Baptist Leon Bates and his Bible Believers Evangelical Association Incorporated. He sold nearly thirty thousand prints in 1980. The postcard form of his painting has sold about one million copies.[20]

Perhaps the most influential charismatic "end time" prophet has been David Wilkerson who rose to fame in the 1950s after writing *The Cross and the Switchblade*. In 1973 Wilkerson published his version of the coming world doom in *The Vision*. Wilkerson's "vision" gave him a glimpse of the future which coincided with dispensational beliefs.

Wilkerson's vision stressed the moral decline of America as a sign of the coming of Christ. Evidences of this predicted moral decline are many: toplessness on television; sex education in senior high schools and colleges; portrayal of the sex act in films; leadership of homosexuals and lesbians in churches; nude dancing in the church; and a growing hatred between children and parents.[21]

In a unique interpretive twist Wilkerson revealed that the flash point of judgment occurred when Americans landed on the moon—an act which assailed the dignity of God. Since that day irreversible moral calamity has set in.[22]

References to Revelation are widespread in secular literature and films. *Armageddon* is the title of a novel by Leon Uris about post-World War II Germany. A widely circulated book on nuclear war strategy is called *The Wizards of Armageddon*. The *London Times* featured an article entitled "The Shadow of Armageddon."

The Seventh Seal is the name of a motion picture directed by Ingmar Bergman on the subject of human mortality. *Apocalypse Now* is the title of a film directed by Francis Ford Coppola on the Vietnam War. All of these titles have their origin in the dramatic symbols of Revelation.[23]

Why Is It Important to Study the Text and the Methods of Interpreting Revelation?

1. In Order to Rescue Revelation from Extreme, One-sided, and Distorted Interpretations

As we have seen, many overspecific and even fantastic predictions have been made in the name of Revelation. Jacques Ellul states that the Book of Revelation has provoked delirium, foolishness, and irrational statements with little relationship to Jesus Christ.[24] Of course, this is not new. Even in the second century, based on their study of Revelation, a group of Montanists retreated to the Phrygian wilderness to see the heavenly Jerusalem descend out of heaven.[25]

Because of such speculative use of texts from Revelation, some Christians have been frightened away from this important book. They write off both the book and its interpreters as a lost cause.[26]

Revelation deserves another look. Serious study is important to show that John's visions, dreams, and revelations are not meant to confuse or confound us. The very word *apocalypse* or *revelation* means to remove the veil, to reveal, and to make clear. John warned us of the coming judgment and of Christ's triumph over evil. John also called us to repentance and faith and action. He declared a mes-

sage for the present as well as for the future. Revelation is also a
pastor's letter to help us in the battle with Satan and to give us personal power. It has a warning and wisdom and a vision. It is an
important book.[27]

2. In Order to Identify and Evaluate the Presuppositions of the Most Widely Held Methods of Interpreting Revelation

According to Robert Clouse, John Walvoord, president of Dallas
Theological Seminary, is the foremost American dispensational
theologian.[28] Walvoord recently explained that the distinctive work
of his school was to train in "expository ministry." He continued:
"An expository ministry is based on what the Bible says. . . . An
expository preacher subjects his ideas to those of the Bible; he does
not subject the Bible to his ideas." In short, argue its supporters,
dispensational premillennialism is the natural product of rigid
open-minded Bible study. Those who reject the theory, wrote John
R. Rice, "do not know what the Bible teaches. They have never entered into the verse-by-verse, chapter-by-chapter, book-by-book
study of the prophecies of the Old Testament and the New."[29]

Dispensational premillennialists are coming to the assumption
that all other views of Revelation are "unbiblical." This assumption
has encouraged fundamentalist separatism. It has undermined creative dialogue between dispensationalism and other schools of prophetic interpretation.[30]

James M. Gray, an early popular teacher of dispensational premillennialism, stated that the inductive method of Bible study which
led to this view eliminated personal bias and provided a foundation
on which to build interpretation. Timothy Weber of Denver Conservative Baptist Seminary, disagrees with Gray. For Weber, in subtle and rather ironic ways, the dispensationalist use of the Bible is
not what it seems.[31]

For one thing, despite the claims that laypeople could study the
Bible for themselves, dispensationalist teachers rarely let them.
Gray, for instance, said that students must first see the Scriptures as
a whole. He really meant that they should view the Bible in dispensational terms. The modern dispensational movement originated in
Great Britain in the 1830s, spreading to America through various
means, including the *Scofield Reference Bible*. The movement developed as an intricate hermeneutic which "rightly divides the word

of truth" into different periods and divine programs and then re-joins them in a complicated way. In 1913 Gray told his students, "Get the whole Bible . . . in its dispensational relations and then you can study it . . . to your heart's content." When he finally published his own synthetic Bible studies everything was arranged in a full-blown dispensational system.[32]

Today, according to Weber, dispensational premillennialists are convinced that their method provides a superior perspective from which to study the Bible. They often claim that nondispensation-alists are incapable of seeing the Scriptures in their fullness. Accord-ing to I. M. Haldeman, "Unless (the Bible student) understands dis-pensational truth he will never fully lay hold of Bible doctrine."[33]

Weber concludes that few people would deny dispensationalists the privilege of reading the Bible in their terms if they are so in-clined. But most would deny that they are being *inductive* when they do this. Whatever may be said for the strengths of a dispensational hermeneutic, the system is anything but inductive. How many stu-dents using purely inductive methods would conclude that the Lord's Prayer and the Sermon on the Mount were intended for the Jews in the millennium and not for Christians in this age? Most peo-ple require extensive persuasion to arrive at such conclusions.[34]

Ironically, dispensational teachers make their students dependent on them for their biblical literacy. Since most laypeople cannot arrive at a dispensational understanding of the Bible on their own, they have to rely on their instructors to unravel the intricacies of the sys-tem. Leaders assure common Christians that they do not need scholarly help in Bible study. However, these teachers then initiate the laypeople into a complicated system that most people could never arrive at without considerable assistance.[35]

In the discussion of other methods of interpreting Revelation, I will identify and evaluate the presuppositions behind these meth-ods. I will also note some of the weaknesses, strengths, and implica-tions of each method.

3. In Order to Point Out the Personal and Social Implications of Representative Methods of Interpreting Revelation

It should be helpful to note the social and political as well as per-sonal implications of postmillennial, dispensational premillennial, and liberal views of Revelation.

a. IMPLICATIONS OF THE POSTMILLENNIAL VIEW

Postmillennialism teaches that the earth shall have in time, through the preaching and living of Christianity, an extended period of righteousness and peace called the "millennium." As the millennium becomes a reality, Christian principles of belief and conduct will become the accepted standard for nations and individuals. Sin will not be eliminated but it will be reduced to a minimum. Political, economic, social, and cultural life will be greatly improved. There will be generally prosperous conditions throughout the world. Wealth will be more widely shared. Nations formerly opposed to one another will work together harmoniously. This golden age of spiritual prosperity will last for a long period of time, probably much longer than a literal thousand years.[36]

Postmillennialism has been widely held from the fifth century AD until recent years. Despite setbacks, it is still held by some. It has had a strong influence. It encourages activism. It promotes a spirit of optimism, confidence, and expectation which is important to success. Furthermore, it combats the spirit of fatalism for this present era that characterizes some dispensational premillennialism.[37]

Significant work by American historians has shown that postmillennialism had a great deal to do with America's unique development.[38] According to S. K. Johannesen, postmillennialism did not allow the United States to see itself as a part of a deteriorating cycle of history. Instead, this view taught that all of the institutions should see themselves as God-ordained American vessels to strengthen moral life. God was working in America to shape the millennium to come.[39]

The colonial expansion of England into the New World must be understood in this light. The Puritan venture in Massachusetts Bay was a self-conscious effort to realize the millennial hope. England had failed in the providential role assigned to her. Therefore, an experiment had to be carried out in the New World to show that a godly people, bound in covenant, could show the way and carry the method back to England. The method by which this hope was sustained was biblical typology. The experience and the messianic hope of Israel and the church were transferred to the Massachusetts Commonwealth. The expectation was that this experiment was to be only the opening episode in the renewal of nationhood and the coming of Christ's kingdom on earth.[40]

Postmillennial language was seen as the proper language of piety by Isaac Watts, the English lyric poet of religious hymns. Watts's hymns are filled with references to "nation"; to the coming triumph of Christ's kingdom; and to the witness of saints now dead to the emerging kingdom of God. Oftentimes his last stanzas point forward, as do the second and last lines in his couplets, to an assurance of a blessed future.[41]

Jonathan Edwards, one of America's greatest minds, believed that a dispensation of divine providence had opened in New England with the Great Awakening. Samuel Hopkins took this one step further, arguing that slavery was not an institution compatible with millennial expectation. The millennium is the end for which the conquering of time in the civic life of men is important. In fact, a population whose moral community is structured in hope and patience is prepared to believe it can solve the ancient problems of luxury and corruption.[42]

But, unlike some dispensationalists, Jonathan Edwards did not say that his vision of a millennium was a deterministic vision. What Edwards achieved was a demonstration of the paradox that election is finally a form of voluntary association. For where the heart leads, he argued, the will necessarily follows and is indeed identical with the wish. When the distance between heart and will is destroyed, the opposition between them is destroyed. We should not use the word *involuntary*. This brilliant teaching allowed Christians to conceive of America as an elect nation at the same time that they affirmed that Americans were free.[43]

Postmillennialism has had a tremendous influence in the history of the United States. Many feel that some of its emphases are needed today.

b. IMPLICATIONS OF THE DISPENSATIONAL PREMILLENNIAL METHOD
(1) Theoretical implications

The Christic Institute, a religious research and action agency, has cited eleven public and private utterances by President Reagan on the possible imminence of Armageddon. These statements, the Christic group concludes, imply that reconciliation with America's adversaries is ultimately futile.[44]

Reagan indicated that he had chatted with people about the biblical prophecies of the coming of Armageddon. He also noted that a number of theologians for the last decade or more have believed that the prophecies about Armageddon are coming together at this time.[45]

Hal Lindsey sees specific political events which signal the "countdown to Armageddon." The establishment of Israel, states Lindsey, calls for a realignment of nations into four spheres of political power. Each sphere will be judged and destroyed for invading the new state of Israel. The first of these prophetic coalitions (the kings of the south) will be fulfilled by an Arab alliance. The three great perils of the Middle East are the power of oil, the power of Islam, and the power of Russia.[46]

The young nation of Israel will soon feel the full wave of attack by the Soviet Union. Russia is the "Gog" nation of prophecy. This great northern enemy will form an alliance with the Arabs only to betray them almost immediately and then invade Israel.[47]

The third confederation of nations, "the kings of the east," is headed by China. The army from the East will wreak incredible havoc once the end-times sequence begins. It will wipe out a third of the earth's population in a thermonuclear attack. China's rise to an executioner's role, like the growth of Soviet power, is being accomplished with the misguided aid of the United States. Soft-headed liberalism is hastening the end-times disaster.[48]

Lindsey has sold a lot of books, and he has discussed his ideas with thousands of people in the past two decades. He has found some remarkable allies. At the publication of *The Late Great Planet Earth*, Lindsey was invited to speak at the American Air War College. He said that "to my surprise the audience responded to the message with enthusiastic ovation." One year later he spoke at the Pentagon to "hundreds of people jamming the room." After his talk, he revealed that "one officer told me that various Pentagon officials had independently come to the same conclusion I had reached regarding the future of the Middle East."[49]

Dispensationalism particularly seems to confirm or even encourage the pessimistic and conspiratorial foreign policy views of American conservatives. The major fears of some are prophetically confirmed. This includes the reduced influence of the United States, the brooding evil of Communist Russia and China, the growth of Arab influence and the spread of Communism in black Africa. Dispensational leaders tend to sanction support of such right wing favorites as Nationalist China and the Republic of South Africa.[50]

William Martin has asked, "What would happen if the President were to appoint one or more dispensational premillennialists to key foreign-policy posts?" What incentive would they have to work for lasting peace in the Middle East since they would regard a Russian-led attack on Israel as a necessary precursor of the millennium? What stance would they assume toward the Tri-Lateral Commission and the Council on Foreign Relations, both of which are viewed as major engines of the one-world Antichrist conspiracy? If the nuclear destruction of Russia is foreordained, as it is in some dispensational schemes, might not a fundamentalist politician or general regard his finger on the button as an instrument of God's eternal purpose?[51]

(2) Practical implications

The most important practical result of dispensational premillennialism has been its support of a rigid pro-Israel stance by some leaders of the new religious-political right. Dispensational premillennialists have been some of the strongest supporters of Zionism and the state of Israel in recent history. Doctrinally, the matter of Israel is simple. God had promised Abraham the land of Canaan for an everlasting possession of his seed. The biblical regathering which was mentioned many times in the Old Testament has taken place in our time. Once the nation of Israel was established "the prophetic puzzle . . . started to come together with amazing speed."[52]

For Jerry Falwell, the dispensational vision of Israel is significant. Although Falwell insists that the Moral Majority is nonreligious, the organization is militantly pro-Israel. Any who do not support Israel, Falwell recently wrote, "are inviting the judgment of God upon themselves." Falwell and other dispensationalist leaders addressed a letter to former Prime Minister Begin stating that "on theological and historical grounds we proclaim that the land of Israel encompasses Judea and Samaria as integral parts of the Jewish patrimony with Jerusalem its one indivisible capital."[53]

According to Mouw, dispensationalists often view God's dealings with Israel in such a way as to imply Christians have no business criticizing the current policies of the Israeli government. This attitude is very different from that which we see in the biblical writers. Whatever the Old Testament prophets had in mind when they articulated the vision of a glorious future for Israel, they were not afraid to criticize Israel. In fact, they often denounced policies and practices with a righteous wrath. Unlike the dispensationalists, biblical prophets did not allow their convictions concerning Israel's future to dull their critical sensitivities with respect to Israel's activities.[54]

c. IMPLICATIONS OF A LIBERAL VIEW WHICH MINIMIZES OR EVEN DE-NIES THE IMMINENT RETURN OF CHRIST, THE FINAL JUDGEMENT, AND THE NEW HEAVEN AND THE NEW EARTH

Under the influence of Origen and Augustine, future eschatology was made to refer either to the spiritual journey of the believer or to the church as the kingdom of God on earth. The impact of this spiritualizing process and the distaste for the apocalyptic speculations of sectarian groups have had a great influence. They have contributed to the overwhelmingly negative estimate of "last things" by biblical and theological scholarship since the Enlightenment of the eighteenth century.[55]

In the nineteenth century, apocalyptic was removed from Paul's thought as an ornamental husk. This was followed in the twentieth century by Rudolf Bultmann. He translated Paul's apocalyptic into existential categories. Paul's writings were directed to the authentic existence of persons in the present. Once future eschatology moved out of the mainstream of church life, it was taken over by extreme movements that proved to be an embarrassment to the truth of the gospel.[56]

In contrast to these liberal views, Revelation teaches that the future involves a definitive closure/completion event in time and space. History is not just an open-ended process. Revelation is opposed to those interpreters who exchange the biblical teaching about a specific end of history for a vague philosophical argument about God as futurity, that is as "always one who comes."[57]

A life of hope is only real when it is anchored in the coming actualization of God's triumph. Is it not also true that the surrender of the biblical teaching about the second coming also causes one to lose the compelling and beckoning power of God's final trial for ethics?[58]

Without a future second coming of Christ, a resurrection of the dead, a final judgment, and a real heaven, there is no ultimate solution to the problem of evil and suffering in the world. The coming triumph of God in Christ offers an ultimate resolution of the contradictions and sufferings of life.

4. In Order to Answer Those Who Contend that Revelation Is Sub-Christian or Less than Christian or Is a Christianized Judaism

From earliest times, some people have contended that certain theological emphases in Revelation are unworthy and sub-Christian. The critics call the cry for vengeance (Rev. 6:10) a "weakly Christianized Judaism." They see Revelation as full of divine revenge and fierce wrath and lacking enough emphasis on God's love and grace.[59]

George R. Beasley-Murray answers the critics. He points out the basic difference in John's views from standard Jewish apocalyptic thought.[60] R. H. Charles states that even though Revelation utilizes many Jewish categories, it is distinctly Christian. In Revelation 5, for example, the redemptive acts of Christ, the Lamb of God, constitute the turn of the ages.

H. B. Swete agrees that the emphasis on judgment in Revelation is more intense and prolonged than in any other New Testament writing. But this emphasis is called for by the nature of John's situation and the prospect which he believed the church of his time faced. In fact, Carl Jung commends John for portraying the judgment side of God which is usually repressed.[61]

Like Swete, many devout scholars now affirm that Revelation is the crown of the Bible. It should be read in conjunction with the other New Testament books. In fact, the other books are incomplete without Revelation.

5. In Order to Establish a Balanced Interpretation of Revelation to Fill the Need for Teaching on "Last Things" in the Main-line Churches

Respectable theologies of main-line churches have continously dismissed last things from their own agendas. This silence has left a vacuum that the neoapocalyptic movement now fills. The popularity of Lindsey's apocalyptic scheme should not only stir us to a correction but also motivate us to a new and positive statement. A balanced view of Revelation corresponds with the truth of the gospel and promises to give the gospel new power among us.[62]

Revelation is not an escapist book. Its apocalyptic categories focus on our present decisions as well as those in the future. Revelation does this because it teaches the motivating and beckoning power of God's final triumph in the second coming of Christ. Revelation opens up to us the horizon of a vision and a hope.[63]

6. In Order to Appropriate Valid Features of Representative Methods of Interpreting Revelation and to Avoid Their Weaknesses

Gordon Fee states that it is necessary to say at the outset of any serious study that no one should approach Revelation without a proper degree of humility. There are already too many books on "Revelation made easy." But Revelation is not easy![64]

We also need to be less than dogmatic. This is true since we will consider at least seven major methods of interpretation, not to mention significant variations within each of the methods. Each method has some strength and value.[65]

The approach which I advocate can be called the combination approach, the synthesis view, the prophetic-apocalyptic perspective, the moderate futurist emphasis, or the historical premillennial method. It will start with a commitment to the truthfulness and inspiration of the text. It will take into consideration the historical, political, economic, and psychological backgrounds of Revelation. An accurate understanding of the "world behind" Revelation is important for an appropriate appreciation of the "world" created by the text itself.[66] Reconstructing the author's intention is not a complete explanation of a biblical book. However, it is essential because it helps distinguish merely possible meanings from probable meanings of the text.[67]

What Do You Need to Know to Understand the Book of Revelation?

1. You Should Understand Its Literary, Dramatic, and Symbolic Nature

For a number of years, I have attended the national meetings of the Society of Biblical Literature and the American Academy of Religion. During these years, I have seen a revolution in the study of the Bible. An important part of this revolution is the contribution which has come to biblical interpreters from the scholars who specialize in understanding imaginative and dramatic literature. Of course, there are some parts of the Bible to which this would not apply since they are straightforward historical accounts and are nonimaginative.[68]

A literary approach is not a substitute for the grammaticohistorical method but a logical extension of it. Furthermore, the literary approach is not just another fad but an important shift in perspective. It affirms that the Bible demands a literary approach because the Bible is literary in nature.[69]

a. FIRST, IT IS IMPORTANT TO NOTE THE EMPHASES THAT MAKE UP THE LITERARY APPROACH TO REVELATION

(1) Revelation should be seen as representing particular literary types or genres

Literary scholars agree on the nature of certain literary genres or types, such as story, poetry, drama, and epic. Each literary type has its own rules or procedures for understanding and interpretation. For example, exaggeration in a story that claims to be factual history is a form of untruth. On the other hand, the same type of exaggeration in lyric poetry is called hyperbole and is a standard way of expressing emotional truth. The reliability of documentary history involves the writer's inclusion of all the relevant historical material. But literary narrative is much more selective and interpretative. It incorporates the material it needs to highlight the specific perspective a storyteller wishes to give to a character or event.[70]

It is important in our study, therefore, to understand the type or types of literature which are used in Revelation. Revelation is not a typical story or ordinary poetry. However, it is related to these categories. Therefore, we will use these categories, as well as the category of visionary writing, in approaching Revelation.[71]

(2) Revelation should be seen from the literary perspective of wholeness and unity

Many scholars tend to divide Revelation into fragments. Liberal scholars look for various levels and parts behind the final work. Conservatives often bring a theological outline to Revelation and then use various verses as proof texts. They divide it into sections and verses. The literary approach, in contrast, assumes the unity of the text of Revelation. This is helpful in grasping the overall pattern of the book.[72]

Revelation should be approached in the same manner in which we approach a work of art. In hearing a symphony, for example, we should first listen to the whole work in order to grasp the full impact of its total composition, its tonal color, its musical forms, and its motifs. Then, after we have listened again and again to the work as a whole, we can go further. We can analyze the elements and details of its composition and study the techniques employed by the composer. We are then prepared to compare it with other works of the same period and listen to different interpretations of it.[73]

When we read the entire Book of Revelation at one sitting (which would take about an hour and a half), it will make its impact on us *as a whole,* like a poetic drama or an opera. Indeed, Revelation in some ways is more like music than discourse. With this approach, we find that the repetition, delays, and changes of key contribute to a total effect which is emotional as much as rational. The proportions of the whole are seen as more important than the individual scenes.[74]

There are other advantages in reading Revelation aloud in its entirety. The hearer of the text is impressed by its archaic and rhythmic language and by its repetition of sounds and formulas. It also contains a wealth of colors, voices, symbols, and image associations.[75]

Revelation is the New Testament book which has received the most attention from artists throughout the centuries. Modern artists, especially, appreciate its almost surrealistic symbols, bizarre images, colors, and forms. Modern literature derives many of its motifs and stylistic elements from the book. The visions of the "new land" and the "new Jerusalem" are also found in the music and poetry of oppressed people. The poetic and dramatic character of the book can be best perceived when the text is read aloud as a whole, as John intended (1:3).

b. SECOND, IT IS HELPFUL TO NOTE THE MAIN ELEMENTS OF THE STRUCTURE OF REVELATION

Literary scholars are agreed that Revelation is the most thoroughly literary and carefully structured long book in the Bible. If our study is legitimate, we must preserve its literary integrity and note carefully the literary elements in the structure of the book.[76]

(1) The first element of structure is the system of contrasts or conflicts which underlies the whole book

The basic conflict is the spiritual struggle between good and evil. Involved in this basic conflict are character conflicts. These include God and Christ versus Satan, Christian believers versus beast followers, and the bride of Christ against the harlot of Babylon. Other conflicts include the Lamb against the dragon, the holy Trinity against the demonic trinity (dragon, beasts from the sea, and beasts of the earth), and Michael's angels against the dragon's angels. Closely related are scenic conflicts between heaven and the bottomless pit and the new Jerusalem and evil Babylon.[77]

(2) The second structural element is the recurrent use of numbers—especially seven

The primary means that John used to achieve an interwoven texture of the whole book was numbers and numerical structures. Leland Ryken sees the sequential structure as a series of six sevenfold units (seven churches, chs. 2—4; seven seals, chs. 6—7; seven trumpets, chs. 8—11; seven great signs, chs. 12—14; seven bowls of wrath, chs. 15—16; and seven events of final judgment and consummation, chs. 17—22).[78]

An awareness of this structural principle makes the book as a whole easy to remember. Following this principle, it is also easy to identify the flow of action.

The numbers which occur most frequently are three, three and a half, four, five, six, seven, ten, and twelve. Three symbolizes the divine or spirit world, either good or evil. The Trinity is an example. Three and one half, or 42 months or 1,260 days, is a cutoff or limited period of time. It is a perfect number divided in half. Four is the earth number. The world has four seasons or four corners. Six is one short of the perfect number. It is the human number. A person is always short of perfection. The number 666 represents total evil.

Seven is the sacred or perfect number and symbolizes completeness. It is four (which is the earth number) plus three (which is the divine number). Seven arms, for example, symbolizes omnipotence or one who is all-powerful. Seven eyes symbolizes omniscience or one who is all-seeing. Ten is the round number. Twelve symbolizes God's redeemed people which refers to Israel or the church. One thousand is a cube of ten. The square of the church number, twelve, multiplied by the cube of the round number, ten, is 144,000.[79]

(3) The third structural element is the linear or conic spiral sequence of visions, images, and events

Few works of literature have such a forward-moving narrative or strong, onward pressure. Revelation propels the reader ever forward. The movement is from promise to fulfillment.[80]

But the linear or forward movement is not a smooth narrative flow from one event to the next. There are many interludes and repetitions. Elisabeth Schüssler Fiorenza pictures the movement in Revelation as a conic spiral moving from the present to a glorious future.[81]

Ryken contends that the general order of events that underlies Revelation is taken from the Olivet discourse of Jesus (Matt. 24—25). The sequence of the five events described in the discourse (witness, wars and persecutions, false leaders, natural disasters, and final judgment) provides the structure for Revelation.[82]

c. THIRD, IT SHOULD BE HELPFUL TO NOTE THE LITERARY ELEMENTS USED IN REVELATION

(1) Revelation uses archetypes extensively

Archetypes are the elemental, universal, recurrent aspects of human experience. They fall into three basic categories. The first is images which include light, mountaintop, or prison. The second is character types which include hero, villain, or tempter. A third is plot motifs, such as the quest, fall from innocence, or rescue. Archetypes are the basic building blocks of the literary imagination.[83]

Revelation is filled with terms and images which name these archetypes. In both literature and life, these archetypes call forth powerful universal responses from humans.

The last half of Revelation, chapters 12—22, places a special emphasis on universal archetypes. These include a woman in distress who is marvelously delivered and a hero who kills the dragon. There is also a wicked witch who is finally exposed and the marriage of the triumphant hero to his bride. Included is the celebration of the wedding with the feast and the description of a palace glittering with jewels in which the hero and his bride live happily ever after.

Especially notable is the journey of the human character, sometimes the narrator, to supernatural realms. In these realms, he encounters spiritual beings and returns to human life newly equipped. This is a classic archetype of literature. Other examples of this type of archetype include Odysseus, Aeneas, Moses, Dante, and the Red Cross Knight. Another archetypal plot device is the use of the vision as a way of narrating supernatural events.[84]

(2) Revelation is closely related to the epic literary form

An epic is a long narrative. It is a hero story on the grand scale. Epic is so expansive that it sums up the whole age. It has been maintained that the supreme role of epic lies in its capacity to focus a society's self-awareness. The great primary epics deal with their cultures at some moment of crisis. Common epic motifs include kingdom, conquest, warfare, and dominion. In one way or another, epic portrays epic-making events in the life of a nation.[85]

Supernatural settings, characters, and events are always characteristic of epic. Events in such stories occur on a cosmic scale that includes the "other" world as well as the earth. Supernatural agents enter the human world and participate in the action.[86]

Epics always have a unifying hero. The action is constructed around a central epic feat which usually consists of winning a battle and establishing a kingdom.[87]

Revelation has many of these epic characteristics. The story is of a great and heightened conflict among spiritual beings using supernatural means of warfare. The setting of the action is cosmic, including heaven as well as earth and hell. References to the earth often extend to the whole earth, not just to a localized part of it. This reinforces the epic expansiveness of the work.[88]

Epic often deals with the establishment of an empire through the conquest of enemies. Revelation pictures Christ's establishment of His eternal kingdom by defeating the forces of evil. Epic is constructed around a heroic leader. In Revelation we find this in the mighty acts of Christ. Epics are often structured on the principle of the quest. The frequently repeated pattern underlying Revelation is the believer's quest for heaven. The movement of history is toward its consummation and goal. The style of Revelation is closer, therefore, to the exalted style of conventional epic than is true of any other book in the Bible.[89]

John's presence in Revelation is typical of the epic narrator's role. It reminds us especially of *The Divine Comedy* and *Paradise Lost*. Furthermore, Revelation opens with the conventional epic formula of announcing the theme and identifying the divine source of the work (1:1-3).[90]

Another feature of epic style that recurs throughout Revelation is the use of epithets, or titles, for people or things. Epithets are a chief means of characterization. Thus, when Christ is called "the Lion," attention is called to His power and headship. On the other hand, the title "the Lamb" evokes an impression of His status as the sacrificial sin bearer.

(3) Revelation makes extensive use of symbolism[91]

(a) The three most timeless and popular uses of symbolism (in addition to numbers) are animal characters, color symbolism, and nature symbols.

i. The animal device is seen in the presence of "living creatures" around the throne in heaven, the divine Lamb, horses of various colors, locusts, a dragon, and terrifying "beasts" from the sea and earth. These creatures symbolize various qualities. The lion conveys strength. The tiger symbolizes fierceness and the goat, evil. The ox or calf conveys patient service, and the eagle is high flight or spirituality. The lamb conveys sacrifice, and the face of man pictures intelligence.[92]

ii. Color symbolism is less prevalent but still important. White is associated with Christ (1:14) and the saints of God (3:18; 4:4; 7:9,14; 19:8). White is also associated with the armies of heaven (19:14) and God's throne of judgment (20:11). Red, by contrast, appears in the context of evil. This includes warfare (6:4), the appearance of the satanic dragon (12:3), and the whore of Babylon and her beast (17:3-4).[93]

In a more general way, white stands for triumph and often purity. Red is strife or war and black is famine. Pale or greenish gray is death. Green stands for eternal life. Purple portrays royalty.

iii. Nature symbols are used to convey the reality of God's judgment. Cataclysms and convulsions stand for God's righteous judgment. The earth is the "seat of false religion." The sea is a basis for false government or separation. It also symbolizes evil or hostile forces. The beast comes up from the sea but in the new Jerusalem there is no more sea (13:1; 21:1). The lake of fire is sometimes called the second death and the final dwelling place for evil. *Gehenna,* the word for hell in the Gospels, is never used in Revelation (20:15). There are also some positive natural symbols. The mountain is the site of visions and revelations (21:10).[94]

(b) The nature and importance of symbolism

Symbolism means that concrete images are constantly used to represent something else. Instead of Christ being pictured as a spirit or a man, for example, He is portrayed as a lion or a lamb. This is not unusual in literature. But this kind of imaginative rendering of experience in history is an obstacle to a reader who responds only to literal fact.[95]

To state that John used symbols is not to deny that Revelation describes historical events that really happen. It can be easily documented by ordinary historical means that the events described in the visionary literature of the Bible are historical in nature. Old Testament prophecy predicted in dramatic terms that Israel and Judah would be carried away into captivity. This happened. Revelation predicts the fall of the Roman Empire. This empire did fall. The question then is not, Are the events historical? Rather we should ask, How did John go about describing history?[96]

Fortunately, chapter 12 sets forth a clearly stated series of historical events. It gives us a glimpse into John's characteristic way of describing historical events that really happen but are not described in literal language. The series of events described in symbolic language include the incarnation of Christ, Satan's attempt to destroy Christ during His earthly life, the eventual triumph of Christ, and His ascent to heaven. There is also a description of the attack of Satan on the church during the rest of human history.

These events in Revelation 12 are not described literally. Instead we read about an unusual woman giving birth to a son, a red dragon of tremendous size, and a great battle between two groups of warring angels. Then the dragon descends from heaven to earth where he makes war upon the descendants of the woman. This chapter shows us how the imagery of Revelation tends to be symbolic rather than literal.[97]

In fact, in describing an actual event in Revelation 12, John drew on the widely known myth of the queen of heaven with the eternal child. The elements of the myth include the woman, the child, his birth and ascension, and the dragon. This myth is international and is found in many places. In Egypt it is known as Hathor/Isis, Horus, and Sed/Tryphon. In Babylon it is known as Demkina, Marduk, and Tiamat. The same myth was popular in Greece as Letho, Apollo, and Python. In Palestine the myth was known as Sion, Israel, Messiah, and Satan/Behemoth/Leviathan.

In each of these examples of the myth, the dragon seeks the child who is not yet born in order to harm him or to kill him. The woman is still pregnant and is pursued for the child whom she carries. She gives birth with the dragon only a short distance away. The child, however, is caught up to heaven and saved from persecution by the dragon.[98]

Geographical names in Revelation are likewise symbolical. Like Guernica and Hiroshima for us, Sodom, Egypt, Babylon, and Jeru-

salem have heavy symbolic meaning. The "great city" in whose
streets the witnesses are slain, cannot, any more than Vanity Fair, be
limited to one place and one time.[99]

(c) The interpretation of symbolism

How does a person know what a particular image symbolizes?
This is perhaps the central problem in the interpretation of Revelation. The best preparation is a wide acquaintance with literature as a
whole. This is true because literary symbolism is to a remarkable
degree a conventional language. It is important to remember that
literary symbols are a universal language whose meaning is usually
intended to be readily accessible to most readers. Such common
symbols as thunder, earthquake, dragon, lion, or harvest occur often enough in visionary literature for us generally to know what they
mean. We do not need a commentary to tell us that a sword symbolizes judgment or a throne is a portrayal of power. The purpose of the
symbols in Revelation is not primarily to conceal but to reveal in an
easily grasped universal form of communication.[100]

A second preparation is to know the Old Testament. John's first-
century readers knew the Old Testament well. John, himself, was
saturated with the Old Testament teachings and symbolism. Knowing Old Testament symbolism is an obvious prerequisite for understanding a book in which there are approximately 350 references to
the Old Testament.[101]

Images and symbols are, of course, less precise and more elusive
than propositional language. They thus preserve a sense of mystery
which is appropriate to a work that pictures spiritual realities that go
beyond ordinary reality.[102]

d. FOURTH, THE USE OF THE PLOT CONCEPT IN REVELATION IS IMPOR-
TANT

The heart of the Bible is its salvation plot. In the beginning is the
creation of the world and the fall of man. The middle of the biblical
plot is the pilgrimage through fallen human history. In Revelation
the great spiritual conflict between good and evil is finally resolved
and the millennium and eternity finally ushered in.[103]

In some ways Revelation follows Northrop Frye's definition of a
comic plot. The comic plot represents a U-shaped sequence of
events that begins in prosperity, descends into potentially tragic
action, and then ends happily. The usual comic ending in literature
is a marriage or a feast or both. Revelation concludes the Bible with

both a feast and a marriage, after the forces of evil have been destroyed.[104]

e. Fifth, it should be helpful to outline guidelines or principles for understanding the imaginative literature of revelation

(1) Be prepared to use your imagination to picture a world that goes beyond earthly reality

Certain sections of Revelation portray a supernatural world. It is usually heaven, but there are also visions of hell. Visions of either type do not primarily take the reader forward in time, but rather beyond this visible spatial world. An example is the scene of heavenly worship in chapter 4. There is also the description of the new Jerusalem in the last two chapters of Revelation. Visionary literature assaults a purely mundane mind-set.[105]

John represented the second coming of Jesus by all kinds of pictures which he did not attempt to harmonize. For example, he portrayed the Word of God descending on a white horse with the armies of heaven following on white horses (19:11,14). How does this picture of the Word of God coming to slay His enemies fit in with a description of a wedding party going to the marriage celebration? How indeed when the Lamb's wife is a city whose height is 12,000 furlongs and wall 144 cubits?

These are actually three mutually exclusive figures. Is it not clear that all of these images are intended to picture from varying points of view one great event? This event is difficult to describe and comprehend from the human perspective, but ardently desired. If we understand the literary nature of Revelation these pictures would not be offensive to us.[106]

(2) Look for the cosmic perspective

In Revelation the scene is usually cosmic, not localized. In Old Testament prophecy, the scene extends to whole nations. In apocalyptic works, it encompasses the entire earth and reaches beyond the earth to heaven and hell. In Revelation, for example, we move in a regular rhythm between heaven and earth. The scenes set on earth involve the entire planet. This action also eventually reaches out to include the whole human race throughout all of history.[107]

(3) Be ready to exercise your imagination when reading of startling scenes and agents in Revelation

Some of the creatures are startling to earthly eyes. Think of the great red dragon in 12:3-4. Then there are the living creatures with

six wings who are covered with eyes all around in 4:8. Again there is
a warrior riding a red horse in 6:4.

Such mingling of the familiar and the unfamiliar, which is a hallmark of Revelation, takes an even stranger form when inanimate
objects and forces of nature suddenly become actors. There is a
breaking down of ordinary distinctions between the human and the
natural realms. For example, in 12:14-16 the woman was given the
wings of the great eagle. The earth helped the woman by opening its
mouth and swallowing the river that the dragon had spewed out of
his mouth.[108]

In this strange and frequently surrealistic world of visionary literature, almost any aspect of creation can become a participant in the
ongoing drama of God's judgments and redemption. Sea, clouds,
earthquakes, storms, whirlwinds, and assorted animals are constant actors in this type of visionary literature. The events symbolically portrayed are not unreal or untrue. Rather, the form in which
they are pictured as happening is highly dramatic and symbolic.[109]

Reading this type of literature requires what the poet Coleridge
called "the willing suspension of disbelief." We know that people do
not fly through the air on wings. When we read such visions in Revelation, we suspend our disbelief and enter into the realm of dramatic symbolism in order to appropriate the truth it conveys about
reality. The best introduction to understanding such visionary literature in Revelation is by reading other similar types of literature.
C. S. Lewis has written this type of literature in his famous Narnia
stories.[110]

*(4) Take note of the purpose of visionary literature (as contrasted with
realistic literature)*

Visionary and imaginative literature has an arresting strangeness.
This literary approach breaks through our normal way of thinking.
It shocks us into seeing that things are not as they appear. Imaginative writing attacks our ingrained patterns of deep-level thought in
an effort to convince us of certain important truths. In Revelation
this genre of literature points out that the world will not always continue as it now is. Furthermore, it tells us that there is something
drastically wrong with the status quo. It also shows us that reality
cannot be confined to the physical world which we perceive with

our senses. This type of imaginative literature is not comfortable fireside reading. It gives us the shock treatment.[111]

Modern communication theory holds that we understand and retain far more of what we see than what we only hear or read. Therefore, today's public speakers often use graphs, maps, overhead projectors, and many other audiovisual aids.

Writers, however, must depend only on the written word to communicate their images. They do not generally sell a package of transparencies along with their books. They depend solely on their use of language to cause the readers to smell, see, hear, and experience their words.

It is obvious that John could not rely on modern communication paraphernalia. Instead, John embraced symbolism and fantasy in word and deed to highlight and illustrate his divine communiqués. Symbolism and fantasy are above all a communication device.[112]

This means that there is nothing to be gained by reading Revelation as an abstract theological essay or as a historical narrative of the kind found in the Acts. Revelation is a different sort of literature. It is an acted word, a dramatized word, a painted word which is set to music. It is a word which you can see and feel and taste.[113]

(5) Despite its literary unity and wholeness, look for a disjointed series of diverse, self-contained units in Revelation

Much of Revelation consists of brief units which are always shifting and never in focus for very long. In some ways, its effects are similar to those of some modern films. The individual units not only keep shifting but also consist of a range of diverse material, including visual descriptions and speeches that the visionary hears and records. There are dialogues, monologues, brief snatches of narrative, and direct discourses by the writer to an audience. There are letters and prayers and hymns. Visionary elements also may be mingled with realistic scenes and events.[114]

This disjointed method of proceeding places tremendous demands on the reader. This characteristic makes Revelation initially resistant to being seen as a literary whole. The antidote for frustration or misunderstanding is to be prepared for this disjointed type of writing.

(6) Avoid allegorizing details in the visionary literature of Revelation

Usually the total impact of a scene or action in the Revelation con-

veys the meaning. John employed visions for much the same reason
that Jesus taught in parables. They drive home in a dramatic and
memorable fashion one significant point. So when we interpret Revelation, we must consider the whole picture just as we study parables in their entirety. The interpreter's task is to uncover the leading
idea or main point of the vision and not try to squeeze from every
detail some allegorical meaning. Details usually serve to supply the
panoramic background for the main event, either for dramatic effect
or to fill in necessary points of reference.[115]

To translate John's message to our own day does not require finding detail-for-detail correspondence between John's symbols and
our present circumstances. It is a futile exercise to try to locate a
person with a fatal head wound which has been healed. Rather,
once we find the main point of John's vision for his contemporaries
we can translate the point to our own setting.[116]

We should also remember that some of the images portraying supernatural reality are meant to convey a sense of more-than-earthly
mystery. The images remain mysterious because their purpose is to
convey the mystery of supernatural reality.[117]

John's type of visionary writing with its blurred edges has been
contrasted to the clarity of outline in Greek statues of the gods. The
very clarity and definiteness of outline in the wonderful marbles of
Greece constitute a limitation. In comparison with the mystical portrayals of John, the representations of Greek art are religiously im-
potent. In the end, the Greek statue of a god, for all its gracious
beauty, is only a glorified and idealized man. The visions of Revelation, on the other hand, go beyond and transcend once for all the
limitations of human nature. As a balance against over attention to
detail, we should be sensitive to the general effect and the central
point of the glorious images of Revelation.[118]

(7) Avoid over literalizing Revelation

As I will contend later in our study, Revelation was not primarily
intended to give a detailed chronological account of the future. Its
message goes beyond that kind of concern. John's larger concern
was that, despite present appearances, God is in control of history
and will undergird and sustain His people. Even though the church
will experience suffering and death, there will be triumph in the
Christ who will return again and judge us individually and save His

people. John's visions must be seen primarily in terms of this greater concern.[119]

The chronological approach tends to distort the core of the Christian gospel. It has sponsored chronological speculations and predictions that have suffocated the primary mandates of the gospel of the incarnation. It has also led in some cases to moral irresponsibility and Christian elitism.[120]

This avoidance of a detailed chronological approach does not prevent Christians from concentrating hope on the concrete occurrence of God's final movement into history in the second coming of Jesus Christ. If we do not accept this truth, our hope in the coming transformation of the world is surrendered. Furthermore, our hope in the conquest of the structures of death in our world is made illusory. Unless Christians expect the coming actualization of God's promises in Christ to occur *in time* our hope loses its passion and realistic character.

This means that Christians cannot simply take for granted time's unending and enduring character. Time as we know it will end and Christ will come and the final stages of the kingdom will be unveiled. This is a central truth of Revelation.[121]

2. You Should Understand the Distinct and Dominant Literary Types or Forms Used in Revelation Which Are Apocalypse, Prophecy, and Letter

Although Revelation is unique, it is related to three distinct literary types or forms. These forms are mentioned in Revelation 1:1-5. The term *apocalyptic* is derived from the Greek word *apocalypsis* (1:1). Apocalypse means a supernatural unveiling or revelation or disclosure of that which is about to take place. This self-description of Revelation has been given to a certain type of literature. John spoke of his work as a "prophecy" (1:3). He indicated that he was writing an "epistle" or letter of instruction (1:4,11). Revelation takes its unusual character from its combination in a unique and finely blended fashion of all three of these forms.[122]

a. First, Revelation is an apocalypse

In contemporary discussion, *apocalyptic* applies to a group of writings which were widely circulated in the biblical world during the period from 200 BC to AD 100. This term also applies to the basic

concepts contained in these writings. There are also some Old Testament writings with some of these characteristics or elements, including Ezekiel, Daniel, Zechariah, and parts of Isaiah. Similar qualities
can be found in the New Testament sections, such as Matthew 24—
25, Mark 13, Luke 21, and 2 Thessalonians 2:1-12. Becoming ac-
quainted with these basic characteristics or elements will be helpful
in understanding Revelation.[123]

(1) Basic theological elements of apocalyptic literature

(a) Future orientation

The great concern of apocalyptic literature is the future time when
God will bring a violent, radical end to history. This end will mean
the triumph of right and the final judgment of evil.

(b) Dualism

There are two opposing supernatural powers, God and Satan.
There are also two distinct ages. The present age, under Satan, is
temporal and evil. The age to come which is under the control of
God is timeless and righteous.[124]

(c) Determinism and pessimism

This evil age is predetermined and must run its course on a definite time schedule. This view leads to a pessimism about this
present age. The result is that God has withdrawn His help for the
righteous in this age. They must wait for salvation in the coming
age.[125]

(d) Ethical passivity

Instead of the righteous remnant being rebuked for their failure,
they were consoled in their undeserved suffering and told that they
were living in the last days. They were not to blame their immediate
plight on their unfaithfulness but on the overwhelming evil of the
world.[126]

(2) Basic literary characteristics of apocalyptic literature

(a) Content normally comes by means of dreams or visions or
heavenly journeys with angelic guides.[127]

(b) Dramatic and even bizarre symbolism and fantasy are used
extensively. For example, apocalyptic language describes beasts
with seven heads and ten horns (Rev. 13:1) and locusts with scorpions' tails and human heads (Rev. 9:10).[128]

(c) Apocalyptic writings were placed in a particular written structure and formed carefully from the beginning. They were formally
stylized into neat packages. This is in contrast to the prophets who

first spoke what they were told or had seen before it was written down or structured.[129]

(d) Pseudonymity

Many apocalyptic writers, in order to validate their message, said that their works were written by Old Testament saints such as Enoch, Ezra, and Baruch.

(3) Similarities between Revelation and nonbiblical apocalyptic writings

There are obviously similarities between Revelation and other apocalyptic writings. John used symbolism, mystical images, and symbolic numbers. God's communication came through visions and auditions. There is a cosmological stage setting for the book. Hope is engendered by the promise of the second coming of Christ in glory.[130]

(4) Basic differences between Revelation and the nonbiblical apocalyptic writings

As indicated, numerous similarities exist between Revelation and the nonbiblical Jewish apocalyptic writings. But Revelation also has some clear differences from these writings. In other words, the non-biblical apocalyptic writings must not be taken as influences on John's thought or method in the same way that the inspired canonical books of the Old Testament influenced him.[131]

(a) John clearly placed himself in the contemporary world of the first century and spoke of the last days at the end of history in much the same way as did Ezekiel and Jeremiah.

(b) Furthermore, Revelation is not a pseudonymous work but bears the name of the author who wrote as a prophet. Unlike the nonbiblical apocalyptic writings, John did not search out some notable person in history, such as Enoch, in an attempt to gain a hearing or to heighten the significance of his writing. Rather, John wrote in his own name. In addition, John made himself known to his readers. Through the seven letters (ch. 2—3), he spoke to known churches in Asia Minor who were his contemporaries and "companions in suffering."[132]

(c) Another difference is that John did not share the pessimism of the apocalyptic writers who despaired of history and saw hope only in the coming age. John did not see this present world as completely dominated by evil, although he did look for an outbreak of satanic activity in the last days. For John, history was the sphere in which God has wrought out redemption.[133]

For the apocalyptic writers, the turning point of history was the future event of the Messiah's coming as the conquering warrior-king. In Revelation, the climactic event has already occurred in the victory of the slain Lamb (ch. 5). Now, however, the Lamb's victory is being worked out in history in the obedient suffering of His followers (12:11; 15:2). Their deaths are seen in Revelation as part of the victory over evil that God is already effecting in the world. This partial victory through the suffering of the saints is combined with the hope of the final and biggest victory of God at the end of history. The pessimism which defers God's saving activity until the end is absent.[134]

John maintained the balance between pessimism and optimism. While the prospects of evil and suffering are realistically set forth, a genuine optimism permeates the entire work. World history is significant as a prelude to God's second great intervention in Jesus Christ.

(d) Another difference relates to the sense of moral urgency which John possessed. We see this urgency as he rebuked a faithless church and demanded repentance to avoid the divine judgment (Rev. 2:5,16,21-22; 3:19). While Revelation is not lacking in words of encouragement to the faithful, it also strongly urges the churches to repent.[135]

These differences show that any identification of Revelation with the writings of the extrabiblical apocalyptic writers must be qualified. Indeed, we should reexamine every method of interpreting Revelation that rests on this assumed similarity. For example, Revelation is more than just a "tract for the times," as are other apocalyptic books.

The Jewish apocalyptic method of producing "tracts for the times" to encourage faithfulness during intense persecution has some truth but is not the whole truth. The beasts of Chapter 13 are identified respectively as Imperial Rome and the imperial priesthood. This is a view held by a majority of contemporary scholars. But I believe that a proper interpretation sees Revelation speaking a prophetic message about realities and events extending beyond the early centuries.[136]

John was no doubt quite familiar with the Jewish apocalyptic writings of the intertestamental period. In some instances, there seems to be a direct allusion to them (compare 2:7) but the relation is, in general, superficial. Only twice is an interpreting angel involved in the explanation of a vision (ch. 7,17). This is a feature constantly present in the other kind of apocalyptic writings. In contrast, John was everywhere dependent on portions of Isaiah, Ezekiel, Daniel, and Zechariah.[137]

As we will see, there is much merit in George Ladd's suggestion that we create a new category called "Prophetic-Apocalyptic" to distinguish Revelation from the late Jewish apocalyptic writings. The form may not be that different but certainly the world view is different. For example, in Ladd's view, the beast of chapters 13 and 17 is historical Rome. But it is far larger than the ancient city. The beast can be seen in recurring Antichrists and in the final Antichrist. The references to the persecutions of Christians likewise have application beyond the known historical situation of John's day.[138]

With Revelation then, as with Mark 13, we must be cautious before classifying it with the nonbiblical apocalyptic writings. We have seen the resemblances, and it would be impossible to hold that John was not indebted to the apocalyptic method. Clearly, he knew this kind of writing. It is equally clear that he did not write just another typical apocalypse. Revelation has its own inspired distinctives. It is a Christian writing, setting forth what God has done in Christ and what He will yet do. John used some of the apocalyptic method to set this forth. But a chief emphasis is on the "Lamb as it had been slain." This means an emphasis on a past event of history as well as on a future event which is the second coming of Christ. This dual emphasis is central to Revelation but is absent from the nonbiblical apocalyptic writings.

b. SECOND, REVELATION IS A BOOK OF PROPHECY

This prophetic emphasis constitutes an additional difference from the pessimistic apocalyptic writings of the interbiblical period. John was not with his Jewish predecessors simply anticipating the end. He knew that the end had already begun with the coming of Jesus.

Crucial to this prophetic understanding is the advent of the Spirit. Very early in Christian history, beginning with Peter's sermon in Acts 3, the pioneer Christians realized that Jesus had not come to usher in the final end but the beginning of the end. Thus they saw that, with Jesus' death and resurrection and with the coming of the Spirit, the blessings and benefits of the future had already come. In a sense, therefore, the end had already come. But in another sense,

the end had not yet fully come. Thus it was *already, not yet*. The early
Christians, therefore, learned to be a truly eschatological people.
They lived between the times. They lived between the *beginning* of
the end and the *consummation* of the end.[139]

The nonbiblical apocalyptic writers wrote in the name of the
former prophetic figures because they lived in the age of the
"quenched Spirit." This meant that they were awaiting the prophetic
promise of the outpoured Spirit in the new age. Thus, they were
living in an age when prophecy had ceased. John, in contrast, belonged to the new age. He was "in the Spirit" when he was told to
write what he saw (1:10-11). He called his book "this prophecy"
(1:3; 22:18-19). Furthermore, he stated that the "testimony of Jesus,"
for which he and the churches were suffering (1:9; 20:4), "is the
spirit of prophecy" (19:10). This obviously means that the message
of Jesus to which John and the churches bore witness is a clear evidence that the prophetic spirit had come. [140]

This combination of apocalyptic and prophetic elements makes
Revelation different. The book is cast in the apocalyptic mold and
has most of the literary characteristics of the apocalyptic writings. It
was born in persecution and speaks about the end with the triumph
of Christ and His church. It is also a carefully constructed piece of
literature, using cryptic language and the rich symbolism of fantasy
and numbers.

On the other hand, John clearly intended for his writing to be a
prophetic word for the church. His book was not to be sealed for the
future. It was a word of God for that present situation. "To prophesy" does not primarily mean to foretell the future, but rather to
speak forth God's word in the present.

At this point, we would do well to remember that prophetic writing is even more common in the Jewish and Christian tradition than
is the apocalyptic. The largest part of the Old Testament prophets is
prophetic writing. Such writing is theological, evangelistic, and ethical by nature. It intends to call people to repentance. The prophetic
message emphasizes the decision-making freedom of the people before God. In contrast, the apocalyptic message emphasizes the freedom of God to act independently of humanity. Prophetic preaching
calls out and affirms the implications of the will of God to the people
here and now. Therefore, it has a more present-tense cutting edge.
The meaning of prophecy is not as mysterious and hidden as is the

meaning of apocalyptic writing. The mark of the prophetic word is its clarity and its immediacy. Revelation is clearly in this great prophetic tradition.[141]

Even the seven letters in Revelation 2—3 bear this prophetic imprint. Thus we have in Revelation God's prophetic word to some churches in the latter part of the first century who were undergoing persecution from without and to some who were decaying from within.

Not only the seven churches but the whole of Revelation is full of ethical admonitions and exhortations for the Christians. This ethical interest of the author prevented the reader of that time, as well as us, from projecting "evil" unto others without holding themselves accountable. Revelation does speak of vengeance against dehumanizing, antichristian demonic and political power. It also calls all of the inhabitants of the earth as well as the Christians to repentance. John insisted that the Christians in no way have "made it" but that they are still in danger of losing their reward in the new Jerusalem.[142]

Revelation could easily be misunderstood in the sense that evil exists only outside the Christian community but not within it. However, John corrected this by beginning with the great vision of the heavenly Christ judging the Christian communities. Furthermore, he interspersed the apocalyptic part with eschatological warnings, blessings, exhortations, and woes. He concluded the whole book with a series of admonitions, announcements, and prayers (22:6-21).[143]

We know Revelation is prophecy because true Christian prophecy responds to the hunger of man for God. In contrast, most of the interbiblical apocalyptic books answer the hunger of man for curiosity about the future. There were more fortunetellers in John's day than there are in ours. John had nothing to do with false prophecy.[144]

Whoever maintains that Revelation was primarily written to satisfy curiosity has not really studied the book. John's visions of the end are those of a great impressionistic artist rather than the pictures of a photographer. For the most part, his visions defy detailed precision. But they do convey sufficient teaching to warn people of the end of state idolatry and enough about the future kingdom of God in Jesus Christ to encourage them to repentance and faith and hope.[145]

c. Third, Revelation is an epistle or letter

This combination of apocalyptic and prophetic elements has been cast finally into the form of a letter or epistle. If you read 1:4-7 and 22:21, you will note that all of the characteristics of the letter form are present. Furthermore, John spoke to his readers in the first person/ second person formula (I . . . you). Thus in its final form, the Revelation was sent by John as a letter to the seven churches of Asia Minor. This means that, as with all epistles, there is an *occasional* aspect to Revelation. It was occasioned at least in part by the need of the specific churches to which it was addressed. Therefore, to properly interpret this book, we must seek to understand the original historical context.[146]

Almost all of the New Testament letters were occasioned from the reader's side (Philemon, James, and perhaps Romans were less so). Usually the occasion was some behavior that needed correcting or a doctrinal error that needed setting right or a misunderstanding that needed further light. Sometimes there was the need of encouragement or a statement of the Christian hope in a fresh way. Many of these needs were obviously met by Revelation.[147]

Revelation was a letter. The primary meaning of Revelation is thus what John intended it to mean, which, in turn, must also have been something his readers could have understood it to mean. Indeed the great advantage they would have had over us is their familiarity with their own historical context that caused the book to be written in the first place. They also had a greater familiarity with apocalyptic forms and images.[148]

But Revelation is also prophetic. It pictures the consummation of the battle between God and Satan and the triumph of Christ in history through His coming in glory. This means that Revelation had a message for the first century and has a meaning for us in terms of its portrayal of the last days of history. It furthermore continues both to encourage Christians and to warn them in every age.[149]

3. You Should Know About the Personal and Social Identity of the Author of Revelation

I have made more than a dozen trips to the Mediterranean island of Patmos and to the ruins of ancient Ephesus. At these historic places, the guides recount in detail the life of John the apostle. There is no doubt in their minds that he was the author of Revelation, the Gospel of John, and the Epistles of John. On Patmos the people have even designated the places where John lived and received the visions which he recorded in Revelation.

What is the external and internal evidence for the personal identity of the author of Revelation? What can we say about the author's social identity?

a. EXTERNAL EVIDENCE

(1) For John the apostle as author

The earliest witnesses are virtually unanimous in identifying the author with John, the beloved apostle, the son of Zebedee. Justin Martyr, the early church father, lived for a time in Ephesus, one of the seven cities in the Apocalypse, around AD 135. He stated in his *Dialogue with Trypho* that Revelation was written by John, one of the apostles of Christ.[150]

Irenaeus is the earliest known writer to attribute both Revelation and the Gospel of John to John, the son of Zebedee. Irenaeus was a native of Asia Minor who spent his youth in Smyrna, another of the seven cities of Revelation. He lived there about forty years after the traditional date (AD 95) of the composition of Revelation. Irenaeus said that, as a child, he heard Polycarp talk about his conversations with John and with the others who had seen the Lord. In another place, Irenaeus affirmed that he had traditions from all of the elders who had met in Asia with John, the disciple of the Lord.[151]

Other major figures in the early church, Hippolytus (d.? 236), Clement of Alexandria (d.? 220) and Origen (d.? 254) followed Irenaeus in their judgments on the authorship of the two works.[152]

(2) Against John the apostle as author

Not until Dionysius, the bishop of Alexandria and student of Origen (d.? 264), was any voice raised within the church against the apostolic authorship of Revelation. Dionysius questioned the apostolic origin of Revelation because the advocates of an early eschatological hope (chiliasts), whom he opposed, appealed to Revelation 20.[153]

From the time of Dionysius, the apostolic origin of the book was disputed in the East. Athanasius of Alexandria (d. 373) turned the tide in the East toward its acceptance.[154]

In the West, John the apostle was assumed to be the author from

AD 150. However, Martin Luther had misgivings about the apostolic nature of Revelation in the sixteenth century. The modern objections to John the apostle as the author of Revelation are twofold.

(a) One objection, held by Moule, is the barbarous Greek style of Revelation as compared to that of the other Johannine writings.[155]

Collins suggests that it is probable that John knew two or three languages. Besides Greek, he seems to have known Mishnaic Hebrew (the Hebrew of his day) or Aramaic or both. It has long been noted that John's Greek is very peculiar. It is more likely that John wrote a peculiar, contemporarily Semitizing Greek on purpose. Such an act may have been a protest against the higher forms of Hellenistic culture. It would have been an act of cultural pride of a Jewish Semite. Such an act fits well with the type of message expressed in Revelation. In protest against white attitudes, some American blacks refuse to "talk right" or use "white English." This could be similar to John's refusal to use sophisticated Greek.[156]

Other scholars suggest that John purposely used an elusive, anthological style. The words, images, phrases, and patterns of the Bible became raw material for a new literary creation and prophetic proclamation. He probably altered the wording deliberately in order to create the desired effect.[157]

There has also been the suggestion that the "bad grammar" in Revelation resulted from an ecstatic state of mind due to John's having received his prophecies in the form of visions.[158]

Another solution to the problem of the Greek style is to remember that John was a prisoner on the island of Patmos in the Aegean Sea when he wrote Revelation. He did not have the advantage of an amanuensis or secretary to smooth out his rough style, as he apparently had for his Gospel and epistles.[159] A similar theory holds that John was the source of the tradition embodied in both the Gospel and Revelation but that he was aided by two different scribes or secretaries. The assumption is that these two assistants were given considerable freedom in shaping the two works.[160]

Others hold the hypothesis that there was a Johannine circle, community, or school which preserved the writings of John and put them in final form.[161]

(b) The second objection relates to the age of John. If John wrote Revelation, he must have done so at a very advanced age. This assumes that the traditional date given by Irenaeus of about AD 95 or 96 is correct. There are some traditions from several times and places which suggest that John the son of Zebedee was martyred or died in some other manner probably before AD 70. This would be a Christian tradition in conflict with the one which first found its full form in Irenaeus that John lived to an old age. It is of course possible to harmonize the two and to argue that John was martyred at a very advanced age.[162]

Once doubt is raised about John the son of Zebedee being the author, curiosity is aroused about who the author actually was. Dionysius concluded that the author had to be another John in Asia. Perhaps he was a prophet named after the apostle who was also a follower of the apostle. He also could have been a member of the Johannine circle or school.[163]

(3) Conclusion

However, despite some of the problems mentioned, a large number of substantial scholars are convinced of the similarity between Revelation and the other Johannine books. They continue to attribute Revelation to the apostle, the son of Zebedee—or at least lean in that direction. This list includes most of the Roman Catholic scholars, Alford, Guthrie, Mounce, Stauffer, Swete, and Zahn. Others leave the question open but do not deny the apostolic authorship. This group includes Beasley-Murray, Beckwith, Bruce, and Morris.[164]

b. INTERNAL EVIDENCE

From the internal evidence a number of things can be said about the author with some confidence.

(1) He called himself John (1:4,9; 22:8)

This is not likely a pseudonym, but instead the author was a well-known person among the Asian churches. It is true that John never referred to himself as an apostle or a disciple of the Lord in Revelation itself.[165]

(2) John of the Apocalypse identified himself as a prophet (1:3; 22:6-10, 18-19)

He was in exile because of his prophetic witness (1:9). As such he spoke to the churches with great authority. He might have been the head of a prophetic school (compare 22:16).

(3) Use of the Old Testament makes it virtually certain that John was a

Palestinian Jew who was steeped in the Temple and synagogue ritual.

(4) Harmony of teaching exists between Revelation and the Gospel of John and the Epistles of John

Others contend that the most telling argument in favor of the writer being John the apostle is the harmony of the teaching of this book with the character of John as he is presented in the first three Gospels. There he is referred to as the "son of thunder" and in Revelation he presented the "thundering judgment of God." John revealed this quality in Luke's Gospel when he and James wanted to call down thunder on a Samaritan village (Luke 9:54). This temperament is expressed in the Apocalypse in John's hostility toward the Jews (2:9; 3:9), toward the "beast," and the "harlot," and in the three cycles of seven plagues which reveal the righteous judgment of God.[167]

Other similarities are noted. Both Revelation and the Gospel of John refer to the Lord Jesus as the Word and the Lamb. Both books use other terms like *witness, tabernacle, keep, overcome, living water, manna, shepherd,* and *sheep.* The same Christology is essentially there—Christ is the Lamb of God who takes away our sin (John 1:29; Rev. 1:5; 5:6).[168]

For those who hold this harmony, the differences are simply a matter of literary form. Since one is a Gospel and the other a type of revelatory literature, they naturally have different subject matter, vocabulary, and perspectives. One looks to the past, to the earthly life of Jesus. The other looks to the heavenly world and to the future.[169]

Palmer concludes that the strongest evidence of all sources from within the document point to John the son of Zebedee as the author of the book, language difficulties notwithstanding. Similarities in theme, style, and theology to the other books of John are very impressive. For these reasons, many scholars, myself included, agree with the early church that John the apostle was the author. Regardless of the problem of authorship, the church universal has come to a knowledge that Revelation is divinely authoritative, inspired Scripture.[170]

c. SOCIAL IDENTITY OF JOHN

Some words about the broader social identity or social location of John will be helpful.

(1) As we have seen, John was likely a Palestinian Jew by birth.

Such a hypothesis helps explain John's massive assumption of continuity. This means that he did not distinguish an old and a new Israel. He had, to be sure, his enemies among the Jewish people. But he claimed indirectly the designation "Jew" for the followers of Jesus (2:9; 3:9). This Jewish background makes John's thorough and deep knowledge of the Jewish Bible understandable. It also explains the similarities in form and content between Revelation and the Jewish apocalypses. His fierce anti-Roman stance also shows that he was heir to certain strands of Jewish tradition.[171]

(2) John apparently claimed (indirectly) to be, and was recognized by at least some as, an early Christian prophet.

The evidence suggests that John was an itinerant prophet who was familiar with all seven communities because he had visited and worked with each of them. John played out his role as a prophet. He saw that his function was to mediate an intelligible message to his fellow Christians, a message that he claimed ultimately derived from God.[172]

John was clearly influenced by the written records and oral traditions of the classical prophets of Israel. At the same time, he saw himself as part of the phenomenon of early Christian prophecy. This prophecy was evidently very widespread in Paul's time. The function had diminished or even died out in some communities. However, it was still alive in the province of Asia as the activities of "Jezebel" and "Balaam" show alongside John's own prophecy.[173]

(3) Some scholars, notably Collins, feel that the itinerant life-style, which involved continual movement from place to place, was typical of Jesus

It was also typical of Jesus' disciples and many leaders in the early church, as those are portrayed in the first three Gospels, Acts, and the Letters of Paul. The motivation and rationale for such itinerant movement apparently varied. The basis for one type of itinerant life-style was the imitation of Jesus.[174]

Some evidence also supports the hypothesis that John was an itinerant or wandering prophet. If this were so, it illuminates much of Revelation. For example, John had rivals in winning the allegiance of the Christians in the seven cities. The major rivals seem to have been the wandering leaders with whom he was in competition. The Ephesians were praised for testing those who called themselves apostles and finding them false (2:2).

Apostles, as we know them elsewhere in early Christian literature, generally traveled from place to place. If John were an itinerant prophet, that fact would explain why he was familiar with each of the seven communities but did not associate himself in any special way with any one of them (tradition states that he died in Ephesus). It would also help explain why he did not mention elders or deacons in any of the communities. He probably knew of their existence but ignored their roles of leadership. This is true because John was a different kind of authority. Perhaps he was in competition with them in influencing the points of view of the other readers.

This itinerant hypothesis also helps explain how John could have advocated teaching which had such extreme political and social ramifications. It condemned the wealth of Rome and the provincial elite with great detachment, integrity, and credibility. He could likewise challenge the readers not to participate in trade guilds and other such associations. He could more easily present continence and the disciplined life as the ideal.[175]

This itinerant hypothesis throws light on the tension between John and the Laodiceans. John did not insist that all his readers adopt the life-style to which he had been called. He probably recognized the need for some followers of Christ to lead settled lives and to earn livings for themselves and to provide hospitality to wandering leaders. But he apparently felt that the Laodiceans had gone too far in compromising with the world. They were too tied to their goods and social status. Therefore, he admonished, "Would that you were cold or hot!"(3:15). That statement reveals the difficulty that one who would be perfect has with the compromises of life in this world.[176]

4. You Should Know About the Date of the Writing of Revelation

Knowledge of the date of the writing of Revelation can help us in deciding how and why the author shaped his raw materials into a new and distinctive composition. To what particular events was he responding? What factors in the historical and social situation did he consider significant? When the date has been fixed as nearly as possible, interpreters can better understand the historical events and social realities reflected in the book's images and narratives. We are then better able to assess the author's purpose in writing the book and see its functions for the earliest readers.[177]

a. EXTERNAL EVIDENCE

One type of evidence is external of the book itself. Such evidence comes to us through the testimony of other early Christian writers. The earliest witness was Irenaeus who stated that the Apocalypse was seen at the end of the reign of Domitian. Since Domitian ruled from 81-96, Irenaeus's comment refers to AD 95 or 96.[178]

Victorinus, who lived in Pettau (modern Austria), died in 303 in the persecution of Diocletian. He wrote a commentary in Latin on Revelation. This is the earliest surviving full commentary on the book. Victorinus and Eusebius said that Revelation was written during the reign of Domitian. They added that John was banished to Patmos from Ephesus by Domitian and that he was released when Domitian died. This fact of the banishment of John tells us a great deal about the attitude of the Roman authorities toward him and his message and about his own probable attitude toward them.[179]

A few late sources date Revelation in the time of Claudius, Nero, or Trajan. These texts show that there were traditions about the date that were apparently independent of Irenaeus. Their historical reliability, however, is doubtful.

There are a number of reasons why the Domitian date of AD 95 is preferred to the earlier date during the time of Nero. Nero's persecution was not on religious grounds. He used the Christians merely as scapegoats to blame for the great fire in Rome. The degenerate condition in the seven churches requires more time than the Neronian date permits. The change in attitude toward Rome from the time of Acts as compared with Revelation fits better with a Domitian date. There seems no good reason for doubting Irenaeus's date of AD 95 on grounds external to the book.[180]

b. INTERNAL EVIDENCE

The next important step is to see if internal evidence in the book itself is harmonious with the external evidence. Revelation announces and describes in several places the destruction of a city called Babylon (14:8; 16:19; 17:5; 18:2,10,21). The dominant city in the Mediterranean world in John's time was obviously Rome. Most commentators agree that "Babylon" in the Apocalypse is a symbolic name for Rome. Rome was called Babylon because her forces, like those of Babylon at an earlier time, destroyed the Temple in Jerusalem. It is probable that John learned this symbolic name from his fellow Jews and that it quickly became traditional.

Use of the name Babylon is an important internal indication of the date. It is highly unlikely that the name would have been used before the destruction of the Temple by Titus in AD 70. Internal evidence thus points decisively to a date after AD 70.[181]

Persecution and harassment also seem to point to the Domitian date. Christians were harassed from time to time in the first two centuries. The fact that the founder of Christianity had been crucified by the Romans made the earliest Christians and their communities suspect. Acts 16:16-24 and 19:23-41 suggest that Gentiles sometimes took the initiative in either unofficial harassment or denunciation of Christians before Roman authorities.

The Christians' refusal to worship any god but their own aroused pagan hostility. The pagans feared that this exclusiveness alienated the goodwill of the gods and endangered the well-being of nature and society.

Relatively few passages in Revelation clearly look back on persecution in the past. One passage, 1:9, implies that the author was banished to Patmos because of his activities as a Christian prophet. Another, 2:13, refers to Antipas's death at Pergamum, probably an execution ordered by the governor of the province of Asia. Most of the rest of the book expresses the author's expectation of persecution. Thus the theme of persecution in Revelation allows a date during the reign of Domitian, but does not establish it in and of itself.[182]

Evidence exists that under Domitian for the first time people began to swear by the genius of the living emperor in public documents. Flatterers apparently began to offer sacrifice voluntarily to Domitian's genius. M. P. Charlesworth suggests that Domitian made the voluntary action of sacrificing to the genius of the living emperor into a test of loyalty. Anyone accused or suspected of disloyalty could save himself or herself by offering sacrifice before the image of the emperor.

The cities of Asia Minor enthusiastically supported the imperial cult. After persistently seeking the honor, Ephesus was allowed to establish a temple and a cult of Domitian as a god during his lifetime. The tendency to flatter Domitian by giving him divine honors and worshiping his person was probably the occasion for John to view the Roman emperor as the adversary of God. Since there is no internal evidence which contradicts the Domitian date of AD 95, it is best to stand with this historic tradition.[183]

5. *You Should Know How Revelation Became a Part of the New Testament Canon*

The New Testament canon or list of authoritative writings was not finally settled until the fourth century. One criterion for selection was apostolic authorship. As we have seen, early in the second century John the apostle's authorship of Revelation was widely accepted.

But the place of Revelation in the canon would not have been upheld if it had not been felt to be apostolic also in content. This means that it was in harmony with the pattern of Christian truth in the other apostolic writings.

Some Alexandrian Christians rejected Revelation in the third century. This rejection was primarily because of the crudely physical millennial expectations which some of their contemporaries drew from Revelation. The rejection of Revelation was part of their overall rejection of apocalyptic Christianity. It could also be said that its apocalyptic character would have been obnoxious to many even in the first century. However, the unusual nature of the book was not a general disqualification, either in the third century or in the first.

Revelation represents an important part of Christianity which stresses Christ's sacrificial death and His imminent return. This type of teaching stamps the first three Gospels and most of the Epistles. In fact, John's Apocalypse can be seen as an updating of Christ's teaching. John gave an elaboration of the themes of Jesus for his own times, much as Jesus had updated the themes of Daniel.[184]

For Christians, the expectation of imminent divine intervention in the coming of the kingdom of God had been partially realized in Jesus' ministry and resurrection. Their belief that the kingdom would soon be completed by His return was rooted in His own prophecy given to His disciples before His arrest, as recorded in Mark 13; Matthew 24; and Luke 21.

This apocalyptic part of Christianity may have been a minority view in the province of Asia at the end of the first century. If this view is right, then John was attacking an influential "gnostic" version of Christianity during a time of comparative affluence and success. At such a time, Christ's return seemed remote and martyrs were few. But as the attitude of the authorities hardened against Christianity and conformity with the world became less viable, the stern apocalyptic version of Christianity which we have in Revelation regained ground. Revelation became the encouragement and solace of martyrs in growing numbers. The spirit and imagery of Revelation sustained the church in its sometimes almost suicidal resistance to persecution. Revelation has sustained and strengthened countless Christians since those early centuries.[185]

Certainly Revelation is not the whole of early Christianity. In fact, it is only one aspect of Christianity and must be read alongside the other books in the New Testament canon. But Revelation does represent what was historically a vital aspect of Christianity. In fact, without Revelation, there might have been no Christianity and no New Testament today.[186]

We can thus see why Revelation, though different from the other books of the New Testament, was seen as an important part of the New Testament canon. Believers saw in Revelation's reinterpretation of the Scriptures the themes of both the Old and New Testaments drawn together. Thus the early Christians saw that it deserved its place as the last book of the Bible. As we study this book, we will come to a deepened awareness of the close relationship of thinking and feeling between John and the other New Testament writers.[187]

6. You Should Know About the Purpose of Revelation

In recent years, Christian scholars have come to realize that this unique and remarkable book has many aspects. These aspects are related to historical, literary, sociological, political, and psychological methods of interpretation. It will be helpful to outline representative aspects of the purpose of Revelation.

a. ENCOURAGE THE EARLY CHRISTIANS WHO WERE BEING PERSECUTED

There is evidence that the Christians of the first century were being harassed or persecuted by both Roman authorities and the Jews. While we do not know of a full-fledged persecution of the Christians before the second century, John knew of the persecutions of individual Christians. The increasing totalitarianism of the reign of Domitian made the future look dark.[188]

Christians were being called upon to join all the inhabitants of the empire to appear before a magistrate. There they would be called upon to pledge their loyalty to Rome by offering a pinch of incense upon the altar of the emperor cult. This act was probably oriented more politically than religiously. Christians, however, interpreted the act religiously and found it difficult to say that "Caesar is Lord." To believers, "Jesus Christ is Lord!" He alone had redeemed them from bondage to sin by His vicarious sacrifice. Because of their unwillingness to compromise their faith, many Christians were banished. Others were condemned to torturous forms of death.[189]

The imperial ruler cult must have been deeply offensive to the Christians. The polytheism with which it was joined was equally distasteful. The imperial cult was enthusiastically supported in Asia Minor, often beyond the expectations of the Roman authorities themselves. The public display must have been traumatic for Christians who opposed its ideology deeply and intensely.

The trouble was compounded by the fact that Gentile neighbors resented the Christians' rejection of polytheism and the ruler cult. The more enthusiastic their neighbors were about the ruler cult, the more precarious the Christians' public status became. The effect upon some Christians and upon John the prophet must have been as intense and as negative as the reaction of contemporary Jews to the emergence of neo-Nazi organizations.[190]

Through the decisions of the Jewish Council at Jamnia in AD 90, the Jewish community separated more and more from the Christian church. This meant that Jewish Christians were excluded from the synagogue. Thus the Christians could no longer claim the Jewish privileges which had been granted by Rome. This meant that they were often regarded as disloyal and atheistic.[191]

This Roman and Jewish persecution aroused many difficult theological questions for the Christians. Why do Christ's followers have to suffer if Jesus Christ is the true Lord and King of the world? Why are the Christians persecuted if God is on their side and the gods of the other religions are powerless? If Christ is really the eschatological regent of God, why does He not revenge the blood of so many Christians who already have had to die? Why has Christ not returned in glory to prevent further suffering of His people?[192]

John, through Revelation, sought to minister to the needs of these persecuted people. His message includes several themes.

The most dominant theme is that Christ *is* reigning as King of kings and Lord of lords in heaven. He will soon appear to usher in the millennial kingdom and the new creation. John warned the faithful in the church to repent and make wrongs right. He further encouraged the faithful to "hold fast" to Christ until the end. Even though fidelity to Christ might result in a martyr's death, it ensured the saints that the victor's crown awaits them. The martyrs (for example, Antipas, 2:13) would be vindicated.

This theme of hope, rooted in the certain triumph of Christ, is emphasized at the end of the Apocalypse when evil is completely destroyed and the eternal kingdom of God is ushered in (chs. 20—22). This living hope, a hope which believers have already experienced in part through faith in Jesus Christ, John held before them. Although the wrong seems quite strong, God is ruling and He will demonstrate His power openly soon.[193]

In addition to these basic themes, John enlarged in Revelation on the background of his message. Jesus Christ, as the Exalted One, is alone in the whole world worthy to take over the seven seal scroll and with it the eschatological dominion over the world. Christ's universal kingship is based on the fact that he was slain and has ransomed from every tribe and tongue and nation people whom he has made to be a kingdom and priests for God. These Christian followers would share in the divine reign on earth in the eschatological future (see 5:9-10).[194]

The imperial cult and image were seen as idols. They were "nothing" but behind them stood Satan, the antidivine power. Final salvation will mean the destruction of the Roman Empire and the idolatrous, dehumanizing forces behind it. In the plagues which will come, and in the second coming of Christ, God's reign extends to the earth. Finally God will destroy all antidivine powers, death, and the underworld. With the second coming of Christ (19:11-16) the second stage of the drama will arrive. Christ and the faithful Christians will reign as kings over the earth (20:4-6). The first heaven and the first earth and the devil and Rome (or its future clone) will at a third stage give room to a new heaven and a new earth.[195]

b. Correct false belief and heresy

Recent studies question how intense, widespread, or sustained the persecution of the Christians was, even under Domitian. Thus, there are reasons other than the persecution of that time for the writing of Revelation.

The letters to the seven churches imply that five of the seven had serious problems. The major problem seemed to be a disloyalty to

Christ. This may indicate that a major thrust of Revelation is not sociopolitical but theological. John was just as concerned with countering the heresy which was creeping into the churches at the close of the first century as in addressing the political situation. Newman suggests that this heresy could well have been gnosticism. He supports this view from a critical study of the statements of Irenaeus in the second century about Revelation.[196]

An important purpose, therefore, of Revelation is to separate true from false belief. John was called to expose the doctrinal failures of the churches of Asia Minor.

c. ENCOURAGE AUTHENTIC CHRISTIAN DISCIPLESHIP

As indicated, many Christians could not understand why Christians were suffering. One purpose of Revelation was to encourage authentic Christian discipleship. This was done by explaining Christian suffering and martyrdom in the light of how Jesus' death and resurrection brought victory over evil. There was a down payment of this victory in power for personal living. God was also judging evil men and nations in the present. But John also taught that the martyrs (for example, Antipas, 2:13) would be vindicated in the future. He disclosed the end both of evil and of those who follow the beast (19:20-21; 20:10,15).[197]

d. PROVIDE A BASIS FOR CHRISTIAN WORSHIP

Some scholars see the great problem in Asia Minor as related to the lack of authentic Christian worship. They see one purpose of Revelation as providing a liturgy for the worship of God. This was needed to counteract the false worship of the pagan gods and the emperor worship.

Revelation is full of worship symbols, liturgical actions, hymnic language, and doxological formulas. Scholars who adopt the liturgical approach propose that the author chose the early Christian paschal liturgy as the blueprint according to which he structured his book. Others postulate that the outline of Revelation reflects the Jerusalem Temple liturgy or follows the Jewish calendar of feasts.[198]

The liturgical approach should not be seen as the chief purpose of Revelation for several reasons. For example, the liturgical pattern represents only one of the structural components of the book. Other patterns and forms are important in the structure of Revelation. Revelation was to have been read in a worship setting, but it had broader purposes than providing a worship manual.[199]

e. Provide a drama for presentation on the Ephesian stage

The dramatic approach has been advanced by John Wick Bowman and James L. Blevins. Blevins, for example, contends that Revelation is an innovative adaptation of Greek tragic drama. This dramatic adaptation accounts for its striking difference from other so-called apocalyptic books.[200]

According to Blevins, John was not able to express his visual experience in ordinary prose. Rather, John needed a dramatic medium. The timeless, poetic forms of Greek tragedy were well-suited to capture John's cosmic vision of another world. As a Christian prophet, however, it was necessary for him to transfer the cyclical nature of Greek history found in Greek tragedy into a prophetic, goal-oriented view of history.

Many recent studies have demonstrated, according to Blevins, how the dramatic forms of Revelation were used in early Christian liturgy and festivity. Drama and divine worship were closely related in the minds of the first-century Greek world. Greek tragedy was a medium well-known in Asia Minor, particularly in Ephesus. The theater in that great city had been both a landmark and a cultural center. Only in that setting can the unique form of Revelation be understood.[201]

Blevins has sought to give support to his idea by examining the unique seven-windowed stage at Ephesus. He has also pointed out the nature of the chorus in Greek drama and the structure of Greek tragedy. The seven acts of Revelation have been located on the Ephesian stage.[202]

The most compelling argument for the dramatic purpose is the way in which John employed choruses. Recent studies of the hymnic materials in Revelation have convincingly demonstrated that the hymns comment on and complement the visions and auditions of the book. They function, thus, in the same way as the choruses in the Greek drama prepared for and commented upon the dramatic movements of the plot.[203]

However, even though Revelation contains dramatic elements, it is evident that it is not written in the dialogue form of the drama, just as it is not patterned after a certain liturgical formulation. Liturgical and dramatic elements are important for the composition of Revelation but they do not constitute its chief purpose. This does not necessarily mean that it was not presented in the Ephesian theater or in other theaters. In fact, Blevins and others have demonstrated the power of a theatrical presentation of this remarkable dramatic book.[204]

f. RESPOND TO A MAJOR SOCIAL CRISIS

(1) Factors contributing to the social crisis

I have suggested that John wrote Revelation at the end of Domitian's reign (AD 95-96). Collins and other scholars have pointed out certain elements in Revelation which imply that John was responding to a major social crisis. A number of factors were involved in this crisis.

(a) Conflict with the Jews

At first, the followers of Jesus and believers in Christ considered themselves to be, and were perceived by Gentiles as, part of the complex diversity we speak of as ancient Judaism. The controversy between the followers of Jesus and other Jews brought more and more to public attention the differences between them. The awareness of differences probably created a crisis of identity for at least some Christians. It also made the public status of some Christian groups precarious.

Revelation contains evidence that controversies between believers in Christ and local Jews had created a social crisis for at least some Christians in Asia. This was especially true for those like John who were Jews by birth. The name "Jews" was denied to the Christian community in Smyrna. Christians in Smyrna thus no longer enjoyed the social, economic, and political security afforded by association with and attachment to the local Jewish community.[205]

(b) Problems with neighboring Gentiles

Rejection by the Jews was especially threatening for Christians. This is true because they had little identity apart from Judaism and because their Gentile neighbors despised them too. There is clear evidence that many Romans and provincials hated Christians for a variety of reasons. Most fundamental was the charge of "hatred of the human race." This was an accusation which was also made against the Jews. The charge grew out of Christian exclusiveness. It was based on their refusal to respect any god but their own. This led to the avoidance of Gentile political and social life. Christians were also accused of vices and crimes, such as arson, incest, and cannibalism.

At stake was the question of simulation. What pagan customs

could Christians adopt for the sake of economic survival, commercial gain, or simple sociability?

Eating meat sacrificed to idols symbolized for the author of Revelation a stance of openness to the surrounding Greco-Roman culture. John regarded such openness as syncretistic and, therefore, idolatrous. The thrust of John is toward even greater exclusiveness.[206]

(c) Conflict over wealth

Crucial tensions resulted from different degrees of wealth and different attitudes toward wealth reflected in Revelation. John criticized the Christians of Laodicea for relying on their wealth. John also attacked the Roman Empire for being a source of wealth. This discussion is found most clearly in Revelation 18. Wealth was one of Rome's faults because Roman leaders and allies were felt to possess it at the expense of others. Whatever John's actual economic situation, he sympathized with those viewed as unjustly at an economic disadvantage.[207]

External evidence also indicates that at the end of the first century and during the first part of the second, there were severe strains between rich and poor in Asia Minor. Revelation was shaped to some extent by these strains.[208]

(d) The offense of the Roman Imperial Cult

The Christians reacted intensely and negatively to the pressure to worship or pay allegiance to Domitian, the Roman ruler.

(2) The results of the rapid development of the social factors

Recent studies point out how cultural disintegration can be brought about by rapid change or contact with a foreign culture, especially if that culture seems superior. In our time, social crisis has arisen from conditions like overpopulation, a shift from rural to urban life, and industrialization. In other cases, the development of a new set of expectations without establishing the means to achieve them causes cultural disintegration. This situation has arisen when primitive societies first come into contact with modern ones.[209]

In the case of Revelation, an additional factor was operative. A new set of expectations had arisen as a result of faith in Jesus as the Messiah and the belief that the kingdom of God and Christ had been established. This situation created an almost unbearable tension for many Christians between what was and what ought to have been. Sociologists speak of such tensions as cognitive dissonance. This is a state of mind that arises when there is a great disparity between expectations and reality. Many of the early Christians evidently expected the social, economic, and political order to be changed speedily and thoroughly.[210]

This perceived social crisis apparently led to certain feelings that are reflected and dealt with in Revelation. A feeling of powerlessness was evoked by the exclusion of Christians from Jewish and Gentile institutions. Fear was generated by the denunciation of Christians before Roman authorities and by the impressions left by the triumph of Nero's persecution. Antipas was executed and John was banished to Patmos. Aggressive feelings were aroused by the various social tensions. Resentment was felt at the rejection and hostility of Jews and Gentiles. Envy of the wealthy and the powerful rankled the Christians. The Imperial Ruler Cult caused persecution, antipathy, and frustration. The violent deeds of the Roman Empire called forth a desire for vengeance.[211]

(3) Methods of responding to the social crisis

(a) Encouraged Christians by showing them how they were related to Old Testament victories and the victory over chaos

John showed the similarity that the seven trumpets and the seven bowls have with the narratives about the plagues against Egypt which God sent through Moses according to Exodus 7—12. The plagues of the trumpets and bowls are presented in Revelation as punishment upon the earth, especially upon the Romans for the unjust shedding of blood and for the murder of faithful Christians. The use of the symbol of the plague suggested to the hearers that they should understand their own situation by analogy with the slavery of the Israelites in Egypt. As God delivered Israel from Egypt, so He would deliver Christians from Rome.[212]

John also presented those who persecuted or opposed Christians as symbols of chaos. He was saying that, as it was in the beginning, as it always has been when the chaos monster rears its head, so it will be once again. God and the Lamb, as representatives of creation, life, and order, will be victorious over the dragon and his two beast allies. Revelation 12 expresses in symbolic form the predicament of the hearers and provides it with a resolution. The hearers are invited to identify with the woman. Like Israel at the time of the Exodus, she is carried to safety by eagles' wings. Like Israel she is nourished in the desert by God. This encouraged Christians to believe that they would not be overwhelmed by the threat that Rome posed to them.[213]

(b) Utilize the method of catharsis.

Collins suggests that in a manner similar to Greek tragedy, Revelation arouses certain emotions and then a catharsis of these emotions is achieved. In Greek tragedy, the emotions of the audience are purged, their feelings of fear and piety are intensified and given objective expression. The feelings are thus brought to consciousness and become less threatening.[214]

Revelation functions in a similar way. Fear of Roman power is evoked or intensified. In various places, conflicts are described. The powers that threaten the Christian are symbolized with a beast from the abyss and the dragon. Then the conflict is projected onto a cosmic screen. This has a cathartic or cleansing effect in the sense that it clarifies and objectifies the conflict. Fearful feelings are vented by the very act of expressing them, especially in this larger-than-life and exaggerated way.

Resentment of Roman wealth and power is evoked or intensified, especially in chapters 17 and 18. The harlot, Babylon, is arrayed in purple and scarlet. She is adorned with gold, jewels, and pearls. She drinks from a golden cup (17:4; 18:16). The merchants are portrayed mourning over their cargo of luxury goods. All these alluring, unattainable goods are to be destroyed by divine wrath.

Feelings of fear and resentment are released by the book's repeated presentations of the destruction of the enemies of the hearers or readers. The persecutors are destroyed by the divine wrath and the persecuted ones are exalted to a new and glorious mode of existence.[215]

Some say that Revelation merely provides a compensation for the relatively disadvantaged situation of the hearers. But the symbols and plot of Revelation, when deeply heard, do affect the actions of the hearers. The book enabled hearers or readers to cope in extreme circumstances. In a situation where direct political action was not practical or feasible, it was a text that kept alive the expectation of a better world.[216]

John also dealt with wealth in a cathartic or cleansing manner. Wealth as such was not rejected in the Apocalypse. The problem was that the wrong people had power and wealth. In order for the feeling of envy to be controlled, the possession of riches in the present had to be presented as evil and hateful in itself. This was done by linking wealth and power.[217]

Collins points out that the process of containing aggression reflected in the Apocalypse was adequate and appropriate. It was adequate in the sense that self-destructive behavior was apparently avoided. As far as we know, the anger of John and the majority of the hearers or readers did not erupt into violence against their non-Christian neighbors. This type of violence would surely have worsened their situation.[218]

g. TELL ABOUT THE LAST DAYS OF HISTORY

This aspect of the purpose will be developed in detail in the discussion of chapters 5 and 6.

In the section on "Eternal and Abiding Truths," I will show in a more specific way how Revelation applies to the contemporary world.

How Do You Interpret Revelation and See It in Broad Perspective?

What Are Representative Methods of Interpreting Revelation?

Before we begin a detailed study of the text of Revelation, I will briefly describe some of the distinctive models or methods for interpreting Revelation. We will look at these methods as they have emerged in the history of interpretation and as they express themselves in the contemporary world. Methods which are not live options for conservative or evangelical Christians will be omitted or only mentioned briefly. However, some elements of truth can be gleaned from less prominent models and should not be overlooked. The models will be presented as fairly as possible. Strengths and weaknesses of each model will be noted.

The easiest approach, of course, is to follow your own inherited or traditional method and see it as the only true view and ignore other approaches. The intelligent and sincere Bible student, however, should be familiar with the various alternative models of interpretation so that he may criticize and purify his own view or adopt a more adequate view.

Each age has its key issues. The *Zeitgeist* or the "spirit of the times" shapes many things, from the awarding of the Nobel peace prize to the ideologies of the day, such as liberation theology. Emphasis on various doctrinal issues rises and falls with this *Zeitgeist*.[1]

Oftentimes the important factor in the development of an approach to Revelation is not the Bible itself, but the spirit of the times. For example, the seed of both postmillennialism and amillennialism were planted about AD 400 by Augustine. The spirit of the times was positive, at least in the early part of the fifth century. Constantine had prepared the way for the legal status of the church. It seemed that God was ruling in the *now*. The millennial kingdom had come or was coming. The lion was reclining with the lamb.

As we have seen, postmillennialism was also undergirded by the optimistic view of the Puritans in the seventeenth century. In fact, the postmillennial view parallels and to some extent is a theological reflection of the optimistic views of mankind's potential and opportunities. The seventeenth and eighteenth centuries saw an expanding geographical horizon and an ever-growing confidence in the powers of human reason.

This idea does not mean that the development of particular views is the result of *only* the sociopolitical climates of their times. In fact, an authentic view should not be shaped by our social milieu but by a proper interpretation of the Bible. But, as we survey the rise and development of seven representative methods, we will note that a number of factors influenced them.[2]

1. Revelation Is Primarily for the Encouragement of First-century Christians. This Is Called the Preterist, Historical Background, or Contemporary-historical View.

a. CHIEF IDEAS

Those who hold this view include such devout scholars as I. T. Beckwith and H. B. Swete. For them, Revelation's chief application is to the days of the Roman Empire when it was ruled by Domitian, about AD 95. They look upon Revelation as a book primarily written to encourage Christians in the days of Roman persecution in Asia Minor. The main contents of chapters 4—22 are viewed as describing events wholly limited to John's own time.

A more recent version of the preterist view sees Revelation as belonging to a distinct type of Jewish-Christian writing called *apocalyptic*. This perspective emphasizes that in the interbiblical period Judaism had many books which are similar in style and emphasis to Revelation. These interbiblical writers were discouraged because of the evils of historical experience and the persecution of God's people at the hands of godless rulers and nations, such as Antiochus Epiphanes and Syria. They saw their own days as growing more and more evil and taught that the end of the age was imminent. According to their understanding, God had turned the evil age over to the powers of evil. However, He would soon intervene to destroy evil and to establish His kingdom. These interbiblical writings, such as Enoch, thus spoke primarily to the discouraged Jews in the age in which they were written.

Interpreted in this apocalyptic way, Revelation expresses the hopes of early Christians of Asia Minor. They were about to be delivered from their troubles at the hands of Rome. Imperial Rome was the beast of 13:1-10. The Asian priesthood promoting the worship of the Caesar of Rome was the false prophet of 13:11-18. John wrote to confirm the faith of believers and to tell them that even though terrible persecution was at the door, God would soon intervene and Christ would return. Rome would be destroyed and the kingdom of God would shortly be established. Although Christ did not return in the first century, for the apocalypticists the book fulfilled its purpose in strengthening and encouraging the first-century church during a time of persecution. This is a view held by a majority of contemporary critical scholars.

b. STRENGTHS

There are obviously elements of truth in the preterist method. This approach stresses the historical background of Revelation. Even though Revelation has meaning beyond the first century, surely it had meaning in and for the first century.

E. D. Hirsch contends that the meaning of a book must be linked to the situation in which it emerged. Interpretations that do not take the original historical context seriously cannot claim to understand the meaning which the text had for the original hearers.

Most contemporary scholars would agree with Hirsch. The symbolic universe of every text is shaped by its historical context and cultural milieu. To ignore these factors is to limit understanding.[3]

To speak of a text as an intermediate link between the past of the author and the present of the interpreter because the text has a certain objective character makes more sense. The logic and the sense of a text is discovered, at least in a primary sense, when it is read in terms of a specific culture and specific historical circumstances. If the interpreter's point of view is not a reconstruction of the original context of the text, it will inevitably be the cultural perspective of the interpreter. And oftentimes this perspective is shaped by some powerful interpretation or influence between the author's and the interpreter's time.[4]

The preterist or historical background view has caused us to regard with careful attention the original historical context as the essential foundation of the interpretation of any text. Such attention is especially important for Revelation since it refers, although at times in a veiled way, to historical, political, economic, and social conditions of its time. Without a precise knowledge of the book's setting, the interpreter is in danger of serious misunderstanding. Therefore, an accurate understanding of the world behind Revelation is indispensable for an appropriate appreciation of the "world" created by the text itself.[5]

In other words, the great merit of the preterist approach is that it understands and interprets the plight of the first-century church in terms of the crisis which had developed at that particular time. By not relegating the book to some future period, the encouragements to the church as well as the warnings are taken with immediate seriousness. It should be noted that preterists hold the major prophecies of the book were fulfilled in either the fall of Jerusalem (AD 70) or the fall of Rome (AD 476).[6]

c. WEAKNESSES

Most evangelical scholars contend that Revelation contains predictive elements as well as encouragement for the first-century Christians. In other words, Revelation is a book of genuine prophecy concerning events extending beyond the early centuries. The major problem with the preterist position is that the decisive victory portrayed in the latter chapters of Revelation was never achieved. It is difficult to believe that John envisioned anything less than the complete overthrow of Satan, the final destruction of evil and the eternal reign of God.

The preterist view, in general, tends to neglect or omit the future significance of the book. In addition to the encouragement and predictive purposes, evangelical scholars also emphasize that Revelation has a moral and ethical purpose for each generation.[7]

2. Revelation Portrays in a Symbolic Way Truths for Each Age and for the End of History. This Is Known as the Amillennial View.

a. DEFINITION OF AMILLENNIALISM

In some ways this is the clearest and simplest view. Actually, the term *amillennialism* is not very precise. It suggests that amillennialists either do not believe in any millennium or that they simply ignore the first six verses of Revelation 20 which speak of a millennial reign. Neither of these two statements is correct.[8]

Some have suggested that this view should be called "realized millennialism." This is more accurate because amillennialists believe that the millennium of Revelation 20 is not exclusively future but is now in process of realization.[9]

b. HISTORY OF AMILLENNIALISM

There was no thoroughgoing amillennialism during the earliest centuries of the church, but there were some amillennial elements present. During the fourth century, when the Christian church was given a favorite status under the Emperor Constantine, the amillennial position was accepted. The thousand-year reign of Christ and His saints was equated with the whole history of the church on earth, thus making for the denial of a future millennium. The famous church father Augustine advocated this position, and it became the dominant interpretation in medieval times. The teaching of Augustine was so fully accepted that at the Council of Ephesus in 431 belief in the millennium was condemned as superstitious.[10]

Details of Augustine's amillennialism may be found in his major work *The City of God*, Book XX. He interpreted the millennium in an allegorical manner that led him to believe that he was already living in the millennium. The first resurrection, interpreted as spiritual, had already taken place for the Christian. The second resurrection would be the resurrection of the body.[11]

With the decline of postmillennialism during the twentieth century, many postmillennialists thought it necessary to adjust their eschatology. Because dispensational premillennialism represented too sharp a break, the majority chose amillennialism.[12]

Today the choice for conservative Christians seems to be either amillennialism, historical premillennialism, or dispensational premillennialism. Conservatives in the historic Reformed groups, such as the Reformed Church of America, the Christian Reformed Church, and the Presbyterian churches are primarily amillennial.[13]

Southern Baptists have those who embrace each of the three approaches mentioned. In *Things Which Shall Be Hereafter* Russell Bradley Jones speaks of the millennium as the indefinite reign of Christ between the cross and the second coming of Christ. Any belief in a reign of Christ upon the earth is classified as "materialism." The same emphasis is found in *The Meaning and Message of the Book of Revelation* by E. A. McDowell (1951). McDowell believed that we already live in the millennium of Revelation 20:4-6.[14]

Two books by Ray Summers are well-known presentations of

amillennialism. His commentary on Revelation, *Worthy is the Lamb* (1951), and *The Life Beyond* (1959) interpret the "first resurrection" in a symbolic way as the triumph of the martyrs, but the "second resurrection" is said to be literal.[15]

H. H. Hobbs in *The Cosmic Drama* (1971) and in *Studies in Revelation* (1971) adopted the Augustinian idea of the millennium as the present reign of Christ. However, he said that the reign is in heaven, not on earth.[16]

The commentary on Revelation by Morris Ashcraft in *The Broadman Bible Commentary* views the reign of Christ during the millennium as confined to the martyrs. *The Revelation of Jesus Christ* by Ray F. Robbins (1975) interprets the first resurrection as spiritual, as in Augustine.[17]

c. TENETS OF AMILLENNIALISM

(1) General perspective on the interpretation of Revelation

Amillennialism usually sees Revelation as composed of seven sections which run parallel to each other. Each section pictures the church and the world from the time of Christ's first coming to the time of His second coming. A well-known exponent of this view is William Hendriksen in *More Than Conquerors*.[18]

This parallel view means that each section recapitulates the events of the same period, rather than describing the events of successive periods. Each section deals with the same era—the period between Christ's first and second comings—picking up earlier themes, elaborating and developing them further.[19]

For Hendriksen the seven sections of Revelation are 1—3, 4—7, 8—11, 12—14, 15—16, 17—19, and 20—22. As an example of the recapitulation approach, chapters 20—22 do not describe what follows the return of Christ. Rather, Revelation 20:1 takes us back once again to the beginning of the New Testament era. [20]

Amillennialism also has its own treatment of the two resurrections referred to in Revelation 20:4-5, "They came to life [the first resurrection], and reigned with Christ a thousand years. The rest of the dead did not come to life until the thousand years were ended [the second resurrection]." The first resurrection, say amillennialists, is spiritual. The second resurrection is either bodily-physical or spiritual. Most amillennialists consider the second resurrection to be physical.[21]

According to Ray Summers, the purpose of Revelation was to assure God's people that Christ will triumph over all opposition. Satan was attempting to deceive believers into worshiping the emperor rather than Christ. The binding of Satan referred to in Revelation 20:1-3 is to keep Satan from effectively continuing this work. The 1,000 years symbolizes the completeness of this binding and restraint.

This same symbol of 1,000 years is used to convey the idea of the complete triumph of the martyrs who have been the objects of Satan's wrath. In Revelation 20:4-5, they are on thrones with Christ for 1,000 years.[22]

This then is the amillennial interpretation of Revelation 20:1-6. It contends that the passage says nothing about an earthly reign of Christ over a primarily Jewish kingdom. Rather, it describes a reigning with Christ in heaven between death and Christ's second coming for the souls of deceased believers. It also describes the binding of Satan during the present age in such a way that he cannot prevent the spread of the gospel.[23]

(2) Summary of the tenets of amillennialism

(a) The second coming of Christ will inaugurate the final age and the final state for both believers and unbelievers. This means that the second coming will be followed immediately by the general resurrection, the judgment of all, and the consignment of all to their ultimate, future estates.[24]

(b) Revelation is a very symbolic and figurative book. Therefore it seems reasonable to conclude that the number 1,000 should not be seen as literal.[25]

(c) The two resurrections of Revelation 20 do not require an intervening millennium.[26]

(d) The Old Testament prophecies will not be fulfilled in a 1,000-year earthly period. They tend rather to be fulfilled within the history of the church, or in some cases in the new heaven and the new earth.[27]

(e) The so-called "signs of the times" have been present in the world from the time of Christ's first coming. However, they will come to a more intensified, final manifestation just before the second coming. The amillennialists also look for an intensified form of tribulation and apostasy as well as for the appearance of a personal Antichrist before the second coming.[28]

d. STRENGTHS OF AMILLENNIALISM

(1) Amillennialism has attempted to take seriously the literary nature of Revelation, and it has sought to learn what was being conveyed within the cutural setting

Amillennialists have also attempted to determine the proper meaning of the symbols by studying the culture rather than assigning them an arbitrary meaning.[29]

(2) Amillennialism has sought to maintain that the Bible is the supreme authority for Christian belief and practice

(3) Amillennialists have maintained a realistic philosophy of history

This view teaches neither that the entire world will be converted prior to Christ's return nor that world conditions will inevitably grow worse.[30]

e. WEAKNESSES OF AMILLENNIALISM

(1) Critics of amillennialism point out that there is a tendency to spiritualize both the Old Testament and the New Testament

National Israel almost disappears. The amillennial exegesis of Revelation 20:1-6 states that there are two different types of resurrection, a spiritual and a physical. Yet upon close examination this interpretation creates a distinction between the resurrections where none exists. The same verb is used of both resurrections, and there is no apparent contextual basis for discriminating between the two.[31]

(2) Critics also suggest that amillennialism is characterized by a lack of interest in prophetic emphasis or predictions of the future

3. Revelation Is Primarily a Forecast of the Development of History. This Is Called the Historicist or Continuous-historical View.

a. DEFINITION

This view affirms that Revelation is a symbolic presentation of the entire course of the history of the Western church from the close of the first century to the end of time. Specific events, nations, and persons are sought in church history that fit the seals, the trumpets, and the bowls. The most important identification, according to this view, is the identification of the beast and the false prophet of Revelation 13 with the medieval pope and the papacy. Other parts of Revelation are seen as describing periods of corruption in the Western church and the various wars through church history.

b. HISTORY

Scholars generally accept that this view started with Joachim of Fiore (d. 1202). Joachim was a monastic who claimed to have received on Easter night a special vision that revealed to him God's plan for the ages. In his scheme, Revelation was a prophecy of the events of Western history from the times of the apostles until his own time.[32]

The various reform movements from the thirteenth through fifteenth centuries, including the Waldenses in France, the followers of John Huss in Bohemia, and John Wycliffe in England, accepted this view. They all agreed that the medieval papacy was the Antichrist and that Revelation was to be directed against the Roman Catholic Church.[33]

Later, Luther, Calvin, and other Reformers came to adopt this view. Martin Luther was, therefore, not at all the first to refer to the medieval papacy as the Antichrist. Interpretation had moved in that direction for three centuries before him. Regarding the beasts of Revelation 13, Luther noted that the second beast had to be the pope who had restored the fallen Roman Empire and conveyed it from the Greeks to the Germans.[34]

In addition to the Reformers, prominent religious leaders advocating this view include Sir Isaac Newton, Bengel, Elliott, Alford, and Barnes. A specific example of the forecast of history approach is found in the writings of Elliott, such as the *Apocalypticae*. According to Elliott, the trumpets of 8:6 to 9:21 cover the historical period from AD 395 to AD 453. In one section Elliott saw a parallelism between Revelation and the attacks on the Western Roman Empire by the Goths and the eventual fall of the Eastern Empire to the Turks. Elliott argued that the hail and fire in Revelation 8:7 had to refer to the Goths because hail comes from the north as did the Goths.

c. STRENGTH

An element of strength in the historical forecast method is that it sees history as under God's guidance and speaks much of the general principles of divine providence.

d. WEAKNESSES

There are many difficulties. As many as fifty different historical interpretations have been given, depending on the time and circumstances of the expositor. A major difficulty, therefore, is that no consensus has been achieved as to what the outline of history foreseen in Revelation really is.

True, prophetic language is somewhat opaque before the predicted events come to pass. However, the fulfilling event should clarify the language enough to prevent the breadth of interpretative variations that exist among the historical forecast advocates. For example, the forecast of history view has variously identified the locusts from the abyss in 9:1 *ff.* with the Vandals, Goths, Persians, Muhammadans, heretics, and others.[35]

Another objection critics raise asks why a general prophecy, which should be universal, is confined to the fortunes of the Western Roman Empire. The historical forecast model stresses chiefly the development of the church in Western Europe and gives little recognition of the Christian development in the East. If the forecast of history method is the correct one, it is clear that no one has found the key.

In fact, Harrison contends that it is doubtful that the Spirit of God would be concerned to inform the apostolic church with a rather detailed picture of events lying beyond their own time and having only a remote bearing on the consummation of the age.[36]

4. Revelation Is a Forecast of Christian Triumph in History Before the Second Coming of Christ. This Method Is Known as Postmillennialism

a. Definition and tenets

Postmillennialism is generally defined as that view of last things which holds that the kingdom of God is now being extended in the world through the preaching of the gospel and the saving work of the Holy Spirit in the hearts of individuals. It affirms that the world is eventually to be Christianized. The return of Christ is to occur at the close of a long period of righteousness and peace commonly called the "millennium."[37]

This view teaches several basic ideas. First, the kingdom of God is primarily a present reality here on earth. Second, all the nations will be converted prior to Christ's return. The preaching of the gospel will be effective. Essentially all persons in each of the areas and nations of the world will come to believe.

Third, there is to be a long period of earthly peace termed the millennium. Conflict among nations will cease, as will friction among the social classes and races. The millennium is a long period of time, not necessarily 1,000 calendar years.[38]

Fourth, at the end of the millennium, there will be a time of apostasy and a flare-up of evil occurring in connection with the coming of the Antichrist. Postmillennialists teach that the great tribulation of Matthew 24 and the apostasy of 2 Thessalonians 2 are already past. Yet on the basis of Revelation 20:7-10, which describes the loosing of Satan at the end of the millennium, they do look for a limited manifestation of evil before Christ returns. Fifth, the millennium will end with the personal bodily return of Christ.[39]

The postmillennialists build their case on biblical texts and emphases. They quote the Great Commission of Matthew 28:18-20 in which Christ commands His people to make disciples of all nations. This commission is not merely an announcement that the gospel will be preached. Rather, it implies a promise that the effectual evangelization of all the nations will be completed before Christ returns.

They use Matthew 16:18, which records Jesus as saying that the gates of hell shall not prevail against the church. They interpret this verse as meaning that the church will take the offensive with the gospel and that it will advance throughout the world. Literally, nothing will be able to resist its onward march.

They also cite passages from the Psalms and Prophets which speak of the universal and triumphant reign of the Messiah. Because nothing that has taken place in history does justice to the glory of the prophetic vision, the golden age must be yet future, but prior to the Messiah's return.[40]

They also mention the parable of the leaven in Matthew 13:33 as pointing to the universal extension of the kingdom. As in all of the parables of growth, the field is the world. Just as natural leaven develops from one atom or segment to the next, the gospel leaven works its way through society from individual to individual. What is true of the gospel spread from individual to individual is true of its spread through society's institutions and activities—physical environment, education, politics, and national and international affairs. In this way, the whole mass of humanity shall be filled with and governed by Christian principles and spirit.[41]

The postmillennialist is not in a hurry. God does not rush matters. He might take a long time to complete His redemptive plan.[42]

Postmillennialists draw from Romans 11 the prospect of the extensive conversion of both Jews and Gentiles. Christ will return after the Great Commission has been fulfilled and all nations have been discipled and baptized.[43]

They acknowledge that the relative growth of Christianity has been slow. But this is blamed on the failure of Christians in general to take seriously the command of Christ to evangelize the world. This slow progress in no sense argues against the power and efficacy of the gospel.[44]

b. HISTORY

This view is generally considered to have its roots, along with amillennialism, in the teachings of Augustine, bishop of Hippo, who worked and taught in the fifth century AD. Augustine tended to identify the visible church with the kingdom of God. He further taught that the church should seek to gradually increase in numbers and in possessions and influence until it could achieve world dominion.

When the political structure of the Roman Empire crashed in the fifth century AD, Augustine felt that survival could be achieved by the church as the city of God. He taught that the millennium is the era or period beginning with the first advent of Christ and continuing until the second advent. The first resurrection is spiritual. The binding of Satan was essentially completed with the resurrection of Christ and the reign of Christ is now in progress. He deduced from this that the present era must continue; Christian influence grows until the church is triumphant.

This view has had advocates for a long time. It is in some ways close to amillennialism. As the Middle Ages developed, it seemed increasingly that only fringe groups viewed the millennium as a future event. What we know today as historical premillennialism came more and more under the suspicion of heresy.

Many major denominations eventually incorporated postmillennialism into their creeds. The Augsburg and Westminster confessions are basically postmillennial. Lutheran, Presbyterian, and Reformed groups have been influenced by this position. The great Princeton School of Theology of the nineteenth and early twentieth centuries, represented by Hodges and B. B. Warfield, held the postmillennial view.[45]

In the seventeenth century, Daniel Whitby (1638-1726) developed another variation of the postmillennial view. Whitby taught that the millennium must occur *before* the second coming of Christ. Scriptures which have commonly been understood to refer to the second coming of Christ, Whitby took to mean a mighty outpouring of the Holy Spirit. As a result, he felt that the Jews, the Roman Catholic

Church, and the Turkish powers would be converted to Christ. Likewise, all of the pagan religions would give way to Christ. After this glorious kingdom had been established, Christ would descend to earth and eternity would begin. The postmillennial viewpoint of Daniel Whitby was widely received in eighteenth- and nineteenth-century England and America.

John Wesley was a postmillennialist. He believed that the pope was the Antichrist and that the papal Antichrist would be overthrown by 1836. Jonathan Edwards was also an advocate of this view.

Most of the popular commentaries of the eighteenth and nineteenth centuries followed the theories of postmillennialism. John Gill used this approach in the eighteenth century. His *Annotations on the Bible* was widely read and is reprinted even now. Matthew Henry's popular commentary on the whole Bible adopted a variation of the postmillennial view. The English Methodist Adam Clarke (1762-1832) published an important commentary on the bible in 1810-1826 which embraced postmillennialism.[46]

The postmillennial movement became an important influence in the South and Southwest. This influence came primarily through the teaching and preaching of George W. Truett, longtime pastor of the First Baptist Church, Dallas, Texas, and B. H. Carroll, the Southern Baptist leader and founder of Southwestern Baptist Theological Seminary in Fort Worth, Texas. Carroll fervently believed that the kingdom of God could and would be "brought in" by evangelism, missions, and social reform. In his basic work, *An Interpretation of the English Bible,* B. H. Carroll adopted the view in which the great harlot is identified with the Roman Catholic Church and the millennium is a triumph over Romanism and other forms of human corruption.[47]

It is interesting that most of Carroll's disciples or students shifted to the amillennialism promoted by conservative Calvinism. George Truett's successor, W. A. Criswell, adopted dispensational premillennialism.

Despite two world wars and a more pessimistic spirit in the world, there are still some defenders of the postmillennial view. Conservative Reformed scholar Loraine Boettner has written a book entitled *The Millennium* which defends a postmillennial view. He maintains that the power of the gospel will win its way and eventually will convert the world before the second coming of Christ. In answer to critics, Boettner states that this view is not based upon a humanistic view of human progress. Rather it is rooted in the supernatural power of God which is working in history.

According to Boettner, dispensational premillennialism loses the deeper spiritual meaning of biblical prophecies by taking them too literally. He contends that properly understood, the Bible teaches that the present day will gradually emerge into the millennial age as an increasingly larger proportion of the world's inhabitants are converted to Christianity. For Boettner, redemption of the world is a long, slow process, extending through the centuries, but it will most certainly come to pass. From the human perspective, the major requirement is that the Great Commission of Christ should be fulfilled through the outpouring of the Holy Spirit and the preaching of the Christian gospel.

c. STRENGTHS

(1) The emphasis on the present power and urgency of the kingdom of God is a strength

Knowing that Christ is present and that His resources are available to us now encourages confidence, optimism, and aggressiveness.

(2) This view encourages an activism on the part of believers

If the kingdom is present now, we can do something to extend it.

(3) It combats the pessimism about the present age which some dispensationalists encourage and which has made some Christians fatalistic

This kind of thinking often makes the churches less effective than they would otherwise be.[48]

d. WEAKNESSES

(1) Inadequate view of continuing evil

If postmillennialism were a prevailing viewpoint in nineteenth-century and early twentieth-century America, it has not continued to be so. Boettner's book *The Millennium* has a chapter entitled "The World Is Growing Better." Today many are convinced that this is not true. For a number of contemporary biblical scholars, there is a lack of adequate scriptural support for this interpretation. For those scholars, you do not have to be a confirmed pessimist to admit that the only final remedy for mankind's problems lies in the intervention of God in and through the second coming of Christ.

In other words, the postmillennial expectation of a future golden age before Christ' return does not do justice to the continuing tension in the history of the world between the kingdom of God and the forces of evil. Its optimism concerning conversion of the world seems somewhat unrealistic in the light of recent world developments.[49]

(2) It neglects biblical passages, such as Matthew 24:9-14, which portray spiritual and moral conditions as worsening in the end times

It appears that postmillennialism has developed its doctrine from very carefully selected biblical passages.[50]

(3) Most of the Old Testament prophecies which are interpreted by the postmillennialists as referring to a future millennial golden age should be seen as referring to the final state of the redeemed community[51]

(4) There is artificiality in the postmillennialist exegesis of the two resurrections and the millennium in Revelation 20

This has been noted in the criticism of the amillennial position.[52]

5. Revelation Is Primarily a Statement of Eternal Theological Principles. This Is also Called the Symbolical or Idealist or Spiritualist View.

a. DEFINITION

This approach sees Revelation as a description, in symbolic terms, of spiritual powers and basic God-ordained principles at work in the world. The message of the book centers in the assurance to the suffering saints of God's final triumph. This assurance is given without prediction of concrete events either in the past or future.

The eternal principles method sees Revelation as being basically poetic, symbolic, and spiritual in nature. Indeed, it is sometimes called the spiritualist view. This does not refer to the cult of spiritualism, but rather to the fact that it tends to "spiritualize" everything in the book. Thus Revelation does not predict any specific historic events. Rather, it sets forth timeless truths concerning the battle between good and evil that continues throughout the church age. As a system of interpretation, it is more recent than most of the other methods. In general, this view is marked by its refusal to identify any of the images with specific future events, whether in the history of the church or with regard to the end of all things.[53]

b. LIST OF PRINCIPLES

Raymond Calkins, an advocate of this view *(The Social Message of the Book of Revelation)*, sees the following general principles in Revelation. (1) It is an irresistible summons to heroic living. (2) The book contains appeals to endurance. (3) Revelation tells us that evil is marked for overthrow in the end. (4) It gives us a new and wonderful picture of Christ. In other words, according to this poetic view, John describes by means of his powers of verbal artistry the sure triumph of God over all evil powers.

c. ADVOCATES

Numerous scholars and writers, apart from the ones mentioned, teach that the importance of Revelation is in its teaching of eternal principles or abiding messages. These include Paul Minear, *I Saw a New Earth*; Thomas Kepler in his work entitled *The Book of Revelation*; and Martin Kiddle in *The Revelation of St. John*. Others who hold this view include William Milligan, who writes in the *Expositor's Bible*, and Cady H. Allen.

d. STRENGTHS

Almost any interpreter of Revelation would give assent to these general principles which have been mentioned. The eternal principles view holds much that is true.

Undoubtedly Revelation does reflect the great timeless realities of the battle between God and Satan and the truth of divine judgment. Obviously Revelation sees history as being ultimately in the hand of the Creator. There is also truth in the emphasis that Revelation employs symbol as its major literary device.[54]

e. WEAKNESSES

This approach continues the allegorical interpretation which dominated exegesis throughout the medieval period and thus minimizes the historical character of the coming consummation. Its weakness, therefore, lies in the fact that it denies to Revelation any specific historical fulfillment. From the eternal principles point of view, the symbols portray an ever-present conflict. The view denies that there is a necessary consummation of the historical process.[55]

In criticism, I would affirm that behind the dramatic language of Revelation there are real occurrences. Revelation portrays the consummation of the battle between God and Satan and shows us the triumph of Christ in history through His coming in glory.[56]

6. Revelation Is Primarily a Forecast of the Very Last Days of History. This Is Known as the Extreme Futurist or Dispensational Premillennial View.

a. DEFINITION

This is one of the most popular, influential, and controversial models for interpreting Revelation in conservative and fundamentalist theological circles. In fact, modern-day America owes a large part of its interest in Revelation to this model called dispensationalism. Advocates of this view did much to renew the interest in the second advent of Christ and Revelation in the late nineteenth century.

According to this view, with the exception of chapters 1—3, all of Revelation relates to a period immediately preceding and following the second advent of Christ at the end of the age. This means that the seals, trumpets, and bowls refer to events still in the future. For example, the beasts of chapters 13 and 17 are identified with the future Antichrist. These beasts will appear at the last moment in world history and will be defeated by Christ in His second coming.[57]

The extreme futurist view was developed in the late sixteenth century by Franciscus Ribeira, a Spanish Jesuit. He held that the beast was the Antichrist of the end time and that Babylon was not Rome under papal rule but a degenerate Rome of a future age.[58]

Dispensationalism is a whole system of theology of which eschatology is but one part. It can also be seen as a method of interpreting the Bible. This means that it affects a person's understanding of even nondoctrinal portions of the Scripture.[59]

The rise of dispensationalism paralleled in a general way the rise of the fundamentalist movement. It has become virtually the official theology of fundamentalism. Some commentators have practically identified the two. Some proponents of dispensationalism consider it not to be an interpretation of the Bible but simply a restatement of what the Bible says. In certain circles, dispensationalists have made it a test of orthodoxy. This means that if you fail to hold all of its points you have denied the Bible itself. In many cases, a whole mind-set or collection of attitudes is involved.[60]

For many people the entire Christian experience is associated with the dispensational way of believing and interpreting the Bible. Of course, this total devotion is true of the adherents of all dynamic systems of belief and life, but it is particularly the case with the dispensationalists. This devotion is enhanced because there is generally a quite extensive and specific program of doctrinal instruction related to it. In some cases, this instruction approaches indoctrination.[61]

b. Key ideas

The first key idea is that God's dealings with humanity are usually divided into seven distinct "dispensations." A dispensation is defined as "a period of time during which man is tested in respect to his obedience to some specific revelation of the will of God." The seventh dispensation of the kingdom is the millennial reign of Christ which will occur after His return.[62]

Second, the Bible must be interpreted literally. This is particularly the case when interpreting biblical references to Israel. The term *Israel* must always refer to the actual nation Israel, ethnic Israel, the Israel that traces its physical descent back to Jacob. God called Jacob *Israel*. The term never refers to "spiritual Israel." All prophetic Scripture is to be treated in a similar manner. All prophecy will be fulfilled literally and in detail.[63]

Third, there is a sharp and definite distinction between Israel and the church. This is regarded as basic to any correct understanding of the Bible. In this view God made a special convenant with Israel (originally with Abraham) that is unconditional. When Christ was on earth the Jews at that time rejected the kingdom. The final establishment of this kingdom, therefore, was postponed until the time of the millennium.[64]

Since the kingdom in its final or "real" form has been rejected by the Jews, Christ proceeded to establish the church. The purpose of the church is to gather believers, primarily Gentiles, but inclusive of some Jews, as the body of Christ. The church, therefore, constitutes a kind of "parenthesis" in the plan of God, interrupting God's predicted program for Israel. The present age (the church age) is a parenthesis or a time period not predicted by the Old Testament. It, therefore, does not fulfill or advance the program of events revealed in the Old Testament foreview.[65]

Fourth, the millennium will feature the restoration of national Israel to its favored place in God's program and the fulfillment of God's promises to Israel. The Old Testament prophets predicted that the people of Israel will at some future time once again be regathered in the land of Canaan. At that time, they will enjoy a time of prosperity and blessing and will have a special place of privilege above other nations. They will live under the benevolent and perfect rule of their Messiah, the descendant of David. Since none of these promises have yet been fulfilled, dispensationalists expect them to be fulfilled during Christ's millennial reign.[66]

Fifth, the true body of believers, called the true church, goes up to heaven with Christ in a pretribulation rapture to celebrate with Him for seven years the marriage feast of the Lamb.[67]

Sixth, those left on earth experience a seven-year period of trial. The last three and a half years of this period is the time of great tribulation. During this time under the Antichrist, 144,000 Jews will accept Christ and become missionaries. The kings of the earth and the armies of the beasts and the false prophet will gather together to attack the people of God in the battle of Armageddon.[68]

Seventh, Christ returns with the church and ends the battle of Armageddon. Christ now begins His millennial reign. He ascends a throne in Jerusalem and rules over a kingdom which is primarily Jewish, although Gentiles also share its blessing. The Jews, however, are exalted above the Gentiles.[69]

Resurrected saints will be living in the new heavenly Jerusalem which is described in Revelation 21:1 to 22:5. During the millennial reign, this heavenly Jerusalem will be in the air above the earth, shedding its light upon the earth. Resurrected saints will play some part in the millennial reign since they will participate with Christ in certain judgments. It would appear, therefore, that the resurrected saints are able to descend from the new Jerusalem to the earth in order to engage in these judgments.

At the beginning of the millennium, only regenerate people are living on the earth. The children born to these people during the millennium will far outnumber their parents. Many of these children will be converted and become true believers. Those who turn out to be rebellious against Christ will be kept in check by Christ and, if necessary, put to death. Those who merely profess the Christian faith but are not true believers will be gathered together by Satan at the end of the millennium after Satan has been loosed from prison. They will then engage in the final attack against the "camp of the saints." This final revolt, however, will be crushed by Christ. God's enemies will be destroyed, and Satan will be cast into the lake of fire. Before the millennium ends, all believers who died during the millennium will be raised. After the millennium has ended all the unbelieving dead will be raised and will be judged before the great white throne.[70]

Eighth, the final state will then be ushered in. God will create a new heaven and a new earth from which all sin and imperfection will be removed. The heavenly Jerusalem, the dwelling place of the resurrected saints, will now descend to this new earth where God and His people will dwell together in perfect peace forever. Although the people of God on the earth will be one, there will remain a distinction throughout all eternity between redeemed Jews and redeemed Gentiles.[71]

c. APPLICATION OF DISPENSATIONAL TEACHINGS TO THE INTERPRETATION OF REVELATION

Statements in Revelation 3:10 and the rapture of John into heaven as described in Revelation 4:1 are usually seen as teaching the rapture of the church at the end of this present age. Chapters 6—18 of Revelation portray the period of the Great Tribulation—that last short but terrible period of history when the Antichrist will seek to destroy God's people. In the dispensational view, God's people during the tribulation period are constituted by Israel restored to Jerusalem. They are protected by divine sealing (7:1-8) and utilize a rebuilt Temple (11:1-3). The church is not on earth during the seven years of the Great Tribulation, for it has been caught up to be with Christ in a secret pretribulation rapture.

For the dispensationalist, most of Revelation (chs. 4—18) has to do with a period of seven years, with the chief emphasis being on the last three and one-half years of the seven-year tribulation period. Chapter 19 of Revelation refers to the second coming of Christ to the earth—not to gather His saints but with His saints. Chapter 20 refers to the future millennial kingdom of Christ on earth which will follow the second coming.

The various judgments of God portrayed in Revelation are poured out on the earth in literal ways. These judgments are described in terms of seals, trumpets, and bowls. The judgments are successive and develop in intensity. Chapter 13 is the prophecy of a great future pagan world empire. The political and religious heads of this empire are represented by the two beasts of this chapter. The harlot of chapter 17 is the final form of the church in apostasy. In a similar way all other events described in Revelation (chs. 4—18) primarily relate to the last seven years of history prior to the second coming of Christ.

d. HISTORY AND DEVELOPMENT

The dispensational movement is of a relatively recent origin. No trace of this theology in a developed form can be found in the early history of the church.[72]

Dispensationalism had its modern origin and development in the context of a small group of Christians known as the Plymouth Brethren about 1830. The primary leader was J. N. Darby (1800-1882), who was an Anglican clergyman. He resigned from the Episcopal Church in 1827 and became a leader of the Separatist group known as the Plymouth Brethren. Darby described the coming of Christ before the millennium as consisting of two stages: the first, a secret rapture removing the church before the Great Tribulation devastates the earth; the second, Christ coming with His saints to set up the kingdom.[73]

Darby also believed that the church is the mystery of which only Paul spoke and that the purpose of God in the Bible could be understood through a series of time periods called dispensations. At his death, Darby left forty volumes of writings and some fifteen hundred assemblies around the world. Through his books, which include four volumes on prophecy, the dispensational system was carried throughout the English-speaking world. A line of continuity from Darby to the present can be traced from his dispensational contemporaries and followers. His contemporaries included C. H. Mackintosh, William Kelley, and F. W. Grant. Those following his teaching include W. E. Blackstone, James Hall Brooks, H. A. Ironside, A. C. Gaebelein, and C. I. Scofield and his *Scofield Bible*. There are many current adherents of his views.[74]

Critics suggest that the French Revolution and its aftermath helped to kindle an interest in prophecy. Biblical students saw the destruction of papal power, the secularization of the state, and the rise of a religion of reason as being remarkably similar to events described in Daniel and Revelation. Those able to break the code of Daniel and Revelation not only could understand what was happening all about them but could face the end of the age with a joy born of the certain knowledge of a pretribulation rapture.

Scholars have pointed out that the dispensational type of thinking influenced the Mormons who think of themselves as Latter-Day Saints. It is also similar to some teachings of the Shakers who viewed Mother Ann Lee as the one who was inaugurating the millennium.[75]

Critics point out the late arrival of this view in Christian history. Dispensational scholars, such as Charles Ryrie, contend that it is understandable that doctrines about last things would not be refined and fully understood until the fulfillment of the events draws near.

J. N. Darby visited America six times between 1859 and 1874 and was warmly welcomed. Beyond the details of his prophetic system, he was seen to have restored the biblical truths of Christ's glorious second coming. The new prophetic emphasis found expression in the prophecy and Bible conference movement of the late 1800s.

Darby's impact on C. I. Scofield (1843-1921) was extremely important since Scofield made dispensationalism an integral part of his Bible notes. Within fifty years, three million copies of the *Scofield Reference Bible* were printed in the United States. In recent days, the popularity of Hal Lindsey's books demonstrates the vitality of the dispensational view.[76]

To understand the impact of the *Scofield Reference Bible*, we must remember that early in the twentieth century few Bibles with "helps" were available. Scofield conveniently combined text and commentary into one volume. It is not surprising that some persons find it difficult to remember whether they had read something in the text or at the bottom of the page in the notes. Scofield's interpretation became widely adopted in fundamentalist circles.

Two types of dispensationalism exist. One could be called extreme or ultradispensationalism. Clarence Larkin is an adherent of this extreme view. His prophetic charts paved the way for many of his disciples. Some scholars in the field contend that Hal Lindsey has done little more than popularize and bring up to date the teachings of Larkin.[77] The old *Scofield Bible* tends to represent this viewpoint.

A revised *Scofield Reference Bible* was published in 1967. It represents the more moderate type of dispensationalism.

In any case, dispensationalism is held by millions of American Christians. It is taught by the leading television evangelists, such as Jerry Falwell, Rex Humbard, Oral Roberts, Kenneth Copeland, and Jack Van Impe. As already indicated, the number one nonfiction book of the 1970s was Hal Lindsey's *The Late Great Planet Earth*.

Another effective means of the propagation of dispensationalism was through the Bible institutes. Many fundamentalist congregations had at one time been part of large denominations and had obtained their ministers from the seminaries of these denominations. When they thought that doctrinal deviation appeared in these seminaries, the churches began to obtain their ministers from Bible institutes, such as Moody Bible Institute in Chicago. Almost without exception, these institutions and their faculties taught dispensationalism. Thus this view spread even more widely. In some cases, the Bible institutes evolved into Bible colleges and then into Christian liberal arts colleges. Some colleges also developed theological seminaries. The Bible Institute of Los Angeles became Biola College which gave birth to Talbot Theological Seminary. Dallas Theological Seminary had a somewhat different pattern of development. Some students obtained their undergraduate education at a Bible college and then went to a dispensational seminary such as Dallas, Talbot, Grace, or Western Conservative Baptist.[78]

e. STRENGTHS

First, dispensationalism takes the future aspect of biblical prophecy very seriously and literally.

Second, adherents claim that the dispensational interpretation of Revelation puts a difficult book into an understandable system which many searching laypeople have found helpful. The system is seen to be orderly and well-organized. Such an approach appeals to the rational, logical mind-set that cannot easily live with ambiguity or understand symbolic language. The fact that meaning is best apprehended, understood, and facilitated within a structure or *gestalt* may account, at least in part, for the great popularity of dispensationalism among laypeople.[79]

Third, dispensationalism discusses the issues of prophecy in terms of specific Scriptures and demonstrates a thorough knowledge of Bible content. Even if we disagree with the method of interpretation, we should appreciate the emphasis on a detailed study of the Bible.[80]

f. WEAKNESSES

The first weakness is the teaching that God has a separate purpose for Israel and the church. In other words, this view fails to take seriously the way in which the New Testament writers saw the Old Testament promises fulfilled in the church. This teaching rebuilds an ethnic-religious wall at the heart of the people of God. This is the touchstone of dispensationalism and, according to Bruce Corley, its greatest flaw. On such a view, the death of Jesus, which is to reconcile Jews and Gentiles and other conflicting groups, has a very limited impact.[81]

Israel has a continuing place in the purpose of God, but this purpose has nothing to do with land or nationality. Paul stated in Romans 11:23 that unbelieving Israel would enter the one saving purpose of God on the condition of faith in Christ. They join Gentiles who are already there by faith. For this truth Paul gave his life in mission and martyrdom. We should be ready to acknowledge the New Testament as God's final word and as our control in the interpretation of the relationship between Israel and the Church.[82]

Second, the New Testament teachings do not indicate that the church will be removed from the earth before the tribulation begins. According to Dale Moody, belief in a pretribulation rapture is not only a deviation that cannot be traced beyond 1830 but also contradicts the three chapters of the New Testament that mention the tribulation and the rapture together. These passages are Mark 13:24-27; Matthew 24:26-31; and 2 Thessalonians 2:1-12.[83]

Third, this interpretation fails to do full justice to the basic unity of the Bible.[84]

Fourth, biblical support is lacking for the theory of the postponed kingdom.

Fifth, biblical teaching is lacking on the parenthesis church.

Sixth, the dispensational teaching about the Jewish nature of the millennium and other Jewish details is not described in Revelation 20:4-6.[85]

Seventh, the dispensational approach leaves Revelation without any particular significance for those to whom it was originally addressed. It would be little comfort for a first-century believer facing persecution to learn that after seven long church ages Christ would return and punish the enemy.[86]

Eighth, as powerful as dispensationalism has been in modern conservative Christian thought, it has also been extremely divisive. Internal squabbling about specific interpretations of the signs of the times has been an embarrassment to the movement. In spite of the warnings of moderate dispensationalists against date setting, extreme dispensationalists find it irresistible.[87]

7. *Revelation Was Written to Encourage, Inform, and Challenge First-century Christians and Christians in Every Generation. Furthermore, It Teaches Eternal Theological Principles and Portrays the Last Days of History and Beyond. This View Is Known as the Combination Approach, the Synthesis View, the Prophetic-apocalyptic Perspective, the Moderate Futurist View, and the Historical or Historic Premillennial Approach. It Is also Called Covenant Premillennialism.*

a. HISTORY

In the early Christian centuries, Revelation was seen as having both present and future dimensions. The view that today is called historical premillennialism was the dominant view during the apostolic period when Christians believed strongly in the approaching end of the world and the second coming of Jesus Christ.[88] Church fathers, such as Justin Martyr (about AD 100-167), Papias of Hierapolis, whose writings appeared around AD 150, and Irenaeus of Lyon (about AD 130-202), made much of this belief.[89]

Beginning in the fifth century, especially under the influence of Origen and Augustine, future eschatology was made to refer either to the spiritual journey of the believer or to the church as the kingdom of God on earth. This view became increasingly dominant during the Middle Ages and historical premillennialism went into virtual eclipse.[90]

During the Protestant Reformation, both Lutheran and Reformed groups, for the most part, followed the amillennialism of Augustine. The more radical segment of the Reformation, the Anabaptists, perpetuated the expectation of Christ's earthly reign, however. Because of what seemed to be rather extreme beliefs, the historical premillennialism of the Anabaptists tended to be disregarded by mainstream Christianity.[91]

Despite general Calvinist opposition, German Calvinist theologian Johann Heinrich Alsted (1588-1638), revived the teaching of historical premillennialism in an academic form in the modern world. Alsted's book, *The Beloved City* (1627), which presented his views caused the learned Anglican scholar Joseph Mede (1586-1628) to become a historical premillennialist.[92]

In the twentieth century, dispensational premillennialism spread in conservative and fundamentalist circles. This resulted in a virtual polarization in conservative groups following World War I. A person had to be either an amillennialist or a dispensational premillennialist. Immediately following World War II, a movement arose which was popularly known as new evangelicalism. It challenged many features of the dispensational-fundamentalist alliance. Many "New Evangelicals" took issue with the doctrine of dispensationalism. Such men as Edward J. Carnell, Dan Fuller, and George Ladd led out in expounding a post- tribulation historical premillennialism as a third option.

Authors teaching the historical premillennial view, in addition to Ladd, Fuller, and Carnell, include George R. Beasley-Murray of Spurgeon's College and The Southern Baptist Theological Seminary in the *New Bible Commentary* and in his more recent commentary on Revelation in the *New Century Bible*. This viewpoint in popularized by Charles de Santo in the *Shield Bible Study* series. F. F. Bruce of England is sympathetic with this viewpoint in his work on Revelation in the *New Testament Commentary*. Oscar Cullmann of Basel was an advocate. Dale Moody teaches a similar view in his books *The Hope of Glory* and *The Word of Truth*. Robert Mounce in the *New International Commentary* is sympathetic with this view. Alan Johnson advocates this view in the *Bible Study Commentary* and in the *New Expositor's Bible Commentary*. This view is also held by Robert H. Gundry, D. H. Kromminga, and Millard J. Erickson.[93]

b. KEY ELEMENTS

(1) First, Revelation is seen as having meaning for the first-century Christians

John's "word of prophecy" was, first of all, committed to the strengthening of the Christian churches in Asia Minor in their severe clash with the antidivine powers actualized in the Roman state and civil religion. Revelation offers a theological-prophetic interpretation of the concrete situation and problems of these communities.[94]

Not just the seven letters but the whole book is full of ethical admonitions and exhortations for the early Christians. This ethical interest of the author prevented the reader of that time, as well as today, from projecting evil only unto others but not to self. Revelation speaks not only of vengeance against dehumanizing, anti-Christian, demonic, and political powers but also calls the inhabitants of the earth, including Christians, to repentance. John insisted that the Christians in no way had "made it" but that they were still in danger of losing their reward in the new Jerusalem.

Revelation could easily be misunderstood in the sense that evil exists on the outside of the Christian community but not within it. However, John began his book with a great vision of the heavenly Christ judging the Christian communities. Furthermore, he interspersed the cosmic-apocalyptic part with eschatological warnings, blessings, exhortations, and woes. He also concluded the whole book with a series of admonitions, announcements, and prayers (22:6-21).[95] Doctrinal errors in the first century (and today) needed correction. John had a word of encouragement and statements of the Christian hope.

(2) Second, Revelation has implications for each generation

This emphasis embraces the truth of the eternal principles view.

As will be noted in the detailed study, the five seals described in Revelation 6 represent the agencies or forces by which God works out His redemptive and judicial purpose in history leading up to the end. In other words, the first five seals represent events which are characteristic of all of history.[96]

The sixth seal brings us to the very last days of history. The first six seals then represent the character of the age and the course of the gospel in the world until the end of the age.

(3) Third, Revelation describes in broad perspective the last days of history

John was allowed to see the logical consummation of the tendencies at work in history. On the canvas of John's age and in the colors of his environment, he pictured the last great crisis of the world. He could do this because of the real correspondence between his crisis and that of the last days. As the church was then faced with the devastating persecution by Rome, so will the church of the last days find itself violently opposed by the prevailing world power. The outcome of that great struggle will be the advent of Christ in glory and, with Him, the establishment of the kingdom of God in power. John clearly regarded the end as at hand (1:1-3). This "foreshortened future," however, no more invalidates his utterances than it does those of the Old Testament prophets and of Jesus, for this concept is characteristic of all prophecy.[97]

The seals show us the forces that operate in history and lead up to the end. The trumpets announce that the divine judgment has arrived and is being executed in part. The bowls are the final pouring out of God's wrath.

Then we come to the detail of the end time itself. First, there is an earthly reign of Christ established by His second coming (Rev. 20:1-6). Believers will reign; the exact nature of their rule is not spelled out. It does appear, however, that a reward for their faithfulness will be to share or participate in what Jesus Christ does.[98]

Satan will be bound (Rev. 20:1-3). Revelation 20:4 tells of a bodily resurrection of martyrs to take part in this manifestation of God's power on earth. The historical premillennialist is not sure about the length of the millennium. But this view teaches that, for an extended period of time, Christ will personally rule upon the earth.[99]

The millennium will be a period of righteous rule. The standard of life envisioned in the Sermon on the Mount will become a reality. The concern will not be merely with what a person does—one's outward actions—but what one is—one's thoughts and intentions. Christ will reign with justice over His subjects. This reign of Christ will involve a political dimension involving a worldwide peace. There will also be harmony within the creation. In the millennium, hostility among creatures will cease. The destructive forces of nature will be stilled.[100]

National Israel will be saved (Rom. 11:15-16)—perhaps at the second coming of Christ. Not every Israelite will be converted, but the nation as a whole will be. Through the agency of Israel, God will bless the whole world, and presumably this will occur during the millennium. The Jews and the Gentiles will become one people of God.[101]

It should be noted that the ethos of historical premillennialism is quite different from that of dispensationalism. In many ways, it is more like that of amillennialism. The millennium, in other words, plays a much less crucial role in this approach.[102]

This teaching by historical premillennialism about the future described above is crucial. Unless Christians expect the coming actualization of God's promises about the future to occur *in time,* our hope loses its passion and its realistic character. Despite the continuation of chronological time, Christians cannot simply take for granted its unending and enduring character. Revelation seriously teaches the power of God's coming triumph without losing us either in chronological speculations or in a denial of the coming actualization of God's promise.[103]

Revelation does have meaning for now, but it does because of the motivating and beckoning power of God's final triumph in the second coming of Christ. In other words, Revelation teaches us that God's kingdom is "already but not yet."[104]

Second, the millennium will be preceded by a deterioration of spiritual and social conditions. The signs of the times have been present from the time of Christ's first coming but will assume an intensified form before His second coming. This view is not given to date setting. Because the length of the tribulation is uncertain, no schedule or timetable is possible.[105]

This period of deterioration is called the Great Tribulation. This is a historic position. Every church father who dealt with the subject expected the church to suffer at the hands of the Antichrist. God would purify the church through suffering, and Christ would save her by His return at the end of the tribulation. Christ would then destroy the Antichrist, deliver His church, and bring the world to an end and inaugurate His millennial kingdom.[106]

Christians will be present during this period of tribulation. The historical premillennial view is not sure that the tribulation will be precisely seven calendar years. Although there is no pretribulation rapture, there is the positive hope that, no matter what may occur, there will be protection from God's wrath and Christ will come and bring all of it to an end. A positive development even during the tribulation period is the continual presence of a dynamic gospel witness.[107]

Third, near the end of the millennium, Satan will be unbound and will launch a final struggle. He will be defeated.

Fourth, Christ will raise the unbelievers, and then both Christians and nonchristians will face the great white throne judgment.

Many moderate futurists have reached their position either in reaction to other views or after becoming disenchanted with other views. Many were dispensationalists who reacted to that view. The historical premillennialist's viewpoint has been constructed to some extent out of portions of the other models which have been described.[108]

The moderate futurists react to the idea that Revelation was only written to give hope to the despairing Christians in the first century.

They believe that prophetic prediction is an important element of the book. They also react to those who say the book is primarily for the future. This would mean that Revelation would have had little relevance for the first century or succeeding centuries. This approach also has a negative reaction to the idea that Revelation is primarily a description of the continuous history of the Christian church.

According to the advocates of the moderate futurist view, biblical theology demands a climax to history. History is being directed by God to an end. This view contends that there could not be a complete fulfillment of God's redemptive purpose without a historical millennium or demonstration of God's glory and power on earth at the climax of history. In fact, a millennium or earthly reign of Christ is a logical necessity according to George R. Beasley-Murray.[109]

Robert H. Gundry and George E. Ladd point out a practical aspect of this approach. Assuming as it does that the church will live through the Great Tribulation, the consequences of failing to prepare the church to face the tribulation could be disastrous. The best possible alternative is to prepare God's people for inevitable suffering. This suffering, however, will not be unbearable and God's people will be protected from Satan's extremes.[110]

c. CRITICISMS AND ANSWERS

(1) Neglects the imminence of Christ's coming

Some scholars, especially dispensationalists, are quick to criticize the moderate futurist position. For these critics, the contention that Christ will not return until after the tribulation destroys the idea of the imminence of His return.

Moderate futurists answer this criticism by calling for an examination of the meaning of Christ's command to watch. *Watch* does not necessarily mean imminence but adequate preparation. George Ladd argues that the command "to watch" relates to the second coming rather than to a secret rapture of the saints.[111]

(2) Lack of biblical support and necessity for the millennium

Those critics who do not believe in a literal or earthly millennium point out that the millennium is only mentioned in one chapter in the Bible, Revelation 20. Accepting the doctrine of the millennium as a major doctrine, therefore, seems to violate the analogy of faith principle which holds that no major doctrine should be based upon minor or isolated passages.

Furthermore, the amillennial critics state that an earthly millennium is theologically superfluous. Why should there be an earthly reign of Christ at all? Why should we not move directly from the second coming of Christ to the judgment and then to the ultimate states of destiny both for the righteous and the unrighteous? Particularly in view of the lack of extensive textual references, the millennium seems dispensable.[112]

In answer, Ladd contends that the millennium plays a definite and integral part in the plan of God. It is a further stage in God's redemptive purpose in Christ. While living on earth, Christ experienced humiliation in progressive stages. Following His resurrection and ascension, He reassumed the glory and power which had been His, reigning at the Father's right hand. His reign of triumph is not yet apparent, however. If it is to be fully exercised and demonstrated, it must become public in power and glory. Ladd believes that it is logically necessary and appropriate for this manifestation of Christ's glory and sovereignty to take place upon the earth. This is a basic purpose served by the millennium.[113]

Ladd further believes that Paul left room for the millennium in 1 Corinthians 15:23-26. Paul saw three stages in Christ's triumph over death described in 1 Corinthians 15:23-26. These three stages are the resurrection, the second coming, and the end (the telos). The interval between the resurrection and the second coming is the church age. The interval between the second coming and the telos—without which the two might as well be collapsed into one—is the millennium. The church age is the age of the Son's hidden rule. The millennium is the age of Christ's manifested rule.[114]

Ladd further contends that the millennium teaching must be seen in light of the entire theological content of the Bible which he believes necessitates or calls for a millennium or demonstration of God's power on earth. This view also points out that numerous other passages, many of them prophecies, refer, directly or indirectly, to the millennium.

(3) Neglects the teachings on the Jews in the Great Tribulation

Dispensationalists accuse moderate futurists of spiritualizing the teaching about the Jews or Israel in order to find a place for the church during the tribulation. An example is seeing the 144,000 in Revelation 7 as a reference to the church.

Moderate futurists answer by saying that in Paul's teaching in Romans the church has in a real sense largely replaced Israel as God's redemptive instrument. Whatever place the Jews are to play necessitates that they will come back to the olive tree by faith in Christ. In Romans 11 Paul did not indicate how or when the Jews would come back. Paul left this accomplishment in the hands of the sovereign God. The Christian mission to the Gentiles, which provokes the jealousy of the Jews, is seen as important in the Jews' return to Christ and the olive tree.

(4) Lack of conviction

Millard J. Erickson, himself a historical premillennialist, believes that advocates of this position appear to lack conviction or even understanding. Because this view considers fine nuances of meaning and precise definitions in eschatology to be less important than does dispensationalism, it does not stress the intensive study of eschatology as does dispensationalism. In the desire to avoid hairsplitting, the moderate futurists have, at times, overreacted and have failed to emphasize sufficiently the great central eschatological facts.[115]

d. STRONG POINTS

(1) It has a strong view of the Bible

The model is conservative. The Bible is accepted as the authoritative Word of God which is final for faith and practice. This view takes exegesis seriously. If we believe the Bible to be authoritative, we must consider this intensive exegesis a very positive value.[116]

This view also has great versatility in dealing with the Bible. It takes into account the broad sweep of Scripture. It offers suitable and plausible interpretations of all types of relevant material—the apocalyptic writings, the prophetic books, the eschatological teachings of Jesus, and much more. In other words, it is not based upon a few skillfully selected proof texts.[117]

In drawing upon a wide group of Scriptures, historical premillennialism seems to handle these Scriptures more naturally than does dispensationalism. By and large interpretations of key passages appear to fit well the natural sense of those passages. It does not depend upon unearthing secret meanings. It seldom finds that it accepts special ideas that one would find only if one came to the text with a preconceived system. The Bible does place great emphasis on the age to come and this view does not neglect this emphasis.[118]

(2) It is positive

Although days of tribulation await the church, the thrust of the model is the Christian's hope for victory and assurance of protection.

(3) It encourages Christian involvement

This active involvement is important because the church will not escape the world in which it lives until the second coming and the rapture. In other words, it does not have a cop-out mentality.

As we have seen, dispensationalism shows strong otherworldly tendencies and dwells upon the hope of a pretribulation rapture and escaped tribulation. In contrast, historical premillennialism offers no escape from hardship. It paints a very realistic picture of the demands and costs of the Christian life. It does this while reminding believers of the resources of power upon which they can draw when living in the midst of hardship.[119]

This view also holds that renewals and revivals can take place in any given church or denomination or era if a response is made to Christ and God's resources are appropriated.

(4) It has a strong future orientation

Although it offers a basis for Christian anticipation, it does not claim to have worked out all of the details of last things or to have explained fully all the symbols involved in biblical eschatology. It has generally exercised real restraint and care in setting dates. In so doing, it has managed to preserve something of a genuine sense of mystery about the biblical revelation. This view has both a confidence in the major facts of eschatology and a belief that when the Lord comes the remaining facts will be revealed.[120]

(5) It has a long history

As we have seen, it can be traced back to the patristic era of church history. It has had many notable exponents.

(6) It is both present and future

At the present time, the church is enjoying the blessings of the future. Christ reigns in the hearts of all who believe in Him and obey Him. The kingdom will be fully realized, however, in the future. Only when Christ returns will every knee bow and every tongue confess Him as Lord. In the judgment of the historical premillennialists, it is important not to neglect either the present or future aspect of the kingdom in favor of the other.[121]

8. Conclusion

Surely God has been working in and through many devout scholars who have developed these seven models or methods of interpretation. I have described the positions and the arguments advanced by advocates of the seven representative views. I have attempted to treat the various options as fairly and as impartially as possible, pointing out both positive and negative aspects of each.[122]

Elements of truth can be found in each model. The historical background of Revelation is important. The book does give expression to basic underlying principles of God's work in history. Revelation does have predictive teachings about the future.

The interpretation of Revelation in this book is based on the prophetic-apocalyptic model or the moderate futurist view which includes elements of the eternal principles approach as our primary model.

How Can You Gain an Overview of Revelation?

Before dealing with the details of Revelation, an overview will be helpful. My working approach follows a literary model. The books of the Prophets in the Old Testament, to a large extent, are collections of individual oracles. In contrast, Revelation is much more like the New Testament Epistles. In the Epistles readers must "think paragraphs" because every paragraph is a building block for the whole argument. Likewise, Revelation is a creatively structured whole and each vision is an integral part of that whole.[123]

1. Prologue and John's Vision (chs. 1—2)

Revelation begins with a brief prologue that is followed by an account of John's vision of the risen Christ on Patmos. John is the narrator throughout. Christ is described in magnificent images, derived partly from Daniel 10, as the Lord of history and the Lord of the church. God has not lost control, despite present persecution, for Christ alone holds the keys of death and Hades.[124]

2. Letters to the Seven Churches (chs. 2—3)

The letters to seven real, but also representative, churches in what was then called Roman Asia follow in chapters 2—3. Persecution is already present and the church is promised more. But there are many internal disorders that also threaten its well-being. Those who overcome are given the promises of final glory.

3. Vision of Heaven and the Dominant Theme (chs. 4—5)

In chapters 4—5, a vision of heaven is described. This vision introduces the main body of Revelation. In the breathtaking vision, which is related to worship and praise, the church is told that God reigns in sovereign majesty (ch. 4). To believers who may be wondering if God is really there acting in their behalf, John reminds them that God's "lion" is a "lamb" who Himself redeemed mankind through suffering (ch. 5). This vision of God and Christ as the Lion and the Lamb supplies the key to the theology of the entire work—hence the title of this book *The Lion and the Lamb*. The songs of chapters 4 and 5 form a dramatic focal point for the book. The remainder of Revelation can be seen as four vast movements.[125]

4. The Dynamics of History (ch. 6)

The next vision initiates the process of events leading to the unveiling of the final kingdom (chs. 6—19). At this point, a decision has to be made on how the remainder of the book is to be interpreted. Are chapters 6—19 to be viewed as a continuous narration of events leading to the second coming? Or are we to regard the three series of messianic judgments set forth under the symbolism of the seals, trumpets, and bowls of wrath as parallel? Or do the seals lead to the trumpet and bowls, which are parallel? I believe that the six seals lead up to the last period of the trumpets and the bowls. The sixth seal brings us to the very last days of history. The first six seals represent the character of the age and the course of the gospel in the world down until the end of the age.[126]

The two series of judgments—trumpets and bowls—describe by the different images a single short period in history, namely, the time of the end which precedes the coming of Christ's kingdom. By repeating his portrayal of the judgments, John builds up to the advent of Christ in an awe-inspiring climax.[127]

5. The First Interlude—Encouragement of the Church (ch. 7)

The descriptions of judgments, however, are themselves not allowed to proceed without interruption. They are interspersed with

114

episodes or interludes of varying length. The chief intention of the interludes is to shed light on what happens to the church and on the nature of her task during the great distress.[128]

The first interlude, between the sixth and seventh seals, is constituted by two visions. The first vision in chapter 7 shows the faithful Christians being sealed for their protection during the time of trial. The second vision portrays a scene of consolation for the faithful in the final coming of the kingdom.[129]

6. The Seven Trumpet Judgments (chs. 8—9)

Chapters 8—9 relate the breaking of the seventh seal and the sounding of the seven trumpets. The seven trumpets relate the beginning of the events of the end itself, particularly the time of the Great Tribulation which will introduce the end. According to Ladd, the content of the seventh trumpet may be the seven bowls. If so, Ladd suggests that we can see in the seven trumpets and the seven bowls an intensification of the woes poured out upon mankind before mankind is overtaken in the final judgments.[130]

7. The Second Interlude—Call to Witness (chs. 10—11)

Another interlude occurs between the sixth and seventh trumpets. This episode confirms John in his prophetic witness and describes the church's call to bear witness in her period of suffering (chs. 10—11).[131]

8. The Third Interlude—Satan's Defeat and Activity (chs.12—14)

The longest interruption or interlude in the flow of the visions occurs in chapters 12—14. This interlude sets the conflict between the church and the Roman state against the background of the age-long conflict between the powers of darkness and the God of heaven. It draws a vivid picture of the kind of pressure to which the church is subject when Caesar demands what belongs to God.[132]

An important theological key to Revelation is found in chapter 12. In two visions, we are told of Satan's attempt to destroy Christ and of his own defeat instead. Thus, within the recurring New Testament framework of the already/not yet, Satan is revealed as a defeated foe (already), whose final end has not yet come. Therefore, there is rejoicing because salvation has come. However, there is still woe to the church because Satan knows his time is limited and he is taking his vengeance out on God's people.[133]

9. The Vengeance of Babylon (chs. 13—14)

Chapters 13—14 then show how, for John's church, that vengeance took the first-century form of the Roman Empire with its emperors who were demanding religious allegiance. There will be other expressions of this vengeance.[134]

10. The Seven Bowl Judgments, the Return of Christ, the Millennium, and the Final State (chs. 15—22)

Next is the description of the judgments initiated by the outpoured bowls of wrath (chs. 15—16). The prophet then holds up once more his description of the coming of Christ and the kingdom in order to show the reader how the antichristian empire falls prey to its own forces of destruction (chs. 17—18). Then at last the revelation of Christ is portrayed and all that is bound up with it in relation to Christ's kingdom—the earthly millennium, the last judgment, the new creation, and the city of God (chs. 19—22).

An epilogue, summing up and pressing home the lessons of the book, brings the whole to a conclusion (22:6-21).[135]

There is progress in the book. But this progress is more of a development that moves the reader to a fuller experience of the divine plan for final victory than it is a progress which ticks off the minutes of an eschatological clock. Each new vision intensifies the realization of coming judgment. Like a mounting storm at sea, each new crest of the wave moves history closer to its final destiny. The numbered plagues reveal this intensification. The seals allow the scroll to be opened and in the process anticipate its contents. The trumpets announce that divine retribution has arrived. The bowls are the pouring out of God's wrath. Morris writes, "It seems to be part of the method of John to repeat his theme, not exactly, it is true, but on another level like a spiral staircase. In this way the same ground is covered, but other perspectives are revealed and fresh facts of the revelation are brought out."[136]

The outline followed in this study does not claim to answer all of the questions which can be raised about exact sequence. It reflects, rather, the literary structure of the book. This is not to say that we cannot anticipate in a general way that course of events which will bring an end to history and usher in eternity. We know that the persecuted church will witness the victorious return of Christ and share in Christ's final reign. We also know that the forces of evil will be totally defeated and Satan and his hordes will forever be destroyed.[137]

So Revelation is not a pessimistic book with a message just for the future. Yes, God shall yet act—evil shall be purged; God's will shall be established.

Sometimes we think that this age is so evil that we despair. Then we see that the One who will one day destroy evil, set up a kingdom, and judge the nations is the Lion. But we also see that this Lion has already come in advance as the Lamb to bring salvation, insights, power, partial answers, and a foretaste of the future kingdom. The powers of the future glorious age have entered into history in advance of their final demonstration and are at work now to save and free us and give victory.

What Are the Eternal and Abiding Truths of Revelation?

The Bible in general, and Revelation in particular, has a meaning found through exegesis and synthesis which goes beyond the meaning for the immediate readers in the first century. However, cultural, social, and personality influences have great impact on the way we find meaning for today. Despite the difficulty of properly discerning the meaning and properly applying it, we will make an attempt. Each generation must repeat this attempt under the guidance of the Holy Spirit. The details of this meaning will be brought out in the study itself. It should be helpful to list a brief summary of these truths.[138]

1. A Vivid Sense of the Majesty of God and the Centrality of Jesus Christ who Triumphed Through His Vicarious Sacrifice

This truth is especially seen in Revelation 4 and 5.

2. A Realistic Statement of the Reality and Power of Evil

This evil persists despite the first coming of Christ. We have seen power as a major issue in Revelation. Christ is seen not only as the Lamb but also as the Judge and Warrior. The significance of the king-

ship of God in Christ can be seen best by remembering that it op-
poses the kingship of the dragon, the beast, and the queenly rule
of the harlot. The symbols of the dragon, the beast, and the harlot
give rise to thoughts on the nature of evil. They teach that sin and
evil are not just matters of individual choices. Rather they show us
that individuals and even groups of people can get caught up in
collective processes with evil with destructive effects. Revelation reveals that there are trends, social structures, ideas, and institutional processes which are human creations, but which get out of
human control and turn against their creator like a Frankenstein
monster.[139]

Jacques Ellul and William Stringfellow have argued that this demonic quality is inherent in all collective human realities and in all
institutions such as cities, corporations, nations, governments, and
even the church. As Peter Berger and Thomas Luckmann have argued, social institutions confront human beings as objective reality.
Revelation insists that the primordial forces of destructive power
and death are embodied in particular institutions.[140]

Social structures and collective processes become demonic under
at least two conditions. When one group achieves or holds personal
dignity and power at the expense of another group, the structures
that support the situation are demonic. When an immediate objective or limited good is pursued without sufficient attention to the
whole picture, the process can get out of control and become demonic. Examples of the first category are social structures that sub-
ordinate women to men and people of color to those who are white.
An example of the second category is the development of nuclear
weapons. Critical reflection on the symbols of the dragon, beast,
and harlot suggest that these evils mentioned and other similar collective realities of our day are analogous to those demonic figures.[141]

3. A Strong Implication that the Christian Churches Should Take a Stand Against Collective Forces of Evil.

Revelation implies that collective forces must be dealt with collec-
tively. Collins sees the Western European and American contexts
where democracy is well established as unique. In this context, the
political theology of Johannes Metz seems to be a promising way of
putting the imperative of Revelation into action. According to Metz,
existential theology has brought the Christian faith into a proper re-

lationship to human existence and subjectivity. He sees two dangers in existential theology. One is that it emphasizes the present at the expense of the future. The second is the concern for the individual's journey of faith at the expense of the social and political dimensions of the believer's faith and responsibility. The emphases of Metz on the future and on the social and political dimensions of faith are also seen in Revelation.[142]

In its role as an institution of a socially critical freedom, the church has two functions. One is to protest the absolutizing of any one political program or system as the full achievement of the ideal social order. Such a protest grows out of the conviction that every stage society has attained is provisional. The church must unmask the pretensions of ideologies. It must name the beast. Second, the church should ally itself with those tendencies in society which hold promise of a movement toward the fulfillment of the eschatological promises of the Bible—freedom, peace, justice, and reconciliation.[143]

There are, of course, significant differences between Revelation and Metz's political theology. But Metz's proposal is one example of what an attempt to take Revelation both critically and seriously might look like in the context of Western Europe and the United States in the second half of the twentieth century.[144]

There is a danger lurking in the shadows. We should not allow social conditions to be the determining factor in our interpretation of Revelation. However, it is important that we allow social and theological issues to challenge our biased and middle-class interpretations and drive us to reexamine the meaning of Revelation.[145]

Cedric C. Johnson believes that the social conditions in the Third World and other places, the indefensible consumptive practices in North America, and the poor and oppressed individuals and systems should call us to a radical discipleship. The characteristic mode of this discipleship should be the servant and not the master. We not only need to be aware of our own culturally determined preunderstanding but also allow the crucial questions of the day to enable us to hear the meaning of the Scripture in a new light.[146]

The danger is that certain new movements in theology also can control or use our interpretation of the Bible. No matter how just our cause, we cannot allow the cause to control the system of biblical interpretation. Rather, we must let the cause direct us to search for a scriptural answer. Ultimately the Scripture must be allowed to give its own message.[147]

4. The Truth of the Doctrine of the Antichrist

That the Antichrist precedes the coming of Christ and His kingdom highlights a doctrine which is as important to the Gospels as it is to Revelation. This doctrine teaches that a power of evil beyond the sinful wills of men and women is at work in the process of history. It destroys that which is good in the world and exceeds the wit or strength of humans to overcome it. Just as Christ by His redemptive deeds delivers from sin and brings the power of the age to come to this world, so the Christ of the second coming alone can bring to its final issue the victory of good over evil.[148]

As the age draws to its close, Satan moves to embody the spirit of Antichrist in a person, the Antichrist to whom he gives power and authority. Whether this Antichrist is a religious leader, political leader, or both is of secondary significance. Perhaps he will be a Jew, deceiving Jews into believing he is the Messiah—only to turn against them. Perhaps he will be the leader of a superecclesiastical system that embraces all religions. We need to be on guard against every spirit of Antichrist that appears, whether in ourselves or in our community.[149]

5. Portrayal of the Church as Embattled

John sees God's people as the embattled church. This emphasis is made in Hans Lilje's book *The Last Book of the Bible,* which was written while he was imprisoned by the Nazis. In light of this embattlement, one of John's important concerns is to strengthen the faith of Christian people and their will to continue in obedience to God. There is accordingly less emphasis on the church's responsibility for the world, which seems extremely hostile, than on the worth of the church to God and its destiny in history and in the eternal ages. Nevertheless, there are teachings in Revelation that the Christian church has a greater duty than simply to survive, even in the time of the Antichrist.[150]

6. An Emphasis on the Fact that Suffering in the World Is the Reverse Side of Fellowship with Christ in Glory

To teach the implications of the conviction that the suffering of this present time is related to the glory that is to follow is a major concern of John's. The church which takes note of John's teaching will not be overtaken by surprise when it meets stern opposition in taking its mission to the nations. Nor will it be brought to despair through its sufferings, for the end of this story is the descent of the city of God from heaven to earth.[151]

7. *Strong Emphasis on Worship*

Revelation is filled with pictures of the worship and adoration of God in heaven. These glimpses of heavenly worship are a model or pattern of the response that people experience whenever they acknowledge the character and worthiness of God.[152]

8. *An Emphasis on the Fact that History Is Linear and Not Cyclical and Is Moving Toward the Divine Destiny*

In other words, history has a definite closure/completion event in time and space rather than being simply a continuous, open-ended process. This view is opposed to those who exchange the specificity of the end-time for a philosophical argument about God as futurity, that is, as one who always comes.[153]

Revelation refuses to turn the coming triumph of God into a never-ending process of history or into a scheme that denies a finality to the future of the creation. The One who has come to us in Christ will come again to complete His redemptive purpose according to His promise.[154]

If we claim Revelation and Paul's letters to be crucially important parts of our Christian confession and as authoritative for us as God's Word, we must accept the second coming of Christ in glory. This concept, instead of being escapist, enhances ethical activity and motivation. Both God's past act in Christ and his future act in the second coming and the manifestation of glory on earth converge on the Christian life in the present. For only God Himself will be able to complete the work that He began in us in Christ (Phil. 1:6).[155]

9. *A Strong Emphasis on Judgment*

Revelation portrays a God of judgment whose ultimate purpose is to destroy all forms of evil.

10. An Important Emphasis on the Separation of True from False Belief

As a prophet, John sees himself as called upon to separate true belief from false. He seeks to expose the doctrinal failures of the congregations in Asia Minor.[156]

11. Implications for Political Perspective, Christian Social Action, and Christian Humanization

a. POLITICAL AND CHRISTIAN SOCIAL ACTION IMPLICATIONS

There are truths to be gained from a sociological and psychological analysis of Revelation. This type of analysis reveals that Revelation has political as well as religious implications. For example, it appears that justice is stressed more than love because of the circumstances at the particular time it was written. However, Revelation seeks to avoid violence. The faithful are called upon to endure, not to take up arms. The violent imagery seems to be intended to release aggressive feelings in a harmless way. Nevertheless, the language of Revelation has been linked historically to violence under certain conditions.[157]

In fact, Rollo May contends that violence may be appropriate in some situations. He has in mind individuals who live at a subhuman level because of their lack of self-consciousness, assertiveness, and personal dignity. He argues that it may also at times be necessary for groups to resort to violence in the form of political rebellions to break out of their apathy and to force the dominant party to make social reforms. For persons in groups living at subhuman levels, anger and violence may be constructive and life-giving, a step toward becoming more fully human. Therefore, the violent imagery of Revelation may be helpful in such situations. The passionate language and call to commitment can support a quest for personal dignity.[158]

However, violence is difficult to control once it is unleashed. These considerations suggest that the limited, rational use of violence in the quest for human dignity is a difficult achievement.[159]

b. CHRISTIAN HUMANIZATION IMPLICATIONS

Collins suggests that the political stance and conflictual tone of Revelation served the valid purpose of raising the consciousness of certain marginal and frustrated early Christians. Their commitment to a hope for the future that involved a transformation of the political and social order was a protest against the injustice of their current situation. One strength of Revelation is the pointed and universal way in which it raises the questions of justice, wealth, and power. Revelation serves a value of humanization because it insists that the marginal and the relatively poor and powerless must assert themselves to achieve their full humanity and dignity.[160]

In fact, the imagery and tone of Revelation encourage attitudes that are necessary in the struggle for justice under certain conditions. These attitudes, however, have a dark side of which interpreters of Revelation must be conscious and whose dangers must be recognized. Revelation needs the rest of the New Testament to balance its message of justice and judgment.[161]

c. PSYCHOLOGICAL IMPLICATIONS

Psychological studies of Revelation contend that meditation on the violent images, symbols, and narratives in Revelation can have a positive effect. These vital aspects of Revelation are helpful in discovering one's own hostile and aggressive feelings. One way of constructively dealing with these feelings is to release them in the imagination in a way analogous to Revelation's resolution of tension. Such an approach may be a step forward toward more self-assertive behavior. If such a process is not needed, a person may attempt to rechannel or defuse the aggression by imagining good things happening to the person or group with whom one is irritated.[162]

12. *Assurance of Triumph*

Assurance of ultimate triumph is the supreme contribution of Revelation to the church of Christ. To all people with little or no hope and to those whose confidence is based on uncertain foundations, Revelation offers strong consolation. It is grounded in the Almighty God who made this universe and whose will cannot be finally frustrated by any power in heaven or earth or hell. The end is assured because it is already begun through God's action in Christ. God will complete that work of grace which He has begun in Christ.[163]

If the present-day Christian cannot be so sure as the first-century Christian that Christ will come soon, neither can one confidently affirm that Christ's coming is far off. To sustain a faith and an attitude about the sure coming and triumph of Christ was the intention of the author of Revelation.[164]

At this point, historical premillennialists see the establishment of a messianic kingdom on earth as a part of John's assurance of triumph. The messianic kingdom on earth is a vindication of God's Christian activity. The triumph of God over the satanic dominion of this planet is necessary for the glory of God. If there were no messianic age, if God simply picked up the redeemed remnant and took them off to heaven, then we would have to conclude that God was not able to complete what he began.[165]

The actual course of those centuries is endurable to Christians only because we know that the desolating godlessness of history shall be halted and that the Kingdom shall triumph. To postulate complete conquest for the church is to expect more than is warranted by experience and the New Testament, which contains also a doctrine of Antichrist. As the kingdom needed an apocalyptic intervention of the Messiah for its initiation in the crucifixion-resurrection and descending of the Spirit, so it needs His apocalyptic intervention in the second coming to bring it to its triumph.[166]

13. The Emphasis on a Christian Philosophy of the Meaning of History

In Revelation 5, John beholds the sealed scroll in the hand of God. This scroll is not identified, but we may assume that it contains the divine purpose for human history. Both to people and to angels the destiny of humanity is a closed and sealed book.

John weeps (v. 4) because no one is found worthy to open the scroll or to look into it. His grief is relieved when he is told, "Weep not; lo the Lion of the tribe of Judah, the Root of David, has conquered, so that he can open the scroll and its seven seals" (v. 5).

But John sees yet another scene (v. 6). He sees a familiar figure. He sees that the Lion is also the Lamb who is still bearing the marks of slaughter. The Lion who will set up the Kingdom in His second coming will be able to do this because He is the Lamb who was slaughtered.

John ties in the working of God in history and the crucified Lamb of God with the working of God at the end of history and the Lion of

Judah. Only one who is both the Lamb of Calvary and the Lion of the tribe of Judah can open the Book and bring God's redemptive purposes for people to their divine end.

Thus we see that the Lion of the tribe of Judah who has become the Lamb has revealed in His life, death, resurrection, and second advent the clue to the meaning of history. He has acted, is now acting in history, and will act in a more dramatic way in the future.[167]

I. Prologue

(1:1-8)

A. Preface to the Book (1:1-3)

1. *God, Jesus Christ, the Angel, and the Source of the Book (1:1)*

The revelation or disclosure or unveiling at the heart of this book was given by God to Jesus Christ. It is sent through an angel to John who, in turn, writes it down for the seven churches in the Roman province of Asia. So it is important to the whole church.[1]

I wrote a book called *Demons, Demons, Demons*. In it, I point out that the Bible indicates that demons are fallen angels. But the Bible also indicates that there are good angels who are mediators from God to people. This is the case in the vision given to John. The Bible presupposes a spiritual order behind this earthly order.

"What must soon take place" implies that the revelation concerns events that are future. However, Revelation itself makes it clear that "soon" does not preclude delay or intervening events. In 6:10-11, for example, we hear the cry of the martyred saints: "O Sovereign Lord, holy and true, how long before thou wilt . . . avenge our blood?" They are told to "rest a little longer."[2]

2. *Nature of the Contents of the Book (1:2)*

Because it has a divine origin, the content of the book can be described as the Word of God and the testimony borne by Jesus Christ. Christians need to be reminded that the neglected Book of Revelation is the very Word of God to us. John's literary activity is present throughout Revelation. However, John claims that he actually "saw" in divinely disclosed visions that which he presents. God Himself bears witness to the readers that these things are not the product of John's own mind (21:5; 22:6; compare 2 Pet. 1:21).[3]

3. *The Happiness or Blessedness Which Results From Understanding the Nature of Prophecy, the Importance of Obedience, and the Foreshortened Future (1:3)*

a. THE NATURE OF PROPHECY
"The prophecy" is John's way of describing his writing and refers to the entire Book of Revelation (10:11; 19:10; 22:7,9-10,18). Prophecy involves not only future events but also ethical and spiritual exhortations and warnings for today.[4]

Hal Lindsey states that John was put into a divine time machine and inspired to give a message just for our period—the last period of history, the terminal generation. John had difficulty, according to Lindsey, in using first-century terminology to describe twentieth-century fulfillment. He used "stars falling" to describe missiles projected from a platform or "fire and brimstone" to describe atomic bombs. In contrast to Lindsey, I contend that John first had a message for the first century and then has a message for each succeeding era of history and for the last period of history—whether that be soon or later.[5]

Biblical scholars have long debated the chief purpose of prophecy. Is prophecy foretelling or forth-telling?

I used to walk with my grandfather to prayer meeting on cold, Ozark nights. There were no street lights. The only light we had was a lantern. There was enough light from the lantern to keep us from falling or stumbling but not enough to give us unlimited vision of the details of the distant horizon. In 2 Peter 1:19, we are told that prophecy has a similar function. "You will do well to pay attention to this [prophecy] as to a lamp shining in a dark place, until the day dawns and the morning star rises in your heart."

Prophecy is like a lamp shining in a dark place. The ancient lamp was a very poor instrument. It was a small clay vessel which one could hold in one's hand. The lighted vessel would show a person how to find his way down a dark path or a dark street but would not illumine the distant horizon in detail. This verse indicates that the primary purpose of prophecy is to shed light on the present from the future, so that God's people may know how to find their way through a rough and dark world.

b. IMPORTANCE OF OBEDIENCE
The blessing which awaits the hearer is not valid unless the hearer

keeps or obeys the word (v. 3). Biblical faith is always an obedient faith. It is not just the hearers of the word who receive the blessing, but, as Jesus said in the Sermon on the Mount, those who both hear the word and do it (Matt. 7:24-27). Jesus further stated that if any man's will is to do God's will, he shall know (John 7:17). We receive religious and moral insight and knowledge as we bend our wills to Christ and become active for Him. The biblical doctrine of knowledge is different from the Greek and Enlightenment emphasis in this regard. Man's basic problem is not just ignorance, but rebellion. The answer is obedience, as well as knowledge.[6]

Excursus on the Foreshortened Future

Notice that John states in verse 3: "The time is near." John, like the other prophets of the Bible, has little interest in exact dates. However, the future is always viewed as imminent.

The Old Testament prophets blended the near and the distant perspective so as to form a single canvas. Biblical prophecy has height and breadth, but there is little concern for the exact time of future events. The biblical prophets maintained a tension between the immediate future and the distant future. The distant future is always viewed as if it were immediate.

The early church adopted this prophetic view. This means that the early church constantly lived in expectancy of the return of the Lord. If we are true to the Bible, we will live in expectancy of the end. To relax and say, "Where is the promise of His coming?" is to become a scoffer of divine truth. The biblical attitude is to take heed, and watch, for you do not know the day nor the hour (Mark 13:33).

In fact, without hope in the imminent coming of God and of Christ as the definitive closure—or completion—event of history, there can be no authentic New Testament theology. But this important New Testament emphasis becomes distorted when that hope becomes the object of human calculation, speculation, and prediction.[7]

We call this the foreshortened future. The apostle Paul taught this view. When Paul preached the doctrine of the imminent second coming of Christ to the Thessalonians on his second missionary journey, the people stopped work. In his second letter to the Thessalonians, Paul corrected their attitude and reminded them that unless they kept on with their normal responsibilities, they misunderstood the meaning of the second coming (2 Thess. 2:1-5). The Thessalonians obviously did not understand this idea of the foreshortened future.

The foreshortened future concept was employed by John. Revelation does not intend to teach a program of events that pinpoints our exact location on the final track of world history. Rather, it teaches the imminence of the second coming of Christ to the churches of Asia Minor and to all churches in history. Thus the theological aims of Paul and of Revelation are quite similar, however different the compositional technique of Revelation is from Paul. Both emphasize the imminence of the second coming and both stress the urgency of the present. This urgency demands a decision about the either/or of allegiance to Christ or to Satan.[8]

Thus the delay of the second coming of Christ was not a theological concern for the early church and should not be for us. It is not an embarrassment. It does not compel the church to shift the center of its attention from the imminence of the second coming to a form of "realized eschatology" which affirms the completed presence of the kingdom of God in our present history.[9]

And so the delay of the second coming of Christ both motivates us and burdens us. It inspires us to continue to work patiently in preparation for that coming reign of God that according to God's purpose and promise in Christ will be our glorious destiny.

But it also burdens us because of the onslaught of the power of sin and death in our world and because of the groaning and suffering of the creation within us and around us. We must continue to be agitators for the kingdom. We must also be joyful that in Christ we may detect and erect signs of the dawning of the kingdom. Yet we are burdened because God's triumph has not yet defeated the awful powers of injustice, suffering, and death in our world.[10]

The biblical people lived with this concept of the foreshortened future and it gave them a dynamic urgency.

B. Greeting and Salutation in the Name of the Triune God (1:4-5a)

1. The Significance of the Seven Churches

The form of address used in letter writing immediately distinguishes this book from Jewish apocalyptic works. These seven churches actually existed in the Roman province of Asia (the western part of present-day Turkey), as the details in chapters 2 and 3 indicate.[11]

Scholars are generally agreed that since the number *seven* symbolizes "wholeness" or "completeness," the seven churches represent not just seven specific churches but all the churches or the entire body of Christ.[12]

2. The Blessing from the Trinity

The greeting voiced by John to the seven churches evokes a blessing from God the Father, God the Son, and God the Spirit. The terms in which he describes the Trinity are unique, extraordinary, and significant.

a. THE POWER OF GOD THE FATHER

The One "who is and who was and who is to come" is God the Father. This title stresses both God's eternity and His vital relationship to history. The title for God evidently refers back to the name of God revealed to Moses at the burning bush (Ex. 3:14 f.). God is the

One who is to come and perform His mighty acts and to achieve His eternal purpose.[13]

b. THE ENCOURAGEMENT OF GOD THE SPIRIT

The seven spirits which are before God's throne symbolize the Holy Spirit, seven again symbolizing completion or perfection.

This image brings great encouragement to the churches, for they serve God "not by might nor by power, but by my Spirit, says the Lord of hosts" (Zech. 4:6). Yet the image also brings responsibility because the history of each church (chs. 2—3) is an unfolding of that church's response to the Holy Spirit—"He who has an ear, let him hear what the Spirit says to the churches" (2:7,11, et al.).[14]

c. THE SUPREMACY OF GOD THE SON

(1) Christ as a faithful witness

In verse 5a Jesus Christ is called the faithful witness, the one who witnessed by His life and death to the whole truth of God (compare John 1:14,17; 14:6; 18:37). This verse reminds us that the first-century Christians were greatly inspired when they remembered that Jesus was a faithful witness in the days of His flesh and that He fearlessly bore His testimony when He was on trial for His life. This helped the members of the early church as they faced the prospect of being brought to trial for the sake of the gospel of Christ (compare 2 Tim. 2:11-13).[15]

(2) Christ as the first-born from the dead

The fact that Christ is the "first-born from the dead" brings further encouragement. As Christ has given His life in faithfulness to the Father's calling, so God has raised Christ from the dead. This pledges Christ as the first of a great company who will follow (compare 7:13-14).[16]

In Colossians 1:15 Paul referred to Christ as the "first-born of all creation." This cannot mean that Christ was the first-created being. Rather, Christ is the source, ruler, or origin of all creation. Christ's being the "first-born" of the dead thus indicates that He was not just the first in time to be raised from the dead but that He is also the first in importance, having supreme authority over the dead (compare 1:18).[17]

(3) Christ as the ruler of the kings of the earth

Jesus is also described as the ruler of the kings of the earth. The emperors of Rome regarded themselves as supreme among the kings of the earth. They used their power to oppose the church of

Christ. John later in this book describes the time when the rulers of
the last days of history will turn over their power to the Antichrist.
This Antichrist will use every means possible to crush the church
out of existence. The risen Christ, however, is superior to and ultimately more powerful than the Caesars or rulers or the Antichrist
himself. The church of Christ should take heart. Their Savior has all
authority in heaven and on earth and over hell.[18]

C. A Doxology to Christ Who Has Made Us
Priests in His Kingdom (1:5*b*-6)

1. *The Present and Future Victory in Christ (1:5 b)*

The mention of the person and work of Christ leads John to a
burst of praise to his Savior. In the present, Christ loves us. Through
all the immediate distresses, persecutions, and even banishment,
John is convinced that believers are experiencing Christ's continual
care. In addition, Christ's love was unmistakably revealed in His
atoning death, by which He purchased our release from the captivity of sin. Christ's power is also revealed in His ability to transform
individual lives through his "blood" (for example, his death; compare 5:9; 7:14). Through His death on the cross and His resurrection, He also defeated the devil; and those who follow Christ in the
battle against the devil share this victory.[19]

2. *The Present and Future Priesthood in Christ's Kingdom (1:6)*

Those who belong to Christ constitute His kingdom. It is not like
an earthly kingdom. This kingdom consists of those people who
have been loosed from their sins by Christ and who live to do His
service. These people are priests, but they are ordinary Christians
and not an ecclesiastical hierarchy. As priests they will mediate or
speak to people on behalf of God. They will also pray, witness, and
offer sacrifice of themselves.

This discussion of priests reminds us of the old covenant made
between Israel and God (Ex. 19:5-6). But Christ has now ushered in
the new covenant by His sacrifice. This has delivered us from bondage of sin and Satan (Heb. 8:1-13; 2:14-15). According to 1 Peter
2:5,9-10, believers are constituted a royal priesthood with both the
privilege of access to the throne of grace and the responsibility of
intercession for others. This is an endorsement of and an encourage-

ment for the lay renewal movement in the churches. As priests of God, we are to be God-centered in our living, and our chief purpose in life is to serve and glorify God our Father.

But here John is not just referring to our present priesthood, but also to the reign of the saints and their priesthood in the millennial kingdom when it is established (compare 20:6).[20]

D. A Solemn Affirmation of Christ's Return (1:7)

1. The Nature of Christ's Return

A basic theme of Revelation is affirmed in the dramatic cry: "Behold, he is coming." This is a clear reference to the return of Christ (22:7,12,20). The divine promise of Christ's return is given by the Father, and the response of the prophet and the churches follows in the words, "Even so! Amen." With this double exclamation, John is saying, "Yes, indeed! So let it be!"[21]

Christ's second coming will be supernatural ("with the clouds") and in some manner open and known to all ("every eye").

2. The Responsibility for the Crucifixion of Christ

When verse 7 states that everyone who pierced Christ shall see Him, it does not refer exclusively to those who physically crucified Him in AD 29 or 30 in Jerusalem, such as Pilate, Annas, and Caiaphas. They were acting as representatives of all humanity in crucifying Jesus. Thus this statement refers to those in every age who share the indifference and hostility behind the act of the crucifixion. In the words of the spiritual, "Were you there when they crucified my Lord?" We were there. We have all helped to pierce Him. If He were to come to the United States again today, we would crucify Him again, or at least a majority of the people would.

Verse 7 also states that all of the tribes of the earth will wail. They will wail because of the judgment which Christ brings upon the world and upon those who reject Him.

3. The Rapture or "Catching Up" of the Church

This verse (v. 7) does not give us details about the rapture or the catching up of the church into the air. In fact, as we shall see, Revelation itself states nothing explicitly about the rapture of the church. Christians assume that the rapture occurs at the time when Christ returns because in Matthew 24 we have our Lord's picture of what is to happen in the end times. Matthew 24:31 states, "He will send out his angels with a loud trumpet call, and they will gather his elect from the four winds, from one end of heaven to the other." In 1 Thessalonians 4:17 Paul stated that "we who are alive, who are left, shall be caught up together with them [the resurrected dead] in the clouds to meet the Lord in the air." We understand this rapture of the church to be at the time of the return of Christ as described in 19:11-16.

E. A Solemn Affirmation of the Power of God (1:8)

Verse 8 makes it clear that the Lord God Almighty has announced Christ's soon return.

Most Christians are aware that Alpha and Omega are the first and last letters of the Greek alphabet. Their meaning here is similar to "the first and the last" in 1:17 and "the beginning and the end" in 21:6 and 22:13. God is the absolute source of all creation and history. Nothing lies outside of Him.[22]

This expression Alpha and Omega also suggests the entirety of a thing. Here John couples it with the three tenses of the copula "is . . . was . . . is to come." The Lord God of history at the very outset assures the saints of final triumph. God not only "is" and "was" but also "is to come."[23]

II. The First Vision of John

(1:9 to 3:22)

A. The Vision of the Glorified Christ
and the Commission to Write (1:9-20)

1. John on Patmos, Tribulation, the Lord's Day, and the Vision (1:9-11)

a. JOHN ON PATMOS (1:9)

John is unlike the Jewish apocalyptic writers of the interbiblical period. They attempted to get people to accept their writings by writing under an assumed name of an earlier "great" like Enoch. John identifies himself as one who is their brother and as one who shared with them the tribulation inflicted by the Roman rulers. He is well-known and has spiritual ties with them.

As we noted in the Introduction, conservative scholars have long identified the John of Revelation as the author of the Gospel of John, the one who was the disciple of Jesus, and the author of the three Epistles of John.

Some conservative scholars have noted the modesty of this "son of thunder." He does not lay claim to his title of *apostle*, but merely identifies himself with his brethren in their suffering.[1]

Patmos is a small island off the coast of Asia Minor which was used by the Romans as a place for prisoners. It is rocky and composed of volcanic hills. It is approximately six miles wide and ten miles long. John was banished for preaching "the word of God and the testimony of Jesus" (compare 6:9; 12:17; 19:10; 20:4).

The early church fathers, such as Irenaeus, Clement of Alexandria, and Eusebius, stated that John the apostle was exiled to this island. Victorinus, another church father, said that John was quite old when he was exiled and worked in the mines of Patmos. This was about the year AD 95. In AD 96, Domitian, the Roman ruler, died. Tradition affirms that John then returned to Ephesus where he lived until he was 102 years of age.

133

Many Bible authors, in addition to John, were in prison or in exile when they wrote: Ezekiel, Jeremiah, and the apostle Paul. David also wrote some of the psalms when he was being pursued by Saul.

I have been to Patmos many times. When visiting this island, the guides and monks emphasize the strong tradition that it was the apostle John, the son of Zebedee, who came to live there. You also hear about this same tradition when you go to Ephesus. In Ephesus, the tradition is that John brought Mary, the mother of Jesus, with him from Palestine, and they both lived there. Justinian, the famous Roman emperor, built a large church in Ephesus in honor of John. The ruins of that church can still be seen today. Because of these associations with John, some of the important early church councils were held in Ephesus.

b. TWO CHIEF CONCERNS OF REVELATION: TRIBULATION AND THE KINGDOM (1:9)

In 1:9 John sets forth two of the main concerns of the book: the tribulation which the church is to experience and the coming of the kingdom.

The tribulation is a present experience as is also the kingdom, but the kingdom is also a future hope. Only those with "patient endurance" will enter into its fullness (compare Mark 13:13).[2]

Tribulation is the lot of God's people in the time between the first and second comings of Christ. Jesus said that in the world we will have tribulation. Acts 14:22 states that through many tribulations we enter into the kingdom of God. John affirms that behind the drama of human history two mighty spiritual powers are in conflict with each other—the kingdom of God and the power of Satan. The church stands between the two. As the people of God, the church is the object of satanic hatred and is destined to suffer tribulation.[3]

The idea of tribulation in Revelation includes all of the evil which will befall the church throughout history. *Foxe's Book of Martyrs* describes the persecution of the Christians in the early centuries. But Revelation also describes the Great Tribulation at the end of history which will be only an intensification of that which the church has suffered throughout all of history. Because of these anticipated evils, a patient endurance, which was exemplified by Jesus, is needed. Jesus said in Matthew 24:13, "He who endures to the end will be saved." At present, Christ's power does not crush opposition.

Rather, Christ uses suffering to test and purify the loyalty of His followers.[4]

c. THE SIGNIFICANCE OF THE LORD'S DAY (1:10)

In verse 10 we find the only place in the New Testament to refer to the Lord's Day. Most commentators, both ancient and modern, have taken the expression to mean Sunday, the first day of the week. Such a reference would bind the exiled apostle to the worshiping churches in Asia through his longing to be with them on Sunday.[5]

This day is also the first day of the week commemorating the resurrection of Christ. Paul made a reference in 1 Corinthians 16:2 to the importance of the first day of the week for the early Christians. Deissmann suggested that Christians deliberately used the "Lord's Day" to deliver a message to the people of Roman Asia. The pagans celebrated the first day of the week as the "Emperor's day." In contrast, the Christians worshiped Jesus Christ and not the Roman caesar as Lord. [6]

d. REVELATION AS THE RESULT OF A VISION (1:10-11)

In verse 10 John states that he was "in the Spirit." He was worshiping. Then he heard behind him a loud voice as of a trumpet. On the Isle of Patmos, the monks show a beautiful cave on the side of the mountain. They even point out the opening in the wall of the cave where they say the voice came to John.

In verse 11 the voice said, "Write what you see." I think that many of us could speak much more vividly if we could speak in terms of dramatic visions or images instead of some of the more abstract words which we use in the Western world. Some scholars suggest that we should think of Revelation as a book of "inspired images" as well as a book of "inspired words."

John is to write down on a papyrus scroll what he sees and send it to the seven Asian churches. This writing would include the substance of the whole book, not just the first vision.[7]

2. *The Vision of the Glorified Christ as the Lord of the Church and the Author of Seven Letters (1:12-20)*

a. THE SEVEN LAMPSTANDS AS THE NEW ISRAEL (1:12)

When John hears the "voice" speaking to him, he turns and sees "seven golden lampstands." In the Old Testament, the seven-pronged lamp was kept in the holy place of the tabernacle and later in the Temple (Ex. 25:31; Zech. 4:2). When the Temple was destroyed by Titus, the lampstand was taken to a heathen temple in Rome.[8]

When John sees a vision, it comes to him in terms of the Old Testament places and occasions where God had already revealed Himself to His people. This should remind us that the best way to prepare for a new revelation of truth is to study the revelation which God has already given.

The lampstand symbolized Israel as God's chosen people who, supplied by divine oil, were to be a "light to the nations" (Isa. 49:6). In this vision, the lampstands symbolize the church of Jesus Christ, the new Israel of God. Christ is the Light of the world (John 8:12), even as God the Father is Light (1 John 1:5). As the children of God, redeemed by Christ, we, too, are "children of the light." We are to let His light shine through us in order that He might be glorified (John 12:36; Eph. 5:8; 1 Thess. 5:5; Matt. 5:14-16).[9]

b. THE SEVENFOLD DESCRIPTION OF THE SON OF MAN (1:13-16)

In verse 13 we have the beginning of the sevenfold description of the Son of man. "Son of man" was Christ's self-designation (Mark 10:45). He fused the concept of the Suffering Servant of Isaiah with that of the Son of man found in Daniel. In His first advent, He suffered, but now He occupies a place of honor and authority at God's right hand (Acts 3:13 ff.; 4:27 ff.; 7:55-56). The Son of man is seen possessing the attributes of God which are found in Daniel 7:13; 10:5-6.[10]

The vision creates an impression of the *whole* rather than of particular abstract concepts. The vision conveys awe, mystery, and deity. John sees Christ as the divine Son of God in the fullest sense of the term. He also sees Him as fulfilling the Old Testament descriptions of the coming of the Messiah by using terms drawn from the Old Testament imagery of divine wisdom, power, steadfastness, and penetrating vision.[11]

(1) The robe and the golden girdle (1:13)

The long robe and golden girdle were worn by the priests in the Old Testament (Ex. 28:4). Here they signify Christ as the great High Priest to the churches in fulfillment of the Old Testament Aaronic priesthood. They may also indicate His dignity and divine authority. The "long robe" could be a judicial robe symbolizing that Christ is the One who will judge people and nations, as well as the church.[12]

(2) The white hair and the flaming eyes (1:14)

In Eastern countries, white hair commands respect and indicates the wisdom of years. This part of the vision may have shown John something of the deity and wisdom of Christ (compare Col. 2:3).[13]

His "eyes" like a flaming fire symbolize His penetrating vision and discerning judgment.[14]

(3) The burnished bronze feet and the voice of many waters (1:15)

In both Ezekiel and Daniel, the firelike brightness of shining metal is one of the symbols connected with the appearance of the glory of God (Dan. 10:6; Ezek. 1:7). "Burnished bronze" could also suggest Christ's strength to overcome all opposition.[15]

His voice which was "like the sound of many waters" symbolizes His irresistible power and the fullness with which the Son of man now speaks (compare Ezek. 43:2).[16]

(4) The seven stars, the two-edged sword and the shining face (1:16)

The "seven stars" which John says are the angels of the seven churches are held in His right hand. In his Gospel, John said that the believer is secure in Christ's hands. This is also true of the church (John 10:28-30).[17]

The "two-edged sword" which issues from Christ's mouth speaks of His judicial power and might both inside and outside the church (compare Isa. 49:2-7; Heb. 4:12; 2 Thess. 2:8). This Word of Christ is able to lay us bare before Him—it strips away all sham and hypocrisy.[18]

But the Son of man is gracious too. John says, "His face was like the sun shining in full strength." Most interpreters see this as a reference to the mount of transfiguration where our Lord's face is said to have "shone like the sun" (Matt. 17:2). John was there—he experienced this foretaste of glory. This could also be an allusion to the glorious truth mentioned by Paul when he said, "The God who said, 'Let light shine out of darkness,' . . . has shone in our hearts to give the light of the knowledge of the glory of God in the face of Christ" (2 Cor. 4:6). Thus judgment and redemption are both part of Christ's ministry.[19]

c. HUMILITY BEFORE GOD AND THE DIVINE RESOURCES (1:17-18)

At the presence of such an awesome vision, John prostrates himself, even as did other prophets who were privileged to have visions (compare Ezek. 1:28; Dan. 8:17; 10:9; Isa. 6:5 *ff*.). But Christ speaks reassuringly to John and tells him to stop being afraid.[20]

The title "the first and the last" belongs to God in Isaiah 44:6 and 48:12. In verse 17 the title is ascribed to Christ. This shows that for John, Christ is identified with God. As John said elsewhere (John 5:26), "as the Father has life in himself, so he has granted the Son also to have life in himself."[21]

These divine qualities of Christ's person in verses 17-18 are now linked to His earthly existence in first-century Palestine. "I died, and behold I am alive for evermore." John's whole view of Jesus and His kingdom revolves around the cross and the resurrection. This is a perspective that sets the tone for all the visions that follow.

Through suffering, death, and resurrection, Jesus won the right to have the "keys of Death and Hades" (compare Rom. 1:4). Keys grant the holder access, and in ancient times the wearing of large keys was a mark of status in the community.

Since Christ alone has conquered death, He alone can determine who will enter death and Hades and who will come out of them—he has the "keys." In Christ, we can gain the victory (17:14).[22]

Not only has our Lord conquered death but has also given us the keys to the kingdom that we, too, might lead men out of death into life (compare Matt. 16:19; John 20:23; Acts 26:18; Eph. 2:2).[23]

d. The Book of Revelation as the description of what is and what is to be (1:19)

The statement of "what is and what is to take place hereafter" applies to the whole Book of Revelation. This is true because there is a perpetual movement between past, present, and future in the visions.

John is told to write down a description of the vision of Christ he has just seen, what it means, and what he will see afterward. This does not mean that all he writes will be about the end-time things. Rather, it means that he will write about the things revealed later to him—whether they are wholly future, wholly present, or both future and present.[24]

This relationship between present and future underlies the entire Book of Revelation. It recognizes that the great throne-room drama of chapters 4 and 5, the vision of the woman giving birth to the man child in chapter 12, and much of chapter 17 belong in the past and the present as well as the future.[25]

This understanding of verse 19 leaves the question open concerning the structure of the book and its chronological progression.[26]

e. The supernatural and Christ-centered nature of the churches (1:20)

The seven stars in Christ's right hand are the angels or heavenly messengers who have been entrusted by Christ with responsibility for the seven churches. The angels of the churches are almost equivalent to the churches themselves. Another way of stating this is that the angels of the churches are the heavenly counterparts of the seven churches or perhaps the ideal church. Angels do not refer to the pastors, for monarchical bishops had not yet evolved.

We can also affirm that the angels of the seven churches constitute a universal symbol to represent the heavenly and the supernatural character of the church. John writes to the people who form earthly communities that they are in Jesus and so are saints of the Most High. Their earthly conduct is a reflection of their heavenly relationship. I would like to think that there is a supernatural character about any genuine church of Jesus Christ.

The emphasis in verse 20 rests on Christ's immediate presence and communication through the Spirit to the churches. The reference to angels in the churches shows that the churches are more than a gathering of mere individuals or a social institution. Rather, they have a corporate and heavenly character (compare 1 Cor. 11:10; Eph. 3:10; Heb. 1:14).[27]

The fact that the seven lampstands are the seven churches shows that the churches are the earthly counterpart of the "stars" and links the vision of Christ with His authority to rule and judge His churches. The Christ who loves His church will reprove it in order that it may fulfill its task in the world and attain its destiny in glory.[28]

Theologically, this portrayal of the Christian church is of decisive importance for the formation of healthy church doctrine for us today. Notice that the churches are not only addressed in their uniqueness, and indeed each one will receive a specific letter, but are also addressed in their connectedness to each other.[29]

Also notice that this connectedness is not a connectedness of government or polity, but of the common center and the common source of life. Jesus Christ united the seven lampstands by the reality of His presence in their midst. This is the only source of vitality and life for the church. This centrality of Christ is more fundamental than the order of the apostolic succession of bishops, or of a common experience of the gifts of the Holy Spirit. It is the unity of the common Savior-Lord. It is the living Word and the gospel that surrounds that Word which give order and unity to the church through the confirming ministry of the Holy Spirit.[30]

We have theologically come full circle back to the centrality of Jesus Christ. His authority makes the church possible in the first place. And as we shall see in the seven messages to the seven churches, our obedience to Jesus Christ as the true center will be the criterion by which the seven churches are judged.[31]

B. Introductory Overview to 2:1 to 3:22

1. General Purpose of the Letters

John addresses seven letters to the seven churches on behalf of the risen Christ. When Christ addresses these seven churches through John, He addresses them as a *true* pastor or shepherd. He does not close His eyes to what is good or evil. However, He seeks to commend them where they have been faithful. But He also condemns them where they have and are failing their mission. As a genuine pastor, Christ calls them to repentance but always holds out to them the forgiving love of God. But He does not fail to warn them of the impending doom if they fail to repent and return.[32]

One unique feature of each letter is the way in which the prophet begins with some appropriate part of the vision of the Son of man (1:12-20) which meets the needs of the particular church. Only in the case of the church at Laodicea does he go back to the introduction of the Revelation (1:5).[33]

These churches were roughly in the circle around Ephesus, which was their center. They were churches that were under John's oversight and supervision. They were churches with which he was familiar. As Christ's representative, he was writing these letters to these churches to exercise apostolic oversight.

The seven letters also provide a representative cross section of conditions in Christian churches. At any time throughout Christian history, it would be possible to find similar problems and conditions. This means that the commendation, condemnation, and the challenge in these two chapters would be applicable not only to John's immediate day but also to the churches that may be going through a similar experience during the course of church history.

2. Dispensational Premillennial View of the Purpose of the Letters

Dispensational premillennialists, such as Dwight Pentecost, not only take these as historical letters to real churches but also see them as a preview of church history in its downward course toward the period symbolized by Laodicea and its lukewarmness and apostasy.

Pentecost states that even the names of these seven churches suggest certain periods in church history. Ephesus means "desired." That would refer to the true church of the apostolic age. Smyrna means "myrrh" which is associated with suffering and death. This was the church in the period of persecution in the early postapostolic age. Pergamum means "thoroughly married." That would refer the the union of the church and state under Constantine.[34]

Thyatira means "continual sacrifice," referring to the church in the period of Roman Catholic domination. Sardis means "those escaping" and so would refer to the Reformation. Philadelphia means "brotherly love" and would be characteristic of the true church of the last days. Laodicea means "people speaking" or "people ruling" and refers to the ecumenical, apostate church of the last days in which the authority of Christ is superseded by the authority of man.[35]

The arrangement of these churches and the order in which John arranges his letters to them, according to Pentecost, reveals the progress of the history of the church through its periods of development in the church age. John Walvoord approves this view and states that to interpret such a remarkable progression as pure accident would be incredible. "The order of the messages to the churches seems to be divinely selected to give prophetically the main movement of history."[36]

3. Criticisms of the Dispensational View

According to Alan Johnson, the text of Revelation itself provides no reason for holding this view. The churches are simply historical churches, typical of those found in every age. If the churches were genuinely prophetic of the course of church history rather than representative of churches in every age, those who held to the imminent return of Christ would have been quickly disillusioned. This would have been true because Christ could not return until the church had gone through the seven periods indicated prophetically by the churches.[37]

George Ladd contends that there is no indication in these seven letters that sustains the dispensational teaching about the churches as indicating a prophetic pattern. Richardson maintains that the idea that these churches are a preview of church history is "based on pure fancy." Richardson does agree, however, that God is at work in history through the churches.

4. The Significance of the Number Seven

In Revelation numbers are almost always symbolic. The reason seven churches were chosen and were placed in this order seems to be that seven is the number of completeness. This emphasis on seven underlies the literary pattern of the book. These seven churches contained typical or representative qualities of both obedience and disobedience that are a constant reminder to all churches throughout every age (compare 2:7,11,17,29; 3:6,13,22; esp. 2:23). Their order (1:11; 2:1 f.) reflects the natural ancient travel circuit beginning at Ephesus and arriving finally at Laodicea.[38]

We know there were other churches in Asia Minor in addition to these seven churches to which John writes letters. The New Testament itself refers to congregations at Troas (Acts 20:5-12), Colossae (Col. 1:2), and Hierapolis (Col. 4:13). John wrote to seven churches, we believe, because they were representative of the whole church in the first century and also are representative of the churches in each age.[39]

Each message to an individual church was apparently also intended for the other six churches (2:7,11,17, etc.; esp. 2:23). By comparing the similar elements of all the letters, we can gain a fuller insight into their messages.[40]

5. The Symmetry and Organization of the Letters

The symmetry and the careful organization of the seven letters has long interested commentators. Each letter is prefaced by a charge to write to the angel of the specific church. This is followed by an identification of the author in descriptive phrases taken from the vision in 1:12-20.

The body of each letter contains an acknowledgment of the

church's positive achievements, except at Laodicea and perhaps in Sardis. Then each letter has words of encouragement, censure, counsel, or warning. Only Smyrna and Philadelphia escaped some note of criticism. The letters close with the exhortation to hear and a promise to those who conquer. The entire sequence is obviously a literary composition designed to impress upon the churches then and in later ages the necessity of patient endurance in periods of persecution.[41]

The motif of patient endurance in tribulation is important and helps to bind these letters to the rest of Revelation. In the final conflict between Christ and Caesar and later opponents, believers will need to hold fast to their confession of faith and stand ready for whatever sacrifice is required. Bruce emphasizes that the letters give a vivid impression of the Christian life in Asia Minor at a crucial time. Pressure is being brought to bear on Christians to be less unyielding in their negative attitude to such socially approved activities as emperor worship and compromising world views.[42]

C. The Letters to the Seven Churches (2:1 to 3:22)

1. The Letter to Ephesus (2:1-7)—The Danger of Leaving the First Love

a. THE CITY OF EPHESUS (2:1)

Ephesus was the foremost city of Roman Asia, even though Pergamum was the capital. It was the gateway to Asia and Rome. Ephesus was important from many perspectives. It was the trade center of the area. It has been called the "Market of Asia" and the "Vanity Fair" of the ancient world.[43]

From a religious perspective, Ephesus was the center for the worship of the fertility goddess known to the Greeks as "Artemis," or "Diana" to the Romans (Acts 19:23 ff.) A temple to Diana, one of the seven wonders of the ancient world, was located there (Acts 19:35). Many of the priestesses were dedicated to cult prostitution. This may be related to the practices of the Nicolaitans (2:6). Ephesus was also one of the chief seats of the emperor cult. Here Paul stayed for three years and faithfully preached the gospel (Acts 19:11-41).[44]

John probably addressed the Ephesian church first because of its strategic importance.[45]

b. THE COMMENDATION: RESISTANCE TO HERESY AND PATIENT EN-
DURANCE (2:2-3,6)

The message of Christ is related to the church's problem and
need. Some itinerant preachers who called themselves prophets
seem to have gained entrance into the churches and probably led
some into idolatry and immorality (Acts 20:29). They were known as
Nicolaitans (2:6). They were also active at Pergamum (v. 15) and at
Thyatira (v. 20).[46]

It is difficult to determine exactly who the Nicolaitans were and
what they taught. Did they mix the Christian faith with idolatry and
cult prostitution? Fiorenza and others identify the group as Gnostics. Whatever the nature of the heresy, the Ephesians had successfully resisted it and remained true to their faith.[47]

Christ also commends them for their hard toil and their patient
endurance. They were willing to bear all manner of trials for Christ's
sake.

c. THE CONDEMNATION: LOSS OF FIRST LOVE (2:4)

Unfortunately, when individuals and churches become involved
in defending the faith, they often lose their original spirit of love. The
Ephesian church "abandoned" or forsook or let go of the love they
"had at first" or their "first love"(KJV).[48]

This could refer to the original Christian love the Ephesians had
for one another. Some commentators, however, see the "first love"
as referring to the inner devotion to Christ that characterized their
earlier commitment, like the love of a newly wedded bride for her
husband. This interpretation is supported by the fact that in the letters to the other churches Christ complains of problems of inner be-
trayal of Him. There is probably truth in both views.[49]

Loving devotion to Christ can be lost in the midst of active service.
And no amount of orthodoxy can be a substitute for love for one
another. "First" love would suggest that they still loved, but with a
quality and intensity unlike that of their initial love.[50]

The first love is also a fundamental first principle for ethics. In
New Testament ethics, we are not so much commanded to love as
we are to experience the love that commands.[51]

How could it happen? Did the Ephesians intellectually outgrow
their most exciting idea? The "Ephesus problem" usually happens
quietly and by gradual shifts of focus. A man or woman first unites
with the Christian church because of an experience of and belief in

Jesus Christ and His love. After a few years of being a Christian, that person becomes a leader in the church with very heavy responsibilities for the fellowship. But something happens along the way. That person finds himself or herself motivated and nourished by the organization or by controversy or by ambition to hold power. The first love has been replaced, while perhaps no one was aware of the replacement.[52]

First Corinthians 13 reminds us of the importance of love. Service without love becomes drudgery. Speaking without love becomes mere noise. Affirming correct doctrine without love leads to harshness, pride, self-righteousness, and legalism. Enduring hardship without love makes one bitter and rebellious. Love for Christ is the ingredient which must control and beautify all our relationships, whether the relationship is with others, ourselves, or God. We need to be careful lest we become so busy with things of the kingdom that we do not have time for the best—abiding in the love of Christ.[53]

d. THE CALL TO REPENTANCE (2:5)

The Ephesians are called on to reflect on their earlier works of fervent love and to compare them with the present situation. They are to ponder how far they have fallen from their former devotion and enthusiasm and to humbly "repent" (totally change) before God and to do the former works motivated by love. These imperatives are all part of a single response that would keep the Ephesians from the judgement of Christ.[54]

Christ says, "I will come" with judgment and remove the lampstand from among the churches unless you repent! When a church loses its love for Christ and the brethren, it ceases to be a church. How many individuals and churches today stand at this same crossroad? This threat of loss of light bearing (or witness) applies also to the other four churches to whom a similar exhortation to repent is given (Pergamum, Thyatira, Sardis, and Laodicea).[55]

e. THE BLESSING: JOYS OF THE ETERNAL KINGDOM (2:7)

To those who hear, that is, respond in repentance and obedience, Christ promises to give the privilege of eating "of the tree of life, which is in the paradise of God."

The "tree of life" is first mentioned in Genesis 2:9 as one of the many trees given to Adam and Eve for food and was off limits to them after their fall into sin (Gen. 3:22,24). It is last mentioned in Revelation 22:19.[56]

The tree of life portrays in a symbolical way the truth of eternal life or the banishment of death and suffering (22:2). Those who truly follow Christ in deep devotion and thus experience the real victory of Christ will share the gift of eternal life that He alone gives.[57]

2. *The Letter to Smyrna (2:8-11)—Suffering and Poor but Spiritually Rich*

a. THE CITY OF SMYRNA (2:8)

Smyrna (modern Izmir) was a real metropolis with one of the largest populations in Roman Asia. It was located thirty-five miles north of Ephesus. The city was known as a center of culture. It claimed to be the birthplace of Homer.[58]

Smyrna was also a center of the emperor cult, having won from the Roman senate in AD 23 (over eleven other cities) the privilege of building the first temple in honor of Tiberius. Under Domitian (AD 81-96), emperor worship became compulsory under threat of death for every Roman citizen. Once a year, a citizen had to burn incense on the altar to the bust of Caesar and say "Caesar is Lord." He was then issued a certificate. Such an act was probably considered more an expression of political loyalty than of religious worship. Yet most Christians refused to do this. Perhaps nowhere was life for a Christian more perilous than in this city of zealous emperor worship. In addition to the temples to the emperors, there were temples of Apollo, Aesculapius, Aphrodite, Cybele, and Zeus.[59] A hostile faction of the large Jewish community at Smyrna was prominent in Polycarp's death and also troubled the church in John's day (v. 9). It was here that Polycarp, bishop of Smyrna, served Christ so long and faithfully. When he was given the choice to either renounce Christ or die, Polycarp replied, "Eighty and six years have I served him and he has done me no wrong. How can I blaspheme my King who saved me?" And so he was martyred, February 23, AD 155.[60]

Thus we see that the Smyrnan church, like many churches in atheistic totalitarian lands since then, had to battle with a hostile environment which sought to crush it.

Humanly speaking one would not expect a strong church at Smyrna. Not only was the Jewish persecution bitter but also the people were materially poor. But, as is often the case, privation and persecution produce a strong faith.[61]

b. COMMENDATION: PATIENT ENDURANCE IN JEWISH PERSECUTION (2:9-10b)

Christ commends this church for her patient endurance in the midst of bitter persecution. But Christ knows her plight and knows the tribulation and poverty and slander she endures at the hands of those who call themselves Jews. This tribulation is not merely the persecution many associate with the end time but is also the persecution which they are experiencing then.[62]

In the first century, the resistance most often originated from the Jews. They refused to accept Jesus as the Messiah and therefore were antagonistic toward those who preached Christ. Paul had said, "He is not a real Jew who is one outwardly, nor is true circumcision something external and physical" (Rom. 2:28).[63]

A certain faction within the Jewish community (not the whole community) used malicious slander to incite persecution of the impoverished Christians in Smyrna. "Who say that they are Jews but are not" shows that, even though these men claimed descent from Abraham, they were not his true descendants because they did not have faith in Christ, the "Seed" of Abraham (Gal. 3:16,29). These unbelieving and hostile Jews probably viewed the Jewish Christians in Smyrna as heretics of the worst sort. Whether the "true" Jews refers to Christians in general or those Jews in Smyrna who became Christians is open to debate.[64]

"But are a synagogue of Satan" in verse 9 reveals for the first time in Revelation the ultimate source of the persecution of Christians— Satan. "Synagogue of Satan" refers to certain hostile Jews in Smyrna who, motivated by Satan, slander the church there. The term should never be indiscriminately applied to all Jewish synagogues.[65]

This period of persecution will not be long (v. 10), but it will be long enough to prove their dedication to Christ. In the last days, a worldwide persecution will break out, but here a local persecution seems to be in view.[66]

The risen Christ speaking through John reveals that some of them will be imprisoned by the devil in order to test them, and they will have ten days of persecution (v. 10b). The "ten days" may be ten actual days, or it may be a Semitic phrase for an indefinite but comparatively short period of time.[67]

c. THE BLESSING: THE CROWN OF LIFE AND NO HURT FROM THE SEC-
OND DEATH (2:10c-11)

Jesus holds before the suffering saints the promise of certain victory. Even though they may die, they can face death with confidence, knowing that the crown of life awaits them (v. 10c). The
obvious meaning is that the crown symbolizes everlasting life, the
ultimate reward of victory.[68]

The saints will receive not only the crown of life but also will not
be affected by the second death (v. 11). The first death is the natural
death to which all people are subject. The second death is eternal
separation from God which will befall all those who reject the
Christ.[69]

Death was a real possibility for these believers. But greater than
the fear of physical death should be the fear of God's eternal judgment (Luke 12:4-5).[70]

3. The Letter to Pergamum (2:12-17)—The Danger of Theological Compromise

a. THE CITY OF PERGAMUM (2:12)

The city of Pergamum (or Pergamus) was the capital of the Roman
province of Asia. It was not as important as Ephesus commercially;
but as a political, religious, and cultural city, it was second to none.
It was fifty-five miles north of Smyrna. Its library numbered 200
thousand parchment rolls, second in size only to the library at Alexandria in Egypt. Here the seat of emperor worship was located. The
first temple to the Emperor Augustus was built in Pergamum as
early as AD 29. The ruins of Pergamum today reflect the glory of this
important city.[71]

In Pergamum stood a great altar to Zeus standing on a platform
cut out of a rock on a hill that was covered with temples and which
dominated the city. There were also shrines to Athena, Dionysius,
and Aesculapius, the god of health and healing. Connected with the
shrine of Aesculapius was the medical college for priests. Sufferers
from all over the Mediterranean gathered at this shrine. R. H.
Charles called Pergamum "the Lourdes of the ancient world."[72]

Because Pergamum was the center for the emperor cult in Asia,
Christ refers to it as "Satan's seat" (KJV). Many Christians at Pergamum were to be added to the list of martyrs because they, like

Antipas, refused to worship the emperor by saying "Caesar is Lord."[73]

b. THE COMMENDATION (2:13): FAITHFULNESS DURING TEMPTATION

Christ praises the believers here for holding fast to the name of Christ. This fidelity is especially meaningful because of the presence of the emperor cult and other pagan shrines and because of the negative influence of those who bowed the knee to the teachings of the "Balaamites" ("Nicolaitans"). One of their number, Antipas, chose martyrdom rather than life without Christ.[74]

The mention of the name "Satan" before and after Antipas in verse 13 makes it virtually certain that his death was instigated by the enmity of pagans in Pergamum. He may have been the first or most notable of Pergamum's martyrs. Christ pays a noble tribute to this hero of the faith: "faithful witness."

Satan tries to undermine loyalty to Christ by persecution. In contrast, Christ strengthens that loyalty by commending those who are true to Him and by exposing those who are deceitful.[75]

c. THE CONDEMNATION (2:14-15): SUCCUMBING TO FALSE TEACHERS

Despite the heroism of most members, some at Pergamum have been led astray. The false teachers are not outsiders who are seeking to gain entrance, as at Ephesus, but they are right there in the church.[76]

Christ identifies the false teachers in Pergamum with clear-cut evil, such as that of Balaam. Balak, king of Moab, could not succeed in getting the seer Balaam to curse Israel directly. But what he could not do directly, Balak achieved through a plan whereby Balaam deceived Israel. Balaam arranged a plan whereby the daughters of the Moabites would seduce the Israelite men. Then the women led the Israelites to sacrifice to the pagan god, the Baal of Peor, and worship him (Num. 25:1 *ff.*; 31:16; 2 Pet. 2:15; Jude 11).[77] Through the worship of the fertility god, Baal, Israel had not only been led into idolatry but also had been led to commit fornication.

In like manner Christ said, "You also have some who hold the teachings of the Nicolaitans." These Nicolaitans are comparable to Balaam of old. They have deceived the people of Pergamum and led them into idolatry and immorality.[78]

The combination of "food sacrificed to idols" and "immorality" may refer to the common practice of participating in the sacrificial meal of the pagan gods (compare 1 Cor. 10:19-22) and indulging in sexual intercourse with temple priestesses in cult prostitution. This is the more normal way to understand the term "sexual immorality" in the context of the pagan gods.[79]

Some feel, however, that the term refers to spiritual unfaithfulness and apostasy from Christ (compare Isa. 1:21; Ezek. 23:37).

There was widespread sexual immorality in first-century pagan society. This makes it entirely possible that some Christians at Pergamum were still participating in the holiday festivities. They saw no wrong in indulging at the harmless table in the temples and in the sexual excitement everyone else was enjoying (compare 1 John 5:21).[80]

d. THE CALL TO REPENTANCE (2:16)

Christ calls them to repent of following the teachings of the false Nicolaitan teachers. If they do not, Christ threatens to come with judgment against these false teachers and the church for their leniency toward them. Christ will judge them with the sword of His mouth.[81]

The message for today is that church members need to know what they believe and why so that when they are challenged by those who claim to have some special revelation from God, they will be able to test those claims by the Word of God. Those who know what God's Word teaches will be able to help others who are floundering in their search for the truth.[82]

e. THE BLESSING (2:17): HIDDEN MANNA AND WHITE STONE

Those who overcome will be given some of the hidden manna. In apocalyptic Jewish teaching, the messianic era will see the restoration of the hidden wilderness manna. To those at Pergamum who refuse the banquets of the pagan gods, Christ will give the manna of His great banquet of eternal life in the kingdom (John 6:47-58).[83]

For Palmer, this blessing has meaning for today's culture. Those who have been malnourished on the falsehoods of hatred, fear, selfishness, sexual narcissism, self-indulgence, and so forth not only need to repent of the falsehood but also need the protein, minerals, and body-building vitamins of God's love, truth, faith, hope, peace. People really need good food. This means that the long-term strategies that seek to share the substantial and health-giving gospel with people, young and old, are those that best express the biblical intent.[84]

Although the blessing is hidden now, it will be manifest at Christ's coming. Jesus, speaking through John, says that if they are victors in the Christian race, they will be given a white stone, and upon it will be a new name.[85]

It seems best to connect the stone with the manna and see it as a reference to an invitation that entitled its bearer to attend the heavenly banquet.[86]

The new name is either the name of Christ Himself, now hidden from the world but to be revealed in the future as the most powerful of names (3:12; 14:1), or the believer's new name or character changed through redemption (Isa. 62:2; 65:15). If this refers to a new name for the believer, it speaks to the identity crisis. He can have a new identity to fulfill the identity distorted by sin.[87]

4. The Letter to Thyatira (2:18-28)—The Danger of Moral Compromise

a. THE CITY OF THYATIRA (2:18)

Thyatira was the smallest of the seven cities. It was known primarily for its dyeing and woolen industries.

Acts 16:4 mentions that Lydia, a proselyte, came from the Jewish settlement at Thyatira. She was a distributor of garments made with the purple dye known today as "Turkey red." She was probably a member of the dyer's guild. It has been suggested that some of Paul's converts at Ephesus evangelized Thyatira (Acts 19:10). The church, like many others, was probably predominantly composed of Gentiles since Jews are not mentioned.[88]

The city was well-known for its trade guilds or labor unions, and it was around these that the trouble centered. If one wanted to enter a trade or advance in it, one had to belong to the trade guild peculiar to one's skill. Unfortunately, these guilds usually had a patron deity. Connected with the guild's activities were communal meals in the temples which began and ended with sacrifices to the deity. Drinking and sexual immorality were usually associated with the festivities at the temple.[89]

Because the Christians felt compelled not to join the guilds, they found themselves ostracized and boycotted. Since earning a livelihood was difficult outside the trade guilds, many Christians were tempted to compromise their faith. After all, had Paul not said that "an idol is nothing" (1 Cor. 8:4; 10:19)?[90]

This threat to the Christians' economic lives makes the letter to Thyatira especially meaningful for twentieth-century readers. The most subtle challenge to faith does not usually originate in public amphitheaters but in the daily places where we earn the money we need to live. The question is: How are we to survive such tests and even turn them toward a new and redemptive direction?[91]

The temptation is heightened by the presence of a false prophetess whom they called Jezebel. She seems to be counseling Christians to surrender to the peculiar temptations of Thyatira. The crucial nature of the problem at Thyatira accounts for the length of this letter, the longest of the seven.[92]

b. THE COMMENDATION (2:19): INCREASED GOOD WORKS AND PATIENT ENDURANCE

The commendable thing about this church is its works. Their love is expressed as works defined as faith, service, and patient endurance. The Thyatireans were doing more for Christ now than they had in the earlier days.[93]

c. THE CONDEMNATION (2:20-24): IMMORALITY RELATED TO FALSE TEACHING

As the Nicolaitans were compared with Balaam so the apostate teacher at Thyatira is compared with the Old Testament character of Jezebel (v. 20). Jezebel was the Canaanite wife of Israel's King Ahab. Jezebel had not only led Ahab to worship Baal but through Ahab had spread her teachings of idolatry throughout Israel (1 Kings 16:31-33; 2 Kings 9:22).[94]

The reason Christ is so severe with Jezebel is that prophets occupied such a prominent place in the early church, even as they did in Israel (1 Cor. 12:28; Eph. 4:11). Since this woman claims the prophet's character and authority, her teaching is all the more dangerous to genuine Christian commitment. She, like the Nicolaitans, is leading believers into idolatry and immorality.[95]

Many commentators prefer to see this "sexual immorality" (v. 22) as spiritual adultery (that is, idolatry). But the possibility of sexual fornication related to pagan god worship should not be ruled out.[96]

The Jezebel of Thyatira continues in her evil work despite the fact that Christ confronts her, warns her, and gives her time to repent (v. 21). Just how Christ confronts her—by messenger or letter—is not stated.

Because she persistently refuses to repent, Christ, using language understandable in reference to one practicing such a vice, says that He will throw her and her followers upon a sickbed and into great tribulation (v. 22). These two expressions are parallel, evidently indicating that both she and her disciples will suffer affliction.[97]

This affliction is seen as an act of God's visitation or judgment. On a bed she sinned and so on a bed she will suffer. Those who committed adultery with her will also "suffer intensely" (v. 22, NIV).[98]

Christ's strongest threat to the offenders concerns not their sin but their reluctance to repent. The Lord is walking among His churches. He judges evil, but He also offers deliverance to those who have fallen if they repent and stop doing Jezebel's deeds (v. 23).[99]

To those who follow Jezebel ("her children") and refuse to repent, a fatal judgment will be handed out by Christ: "I will strike her children dead" (perhaps a Hebrew idiom denoting "pestilence"; compare 6:8). Some understand "her children" to refer to her actual children, born of her sexual sins, rather than to her followers. Whatever the exact nature of the judgment in verse 23, it is announced beforehand by Christ so that when it takes place not only Thyatira but "all the churches will know that I am he who searches hearts and minds" (NIV), since they will read the same letter and will later hear of the historical outcome.[100]

The teachings of Jezebel are referred to as the deep things of Satan (v. 24). This reference is frequently interpreted as an attack upon an incipient Gnosticism. The "gnostics" were those who believed that God had given to them some special knowledge which automatically made them children of God.[101]

Johnson suggests that the reasoning of some in the early church (the Nicolaitans) may have suggested that the only effective way to confront Satan is to enter his strongholds. The real nature of sin can be learned only by experience. In fact, only those who have really experienced sin can truly appreciate grace. Thus by experiencing the depths of paganism ("the deep secrets of Satan"), one would be better equipped to serve Christ or to be an example of freedom to his brothers (compare 1 Cor. 8:9-11). If this is true, the sin of Jezebel is deadly serious because of the depths of its deception. Only a few perceive where the teaching is leading (v. 24).[102]

d. THE CALL TO REPENTANCE (2:22-25)

Although no explicit call to repentance is given, it is implicit. The church is tolerating Jezebel since they are permitting her to occupy a place in their midst. If they are to inherit the blessing of the messianic kingdom, they must act now (v. 25).[103]

Someone has likened the church to a ship sailing in the ocean. As long as the ship is in the ocean, it can fulfill its function. But if the ocean gets into the ship, it will mean disaster. So, too, if the spirit of the non-Christian world floods the church it will sink.

Jesus is warning the church today that unless it stands against all forms of sin and heresy, there will be judgment. The individual Christian needs to examine his or her own life-style. Are you taking a firm stand against that which God declares is sin, or are your views being conditioned by the hard sell of the world?[104]

e. THE BLESSING (2:26-29): POWER TO RULE AND THE MORNING STAR

To those who conquer, that is, overcome the temptations of Jezebel and keep performing good works until Christ returns, there will be given power to rule by Christ (vv. 26-27).[105]

The first promise is a fulfillment of Psalm 2, which is messianic and tells how the Father gave the Messiah the rule over the nations of the world (vv. 8-9). The coming reign of the Messiah over the world is to be shared with His disciples (1:6; 3:21; 20:6; 1 Cor. 6:2). The prospect of such a reversal of their present experience of oppression and persecution is constant encouragement to suffering Christians.[106]

The second promise is that believers shall be given the morning star (v. 28). Some link this expression to Christ Himself (compare v. 16). Believers would then receive Christ as their very life. Or it may refer to the resurrection in the sense that the morning star rises over the darkness of this world's persecution and offers victory over it. The promise of Christ's return is like the "morning star" (2 Pet. 1:19). In verse 16 Jesus calls himself "the bright morning star" in apparent reference to his return.[107]

5. *The Letter to Sardis (3:1-6)—The Danger of Spiritual Deadness*

a. THE CITY OF SARDIS (3:1a)

Sardis enjoyed prominence as a commercially prosperous and militarily strategic city throughout its history. Her greatest king was Croesus who lived in the sixth century BC. His wealth is commemorated in the proverb, "As rich as Croesus."[108]

Under the Romans, Sardis became an important industrial center, famous for dyeing and woolen industries. Sardis never freed herself from her bad moral conditions.

Christ is fully aware of the spiritual slumber of the church members at Sardis. Although they may have a form of godliness, there is no real power of substance there.[109]

b. THE COMMENDATION (3:4): RESISTANCE TO IMMORALITY

This is a pathetic church. There is not much good that can be said about it. Fortunately for Sardis there are a few who had not soiled their garments. The soiled garments seem to refer to contamination in general, which results from yielding to the many temptations in their society.[110]

Soiling here then appears to be a symbol for mingling with the pagan life and thus defiling the purity of one's relation to Christ (Rev. 14:4; 1 Cor. 8:7; 2 Cor. 7:1; 11:2; Jude 23).[111]

c. THE CONDEMNATION (3:1b-2): SPIRITUAL DEADNESS

Christ knows their true condition. They are dead. Dead is not to be interpreted as complete spiritual death, but as at the point of death (v. 1b).[112]

"Wake up!" (NIV) or "Be (constantly) watchful" (author) is a call to reverse radically their attitudes (v. 3:2). The congregation must be alerted to the seriousness of the situation, which is bad but not totally hopeless. Immediate steps are to be taken to "strengthen what remains." Some persons and things are salvageable if quick and decisive action is taken. Otherwise death will follow. "As a thief" (v. 3) should probably be taken as referring not to the second coming but to Christ's coming against them (opposing them) in judgment.[113]

As Jesus walks in the midst of our churches today, does He find areas of outward form which are devoid of inner power and meaning?

d. THE CALL TO REPENTANCE (3:3)

Christ calls for the church to continue to hold fast and to bring itself to repentance. If the church refuses to awaken from her stupor, Christ promises to come with judgment at a time when they least expect it—as a thief comes in the night.[114]

e. THE BLESSING (3:5-6): NEW GARMENT, ETERNAL NAME, ETERNAL CONFESSION

The blessing awaiting the faithful person who conquers evil in Christ's name is threefold: (1) He will be clad in a white garment; (2)

his name will be written in the book of life; (3) and his name will be confessed before the Father and the angels (v. 5)[115]

The pure relationship to Christ is permanently guaranteed: "I will never erase his name from the book of life" (NIV). Christ's statement that He will never blot out or erase the overcomer's name from the book of life is the strongest affirmation that death can never separate us from Christ and His life (Rom. 8:38-39).[116]

Finally, to the overcomer Christ promises to "confess his name before my Father and before his angels." Christ's confession of our name before the Father and His angels (implying our fellowship with Him) assures our heavenly citizenship (Matt. 10:32; Luke 12:8).[117]

What ultimately counts, then, is not our acceptance by this world's society but whether our relationship to Christ is genuine and loyal. If it is, then we will merit His approval in the coming kingdom.[118]

6. *The Letter to Philadelphia (3:7-18)—The Importance of Loyalty*

a. THE CITY OF PHILADELPHIA (3:7)

The name *Philadelphia* means "one who loves his brother" or "brotherly love." The city of Philadelphia was established by the Pergamenian king Attalus II (159-138 BC), who had been given the epithet "Philadelphus" ("brother lover") because of his loyalty to his brother. The city was to be a mission city for disseminating Greco-Asiatic culture and language in the eastern part of Lydia and in Phrygia.[119]

In this city, a number of Jews persecuted Christians, claiming that they were the true Jews. Christ in addressing the church declares that the Jews who rejected Him are really of the synagogue of Satan. Those of the synagogue of Satan do not acknowledge Him as the Messiah, but they will be compelled to do so some day (v. 9).[120]

Christ also says that He possesses the key of David (v. 7). The "key of David" refers to Isaiah 22:20 *ff*. Keys were normally held by the king himself, unless delegated to another. The use of the name "David" points to Christ as the Messiah, who alone determines who will participate in his kingdom and who will be turned away: "He opens, no one can shut; . . . he shuts, not one can open" (v. 7, NIV).[121]

No self-styled child of Abraham can enter, but only the person who is circumcised of heart and who confesses Christ as Lord.[122]

b. THE COMMENDATION (3:8-9): KEPT THE CONFESSION

Even though the church at Philadelphia was small in number and had little strength, yet Christ commended it because it had kept and not denied His name (v. 8). The "little strength" (NIV) or "power" referred to here does not refer to spiritual strength, but to numbers, material wealth, and influence. On a given occasion they had been tried and sorely tempted to deny Christ, but they had held fast to Christ and did not deny His name.[123]

The sentence, "Behold, I have set before you an open door, which no one is able to shut" (v. 8), is regarded by most interpreters as a parenthesis. The open door may refer to the fact that the Christians have the door (compare v. 20; Acts 14:27; John 10:7,9). This is in contrast to the Jews who claimed they alone had access to God. The context favors this view. Christ assures the faithful that the door into His kingdom is open to them and no one can rob them of the right of entrance.[124]

Others suggest that the door may refer to opportunities which this church had for witnessing (1 Cor. 16:6; 2 Cor. 2:12; Col. 4:3). Christians are not asked to open the heavy doors, but to walk through doors that Christ opens. The task is too hard unless the Lord of the mission empowers His people. On the other hand, Christians are granted a realistic, down-to-earth strategy. This strategy calls upon the Christians to find ways to proclaim the gospel source of their identity and salvation. This is the direct implication of the open-doorway imagery.[125]

Christians are instructed to welcome people who come to the people of God as a result of this combined divine and human evangelical strategy.[126]

But what of those Jews of the synagogue of Satan? There are evidently Jews in Philadelphia who deny that Christians are really God's chosen people (v. 9). We catch a picture here of the ever-widening gap between Judaism and Christianity toward the end of the first century.[127]

Christ clearly states in verse 9 that the Jews who have rejected Him as the Messiah are in reality not Jews at all. The true Jew is one who recognizes Jesus as the Christ (Rom. 2:28-29; Gal. 6:16). Those

Jews who refuse, says Christ, will be compelled to bow at the feet of Gentile believers. What a shock this will be to unbelieving Israel when the tables are turned.[128]

John is saying in verse 9 that not everybody who is born of a Jewish mother and is circumcised is part of the true spiritual Israel. This will lead us to understand, when we discuss Revelation 7 where John talks about the 144,000 Jews, that he is talking about the true Jews who are the Christians or the church.

Verse 9 implies that some of the Jews are persecuting the Christians. He calls these persecuting Jews the synagogue of Satan. They are not the real Jews in the New Testament sense of the word as Paul indicated in Romans 4:16 and Galatians 3:7. One who is a true Jew in the New Testament sense, and is a true descendant of our spiritual father Abraham, is not someone whose mother is Jewish, but is someone who has accepted Christ as the Messiah. Paul stated in Galatians 3:7 that "they which are of faith, the same are the children of Abraham" (KJV).

Excursus on the Jews and God's Redemptive Purpose

All of us are grateful for the place that the Jews have played in God's redemptive purpose. Karl Barth said that we ought to thank God every time we pass by a Jewish synagogue because it reminds us of the beginnings of God's redemptive work and the place of the Jews in this redemptive plan. But as Christians, who believe that Christ is the climax of God's revelation to man, we must interpret the Old Testament in the light of the New Testament.

The unity of the people of God and the fulfillment of the Old Testament

The New Testament indicates that there is a unity of the people of God. Paul stated in Romans 9—11 that we can compare God's redemptive work to an olive tree. First, the Jews constituted the olive tree. Then, when they did not accept Christ as the Messiah, God grafted the Gentile Christians into the olive tree. Christians now constitute the olive tree. Paul did say in Romans 9—11 that in some way God is going to graft the Jews back into the one olive tree. But they will have to come back as does everyone else, by accepting Jesus as the Messiah. There will always be one olive tree, not two.

God promised the Jews that they would have a new exodus and redemption. They would again possess the land and dwell therein as God's people. This promise was explicit. From an external point of view, this promise was fulfilled in the return of the Jews to Palestine from the Babylonian captivity. From an external point of view, the prophecies spoken by many men were fulfilled. That promise does include the promise of the land.

If there is an unfulfilled element in the prophecy of Isaiah, Jeremiah, and Ezekiel, and there most certainly is, the fulfillment, in the light of the New Testament teaching, would not just be in terms of a physical possession of the land. Rather it would be in terms of spiritual reality which is the goal of the covenant made with Abraham and fulfilled in Christ. Even the main concern of the prophets was not primarily with Israel's possession of the land but with the spiritual rebirth of Israel as the true covenant nation.

For John P. Milton, the safe rule to follow in interpreting the Bible is the one that states that a promise is to be regarded as completely fulfilled when its central idea is fulfilled. Which is the more important stress in the Bible—the promise of the land or of the spiritual blessing? Which is the central ideal in the covenant promise?[129]

In a Jerusalem conference on biblical prophecy, Herman Ridderbos of Holland pointed out that he is an evangelical Christian, and that means that he can only understand God's revelation in the Old Testament in the light of the New Testament. He admits that Israel's position among the people of the world is unique because it pleased God to set Israel apart from all people in order to reveal His redemptive love plan. In the second place, however, the privileged place of Israel is valid only to the extent that Israel fulfills her divine vocation, namely to be the people of God's special revelation and thus to be the light of the nations. Election is for redemptive service said W. O. Carver.

Continuing purpose and hope for Israel

Ridderbos believes that God's ordination has left a mark on Israel and has given Israel an identity even though this religious calling and purpose has faded away for most Jews in modern times. This feeling of uniqueness on the part of the Jews has been encouraged by the opposition and hatred and persecution of the Jews by other nations. Ridderbos states that more important than this national consciousness on the part of Jews is the viewpoint that Israel may miss the real aim and purpose of her election as the people of God if she does not yield to her divine vocation.

Ridderbos does admit that God could in some way use Israel even when she does not accept her universal spiritual vocation. For example, at the very moment when Israel rejected the Messiah, Jesus, the breakthrough to the Gentiles became a reality. The church is indebted to Israel according to Romans 9—11.

Ridderbos further states that he cannot find any spiritual guarantee for the national restoration glory of Israel as the people of God. Romans 11:26 does proclaim that all Israel will be saved. From that perspective, he suggests that there will be no consummation of the world before the full number from Israel will be gathered into the kingdom and grafted into the olive tree. On the other hand, Israel's future and salvation depend upon her response to God's final revelation in Jesus Christ.

Robert L. Lindsey, a Southern Baptist missionary who has spent most of his life in Israel, contends that the New Testament promises no salvation or choosing for Israel outside her positive assent to the person and name of Jesus Christ. He states that a strong mission to the Gentile world is an indirect method of provoking the Jews to jealousy.

When Paul recognized that an Israel without Christ was unsaved, he was not saying at all that Israel remains meaningless in history. Israel retains the divine artifacts which were produced as a result of the encounter of God and Israel in the

Old Testament history. In Romans 11:28, Paul stated that the Israelites are loved because of their fathers. This means that God loves the Jews. The Jews are not just puppets which are being used as God's playthings in the working out of a divine plot. A point of contact between Jews and Christians lies in the fact of our sharing of redemptive history.

We must recognize that whether we are committed or nominal Christians, we share with the Jews redemptive history, and on this plane Christians and Jews are inseparable.

c. THE BLESSING (3:10-13): KEPT FROM THE HOUR OF TRIAL; THE CROWN, THE PILLAR, AND THE NEW NAME

(1) The meaning of the hour of trial (3:10)

The reward for patient endurance is Christ's promise to keep them from the hour of trial or testing which is to come upon the entire world (v. 10).

This promise presents two problems. First, what is the identification of the "hour of trial"? Second, what is the precise meaning of the phrase "keep you from the hour of trial"? Both problems relate directly to the ongoing debate among conservative Christians concerning the tribulation-rapture question.[130]

According to dispensationalists, the "hour of trial" is a time of intense trouble. It is known as the Great Tribulation that will befall the world before the coming of Christ (Dan. 12:1; Joel 2:31; Mark 13:14; 2 Thess. 2:1-12; Rev. 14:7). These interpreters understand the promise of the overcomers that they will be "kept from the hour of trial" to mean that they will be removed from the earth (raptured) before the Great Tribulation begins.[131]

In contrast, the historical premillennialists note that the phrase "those who dwell upon the earth" or "the whole world" is repeated a number of times in Revelation and refers not to believers but to unbelievers who are the objects of God's wrath. This is apparent in the references to the worshipers of the beast (6:10; 8:13; 11:10; 12:12; 13:8,12,14).[132]

Much confusion, therefore, may be avoided by clearly identifying "the hour of trial" as the wrath of God upon unbelievers. Christ does not promise immunity for Christians from trial or persecution in general. However, Christians are protected from a specific type of trial (God's wrath) that is aimed at the rebellious on the earth.[133]

Furthermore, by urging the Philadelphian Christians to hold fast (v. 10), Christ seems to imply that they will pass through this period of tribulation. John 17:15 is perhaps the best commentary on Revelation 3:10. Christ prays not that the believers be taken out of the world but that they be kept from the evil one.[134]

In fact, the danger of martyrdom is nothing the church should fear. Jesus said that when His disciples are hated and put to death, not a hair of their head will perish (Luke 21:17). Physical death, even as a martyr, has no eternal significance. Indeed, in the time of the Antichrist the martyrdom of the saints will prove their salvation. In the very act of martyrdom, the saints conquer the beast (Rev. 15:2).[135]

(2) The subjects of the wrath of God

On the other hand, God will pour out His wrath on the followers of the beast and try to drive them to repentance before it is too late (Rev. 9:20; 16:9,11).

The outpouring of God's wrath is pictured symbolically by the plague of the seven trumpets (8:1 to 9:19) and the seven bowls (16:1-20). Before these terrifying judgments, the people of God are sealed so that they will not be hurt by these plagues. These fearful divine judgments are directed upon those who follow the beast (16:2). Those who have the seal of God will be divinely sheltered (9:4). Although the church will be on earth in these final terrible days and will suffer fierce persecution and martyrdom at the hands of the beast, she will be kept from the hour of trial which is coming upon the pagan world. God's wrath, poured out on the kingdom of the Antichrist, will not afflict His people.[136]

(3) The soon coming of Christ as encouragement (3:11)

"I am coming soon" (v. 11) is a basic emphasis of Revelation. It is sometimes used to warn the unfaithful, at other times to encourage the faithful. Here it is used in terms of encouragement. Since He is coming soon, they are to hold fast and see that no one seizes their crown (v. 11).[137]

After the hour of trial, Christ will come again, and the conquerors will be made a pillar in the temple of God (v. 12). The ancient cities were constantly threatened by earthquakes. Often the only parts of a city left standing after a severe quake were the huge stone temple columns. Christ promises to set believers in His temple in such a secure position that no disturbance can ever force them out.[138]

(4) The meaning of the pillar and the new name (3:12-13)

A faithful municipal servant or a distinguished priest was sometimes honored by having a special pillar, inscribed with his name, added to one of the temples. This may well be the sense of the second promise, "I will write on him the name of my God and the name of the city of my God, the New Jerusalem, . . . and my new name" (v. 12, NIV). The inscribed name would then signify identification, ownership, and recognition. To those who have little influence because of being ostracized, Christ promises recognition in His kingdom worthy of the most noble hero of any society.[139]

Christ's "new name" could be the new name of Christ given to the believer, reflecting Christ's ownership through redemption (Isa. 62:2; 65:15).[140]

7. The Letter to Laodicea (3:14-22)—The Danger of Complacency, Lukewarmness, and Apostasy

a. THE CITY OF LAODICEA (3:14)

Laodicea was located on the banks of the Lycus River at the junction of several branches of the great trade road from Ephesus to the inland of Roman Asia. This great Roman road ran straight through its center, making Laodicea an important center of trade and communication.

It was the judicial center for that district. It was also an important commercial city with banking, manufacturing of woolen garments and rugs made from its famous black wool, and medicine. The god of health and healing, Aesculapius, was worshiped at Laodicea, and there was a medical school attached to his temple. In connection with the manufacture of medical products, a specialty was the production of a "Phrygian powder" which was a cure for weak eyes.[141]

A six-mile-long aqueduct brought Laodicea its supply of water from the south. The water came either from hot springs and was cooled to lukewarm or came from a cooler source and warmed up in the aqueduct on the way. For all its wealth, the city had poor water.[142]

We know something of the Christian church in Laodicea from Paul's letter to the Colossians. The church at Laodicea is mentioned four times (Col. 2:1; 4:13,15-16). Many interpreters speculate that Epaphras was the founder of the Christian church in Laodicea and that the Christians in the three cities of Colossae, Hierapolis, and Laodicea were yoked in special friendship.[143]

The inevitable apathy and stagnation which sometimes accompanies affluence infiltrated the church at Laodicea. Although there was a sizable Jewish population, they evidently did not cause any trouble for the Christians.[144]

b. THE CONDEMNATION (3:15-17): LUKEWARMNESS

The Laodiceans received no commendation from Christ; instead they received the most scathing attack of all the churches. Yet behind this attack is seen the loving concern of Christ in verse 18 and following.[145]

Christ condemns the church as a whole for its lukewarmness—it is neither cold nor hot. Lukewarmness, when it becomes a way of life, so completely blurs and dulls the colors that it becomes almost impossible to recognize differences when they occur. Lukewarmness is low-grade paranoia, low-grade cynicism, low-grade immorality. The result is always fatigue and finally despair. Their insipid condition gives Christ a sense of nausea.[146]

The two adjectives in "neither hot nor cold" should be understood together as equivalent to "lukewarm" (v. 16). This means that they were useless to Christ because they were complacent, self-satisfied, and indifferent to the real issues of faith in Him and of discipleship.[147]

In an attempt to shock them out of their apathy and pride, He warns them by saying: "So [therefore, because you are in this insipid state], I will spew you out of my mouth" (v. 16). This seems to refer to the lukewarm water. Laodicea, for all its wealth, had an insipid water supply—one that induced vomiting! Christ detests a Laodicean attitude of compromise, one that seeks easy accommodation and peace at any cost. With such a condition, He must deal harshly. That this is not a total rejection is clear from the admonition and invitation to renewal (vv. 18-22).[148]

Why are the Laodiceans so lukewarm? The deeper problem in the Laodicean church is not simply their indifference. It is their ignorance of their real condition: "You say, 'I am rich; I have acquired wealth and do not need a thing'" (v. 17, NIV).[149]

The answer to their lukewarmness is thus seen in the prideful boasting of verse 17. They feel as though they have arrived, and this by their own efforts. Their boasting seems to be related to the industries of Laodicea. Rather than being spiritually rich, they are materially prosperous and so in need of nothing.[150]

Christ sees them as they truly are: the wretched and pitiful—poor, blind, and naked (v. 17). The reference here is emphatic and is to the spiritual condition of the believers, since the material wealth of the Christians at Laodicea is well known.[151]

Other scholars see "lukewarmness" as not referring to the laxity of Christians but rather to the condition of not really knowing Christ as Savior and Lord and thus being useless to Him.[152]

The word for "blindness" is often used of spiritual blindness and is probably used here in anticipation of the figure of eye salve. Christ is referring to the inability of the Laodiceans to see their spiritual poverty. Likewise, Christ uses the analogy of clothing, with which they are familiar, and declares that they are spiritually naked.[153]

Excursus on Lukewarmness

The dispensationalists contend that we are now in the Laodicean period of church history. One dispensationalist reported to me that we are living in the days of Laodicea, the seventh church, or the apostate church. Things are getting worse and worse. Efforts to work out even temporary frameworks of justice for our communities and country and world are outside of the concern of God's elect in these very last days of history.

The twentieth-century church in the United States faces the same problems and temptations as did the Laodicean church. We, too, are living in an affluent society. We have beautiful buildings, efficient organizations, and thriving, working congregations. Our great danger is that we too become self-satisfied and lukewarm, letting the world squeeze us into its mold.

I do not think that it is inevitable that any particular church or any particular denomination should get lukewarm and continue to stay in a lukewarm condition. Built into the very nature of Christianity is the Holy Spirit and His renewal work. God is constantly renewing His church, both in terms of individual churches and denominations.

It is true that any church or denomination, as it gets older, does tend to become fossilized. Richard Niebuhr, the famous Yale theologian, discussed the social sources of denominationalism. He pointed out that many of the churches which were once socially and spiritually insignificant have now, by the very virtues which were given to them by Christ, become prosperous and prominent. There is always the danger of apostasy both in spirit and in doctrine.

But built into the very structure of the Christian movement is the Holy Spirit and His constantly renewing and reviving power. There is renewal and revival going on in many of the so-called mainline churches. We cannot say that all mainline denominations are inevitably becoming lukewarm.

c. THE CALL TO REPENTANCE (3:18-19)

Christ says, therefore, in the light of your spiritually precarious position, "buy from me gold refined by fire, that you may be rich" (v. 18). Gold, which is a source of the city's wealth, is to be bought from Christ and to become the true wealth of the spiritually poverty-stricken Laodiceans. Their shameful nakedness is to be clothed, not by purchasing the sleek, black wool of Laodicea, but by buying from Christ the white clothing that alone can cover shameful nakedness (16:15). For those who are blind to their true condition, the "Phrygian powder" is useless. They need to buy salve from Christ so that they can truly see (v. 18). The three figures all point to the Laodiceans' need of authentic salvation through Christ.[154]

That Christ has not completely cast His people off becomes clear in verse 19. Actually, He says that He loves them. This is why He has spoken so severely to them (v. 19). Because He loves His proud and rebellious children, He reproves and chastens them.[155]

The difference between the expelled and the disciplined lies in their response: "So be earnest ['zealous,' 'enthusiastic'] and re-pent" (19, NIV). The Laodiceans' repentance would come from a rekindling of their loyalty to Christ.[156]

Christ thus calls for an about-face in the Laodicean attitude toward Him. "Be zealous" is in the present tense which means that they should begin to be zealous, on fire, and continue to maintain this spirit.[157]

d. The blessing (3:20-22): salvation, renewal, fellowship, and eternal reign

(1) The identification of the subjects of the appeal of the open door (3:20)

The context of verse 20 is one of a summons to repentance. Some commentators hold that the figure represents Christ standing at the door to the hearts of the members of the congregation at Laodicea. Christ will come and have fellowship with anyone who hears His voice of rebuke and thus proves to be Christ's friend by zeal and repentance.[158]

This view, then, sees Christ summoning the lapsed members of a lifeless, complacent church to spiritual life. Even though the church is in a sad and deplorable state, Christ still stands at the door of the heart of each individual seeking admission. The repentance of verse 19 is implemented by the admission of Christ into one's life.[159]

Other scholars believe that the context of verse 18 suggests that the Laodiceans are, for the most part, mere professing Christians. They lack the essential prerequisite for true discipleship which is an authentic conversion to Christ. This approach sees verse 20 as more evangelistic than an admonition to lukewarm Christians.[160]

Although they bear the name of Christian and formally constitute a Christian congregation, the Laodiceans are, in fact, spiritually naked and poor and blind. Therefore, like any new convert, they must respond to the appeal of Christ and open their life to His incoming.[161]

Next, a promise is given by Christ: "If any one hears my voice and opens the door, I will come in to him, and eat with him, and he with me" (v. 20). A shared meal in the ancient Jewish world had far more significance than it has today. It was a symbol of affection, of confidence, and of intimacy. So verse 20 contains a promise of the most intimate fellowship possible.[162]

(2) The promise of a place on the throne (3:21)

In verse 21, to the conqueror, Jesus promises that "he . . . will sit with me on my throne, as I myself conquered and sat down with my Father on his throne."

Christians who suffer with Christ even to the point of death will share in the honor of Christ's exalted position. The distinction between the Father's throne and Christ's throne is no mere rhetoric. On the contrary, it points out the difference between two aspects of God's program in history (1 Cor. 15:24-28). Christ is reigning now, for there is a sense in which the eschatological or messianic kingdom of God was inaugurated with Christ's earthly ministry, death, and resurrection. But the promise here, as elsewhere in the New Testament, foresees a final earthly manifestation or consummation of the kingdom that awaits the return of Christ.[163]

Here is a message for every church which faces persecution: assurance that their evil plight is only temporary. Even though human experience may seem to contradict it, Christ is already enthroned as Lord and King. In the next stage of His kingdom, His kingly rule will put all His enemies under His feet.

The conqueror is assured that he will have a share in this reign in the final consummation. Just how this is to be fulfilled is not altogether clear, but probably during the millennial rule of Christ (20:4 *ff.*). However, the promise is not limited to the millennium, for in the new order of the age to come "they shall reign for ever and ever" (v. 5).[164]

There is no need to restrict this promise to martyrs. The promise in each of the seven letters to the conqueror is addressed to all the disciples of Christ with the expectation that all faithful disciples will overcome.[165]

To return to Revelation 3:20, Jesus says, "I am standing at the door and I am knocking. I am not finished with you who are at Laodicea. One of the reasons why I am chastening you and punishing you is to try to awaken you" (author's translation).

Christ is continuing to knock on the door of our individual lives, both through blessings and through sufferings. He is knocking through world conditions. He is knocking through the Holy Spirit. He is knocking through world need. He tells us that if we will open the door He will come back into our hearts and into our churches (compare John 10:9).

Revelation 3:20 is the verse which inspired Holman Hunt to paint his famous picture in Saint Paul's Cathedral in London entitled *The Light of the World*. In this picture, Christ is standing at the door knocking, but there is no knob on the door on His side. The only way it can be opened is when we respond and open the door and yield to Him as our Savior and Lord.

III. The Second Vision

(4:1 to 16:21)

Introduction: Why Is the Vision Needed?

Chapter 4 is a crucial section of Revelation. Here we have a vision of God the Creator and a vision of the sovereignty of God. God is seen as enthroned over all in eternal majesty and power.

In Revelation 4, John receives a vision of what must take place in the days ahead (v. 1). This revelation tells of the destruction of the powers of evil, of Satan, and of death. But before these evil powers are destroyed, they will break forth in a final desperate effort to frustrate the purposes of God by seeking to destroy the people of God. There will be a terrible conflict that will take place on earth between the church and the demonic powers embodied in an apostate civilization.[1]

This conflict is an expression in historical form of a fearful conflict that is going on in the spiritual world between the kingdom of God and the kingdom of Satan. Therefore, it is important at the outset for John to give embattled Christians a vision of God who is on the throne of the universe. However fearful or uncontrolled the forces of evil on earth may seem to be, they cannot annul or blot out the greater fact that behind the scenes God is on His throne governing the universe.[2]

On the plane of history, the church appears unable to resist the might of hostile worldly powers. But the course of history is not finally determined by evil political powers but by God enthroned and active. At the appointed time, the scroll of destiny is to be handed to the Lamb of God, who Himself will open the seals. He will then provide the key to understand ongoing history, bring history to a close, and usher in the eternal state. The great throne room vision of chapter 4 serves to remind believers living in the shadow of impending persecution that an omnipotent and omniscient God is still in control.[3]

A. The Vision of God the Creator and Sovereign (4:1-11)

1. *The Call from Heaven (4:1-2a)*

Revelation began with the dramatic vision John experienced at Patmos: "Then I turned to see . . ." (1:12). The unfolding of John's second vision begins in chapter 4 with a similar phrase, "After this I looked . . ." (v. 1).[4]

a. THE DOOR OF REVELATION (4:1a)

John is taken to the supreme headquarters. The door that is opened to him this time is obviously a door of revelation (compare Ezek. 1:1; Acts 7:56; 10:11). This is not the door of the heart to which he referred in the letter to the church in Laodicea (3:20).[5]

b. THE CONTROVERSY OVER THE RAPTURE (4:1b)

"Come up hither" is the phrase which Hal Lindsey and some dispensationalists believe teaches what they call the pretribulation rapture. According to this view, the mystery church will be taken up into heaven in a secret "great snatch" before the last days of persecution.[6] This view infers that the absence of the word "church" in Revelation 4:1 to 22:15 and the continued references to the "saints" indicate that at this point the church departs from the earth.[7]

But "church" or "churches" in Revelation always stands for the historic seven churches in Asia and not for the universal body of Christ. Since 4:1 to 22:15 concerns the believing community as a whole, it would be inconsistent with John's usage to find the narrower term "church" in this section (compare 3 John 6,9-10).[8]

Furthermore, the overall teaching of Revelation does not allow this interpretation. Revelation 4:1 introduces us to the frequent interchange between heaven and earth found throughout Revelation. There is a constant movement from heaven to earth. What happens on earth has its heavenly counterpart.

John is caught up to heaven in a vision at 4:1 and remains there until the end of chapter 9. In chapter 10, he has returned to earth, for he sees an angel "coming down from heaven" (v. 1). He remains on earth until 11:13. But in 11:15-19, the scene of the vision is again in heaven. In chapter 12, John seems to be on earth again, but 14:18-20 implies that he is back in heaven. In a trance-like state, one can move without difficulty from earth to heaven through a series of visions.[9]

The "after this" in 4:1 is revealed when Christ breaks the seals of the scroll (6:1). "At once I was in the Spirit" in 4:2 is a continuation of the same ecstatic experience referred to earlier (compare 1:10).[10]

2. God Seated on the Throne Surrounded by Twenty-four Elders (4:2b-6a)

John then has a vision of the One who is seated upon the throne (v. 2). The throne symbolizes God's majesty and power. This vision is filled with movement and sounds and color. The vision is related to many Old Testament symbols and experiences from Old Testament prophetic and apocalyptic visions. There are similarities to the vision of Isaiah in the year that King Uzziah died (Isa. 6:1-5). There are even more similarities to the vision of Ezekiel (Ezek. 1). The green jasper (jade) and red sardis (carnelian) remind us of the breastplate stones of the high priest (Ex. 28:17-21). The rainbow reminds us of both Noah's rainbow (Gen. 9:16) and Ezekiel's bow (Ezek. 1:28). Although Isaiah, Ezekiel, and Daniel provide the background for this throne vision, John himself, inspired by the Holy Spirit, is responsible for this majestic description.[11]

The brilliance and beauty of the throne vision is conveyed by the use of precious stones and the rainbow (v. 3). The glory of God appearing as "jasper" suggests translucence—brightness; probably symbolizing the holiness of God. The "fiery-red sardis," or "carnelian," suggests the wrath of God. The "emerald rainbow" (Phillips) is thought to be the rock crystal which shows a rainbow of prismatic colors. It is best to see the rainbow as the covenant promise of God to Noah never to destroy the earth with water (Gen. 9:8 ff.).[12]

Some say that the twenty-four elders are symbolic of the church in its totality—a combination of the twelve patriarchs and the twelve apostles. However, this seems unlikely in that their song of praise (5:9-10) definitely sets them apart from those who were purchased by the blood of Christ (most certainly the church!). It thus seems best to take the elders as a jubilant group of heavenly spirit-beings belonging to the general class of angels (v. 4). They are performing some kind of mediating function, such as expediting the prayers of the saints to the throne of God.[13] In the Bible, "twelve" is often the number of divine government. Multiples of twelve—such as twenty-four—probably have the same significance.[14]

From this viewpoint, the "angels," the "twenty-four elders," and "the four living creatures" all designate actual supernatural beings involved with the purpose of God on earth and His worship in heaven. They are always distinguished from the "saints" (5:8; 11:17-18; 19:1-4).[15]

The white garments of the elders (v. 4) symbolize purity and victory. The golden crowns refer to the fact that the elders have royal dignity and are privileged to reign with God.[16]

Revelation 4:5 reminds us of Exodus 19:16. The flashes of lightning and the voices signify God's awe-inspiring majesty and power. The seven torches of fire are the seven spirits of God, or the Holy Spirit. The pavement of God's throne room was like a sea of glass. This suggests the waters above the firmament and thus could symbolize God's transcendence (4:6; compare Ex. 24:10; Ezek. 1:26; Gen. 1:7). The mirror-like reflecting quality of the sea of glass could also symbolize the fact that before the sight of God all is revealed.[17]

3. The Four Living Creatures and Their Praise (4:6b-11)

The vision of the four living creatures is splendid. It is also unsettling and strange with the sight of the four living creatures "full of eyes in front and behind" (v. 6).[18]

The background for this is primarily Ezekiel 1:4 and following and Isaiah 6:2 and following. These four creatures are significantly different from those in Ezekiel. In Ezekiel, they each have four faces, here only one. In Ezekiel, they have wheels full of eyes, but here the creatures have eyes "in front and behind" (v. 6b).[19] These creatures are angelic beings. They are the highest order of angelic beings because they apparently stand nearest the throne. Each of the creatures mentioned in 4:6-8 is the chief of its class. Together they embody the reflection of God's nature as the fullness of life and power. Their six wings (compare Isa. 6:2) give the impression of unlimited mobility in fulfilling God's commands.[20]

The four living creatures ceaselessly proclaim the holiness of God in hymnic fashion: "Holy, holy, holy" (4:8; Isa. 6:3). In Hebrew, the repetition of a word adds emphasis. The living creatures celebrate God's holiness and power as manifested in His past, present, and future activity.[21]

The second hymn praises God for His creation and is sung by the twenty-four elders (4:9-11). When the four living creatures sing their song of praise, giving glory and honor and thanks to God (v. 9), then the twenty-four elders prostrate themselves before God's throne. They cast down their crowns and join in praising Him who alone is worthy "to receive glory and honor and power" because He is creator and sustainer of the universe (vv. 10-11).[22]

Praise shifts the focus of our attention away from ourselves to God. Praise is the highest form of faith; for when we cannot see the answer and yet praise, we are telling God that we trust Him, love Him, and dare leave the final and ultimate answer to Him.

Excursus on the Biblical Doctrines of Creation and God's Sovereignty

The famous chorale or song of Revelation 4:8-11 teaches that the God of Jesus Christ is the God of creation. The song teaches that everything that exists in heaven and earth exists because of the decision and creation of God (v. 11).

The biblical view of creation

The Hebrews have always believed in creation, and they have rejoiced in its implications. This is why Jewish piety is not congenial with an exclusively inward spiritualism of the heart or with theological flights of intellectual escapism.

Old Testament ethics are practical, definite, and earthy. This emphasis is rooted in the fundamental teaching of the biblical world view that God made the earth by His good decision. Therefore, biblical piety has a practical earthy implication. The Law tells about harvests and work schedules. This is true because the God of creation cares about the earth He made.[23]

The Greek and gnostic view of creation

The biblical world view and the Greek world view that has been permanently influenced by the perspective of Plato have a basically different way of looking at the earth. The difference becomes a very sharp and open cleavage by the time of the first and second centuries. This difference forced the Christian churches to decide whether Jesus Christ was a real man who really suffered and died or a phantom man—a spirit man who only appeared to be physically human and who only appeared to suffer the humiliation of death.[24]

The Greek world of thought prefers its highest deities to live above creation. They are above the concrete, earthy reality of the daily twenty-four-hour cycle within which we humans live out our physical existence. The Platonic Greek concern for the spiritual sought to transform the Jesus Christ of Christianity into a spiritualized Christ of pure idea. The movement that grew up in the later first century around this spiritualization effort is known as incipient Gnosticism.[25]

As a result of the recent discovery of the Gnostic library at Nag Hammadi, Egypt, we now know that the "gnostics" went on to develop a complete system of cosmology. This system contradicted the biblical world view of the Old and New Testaments. For the "gnostics," redemption happens when the "believer" discovers the true secret and knowledge *(gnosis)*. This knowledge will make possible an escape from this meaningless physical prison to the higher spirit world levels of enlightenment. It regrets the earth. Therefore, relationship to the earth has very little real meaning. But this Gnostic view is not the vision that confronts John in Revelation 4:8-11. The "gnostics" who read his vision would be profoundly disappointed. Their whole system is under direct assault.[26]

The Christian view of creation and its implications

This amazing song has profound meaning for those of us living in the twentieth century. We are confronted in Revelation 4 with a fresh vision of our origins. This means that we can never take creation lightly nor despise it because of its brokenness. Here we have the biblical doctrine of creation restated in the last book of the Bible, just as it was stated at the beginning in the first book of the Bible. The last words of the song (v. 11) state that God created all things and because of His will all things continually exist and come into being.[27]

As a result of this song, we know that redemption, when it happens to us by the grace of God, will not remove us from the twenty-four-hour cycle within which we live. Rather, this redemption will forgive, enable, and offer compassion to us in the midst of the days and months and years that exist by the will of God.[28]

Before John shows to these people that they are going to suffer at the hands of the demonic forces of Rome or of any Antichrist figure, He wants to assure them of the glory and sovereignty of God. Believers are encouraged in a moment of discouragement to know that God is on the throne.

Christians are being persecuted in our world today, and they also need the comfort and encouragement of this vision as do we. We need to remember that God is on the throne and that any government (including our own) that seeks to stamp out authentic Christianity will ultimately go down to defeat. As we see forces at work which are corrupting our own nations, we need to pray for America that it may be cleansed from evil.

When discouragement, illness, personal problems, and unanswered whys confront us, we need to know that the God of the universe is in control and that He is interested in every detail of our lives. We need to learn to trust Him, believing that He cares and that He can help us. We need to learn to worship and praise Him, even as the hosts of heaven do. It is not surprising that the hymn "Holy, Holy, Holy," based on Revelation 4:8-11, continues to be important in Christian worship.

B. The Seven Seals (5:1 to 8:1)

Chapter 5 constitutes the fulcrum or pivot of the Book of Revelation. It is also one of the most dramatic parts of this book. It tells us that the God of creation is also the God of redemption. God is accomplishing His redemptive love plan through the Lamb of God who is also the Lion of God.

1. *The Vision of the Lamb Who Alone Can Open the Sealed Book (5:1-14)*

a. THE SEALED SCROLL IN GOD'S RIGHT HAND (5:1-5)—THE MYSTERY OF THE MEANING OF HISTORY

(1) The puzzle of the meaning of life and history (5:1-3)

The sealed book in verse 1 indicates in a very dramatic way that the mystery of the meaning of history is absolutely unknown to anyone from a human or secular perspective. This book is like a last will. Seven seals mean that the book is completely sealed. This is not the Lamb's book of life. It is not only about judgment or the inheritance of the kingdom. Rather, this scroll is a prophecy of end events which tells about salvation for God's people and the judgment of the wicked. The contents of this scroll are found in chapters 7—22.[29]

A strong angel (v. 2) shouts out a challenge for anyone to come forth who is "worthy" to open the great scroll and its seals. In verse 3 all creation in heaven and on earth and under the earth stands motionless and speechless. No one is worthy to open the scroll (v. 4). No one in the whole of creation from heaven to hell is able to open the seals. The one who must open them cannot be found within creation.[30]

Here is a simple but profound biblical truth which cannot be over-emphasized: Apart from the person and redeeming work of Christ, history is an enigma or puzzle. Since the Enlightenment in Europe, many philosophers have rejected the Christian view of life and history. But, in so doing, history has become a problem for them. The view of man's inevitable progress has not proven to be true. Indeed, some advocates of inevitable progress have become prophets of doom who see nothing but darkness ahead. The problem of the meaning, purpose, and goal of history has become one of the most disturbing and difficult questions of our time.[31]

In the face of this modern dilemma, the fact that the scroll is so tightly sealed that no human eye can read its contents is highly significant. It is, therefore, not surprising that many modern secular thinkers are pessimistic.[32]

(2) The trauma over the loss of meaning (5:4)

In verse 4 John tells us that he weeps loudly because no one is found to take authoritative hold of the scroll to open its seals as their rightful owner. The dramatic tension in this vision of chapter 5 is both emotionally and physically expressed by John.[33]

John weeps because he senses the profound significance of the scroll and of the great question which it raises. This is a question that has haunted humanity from the opening of the story of life. It is the philosopher's question, and it is the child's question: What is the meaning of my life, my name, my past, my present, my future? What is the meaning of the world? That form of the question asks about the great nouns.[34]

The question raised by John has also been asked even more urgently about the verbs: "Why do I want to live? Where am I going?" When John hears that the scroll that contains these ancient and new questions cannot be opened and known, he breaks down and cries in the same way that men and women before and since John have cried in the face of the question of meaning. If the scroll contains both the revelation and the implementation of the final drama of history, then John's despair can be appreciated.[35]

(3) The significance of the Lion (5:5)

In verse 5 John is comforted by an elder who speaks to Him. "Weep not; lo, the Lion of the tribe of Judah . . . can open." He can open because He has conquered. Two titles are used of the One who is worthy—"the Lion of the tribe of Judah" and "the Root of David." Both are familiar Old Testament messianic titles (Gen. 49:9-10; compare Isa. 11:1,10; Jer. 23:5; 33:5; Rev. 22:16), but they are linked together only here and in the Qumran literature. The lion is the most often named animal in the Bible, yet only in this place in the Old and New Testament documents is the lion given unmistakable messianic meaning.[36]

In verse 5 is a vivid summary of the Old Testament promise of a divinely endowed messianic King who will be so mightily equipped that He will destroy all evil. He will deliver God's people from their affliction by evil powers, both spiritual and political. He will establish a new order on earth in which peace, righteousness, and blessedness will reign. This biblical hope includes individualistic salvation. It also refers to the salvation of the people of God as a society dwelling on the earth and their deliverance from all evils— spiritual, social, political, and physical. John is assured that this mighty Messiah has already won a great victory.[37]

b. THE VISION OF THE LAMB (5:6-14)

(1) The significance of the Lion becoming a Lamb (5:6a)

As John looks to see the mighty Lion (the conquering Warrior-Messiah from the root of David) he sees instead the striking figure of a Lamb (v. 6). This new image portrays sacrificial death and links the Messiah to the Old Testament Passover lamb (Ex. 12:5 *f.*; Isa. 53:7; John 1:29, 36; Acts 8:32; 1 Pet. 1:19).[38]

Here John joins the Old Testament royal Davidic Messiah and the Suffering Servant of Isaiah (Isa. 52-53). Both prophetic themes come together in Jesus of Nazareth, the true Messiah. The "lamb" metaphor dominates John's thought in the rest of the book (for example, 6:1 *ff.*; 7:9 *ff.*; 12:11; 13:8; 21:9).[39]

John sees a *little lamb*, but the remarkable language of the text tells that this Lamb is alive though He was dead! He bears the marks of death, but He has triumphed over death. John sees that this Lion is also a Lamb who is still bearing the marks of slaughter. The Lion who will set up the kingdom in His second coming will be able to do this because He is the Lamb who was slaughtered.[40]

(2) The place of the Holy Spirit (5:6b)

This Lamb is able to see all seven of His churches and the whole world through the Holy Spirit who proceeds from Him. In fact, the eyes are identified as the "seven spirits of God sent out into all the earth." This is probably a symbolic reference to the divine Holy Spirit who is sent forth by Christ into the world (1:4; 4:5). The teaching of John's Gospel is similar: The Spirit is sent forth to exalt Christ and to convict the world of sin (John 14:26; 15:26; 16:7-15).[41]

(3) The Lamb and the scroll (5:7)

The Lamb acts. "He went and took the scroll" (v. 7). The Greek conveys a dramatic action in the tense of the verb "took": "He went up and took it, and now he has it!" This means that the One on the throne authorizes the slain messianic King to execute His plan for the redemption of the world. In and through the Lamb, God is at work in history for the salvation of humanity. Christ's victorious death on the cross is the basis of His authority to redeem the world and to take and open the seven-sealed scroll.[42]

In 5:1-7 John ties in the working of God in history in the crucified Lamb of God with the working of God at the end of history in the Lion of Judah. Only one who is both the Lamb of Calvary and the Lion of the tribe of Judah can open the book and bring God's redemptive purposes for humanity to their divine end.

Here John links together, as no Jewish interbiblical writer did, present history and the future. The windup and fulfillment of history are in the hands of Him who appeared in history as the Lamb of God who takes away the sin of the world.

The Lamb took the focus of human sin and tragedy and bore it in His own body. By a redemptive act in history, the powers of the future glorious age have entered into history in advance of their final demonstration and are at work now to save and give victory.

The present age is evil. But the one who will one day destroy evil—the Lion—has already come in advance as the Lamb to bring the spiritual blessings of the future kingdom.

The Lion became the Lamb and so now we can know forgiveness of sins and the powers of the age to come in this present evil age. We can know partial answers, claim significant victories, and experience preliminary healings, but the ultimate victory is yet to come.

(4) The response of praise (5:8-14)

The Lamb's act in taking the scroll calls forth three hymns of praise from the living creatures and elders. John sees them fall down in worship before the Lamb, as they had earlier done before the One on the throne (4:10). They have "harps," which are the "lyres" used for the older psalmody (compare, for example Pss. 33:2; 98:5) but will now be used for the "new song" of praise to the Lamb (v. 9).[43]

The "bowls full of incense" represent the "prayers of the saints" (8:3-4). And since verse 10 refers to the coming kingdom, it may be that the prayers are petitions to God to judge the world and to extend His kingdom throughout the earth (Luke 18:7-8).[44]

In verses 9-10 the first chorale is sung for John. They sing a "new song" stating that the Lamb has died to redeem not only the Jews but all people. The death of Jesus broke the stranglehold of the "powers and authorities"(NIV) over the creation and produced a great victory liberating humanity (Col. 2:15). This victory, obtained through suffering and death, entitles Christ to execute the unfolding of the mystery of God's consummation of history. The centrality of the cross and its meaning as a redemptive act come repeatedly to the fore and dominate throughout our understanding of Revelation.[45]

The Lamb's right to open the scroll rests also on the fact that He has made the ransomed into a "kingdom" and made them "priests" (v. 10; compare Heb. 13:15-16). Christians "will reign on the earth" with Christ because they have been given "kingly authority" (author's translation) through His death (1:6; 20:4-6). While not excluding the present reign of believers, the reference to "the earth" is best taken to refer to the future millennial kingdom reign of Christ.[46]

In verses 11-12 the second chorale is sung for John as all of heaven rejoices. Thousands of thousands, myriads of myriads sing this chorus of praise. The numerical description in the Greek text is constructed in a way to discourage any precise numbering of the great company. The meaning of the word usage is of a number beyond counting. John has his eyes on the Lamb, not on the crowd. These thousands have a sevenfold shout: power, wealth, wisdom, might, honor, glory, and blessing. All these are qualities of Christ except the last, which is the expression of the creatures' worship.[47]

In verses 13-14 the final chorus is an exalted affirmation of the worth and authority of both God and Jesus Christ the Lamb. The song ends with the whole of creation joining in praise. John beautifully blends the worship of the Father (ch. 4) and the worship of the Son (5:8-12) together. In appropriate response, the four living creatures utter their "Amen," and the elders fall down in worship.[48]

Excursus on the Meaning of the Messiah

The Jewish view of the Messiah

I once read a paper at Hebrew Union College in Cincinnati, Ohio. This is the leading Reformed Jewish seminary in the United States. The subject of the paper was "The Christian Understanding of the Messiah." I quoted Revelation 5. In the same meeting several of the Jewish leaders spoke on the Jewish meaning of the Messiah.

The Jews have considerable difficulty with the messianic concept. The Old Testament does not put together in an organized and systematic way all of its teachings about the Messiah. As is indicated in 5:5, in one place the Old Testament says that the Messiah will come in power. He will come as the Son of man and as the Lion of the tribe of Judah. Some Jewish scholars believe that the Messiah, when He comes, will elevate the Jewish people to rule the world. One of the reasons Jesus Christ was not accepted as the Messiah by the Jewish leadership of His time was that He did not fit into this pattern.[49]

John 6:14-15 states that after Jesus fed the 5,000 many Jewish followers tried to make Him into a political messiah or king. With this demonstration of power, Jesus was exhibiting some of the qualities which the Jewish people thought the Messiah should have. But Jesus turned away from them and retreated to a mountain alone, even as he rejected Satan's invitation at the mount of temptation to use His power in an outward demonstration.

John is saying that this One who is the Lion of the tribe of Judah is able to be the true Messiah and is able to be the clue to the meaning of history because He has suffered as the Lamb.

There is another strand in the Old Testament, Isaiah 53, which the Jews were unable to identify clearly as the Messiah figure. We remember this passage as we sing the words of Handel's *Messiah*. It tells us that the Messiah will be One who is to be wounded for our transgressions and bruised for our iniquities and who will heal us by His stripes.

The Christian view of the Messiah

In Revelation 5, John fuses the Davidic king and the Suffering Servant concepts of the Messiah, as was not done in the Old Testament or in the interbiblical period.

In these two great visions in Revelation 4 and 5, John is saying that the power that will one day be demonstrated openly and outwardly in Christ's second coming is now being demonstrated through the cross, through the cross way of life and through the indwelling Spirit. This is what we call the way of suffering love. This way of suffering love is the primary way in which God's power and purpose are now being demonstrated to the world. Sometimes we get quite discouraged as we seek to demonstrate and incarnate suffering love. But before we become discouraged, we should remember that this is the clue to the meaning of history—the way of the cross.[50]

The theological meaning of the Christian view of the Messiah

The theological importance of John's dramatic vision for us today cannot be overemphasized. The conviction of every New Testament writer was that the whole of human history finds its meaning and its convergence point in the slain and resurrected Jesus Christ. He is the critical center from which all of the parts make sense and toward which all of the parts converge.[51]

At the school where I teach, an annual custom is for the music school to present the Christmas portion of the *Messiah*. Many feel that there is no single musical work as compelling and grand as G. F. Handel's "Worthy Is the Lamb" at the end of his *Messiah*. Handel caught the surprise and joy of the vision of John in Revelation 5. He even caught the exciting incongruity of the mighty Lion who is the little Lamb. He portrayed the Lamb, despised and rejected, broken at Calvary, now alive and rightly honored. God is so sure of Himself that He came in humility. He came alongside our lives to find us. Augustine said, "Proud man would have died had not a lowly God found him."[52]

In the light of this vision in Revelation 4 and 5, history is not as ominous and frightful as it seemed before. And whatever may come, we have met the Lion who became the Lamb to give life and history meaning and hope. We must not forget this chorale in the journey ahead as the seven seals are opened.[53]

2. *The Six Seals (6:1-17)*

a. THE FIVE SEALS AND ONGOING HISTORY (6:1-11)

We now come to the seals. One of the most controversial areas of Revelation is the question of how to interpret the seals, the trumpets, and the bowls. I have already given a brief statement in the Introduction of the approach to be followed in this study. A more detailed outline is appropriate before we examine the text itself.

The content of the seventh seal (8:1) is constituted by the actions caused by the blowing of the seven trumpets (8:6 to 9:21; 11:14-19). This leads to the suggestion that the breaking of the seven seals and the following events do not make up the contents of the scroll (5:5). Rather, this seal breaking and related events are preliminary and preparatory to the final opening of the scroll. John emphasizes that the scroll was completely sealed within and on the back with seven seals (v. 1). This means that the scroll itself is not opened and its contents disclosed until all seven seals have been broken.

Although we are dealing with a vision, we must assume that its details are patterned after reality. If the scroll is sealed in a normal fashion, it cannot, of course, be opened until *all* of the seals are broken. Therefore, the seven seals cannot represent the content of the scroll. Rather, the seals represent preliminary events, the things that must take place *before* the scroll is opened.[54]

Thus, the five seals are essentially *preliminary signs*. They constitute characteristic events that must take place before the final stages of the kingdom. There is Christ's victory in His first coming. But ongoing history will see war, famine, pestilence, and a dynamic gospel mission as we move toward the end.

To a church facing the prospect of suffering, these images convey a strong word of consolation. Christians can take heart, knowing that the gospel will be preached and that when fearful things happen to them God is not taken by surprise. On the contrary, these victories and hardships are intrinsic parts of God's redemptive plan. They are necessary precursors of His final victory.[55]

At most, the seals are *signs* of the end, not the end itself. As each seal is broken, something happens. After the first seal, conquest rides forth over the earth; after the second, war; then famine, death, and martyrdom. This structure is parallel to Matthew 24:1-35 and Mark 13:1-37.[56] In these passages, the events of the last days fall into three periods: (1) the period of false Christs, wars, famines, pestilences, earthquakes, and death, called "the beginning of birth pains" (Matt. 24:8, NIV); (2) the period of the Great Tribulation (Matt. 24:21); and (3) the period "immediately after the distress of those days," when the sun, moon, and stars will be affected and Christ will return (Matt. 24:29-30, NIV). This parallel to major parts of Revelation is too striking to be ignored. Thus the seals would correspond to the "beginning of birth pains" in the Olivet discourse. The events are similar to those occurring under the trumpets (8:2 to 11:19) and bowls (15:1 to 16:21), but they should not be confused with those later and more severe judgments. Moreover, in the eschatological reckoning of time, the events immediately preceding the end can stretch out over the whole age of the church, from John's time until now. They can still be viewed as "next" (see 4:1) in the sense that the "last days" began in the first century and are still continuing (compare 1 John 2:18).[57]

In this interpretation, the seals would correspond to the "beginning of woes" and not the end itself (Matt. 24:8). Furthermore, the conquering white horse parallels Matthew 24:14. It pictures the victories to be won by the preaching of the gospel in the world.[58]

The breaking of the five seals reveals the agencies God uses before the end to lead up to the fulfillment of salvation and judgment. These agencies are the preaching of the gospel and the evils of war, death, famine, and martyrdom. These seals are anticipations of the completed salvation and judgment that are contained within the sealed book. The seals represent the forces in history, however long it lasts, by which God works out His redemptive and judicial purposes in history leading up to the end. The events beginning with chapter 7 lie in the future and are related to the final outworking of the divine will for human history. As Jesus told His disciples on the Mount of Olives, "Do not be alarmed; this must take place, but the end is not yet"(Mark 13:7).[59]

Here a caution must be sounded. These signs do not form a chronological sequence of datable happenings. The signs cannot be ticked off in a way which enables the curious to predict the future. The first five at least have always been with us. They characterize John's age and our own. The point of the opening of the seals is simply to demonstrate Christ's sovereignty over them. The prophetic viewpoint allows us to see them in the widest possible scope, to get the "big picture." From this perspective they are the work of Christ. They belong to Christ's timetable, not ours.[60]

b. The sixth seal and the threshold of the end of history (6:12-17)

The sixth seal is different. It corresponds with nothing that we have experienced, only with what we can imagine. We have no categories for the stars falling or the sky rolling up like a scroll. This is not part of our past or present. It must belong to the future. Here the focus moves beyond the events of this age to those catastrophic signs that immediately precede the second advent, or *parousia*, of Jesus Christ as He comes to rule the world (compare Mark 13:26-27).[61]

The breaking of the sixth seal (v. 12) clearly brings us to the threshold of the end. The five seals must precede it. As soon as the seventh seal is opened (8:1), the book or scroll can at last be opened and its contents disclosed. Then the end can be described in terms of the seven trumpets and the seven bowls.

c. FIRST FOUR SEALS: THE FOUR HORSEMEN (6:1-8)

(1) Background of the seals (6:1)

You will remember that in chapter 1 John had his first vision. Then Jesus through John gave the message to the churches in chapters 2 and 3. Next John gave us the vision of God in chapter 4. In chapter 5 John gave us the vision of the Lion who has already come to earth as the Lamb. Now John in chapter 6 is going to unfold the dynamics of history in terms of the horses.

As the Lamb breaks each of the first four seals, four horses ride forth on the earth as instruments of the divine purpose: the first is white, the second red, the third black, and the fourth pale. The background for this symbolism is found in Zechariah 1:8 and following verses and 6:1-8. The Old Testament prophet is given a vision of four chariots drawn by horses of different colors: red, black, white, and dappled gray. In Zechariah's portrayal, these four chariots ride out to the four winds to patrol the earth as instruments of God's wrath upon the enemies of His people. According to Zechariah and now John, history is going to get intense. There is going to be a lot of trouble in history.[62]

John's treatment of the white horse is peculiar to this new revelation. Again caution must be exercised, and we must reject the temptation to read Old Testament meaning into this new revelation. God did something *new* in Christ, and we must look for what He is saying in this new revelation.

(2) The first seal (6:1-2)—conquest (white horse)

(a) The emphatic call (6:1)

The emphatic call "Come!" (vv. 1,3,5,7) should not be viewed as addressed either to John or to Christ but rather to each of the horsemen. An analogy may be a first-century amphitheater or circus with various charioteers being summoned forth into the arena by the call "Come!" or "Go forth!" The word "come" refers primarily to the fact that the four living creatures are now ready to call out the four horses.[63]

(b) The white horse (6:2)—evil conquest or dynamic gospel witness?

Revelation 6:2 is one of the most controversial verses in Revelation. What is the white horse? Most interpreters insist that the first horseman must be understood consistently with the other three. Since the other three are evil powers of destruction and death by which God executes His judgment, the white horse must be similar in kind. Usually, this white horse is said to be conquest, in general, while the red horse is war, in particular. The crown worn by the rider is thought to be a symbol of conquest.[64]

One of the main difficulties with this interpretation is that it does not do justice to the white garb of the rider and the white horse on which he rides. In the identification of the other three horsemen, the color is of great significance. The color white may be taken, therefore, as a major clue to the identity of the first horseman. In Revelation, white is always a symbol of Christ or of something associated with Christ or of spiritual victory (for example, 1:14; 2:17; 3:4-5,18; 4:4; 7:9,13-14; 20:11). Furthermore, no woe is mentioned as is the case with the other horsemen.[65]

(c) Clues about the white horse from the teachings of Christ

A further clue to the meaning of the seals may be found by looking at similar types of teaching in other parts of the Bible. We should be especially careful of overusing the concept of the "analogy of Scripture" in the exegesis of Revelation. The analogy of Scripture means that Scripture is to be interpreted in the light of other Scripture. We hold this to be self-evident, based on our stance that all of Scripture is God's Word and has God as its ultimate source. However, to interpret Scripture by Scripture must not be tilted in such a way that one *must* make other Scriptures the hermeneutical keys to unlock Revelation.[66]

But many commentators have pointed out that there is a similarity between the structure of the seven seals and the discourse on the Mount of Olives by Jesus as recorded in Mark 13 and Matthew 24. The parallel of these chapters to major parts of Revelation is too striking to be ignored. In these passages there is a time of preliminary troubles marked by evils in human society and in nature (Matt. 24:8—similar to the seven seals). This is followed by a short but terrible time of Great Tribulation (Matt. 24:21—similar to the seven trumpets and bowls, and the beast).[67]

There is, however, in the preliminary evil period, one positive note reported by both Mark and Matthew. According to Mark 13:10, before the end, "the gospel must first be preached to all nations." And according to Matthew 24:14, "And this gospel of the kingdom will be preached throughout the whole world, as a testimony to all nations; and then the end will come."[68]

That the preaching of the gospel is associated with plagues is here no more incongruous or out of place than it is in Matthew 24:1-14. It is no effective objection to say that the gospel in this present order will never be triumphant. This is true, but the gospel does win victories.[69]

Thus the rider in Revelation 6:2 is not necessarily Christ, but symbolizes the dynamic proclamation of the gospel to the end of history.[70]

Hal Lindsey, in contrast, says that the white horse represents a European Antichrist who is going to head up the Common Market in Europe from the city of Rome. At first the Antichrist will be looked upon as a savior but he will then turn and persecute the Christians.[71]

Excursus on the Place of Christian Witness
and Missions in the Christian View of History

Revelation 6:1-2 and other important biblical passages indicate that the course of the age is not to be one of unrelieved evil in which God's people are surrendered helplessly and passively into the hands of hostile powers. It is true that the kingdom of God will not be completely established until the return of the Son of man in glory. This age, however, will be characterized by two emphases—one is evil which will continually afflict the followers of Jesus. The other is an active and aggressive proclamation of the gospel of the kingdom by those same disciples until the end.[72]

This view may be supported by the later vision in Revelation of the angel who appears with the eternal gospel and issues a final call to repentance to the pagan nations (14:6-7). Once more we are reminded that the preaching of the gospel, as well as the processes of historical judgment upon sin, are necessary preconditions of the end.[73]

The teaching of Paul

The apostle Paul had a similar emphasis. There is no conflict between missions and evil end time signs in Paul's writing and life. Interest in end times and missionary strategy go hand in hand. In carrying out his missionary plans, Paul spent one and a half years at Corinth, three years at Ephesus, and contemplated a mission to Spain (Rom. 15:24). And so, for Paul, last things and missionary strategy did not contradict each other, as if the one paralyzes the strength of the other. Paul could project and implement a universal mission and yet think in terms of the signs related to the second coming of Christ.[74]

Hope was for Paul accompanied by both impatient fervor and patient missionary strategies. The apocalyptic vision of the future coming of Jesus is related to this worldly and cruciform activity. For Paul there was no detailed secret knowledge about the future, ethical passivity, disdain for God's world, and an elitism of the in-group. Rather, there was missionary ethical fervor and a belief in the outworking of revealed end time principles in history.[75]

This truth of dynamic missionary fervor amid the evil developments of history is well portrayed by John in the vision of the white horse (6:1-2). The rider is not Christ Himself. Rather the rider symbolizes the proclamation of the gospel of Christ in all the world.

The teaching of biblical symbols

The bow and the crown given to the rider of the white horse are significant (6:2). Both the sword (Heb. 4:12; Rev. 2:12) and the bow (Isa. 49:2-3) are symbols of God's working among people. A bow is often used in Scripture as a symbol of divine victories. The crown is a symbol whose meaning is expressed in the words "he went out conquering and to conquer." This does not necessarily mean complete and utter conquest. It does mean that the proclamation of the gospel will win its victories. It will be preached effectively in all the world. In spite of an evil and hostile environment characterized by human hatred, strife, and opposition, the gospel will make its way victoriously in all the world.[76]

The importance of a dynamic gospel mission

Here is a word of confidence, combined with a realistic note, for the church of the first century and for every other age. How can any people be devoted to a cause which they believe will experience only defeat? The first generation of believers suffered. At the hands of some of the later emperors, such as Domitian, they met determined efforts to root them out and to destroy them completely. But in spite of every form of opposition, the church effectively and victoriously established the gospel in all the Roman world until the empire ceased its violent opposition. We do not look for the complete coming of God's kingdom and the righting of the world's evils short of the return of Christ. But we are, as the modern bearers of the gospel of the kingdom, expectant of seeing victories won by the power of this gospel.[77]

Paul wrote in 2 Thessalonians 2:7 that something is holding back the coming of the final Antichrist whose appearance will be the prelude to the end. What is this restraining power? Some say the Holy Spirit and others say the Roman government. But others say that the thing that is holding back the final Antichrist is that there has not yet been this dynamic gospel proclamation that Jesus wants preached to the end of the world.[78]

Thus many devout scholars, such as Oscar Cullmann, J. Munck, and others, suggest that the white horse of Revelation 6:1-2 refers to a dynamic gospel mission that will characterize the last days of history. Along with the war, famine, and death, there will be to the very end a dynamic gospel mission. And we have seen such a promise happen. In the twentieth century, it appeared that Christianity in certain countries, such as the Soviet Union, China, and other places, would be completely suppressed and even eliminated. But even in these dangerous and difficult areas of the world, there continues to be an underground church and a resurgence of Christian witness. There continues to be a dynamic gospel work.[79]

(3) The second seal (6:3-4)—strife (red horse)

The second horseman is war and bloodshed. He rides on a steed whose "fiery red" (NIV) color symbolizes slaughter (2 Kings 3:22-23). He is given a "large sword" because the number of those he kills is so great (compare 13:10,14).[80]

Hal Lindsey contends that the red horse refers to Russia who is the rider of the red horse. He relates this to Ezekiel 38 and Daniel 11. Russia will snatch away peace from the earth by making an alliance with the Arabs to invade Israel. This war will escalate until it leads to the battle of Armageddon which is described in Revelation 16. The red horse does represent war, but it cannot be pinpointed in the way proposed by Lindsey.[81]

(4) The third seal (6:5-6)—famine (black horse)

The third horse is black. The rider holds a balance. The third horse is the specter of famine. The saying, "a quart of wheat for a denarius [a day's work]," implies overwhelming poverty and hardship—the runaway inflation of an economy in ruins.[82]

Famine was a normal result of warfare in ancient times when invading armies lived off the lands they were conquering. The warning against hurting the oil and wine sets limits to the destruction about to be carried out by the horseman. Since the roots of the olive and vine go deeper, they would not be affected by a limited drought which would all but destroy the grain. This interpretation is in harmony with the increasing intensity of the three cycles of judgment. The fourth seal affects "the fourth part of the earth" (v. 8, KJV), the trumpets destroy a third (8:7-8,10,12), and the destruction by the bowls is complete and final (16:1 *ff.*).[83]

Hal Lindsey again makes a great deal of this verse. He contends that it refers to our time because there is now a worldwide famine of food and fuel. The rich are selling out to the Antichrist in order to get precious commodities.[84]

(5) The fourth seal (6:7-8)—death (pale horse)

The fourth seal reveals a rider on a "pale horse." "Pale" denotes a yellowish green, the light green of a plant, or the paleness of a sick person in contrast to a healthy appearance. This color fits in well with the name of the rider—"Death." This probably refers to the death resulting from pestilence, or plague, which often follows famine.[85]

Hades was following close behind Death—whether it was on foot, on the back of the same horse, or on a separate horse, the Bible does not say. Hades in the New Testament usually refers to the place of the departed wicked (Luke 16:23; Rev. 20:13-14). Death by wild beasts (the "evil beasts" of Ezek. 5:17; 34:25) would be expected in a land decimated by war and famine.[86]

Hal Lindsey states that this verse means that one fourth of the population of our era is going to be killed by the atomic bomb.[87]

d. FIFTH SEAL (6:9-11)—SUFFERING OF GOD'S WITNESSES

The fifth seal refers to the martyrs who have been killed as the Antichrist figures are persecuting the Christians in the last days. These martyrs were under the altar because they had been killed.

The question sometimes arises why the martyrs alone receive so much attention, rather than all suffering or persecuted Christians. John may be referring to all those who so faithfully follow Christ that they may be characterized as the slain of the Lord. They may or may not actually suffer physical death for Christ. However, they have (like John) so identified themselves with the slain Lamb that they have, in effect, already offered up their lives ("because of the word of God and the testimony they had maintained," NIV; compare 1:2,9; Rom. 8:36).[88]

John says that he saw the "souls" of those slain (v. 9). This is oftentimes understood to mean the disembodied souls of these saints. However, the Greek word *psyche* has various meanings and probably stands here for the actual "lives" or "persons" who were killed rather than for their "souls." They are seen by John as persons who are very much alive though they have been killed by the beast.[89]

"Under the altar" in verse 9 places the scene in the temple of heaven. In 8:3,5 and 9:13, "the altar" is the golden altar of incense that stood in the tabernacle in front of the Most Holy Place (Ex. 30:1 *ff*.; Heb. 9:4). If this is the altar John sees the prayers of the saints will be for God's vindication of the martyrs of Christ (compare Luke 18:7-8).[90]

Revelation 6:10 is often seen as being too bloodthirsty. But when you pray for deliverance from the enemy, it follows that you usually pray for judgment on the enemy. It is difficult for Americans who have never suffered as the Christians did in the early centuries, nor as many do in some parts of the world today, to truly empathize with the martyred saints.

It should also be noted that these Christians are following the teaching of Paul in Romans 12:19 (NIV): "Do not take revenge, my friends, but leave room for God's wrath, for it is written: 'It is mine to avenge, I will repay,' says the Lord." Though believers are forbidden to take revenge, God will vindicate His elect by punishing those who kill them (Luke 18:7 f.; 2 Thess. 1:8).[91]

In verse 11 we note that the martyrs are each given a "white robe" as an evidence of their victory and righteousness before the Judge of all the earth, who will speedily avenge their deaths. They are to wait a "little longer." In God's estimate, this may be but a fleeting moment. However, for us, it may stretch out for ages (compare 12:12; 20:3).[92]

Fortunately we do not live in a country where, at this time, Christians suffer serious persecution. But we should not overlook what constitutes the essence of Christian discipleship in John's eyes. As Lilje, a former Nazi prisoner, says, "Every believer in Christ ought to be prepared for martyrdom; for Christians . . . cannot express their priestly communion with their Lord more perfectly than when they accept the suffering and the glory of martyrdom."[93]

e. The sixth seal (6:12-17)—the threshold of the end

After the fifth seal, Christ opens the sixth seal. Then John witnesses the dreadful signs heralding the imminent, final Day of the Lord so often described in the New Testament.

In verses 15-17 John describes three types of signs: (1) the great earthquake and its storm affecting the sun and moon, (2) the stars falling, and (3) the terror on earth.[94] As usual, John uses Old Testament references for background: "earthquakes" (compare Ezek. 38:19 f.; Isa. 2:19; Hag. 2:6); "sun" blackened and "moon" like blood (compare Joel 2:31; Ezek. 32:7); "stars" falling like fig leaves in a winter gale (compare Isa. 34:4; Nah. 3:12); the "sky vanished like a scroll" (compare Isa. 34:4); "mountains" and "islands" moved (compare Ps.114:4; Jer. 4:24).[95]

It is difficult to know how literally the whole description should be taken. Some of the events are described from the standpoint of ancient cosmology.[96]

The scene, whether taken literally or figuratively, is one of catastrophe and distress for the inhabitants of the earth. John uses the language of cosmic turmoil to describe the condition of the world when God comes to judge the earth.[97]

The sixth seal has to do with physical convulsions. Whenever God becomes angry, whenever God's holiness is demonstrated, God's power over nature is portrayed. The Old Testament constantly pictures the divine visitations of God to His people in terms of a theophany, that is, in terms of majesty and power and glory so great that the physical world is shaken.

The most notable illustration of this in the Old Testament is the visitation of God at Mount Sinai. However, this is not all. The Old Testament pictures the physical world in some way as sharing man's fate, as having fallen under the burden of violence, decay, and death. Paul had a similar emphasis in Romans 8:21-22.[98]

The earth is, therefore, subject to the divine judgment and in need of the divine salvation. This language of cosmic catastrophe which will occur at the end of the age is the Bible's picturesque way of describing the divine judgment falling on the world. The language is semipoetic. That means that it is symbolic language which can hardly be taken with stark literalness.[99]

However, the language is not merely poetic or symbolic but describes a real cosmic catastrophe whose actual character we cannot conceive. Out of the ruins of judgment will emerge a new redeemed order which John describes as the new heaven and a new earth in chapter 21.[100]

Hal Lindsey puts a great deal of emphasis on this section because he lives in California where there are many earthquakes. He states that the reason we are having earthquakes is that we are beginning to experience the fulfillment of this part of Revelation in our time. This section also, according to Lindsey, refers to an all-out nuclear exchange. He states that John is describing in verses 12-17 an earthquake set off by a nuclear explosion. He admits, however, that John had to describe this phenomenon of our very advanced technical age in terms of his first-century understanding.[101]

Since all kinds of people are included in this final catastrophe described in verses 15-17, we cannot say that God's wrath is directed only at the powerful, at the rich, or at false Christians. His judgment will fall on all who refuse to repent and instead worship demons and idols and persecute Christ's followers (9:20-21; 16:6,9).[102]

(1) The wrath of the Lamb (6:16)

The wrath (anger) of the Lamb is not only a new metaphor but also a paradoxical one (7:16). Lambs are usually gentle. But we should note that this Lamb shows wrath against those who have refused His grace (compare John 5:27). The wrath of God and of the Lamb is a continuing theme in Revelation and is later described under the images of the trumpets and bowls (8:7 to 9:21; 16:2-21). Moreover, God's wrath is a present historical reality, as well as reality at the last judgment (compare Rom. 1:18 *ff.*; 2:5).[103] The wrath of God is neither personal vindictiveness nor an impersonal process of retribution which works itself out in the course of history. It is rather the response of God's holiness to persistent and impenitent wickedness.[104]

Some people do not like the teaching that Jesus who is the Lamb of God will exhibit wrath. Devout scholars, however, point out that if you read the Bible carefully, you will find that the Bible says that God is holy as well as love. It is true that Jesus is the Lamb of God, the One who loved us and who has given every evidence that He is the Messiah. Verse 16 also teaches that those who despise Him and turn from Him will one day call for the rocks to cover their faces from His holiness and His judgment.

(2) The great day of wrath (6:17)

The "great day of their wrath" in verse 17 was spoken of in Joel 2:11,31*b*; Nahum 1:6; and Malachi 3:2. That day will be so fierce, none of the ungodly will be able to endure it. The symbolism employed here is that, *symbolism*, but the event describe is anticipated as *real*. Judgment is sure and certain, and it will be catastrophic in its effect. God and the Lamb shall execute righteous judgment (compare v. 10).[105]

From the day when Adam and Eve hid themselves from the presence of God (Gen. 3:8), the guilty conscience has made man a fugitive from God. But now there is no longer a place to hide. God will confront in judgment all those who have rebelled against His sovereign authority. Better death by a crushing avalanche than face the wrath of the Lamb.[106]

Elsewhere in Revelation man is pictured as so adamant in pursuing his own goals that neither demonic plague (9:20) nor scorching heat are sufficient to make him repent. Nothing short of the awe-some dissolution of the world itself will strike terror to the heart of man in the last days.[107]

(3) The beginning of the end

The sixth seal brings us to the threshold of the opening of the book of destiny and the great events of the end. The breaking of the seventh seal (8:1) makes it possible for the book to be opened and its contents disclosed. The book or scroll contains the prophecies of the end of the world.[108]

We will see, however, that the end is not a single event but rather consists of a series of events. It includes the outpouring of God's wrath upon a rebellious civilization, the judgment of the Antichrist, and the destruction of his hosts. It also includes the resurrection of the dead, the establishment of the millennium, and the coming of the new heaven and the new earth. So we see that the sixth seal brings us to the beginning of the end. Then John stands back to tell the story again in greater detail. The breaking of the seventh seal opens the book and begins the story of the events of the end time. These end time events thus constitute the substance of the remain-der of Revelation.[109]

3. An Interlude (7:1-17)—Visions of Security and Salvation

When we come to the dreadful opening of the sixth seal, we wonder how anyone will be able to survive such upheaval. Then comes a surprise in the form of a dramatic pause or a halt at the very last moment. And this interlude comes none too soon.[110]

The change in tone from the subject matter in the sixth seal (6:12-17), as well as the delay until 8:1 in opening the seventh seal, indi-cates that chapter 7 is a true interlude. John first sees the angels who will unleash destruction on the earth restrained until the 144,000 servants of God from every tribe of Israel are sealed (vv. 1-8). Then he sees an innumerable multitude clothed in white standing before the throne of God. These are identified as those who have come out of the Great Tribulation (vv. 9-17).[111]

The principal difficulties in Revelation 7 center around the identi-fication of the 144,000 (vv. 1-8) and the identification of the innumer-able multitude (vv. 9-17). Is the reference to the tribes of Israel symbolic, representative, or literal? What is the Great Tribulation

(v. 14)? Are those described in verse 9 and following verses martyrs? There is considerable disagreement among interpreters on these questions.[112]

a. THE SEALING OF GOD'S SERVANTS (7:1-8)

Revelation 7 presents two visions. One is the sealing of the 144,000, and the other is the blessedness of the great multitude before the heavenly throne. The modified futurist method of interpretation affirms that in both visions the church is in view, but from two vantage points. Prior to the trumpet judgments, according to verses 1-8, the last generation of believers is sealed. This will ensure that they will be saved from the destruction coming upon the earth. Futhermore, it will assure them that they will be brought safely into the heavenly kingdom. The second vision (vv. 9-17) anticipates the eternal blessedness of all believers, when in the presence of God they realize the rewards of faithful endurance.[113]

Before John begins the story of the actual end, he interrupts the flow of his narrative. He inserts an interlude. In this interlude he paints a picture which is essential background to the flow of the narrative. In this interlude, as the church stands on the threshold of her time of great tribulation, she is reassured that God will safely see her through her terrible ordeal. Those whom God has sealed will be safely preserved from the outpouring of divine wrath, even though many will suffer martyrdom.[114]

God is about to visit the earth in wrath, afflicting an apostate and rebellious society with fearful plagues before the final judgment falls. In the midst of this apostate society are God's people. But the wrath of God does not fall on them. They are sealed and thus delivered from the wrath.[115]

"After this" marks a logical transition and not a chronological one. John sees "four angels standing at the four corners of the earth, holding back the four winds of the earth" (v. 1). The Jews believed that angels were in charge of the elements. Here the four angels hold back the four winds.[116]

I cannot emphasize too often that apocalyptic language does not convey its message in precise photographic style. For example, the four winds in verse 1 may be taken as representing the earthly catastrophes that occur under the trumpets and bowls (compare chs. 8 and 16). This shows how the language is more in the style of modern surrealistic art with great fluidity and imagination. The message of verses 1-3 is simply that the judgment of the first plagues is to be withheld until God's people are sealed.[117]

(1) The sealing of the Christians (7:4)

Verse 4 is a controversial verse. The historical premillennial perspective is that this is seen not to refer to physical Israel but rather to the Christian community. The background of this section is the great plagues of Egypt. God's people were to put the seal of blood on their doorposts so the death angel would then pass over them. God protected the Israelites when the death angel passed over them. He will do the same for the Christians. Verse 3 indicates that it is not merely the martyrs who are sealed but *all* the servants of God.

It is difficult to know exactly what sealing means. Such a seal surely indicates ownership by God and the Lamb (14:1). Furthermore, a seal may offer protection or security for its bearers. Such seems to be the emphasis in 9:4, where the demonic forces are told to harm "only those people who did not have the seal of God on their foreheads" (NIV).[118]

(2) The mark of the beast

The matter may be clarified by examining what happens to those who, by contrast, have the "mark" of the beast (13:16-17). Those who have the mark of the beast are not only identified as beast worshipers but also become the objects of the irreversible wrath of God (14:9,11). This implies, by contrast, that those who have "the seal of God" are God worshipers and will be the objects of His abiding grace.[119]

In 16:2 the bowl of God's wrath appears to be directed exclusively toward those who have the mark of the beast, thus excluding those with the seal of God (compare 16:6). Those having the mark of the beast are deluded by the beast (19:20), implying that the sealed of God are not thus deceived. Finally, the martyred group is seen just prior to their resurrection and 1,000-year reign with Christ and are described as not having the mark of the beast or worshiping him (20:4).[120]

In the light of these passages, we may say that the "sealed" are the people of God and that their sealing must be related to their salvation, as in the comparable figure used by Paul (2 Cor. 1:22; Eph. 1:13; 4:30). This is also evident in 14:3-4, where the sealed are described as those who were redeemed from the earth as firstfruits of God (compare Rom. 8:23; Jas. 1:18).[121]

Also note that while the seal may not protect the sealed against harm inflicted by human agency (13:7; 20:4), they are protected from the divine plagues (16:2).[122]

(3) The nature of sealing

Certainly this sealing is a spiritual fact and not a visible bodily phenomenon. An analogous idea is found in the spiritual sealing by the Holy Spirit of all Christians, who "were sealed with the promised Holy Spirit, which is the guarantee of our inheritance until we acquire possession of it" (Eph. 1:13-14).[123]

The sealing of believers is also an assurance of spiritual safety on the grounds of divine ownership. It is an inner spiritual fact which cannot be observed with the outward eye. So will God's people in the Great Tribulation be sealed and protected from His wrath and the demonic forces.[124]

Verses 1-3 would also assure the people of God of His special concern and plan for them. Even when facing persecution and martyrdom at the hand of the beast, they can be certain that no plague from God will touch them. Rather, they will be in His presence forever because they are His very own possession.

This act of sealing will also fulfill the promise to the Philadelphian church: "Since you have kept my command to endure patiently, I will also keep you from the hour of trial that is going to come upon the whole world to test those who live on the earth" (3:10, NIV). This means that those thus sealed must be Christians and not unconverted Jews or Gentiles.[125]

(4) The dispensational view of the 144,000 (7:4-8)

In contrast, the dispensationalists see the 144,000 as the select group of Jews who will be converted to Jesus shortly after the rapture of the church to heaven. These Jewish evangelists will preach the gospel to the world during the tribulation. As a result of their preaching, a great multitude of Gentiles will be converted to Christ.[126]

According to Hal Lindsey, the 144,000 are Jews who may have been witnessed to by some Christians prior to the secret rapture of the Christians. When these Jews discover that all the believers are gone, they will turn in faith to Christ, the Messiah. God's original promise to bless the world through the Jews will be fulfilled. The Jews once again will be responsible, as God's representatives, to take His message to the world. But this time the 144,000 Jews will do in only seven years what their nation has failed to do in all its history—evangelize the whole world. Lindsey states that the effectiveness of the evangelism during the seven-year tribulation period will be overwhelming.[127]

From the dispensational perspective, the second multitude (vv. 9-17) is a great host of Gentiles who are supposed to be saved as a result of the preaching of the Jewish remnant, but who, in turn, are martyred by the Antichrist.[128] This view, however, depends upon the view that the church has already been raptured—a theory for which I have found no evidence.

(5) The 144,000 as the church (7:4)

I believe the 144,000 are best identified with the whole body of Christ, the church, both Jews and Gentiles. The New Testament clearly conceives of the church as the true, spiritual Israel. It is beyond debate that "if you are Christ's, then you are Abraham's offspring, heirs according to promise" (Gal. 3:29). Again, Abraham is the "father of all who believe" (Rom. 4:11), whether they be circumcised or uncircumcised. "He is not a real Jew who is one outwardly, nor is true circumcision something external and physical. He is a Jew who is one inwardly, and real circumcision is a matter of the heart, spiritual and not literal" (Rom. 2:28-29). If believers are the true sons of Abraham, the true circumcision, then we must conclude that the church is the true spiritual Israel, even though the word itself may not be used of the church. This I believe to be confirmed by the expression, "the Israel of God," in Galatians 6:16.[129]

Even in Revelation John confirms this distinction between outward, literal Israel and inner, spiritual Israel. In Smyrna there are "those who say that they are Jews and are not, but are a synagogue of Satan" (2:9). That is, there are men who are actually and outwardly Jews—literally Israel—but in reality they are not true Jews—spiritual Israel—but follow the ways of Satan rather than God.[130]

Also, it should be noted that the Old Testament image of the people of Israel as a kingdom and priests to God is applied by John to the followers of Jesus (1:6). Similarly, many of the promises to the victors in the churches of Asia (chs. 2—3) are fulfillments of Old Testament promises given to the true people of Israel. In Christ's rebuke to the churches, we have the Old Testament imagery of Balaam and Jezebel describing error that had influenced not the Old Testament Israel but the New Testament church.[131]

In Revelation 21:9-21, the church is called the "bride, the wife of the Lamb" (v. 9). In this passage, the church is identified with the New Jerusalem, and on its twelve gates are inscribed the "names of the twelve tribes of Israel" (v. 12, NIV). Jesus claims to be the true Israel. The followers of Jesus, the branches, would then be related to the true Israel (compare Rom. 11:17-24). All this strongly suggests that in John's mind the followers of Jesus (14:4) are the true servants of God, the Israel of God (compare John 11:15-52).[132]

(6) The symbolism of 144,000

The identification of the 144,000 with the whole elect people of God who will face the Great Tribulation, including Jews and Gentiles, does not contradict Paul's teaching that the majority of the Jews themselves will one day be brought back into a relationship of salvation before God. John is not dealing with Paul's emphasis at this point in Revelation.[133]

The number 12 times 12,000 which equals 144,000 is a symbolic number and affirms a full number of the people of God who will be brought safely through the time of tribulation. The number is the multiple of the square of twelve and the square of ten. It represents a completeness, as each number is multiplied by its own kind.[134]

The number 144,000 is obviously obtained by adding 12,000 from each of the twelve tribes of Israel (vv. 5-8). Earlier in Revelation (compare 4:4), twenty-four (a multiple of twelve) serves as a symbolic number. This meaning also applies to the redeemed 144,000 who stand on Mount Zion with the Lamb (14:1-5). The same multiple of 1,000 is found again in the size of the Holy City (21:16). Thus 12,000 is symbolic of completeness and perfection. By using 144,000, John signifies the sealing of *all* or the *total* number of God's servants who will face the Great Tribulation.[135]

(7) Interpretation of the twelve tribes (7:5-8)

In verses 5-8 John goes even further. He enumerates each of the twelve tribes and their number. Why was it necessary to provide this detailed enumeration? And why this particular selection of tribes?[136]

Various efforts have been made to explain the reasons behind John's list and especially to explain the absence of the tribe of Dan. The early church held that the Antichrist would arise from the tribe of Dan. Furthermore, in the Old Testament, Dan was associated with idolatry (Judg. 18:18-19; 1 Kings 12:29-30). This may be the clue. John seeks to expose Christian idolatry and beast worship in his day by excluding Dan from the list of those sealed.[137]

We remember that the description of the judgments under the sixth seal (6:12 *ff.*) ended with the question, "The great day of their wrath has come and who can stand before it?" (6:17). Chapter 7 answers this question by implying that only the true servants of God, who are divinely sealed, can be protected from the wrath of God and the Lamb.[138]

b. BLISS OF THE REDEEMED IN HEAVEN (7:9-17)

In verse 9 John sees a great multitude from every nation and cultural background, standing before the throne of God and clothed in white robes. They are identified by one of the elders as those "who have come out of the great tribulation" (v. 14). Who are these people? They cannot be the Gentiles who are saved in the tribulation in contrast to the Jews in verses 1-8. This is true because they are described as coming from every nation and tribe and language, which would mean both Jews and Gentiles.[139]

There is evidence that the identification of this second group is related to the identification of the first group (vv. 1-8). Some argue that the two groups must be different because the first is numbered and the second is innumerable. And as already indicated, some see the first as limited to Jews and the second referring to every nation.[140]

These objections can be answered by recalling the earlier explanation of verses 1-8. First, the number of the sealed was symbolic and not literal. Second, the use of the twelve tribes was John's deliberate attempt to universalize the election of God. Thus, there is a continuity or unity between the two groups. John's vision in verses 9-17 leaps above to a scene in heaven where the saints have been delivered from the Great Tribulation. Here he views the glorified tribulation saints as being in God's presence, at rest from their trials, and serving Him continually.[141]

Thus we see that verses 9-17 refer to Christian people after their entry into heaven. It is the church triumphant around the throne. This is the Christian multitude seen after their trial is over, saved in the kingdom of God.

In verses 9, 13-14, John is impressed with white robes worn by the multitude. The white robes symbolize salvation and victory (v. 10). Those who wear them obtained them because "they have washed their robes and made them white in the blood of the Lamb" (v. 14). This implies that they are true recipients of Christ's redemption in contrast to others who, though professing belief in Christ, are not genuine overcomers (compare 3:5-6,18). Palms (v. 9) were also emblems of victory. In John 12 they denote the triumph of Christ; here in Revelation, the reference is to the victory of the servants of Christ.[142]

In verses 13-14 and in 5:5 are the only references in Revelation to an elder speaking individually. This supports the view that the elders in Revelation are angels and not a symbolic group representing the church.[143]

In verses 15-17 John describes the activity and condition of the true servants of God in their future and eternal relation to the Lamb. The scene is one of the most beautiful in the Bible. Those who have washed their robes in the blood of the Lamb are described as being before the throne of God without fear or tremor. They are fully accepted by the divine Majesty and are continually serving God in praise and worship.[144]

The idea of the Lamb as the Shepherd of God's flock in verse 17 is an intriguing picture. Elsewhere in the writings of John, Christ is pictured as the Good Shepherd. The metaphor builds on the Old Testament picture of God as the shepherd of Israel. Such passages as Psalm 23:1 ("The Lord is my shepherd , I shall not want") and Isaiah 40:11 ("He will feed his flock like a shepherd") speak of the gentle care and daily provision of the ancient shepherd.[145]

The Lamb as heavenly Shepherd leads His flock to the wellspring of life and wipes away the last trace of earthly sorrow. He directs the heavenly multitude to the fountain and source of life—that is, to the immediate presence of God. As a fresh-water spring in a semiarid land would be to a shepherd and his thirsty flock, so will be the eternal presence of God to redeemed man in his longing for spiritual wholeness.[146]

The vision of John portrayed in this beautiful interlude has many points of significance. It assures us that God's faithfulness stretches beyond the times and seasons of our own measurable existence here on earth. God's promises extend beyond these time-space dimensions that we watch so closely. John is privileged to hear a great song that bears clear witness to this fact. This song gives us a glimpse beyond death into the mystery of vindication.[147]

A long-lasting motivational influence comes from the assurance that the Christ of our daily walk of faith today is the same Christ we shall meet at the end of our journey. Jesus Christ reigns at the end boundary just as He reigns at the beginning and at the middle. Ideology does not sustain Christians with the kind of hope that produces relevant ethical and interpersonal action in the present and real world of our daily twenty-four-hour cycle. The living Jesus Christ motivates us from the past, present, and future as we look toward the vindication of truth, justice, love, and faith. This is the ethics of hope, and it has staying power that ideology and mysticism have never known.[148]

Excursus on Tribulation

Revelation 7:14 raises the controversial problem of tribulation. The Bible speaks of three different types of tribulation or distress, and it is important to distinguish between them.[149]

First, there is tribulation that is inseparable from the Christian life in the world (John 16:33; Acts 14:22; Rom. 5:3; 2 Tim. 2:11-12; 1 Pet. 4:12; Rev. 1:9; 2:10). All Christians during all ages experience tribulation, thus sharing in the continuing sufferings of Christ (Col. 1:24).

Second, the Bible also speaks of an intense tribulation that will come on the final generation of Christians. It will be the climax of all previous persecutions. Jesus likewise predicts such an unprecedented persecution: "For then there will be great tribulation, such as has not been from the beginning of the world until now, no, and never will be" (Matt. 24:21). Paul's teaching about "the rebellion" and "the man of lawlessness" apparently refers to this time period (2 Thess. 2:3 *ff.*).[150]

In Revelation this more intense persecution is mentioned in 7:14; 11:7-10; 13:7; and 16:6. The events under the fifth seal should perhaps also be included here (6:9-11). This future tribulation is distinguished from previous persecutions of the church in its intensity and in its immediate connection with Christ's second coming. It is also related to the presence of the final Antichrist.[151]

Third, the Bible also speaks of a future time of God's intense wrath on unbelievers. Revelation refers to this as "the great day of their wrath" (6:17) and "the hour of trial that is going to come upon the whole world to test those who live on the earth" (3:10, NIV). Such wrath from God is especially seen during the time of the trumpets and bowls (8:2 *ff.*; 16:1 *ff.*). Paul referred to this punitive action of God in 2 Thessalonians 1:6-10. Paul probably drew on the teaching of Jesus in the Olivet discourse (Matt. 24) in his teaching about God's wrath on unbelievers.[152]

For Christians, there could be an overlapping of the Great Tribulation with a portion of the period of God's wrath on rebellious humanity. However, this final, more intense judgment of God seems to follow the Great Tribulation itself and is directly connected with the coming of Christ (Matt. 24:29; Rev. 6:12 *ff.*; 19:1 *ff.*).[153]

Thus the Great Tribulation will be but a concentration of the same satanic hostility which the church has experienced throughout her entire existence. In this last period, Satan, in one final convulsive effort, tries to turn the hearts of God's people away from Christ.[154]

If this great company in verses 9-17 has come out of the Great Tribulation, the assumption is that they have suffered martyrdom. However, they have not surrendered their faith in Christ nor permitted themselves to be stained by unbelief or by worship of any false gods. They have remained steadfast in their faith in Christ.[155]

4. The Seventh Seal (8:1)—A Dramatic Pause

In 8:1 John shows us the beginning of God's execution of His wrath—the trumpets and the bowls. The statement in verses 1-2 clearly implies that the trumpets follow the seals: "When he opened the seventh seal, . . . I saw the seven angels . . . to them were given seven trumpets" (NIV). The seventh seal has no plagues. The seven trumpets are the *content* of the seventh seal. Trumpets are frequently associated with eschatological messages. And in Revelation 8 they are used to announce the impending judgment of God. Before the trumpets sound, there is an attitude of suspense—silence for half an hour.

This quietness has as much dramatic impact as the sounds and colors that have dominated the vision of John up to this point— perhaps even more. It is not the silence of emptiness or the yawn of boredom. Rather it is the silence of mystery and intense waiting. But most important of all, it is the silence of God's sovereignty. There is communicated in a very dramatic way in this quietness the full and awesome authority of God. Everything must wait for His kingly move. Once again, the vision of John has taught the gospel to us. This time it is taught by the strange silence which waits for the Lamb and His Father to give the trumpet to the angel. History is not a jumble of chances. There is in this interlude in verse 1 the portrayal of holy restraint. The sabbath of stillness proves God's might.[156]

Most scholars would agree that the best suggestion is that silence represents an attitude of trembling suspense on the part of the heavenly hosts in view of the judgments of God which are about to fall upon the world. It is the silence of the dreadful anticipation of the events that are about to take place, now that the time of the end has come.[157]

C. The Seven Trumpet Judgments and the
Two Interludes (8:2 to 14:20)

1. The Six Trumpet Judgments (8:2 to 9:21)

a. THE RELATION OF THE SEALS, TRUMPETS, AND BOWLS

Chapters 8 and 9 describe the breaking of the seventh seal and the sounding of the seven trumpets. Both the seals and the trumpets bring us to the end of history. This fact requires us to recognize some measure of recapitulation in Revelation. John's presentation backs up and covers some of the same ground again. The seven trumpets seem to constitute, in fact, the content of the seventh seal. The six seals describe the forces leading up to the end. The seven trumpets relate the beginning of the events of the end itself, particularly the time of the Great Tribulation which will introduce the end.[158]

The visions of John obviously do not follow one another in a strict chronological sequence nor do they systematically recapitulate one another. The seven bowls (16:1-21), after some intervening visions, follow the seventh trumpet. There is progression, but not without considerable restatement and development of detail. The further one moves toward the end, the greater is this enlargement.[159]

All attempts to press the material into well-defined patterns leave the impression that John was less interested in producing a work of literary subtlety than sharing with his fellow believers the awe-inspiring visions God had dramatically revealed to him. E. F. Scott wisely remarks that a perfectly logical apocalypse would be a contradiction in terms.[160]

b. THE SYMBOLIC AND BIBLICAL LANGUAGE DESCRIBING THE TRUMPETS

The problem of literal interpretation of the language in such a highly symbolic book of Revelation is seen as we read and study the descriptions of the events related to the seven trumpets. The crucial question is not literal versus nonliteral but what did John intend? Some things may need to be understood more literally and others symbolically. For example, the reference to the army of 200 million (9:16-19) can hardly be literal. Either the number is figurative or the army refers to demonic powers rather than human soldiers. It is also difficult to take literally the reference to the eagle that speaks human words (8:13). The approach I take will attempt to steer between a literal approach and a totally symbolic one.[161]

An awareness of the biblical origin of most of John's language reduces the element of strangeness and helps the reader understand what is being said (perhaps a part of our problem relates to our general ignorance of the Old Testament). Most of the judgments described in the trumpets are closely related to the plagues preceding the Exodus. By means of the plagues, the Egyptian pharaoh was "persuaded" to give the Israelites their freedom (Ex. 7—12). This analogy between God's end-time judgment on human history and the deliverance of Israel from Egypt also shows that through all of the "blood and thunder" the purpose of God continues always to be a saving purpose.[162]

An intensification or progression in the judgments can be seen. The seven bowls, while describing the same sequence of events as do the trumpets, exhibit this greater intensity from the very beginning. However, like the trumpets, the bowls build in their own sequence to increasingly terrible scenes of judgment.[163]

c. PREPARATION FOR THE TRUMPETS (8:2-5)—GOD HEARS HIS PEOPLE'S CRY

The seven angels who stand before God (v. 2) are believed to be the angels of His presence: Michael, Gabriel, Raphael, Uriel, Raguel, Sariel, and Remiel. Each angel is given a trumpet which is connected with the next cycle of seven woes or plagues. Trumpets are frequently associated with end-time messages. Here, as elsewhere, they are used to announce the impending judgment of God (compare Isa. 27:13; Joel 2:1; Matt. 24:31; 1 Cor. 15:52; 1 Thess. 4:16).[164]

Before the trumpet judgments are executed, another angel enacts a symbolic scene in heaven (v. 3). He takes a golden censer filled with incense and offers the incense on the altar in behalf of the prayers of all God's people (vv. 3-4). Earlier, in connection with the martyred saints (6:9), John mentioned the altar that was near God's presence. At that time, the saints were also crying to God for deliverance.[165]

Here a strong assurance is given to the suffering followers of Christ that their prayers for vindication are not forgotten. God will speedily vindicate them and avenge their enemies' assaults. So close is the altar to God that the incense cloud of the saints' prayers rises into His presence and cannot escape His notice (compare Ps. 141:2). The incense evidently helps to make the prayers more acceptable to

God (v. 4). There is no thought of mediatorial angels here. The prayers rise directly to God.[166]

In verse 5 the angel takes the censer and fills it with fire from the altar and throws it on the earth. The casting of the fire upon the earth symbolizes the impending wrath and judgment of God in response to the intercession of the saints. This is indicated by the physical signs, such as thunder and lightning, which follow.

Dramatic upheavals in nature also follow the seventh trumpet (11:19) and the seventh bowl (16:18). Ezekiel 10:4 records a somewhat parallel scene in which live coals are scattered over Jerusalem as a symbol of God's judgment.[167]

d. THE FIRST FOUR TRUMPET JUDGMENTS (8:6-12)—JUDGMENT UPON NATURE

There is a recognizable *literary pattern* in the unfolding of the trumpets. The first four trumpets are separated from the last three (which are called "woes": 8:13; 9:12; 11:14).[168]

The first four trumpets are judgments of God on nature. The last three are directed specifically upon people. The background for these plagues is the experience of the plagues in Egypt.[169]

The first trumpet (v. 7) calls for hail and fire to fall over a third of the earth. This should be compared to the plague of hail in Exodus 9:23-26 and the fire and blood in Joel 2:30. This is a judgment on vegetation.

For Hal Lindsey, the second trumpet prophesies that a super-thermonuclear weapon will be set off in the ocean and destroy a large percentage of the marine life. He thinks one of the reasons such devastation will occur on the ocean is that thermonuclear missiles are targeted toward large armadas of naval vessels.[170]

The second trumpet (vv. 8-9) states that one third of the sea turns to blood, and the fish and the ships are destroyed. We should compare this with the turning of the Nile River into blood in Exodus 7:20-24.

The third trumpet (vv. 10-11) brings fresh-water pollution. A "great star" blazing like a torch falls from heaven and pollutes one third of the rivers and fountains of water. This star was named "Wormwood" which refers to a bitter herb found in the Near East. The fact that "many men" die from the bitter water indicates that the water did not literally become wormwood (v. 11*b*).

This plague is like that of Marah in reverse (Ex. 15:23). The corruption of drinking water reminds us of the first Egyptian plague, but here wormwood is the means used. Wormwood symbolizes divine punishment, as Jeremiah's words indicate: "I will feed this people with wormwood, and give them poisonous water to drink" (Jer. 9:15; compare 23:15; Lam. 3:15,19). Hal Lindsey contends that this star is a thermonuclear weapon which will contaminate all of the fresh water sources on earth.

The fourth trumpet (v. 12) affects the luminaries—the sun, moon, and stars. The background for this is the Egyptian plague of darkness (Ex. 10:21-23). In this case, Lindsey states that this will be a light reduction which will result from the tremendous pollution in the air left from nuclear explosions.[171]

e. THE EAGLE'S WARNING (8:13)

John states that an eagle comes to warn the wicked inhabitants of the earth of the severity of the last three judgments. The eagle is an omen of danger in other places in the Bible. There may be a reference to the eagle as a sign of danger in Matthew 24:28: "Wherever the body is, there the eagles will be gathered together." This bird could be a vulture since there is this reference to carrion or a dead body. The eagle is a bird of prey. For a traveler in the desert, the sight of an eagle is a sign of danger. The implication of this sign is that the cry of the eagle signals even worse dangers ahead.[172]

In verse 13 the eagle's cry introduces the demonic hosts or demonic locusts. They will torment the people who have not the seal of God on their forehead. The description of the following plagues (9:1-19) is highly imaginative. It is possible that John wishes to suggest the troubling of humanity by demonic powers.

f. THE FIFTH TRUMPET JUDGMENT (9:1-12)—FIRST WOE: DEMONIC LOCUSTS

(1) The fallen star (9:1)—angelic agent

The fifth trumpet blows (v. 1), and John watches a strange thing happen. "A star fallen from heaven to earth" opens the shaft of the bottomless pit. Then the warriors which are described as locust-horse-scorpion-human hybrids are loosed upon the earth. The star probably symbolizes an angel employed by God for a specific task and not Satan himself. The star appears to be an angelic agent who comes down to perform God's judicial and redemptive purposes at the end of the age.[173]

(2) The bottomless pit and the locusts (9:1-6)

The bottomless pit in verses 1-2 is a provisional place of punishment for Satan until the end when he is thrown into the "lake of fire" (20:1-3,10). The bottomless pit is also the abode of the beast or Antichrist before he appears on earth (11:7). This pit will also be the temporary prison of Satan during the millennial reign of Christ (20:3). The pit is sometimes represented as either the home or the place of imprisonment of demons (Luke 8:31).[174]

In this particular case, it is the abode of hosts of demons who fly forth, like scorpions, to plague people (v. 3). It should be noted that Revelation does not uniformly represent Satan as having his abode in the underworld. In chapter 12, Satan is represented as a fiery red dragon who engages in a fearful conflict with the angel Michael in the upper heavens.[175]

The objects of the locusts' attack are people, but only those people who do not have the seal of God upon their forehead (v. 4). This takes us back to chapter 7 where John sees the sealing of the people of God before the last terrible period of tribulation.[176]

Verse 5 gives the purpose of the sealing. The tribulation will be a time of the beginning of the wrath of God upon a rebellious society. It is a time of fearful persecution of the church by the beast and, as this trumpet judgment shows, a time of demonic activity. But God's wrath will fall only on the worshipers of the beast (16:2). God's people will be sheltered by a divine protection from demonic activity. However, the church in the tribulation will be the victim of persecution and martyrdom as she has been throughout her entire history.[177]

We are reminded of Israel and Egypt. God sent the plagues upon the Egyptians. They suffered terribly, even to the loss of the first-born, but Israel was preserved. When the blood of the lamb was sprinkled over the door of an Israelite family, the angel of death passed over the family. The judgment of God did not fall upon the members of that family.

In a similar way the church will be in the world during the time of tribulation. The church will suffer martyrdom. The church will suffer persecution, but it will be preserved from the terrible experience of the wrath of God. This wrath is poured out only upon those who have not the seal of God upon their foreheads.

(3) The description of the strange horse-like locusts (9:7-10)

The appearance of these locusts is "like horses arrayed for battle" (v. 7). The fact that their faces are like human faces is to convey the idea that these are not ordinary locusts. Rather they are symbolic representations of the demonic forces of evil (John uses frogs to represent demonic powers in 16:13). Their lion-like teeth refer to the way in which locusts devour vegetation (v. 8). The demonic power of the locust to inflict punishment is in their scorpion-like tails. They are directing their hostility against people and not vegetation (v. 10).[178]

(4) The leader of the locusts (9:11)

The leader of these demonic forces is not Satan but an angel who presides over the bottomless pit (v. 11). This leader is called "Abaddon" in Hebrew and "Apollyon" in Greek. Apollyon appears to be an angel entrusted with authority over the abyss. The creature, his name, and his responsibility seem to be original with the author of Revelation. These creatures are part locust and part scorpion which obviously is a symbolic representation of demonic powers (vv. 7-11).[179]

The Old Testament background for this picture is Joel 2:1-11. In Joel the Day of the Lord is described under the figure of a devastating plague of locusts. For Joel the judgment is directed against Israel, but here it is directed against the enemies of God. The symbolism employed by John in his vision is different from that in Joel, but its message is no less frightening. Both point to the day of wrath and judgment.[180]

Hal Lindsey agrees with one of his friends that this description in verse 10 fits a machine like a Cobra helicopter, such as those which were used in Vietnam. The means of torment will be a kind of nerve gas sprayed from the tail of the helicopter.[181]

In verses 1-12 the judgment of God has shifted from the world of nature to the world of wicked people. God has permitted these demonic forces of hell (the "bottomless pit"), with which people in their rebellion against God have been in league, to vent their diabolic powers against the people.[182]

John is saying here that there is an actual troubling of humanity by demonic forces. This may already be happening in our time in a preliminary way. At the end of the age, it will be even more intense. However we interpret this passage, we know that John is using dramatic and symbolic language to portray something that is very powerful.

g. THE SIXTH TRUMPET (9:13-19)—SECOND WOE: FIENDISH CALVARY

(1) The significance of the Euphrates (9:13-15)

With the sixth trumpet blast, a voice cries out "from the four horns of the golden altar before God" (v. 13). It was from this altar that the prayers of the saints, mingled with incense were raised to the throne of God (8:4-5). Now God is answering their prayers in this and the other plagues. The voice commands the sixth angelic trumpeter to "release the four angels who are bound at the great river *Euphrates*" (v. 14, author's italics; compare 7:1-3). These four angels were to lead the devastating armies of 200 million cavalry from beyond the Euphrates to kill one third of humanity (v. 15).[183]

In terms of background, we know that large devastating armies from the region north of Israel, from around the great river Euphrates, are closely associated in prophecy with the final conflict. There are numerous references to fierce armies of destruction in Ezekiel 38—39; Joel 3:9 and following verses; Jeremiah 1:14-19; 6:22-23; Isaiah 5:26-30; and Zechariah 14:2.[184]

Beyond the Euphrates were the hordes of the heathen kingdoms, particularly Assyria. Thus the river Euphrates became symbolic in Isaiah and Jeremiah of the enemies of Israel and of God. So the angels are bound on the banks of the Euphrates until the time of judgment when they will be loosed and a flood of demonic powers will burst forth upon the civilized world (v. 14). These evil angels are obviously instruments of the divine judgment. They are a part of carrying out the unfolding of the divine plan for the rebellious world.[185]

In this context, John sees these powers coming upon the enemy of the Christian community. By stating that the four angels were restrained until a precise moment points up the apostle's conviction that God is in control and that He has planned a precise time for each event.

John here makes use of ancient geographical terms to picture the fearful character of the coming judgment of God on a rebellious world. In addition to the Hebrew background, the first-century Mediterranean world would have understood the Euphrates cavalry image. The Roman world feared the cavalry forces of the Parthians who came from the region of the Euphrates River. In a similar way, the late twentieth-century world fears the nuclear intercontinental weapons of the USA and the USSR. While the language of verses 13-19 is drawn from historical-political events of the Old Testament, it describes realities that far transcend a local event.[186]

(2) The army of 200 million (9:16-19)

Verse 16 rather abruptly introduces a mounted army of some 200 million horses and riders. While some argue for a literal, human army here, several factors point to their identity as *demonic* forces. First, the horsemen are not in themselves important. They wear brightly colored breastplates of fiery red, dark blue, and sulfurous yellow, more suggestive of supernatural than natural riders (v. 17).[187]

More important are the horses. They have heads resembling those of lions. The horses, rather than their riders, are the instruments of death by the plagues of fire, smoke, and sulphur that come from their mouths (vv. 17,19). Furthermore, these horses have tails like snakes that are able to kill. Contrast this with the locusts' scorpion-like tails which inflict injury but not death (v. 5).[188]

As leaders of the demonic horses, the evil angels kill one third of humanity (v. 18). Their mission was not the destruction of the race. Rather, as agents of divine judgment, they were to warn people of the terrible judgment which awaits those who do not repent of their evil deeds and who reject God's love and mercy. It is difficult to believe that a literal number is intended. The demonic hosts are simply innumerable.

(3) Theories about the meaning of the army of 200 million

One of the attractions of Hal Lindsey's book is the way in which he attempts to relate the teaching of this passage to the contemporary scene. He states that this passage tells us that in our time 200 million troops of Red Chinese soldiers accompanied by other Eastern allies will come into Palestine. He thinks that it is possible that the industrial might of Japan will be united with Red China to form this army. For the first time in history, there will be a full invasion of the West by the Orient.[189]

The armed militia of China is estimated now to be at least 200 million people. The significance of this fact, for Lindsey, is that in our time, for the first time in history, there is an Oriental power which can do exactly what John says will happen. He points out that at the time when John wrote this prophecy there were not yet 200 million people in the whole world![190]

Lindsey also conjectures that the horses with heads like lions which belch out fire, smoke and brimstone (v. 17) prophesy some kind of mobilized ballistic missile launcher. He states that this army will destroy one third of the world's remaining population while they are coming from the Orient to the Middle East (v. 18).[191]

Lindsey thinks that the attack on the United States will be a long-range strike. This must be true because the United States is nowhere intimated as being present in the Bible's prophecies of the last war of the world. This destruction of the United States can happen because Red China is a thermonuclear power.

The *New Scofield Study Bible* also teaches that the army described in Revelation 9:16-19 is a military host coming from the Orient across the Euphrates River (16:12). The loosing of the angels (vv. 14-15) and the drying up of the Euphrates are a preparation for the invasion of the Holy Land by the "kings from the east" (16:12) in anticipation of the battle of Armageddon (vv. 14-16). The detailed identification with current events is avoided.[192]

In answer to the *New Scofield Study Bible*, Alan Johnson draws upon the expertise of General William K. Harrison. According to Harrison, an army of 200 million could not be conscripted, supported, and moved to the Middle East without totally disrupting all societal needs and capabilities. God has made people with certain limitations. The actual raising and transporting of an army of the size spoken of in verse 16 completely transcends human capability. All the Allied and Axis forces at their peak in World War II numbered only about seventy million.[193]

Thus it seems better to understand the vast numbers and the description of the horses as indicating demonic hordes. Elsewhere in Scripture such large numbers do occasionally indicate angelic hosts (Ps. 68:17; Rev. 5:11; compare 2 Kings 2:11-12; 6:17). This would not eliminate the possibility of human armies of manageable size also being involved. But the emphasis in verses 16-19 is on the demonic character of the army. The horses are cruel and determined and show no mercy to man, woman, or child. These demons, besides constituting an army, could also manifest themselves in pestilences, epidemic diseases, or misfortunes. This would explain the use of "plagues" to describe these hordes (vv. 18,20; compare 11:6; 16:9,21).[194]

h. THE PURPOSE OF GOD'S JUDGMENT (9:20-21)

Although these demonic plagues seem to be terrible, they do embody a merciful purpose (vv. 20-21). They are designed to turn people to repentance before it is too late. Throughout history, it has appeared on the surface that persons have been able to pursue a path of sin and to defy God with limited consequences. As the end approaches and the time of judgment draws near, God pours out on people a taste of His final judgment and wrath. This is not because He takes pleasure in wrath but in order to warn people that the way of sin and defiance of God can lead only to disaster.[195]

God does not desire that any person should suffer His judgment but that all should repent and turn to Him (Luke 13:3,5; 2 Pet. 3:9). But when God's works and words are persistently rejected, only judgment remains (Eph. 5:6; Heb. 10:26-31).[196]

One would think that the rest of mankind, who were not killed by these plagues (v. 20), would learn a lesson from the one third who were killed. Surely they would repent in fear and trembling. But this is not so. They do not repent because they continue in their defiant path of worshiping demons and idols (v. 20).[197]

Since John in verse 20 distinguishes the cultic objects (idols) from the demons, he no doubt shared Paul's concept of demons as evil spirits (Rev. 16:14; 18:2). Thus, there is a twofold evil in idol worship. First, it robs the true God of His glory (Rom. 1:23). Second, it leads to consorting with evil spirits which corrupt people. "Sorceries" in verse 21 means "a practice of magic arts," or "witchcraft" in degraded religious practices (Ex. 7:11; 9:11; Gal. 5:20; Rev. 21:8; 22:15).[198]

The defiance of the rest of humanity is reflected not only in their idolatry but also in their immorality (v. 21). Here is the same theology taught by Paul in Romans 1:18 and following verses. Ungodliness issues in all kinds of unrighteousness and wickedness. The word "immorality" designates sexual sin in general.[199]

Hal Lindsey entitles the sins listed in verse 21 as the "big-four sins." The first of these is murder. The second is drug-related occult activities. The third prominent sin of the tribulation will be rampant immorality. And the fourth characteristic of the tribulation will be thievery of all kinds.[200]

Excursus on the Biblical Philosophy of History

I think most careful Bible students would agree that no good result can be achieved by interpreting Revelation in order to set dates or insist arbitrarily that the twentieth century is prefigured in some exact way by some one of the seals, trumpets, or bowls. The history of this type of interpretation is its own best refutation.

On the other hand, the biblical philosophy of history would state that each succeeding year brings us constantly closer to the climax of history about which Revelation speaks. It is easy to see why sensitive people in our generation can note many of the evils described in Revelation as increasing in our time. There is an increasing ability of man to destroy himself and his world by the powers of nature which he has harnessed. Legislation and diplomacy and conferences have not permanently been able to get into the hearts of people. In other words, the world process has accelerated greatly in the last fifty years. The Bible describes a climax when mankind asserts its independence of God under the leadership of one genius, the beast, and when God decides to reveal His ultimate authority through Christ, the Redeemer and Conqueror.

If the historical premillennial interpretation is correct in terms of the four horsemen (6:1-8), then the growth of good and evil will tend to keep pace with each other. As the gospel reaches out to the uttermost parts of the earth, rebellion against it becomes even more widespread. Airplanes and new communication instruments can be used by Christian workers, but they can also be used in the service of evil. Whatever the place of Israel in prophecy, it is true that the return of Israel to Palestine has produced an international crisis. It is also true that much of the growth of the churches is based on a superficial type of Christianity which can be called apostate.

No one of us can say exactly in which generation the end will come. But according to the biblical teaching, the end must come, and each year is bringing this end constantly nearer. We are not to set dates, but we are to be faithful in proclaiming and incarnating Christ's Word and seek to maintain structures of justice and love until the end.

2. An Interlude (10:1 to 11:13)—Visions of the Prophetic Role

Excursus on the Dramatic Nature of Revelation and Its View of History

I have tried to think of an analogy to help us understand Revelation. I am interested, as are some of you, in visual art. I feel that this book could be compared to some types of expressionistic art, such as an early Kandinsky. Revelation is expressionistic and dramatic. It overstates for emphasis; it repeats; it recapitulates. It says the same thing over and over and progressively makes its statements in more intense terms. We Western people should not try to force this ancient book into some type of highly regimented or structured twentieth-century scheme.

Paul Ricoeur, the eminent French philosopher, states that we can approach the Bible in three ways. First, we could take all the parts of the Bible literally without allowing for symbolism, metaphor, or analogy. Second, in reaction to such literalism we could, like Bultmann, demythologize the Bible. He sees little reality behind the dramatic stories in Revelation. However, a third option is to view the Bible with a new appreciation for its authentic nature as an inspired book of salvation and doctrine. We could see a definite message and important doctrine and reality conveyed in the dramatic parts of the Bible, such as Revelation, through symbols, metaphors, and analogies. With this approach, the dramatic or symbolic parts of the Bible once again become meaningful and relevant for these people. I believe that there is reality behind the metaphors and symbols of the Bible.

A man called in on a radio talk show which I conducted in Houston, Texas. He gave me developments which he said proved to him that these had to be the last days of history predicted by Revelation. I said, "Sir, I just cannot say dogmatically that these are the very last days. I do believe in what I call purposive history, that history is moving toward a climax. As a person who believes very sincerely in the biblical understanding of history, I believe that history is moving toward a climax. As a person who accepts the biblical understanding of history as divinely revealed, I believe that history has a beginning, a middle point which was the coming of Christ, and is moving toward a crescendo which we call the second coming of Christ."

There are Antichrist figures in every generation. For example, Jim Jones of the Guyana movement had many of the characteristics of the Antichrist which are described in Revelation 12—14. He claimed to be a god. He actually said, "I am God." He called for the worship of himself in the manner in which the false prophet will call for the worship of the beast. Jones used psychic powers. He distorted sex. He used power. He used money. All of this is a part of the panorama of Revelation. But I could not say that he was the final Antichrist when he was active in the late 1970s.

Incidentally, Jim Jones used Revelation as one of the means by which he guided and controlled his followers. When he left Indianapolis in 1964, he did so on the basis of prophecy. He said that it had been revealed to him that the world was coming to an end with an atomic holocaust. There were only two safe places in the world, Brazil and Ukiah, California, north of San Francisco. He persuaded 150 people to leave Indianapolis and follow him to the Redwood Valley of California, where he established his settlement. At the time that he made a visit to Brazil he also visited Guyana. He persuaded the people to follow him to Guyana by using apocalyptic prophecies from Revelation and by saying that those were the very last days of history. He even went so far as to set a date for the end. He told the people that the world would come to an end in 1977.

The biblical teaching does give a dynamic view of history and does teach that there will be many Antichrists and a final Antichrist. We can identify those in every generation who have Antichrist characteristics and who could have been or could be the final Antichrist. But in our human limitations, we cannot dogmatically say that this or that person is the final Antichrist or that this or that sign indicates that this has to be the last period of history.

a. INTRODUCTION TO THE INTERLUDE

At the close of chapter 9, John described six of the seven trumpets with the plagues or woes accompanying them. We would expect him now to describe the sounding of the seventh trumpet. Instead, once again, John gives us an interlude of two related visions. The first vision of the angel with the little book is addressed to John (10:1-11). The second vision has to do with the two witnesses and is addressed to the persecuted church (11:1-13). These interludes are not so much pauses in the actual sequence of events as they are literary devices by which the church is instructed concerning its role and destiny during the final period of church history.[201]

The literary procedure which uses interludes is an essential factor in the artistic structure of Revelation. Between the sixth and seventh seals, you will remember that John inserted the interlude of the two multitudes and the 144,000 (7:1-17). Between the seven trumpets and the seven bowls, we will note that John will insert the interlude of the dragon and the woman (12:1-17). He will also at that time insert the vision of the two great beasts (13:1-18) and the vision of the Lamb on Mount Zion (14:1-20).[202]

G. Beasley-Murray notes that by means of the interlude in chapters 10 and 11, John wishes to make two points completely clear. The first point answers the perennial question of the martyrs, "How long will we have to suffer?" (10:7). The second point answers a question not yet raised in the visions, "What is the task of the church in these troublesome times?" (11:1-13).[203]

There will be no corresponding interlude between the sixth and seventh bowl judgments which are the final series of judgments yet to come. This is because all the warnings and the preliminary judgments will be over. When the bowls of divine wrath are poured out, the very last days will have been set into motion.[204]

Each of these series of seven (seals, trumpets, bowls) moves us closer to the end. Each of the series heightens and intensifies the final and climactic confrontation of God and the forces of evil.[205]

b. THE MIGHTY ANGEL AND THE LITTLE BOOK (10:1-11)

(1) Announcement of the proximity of the end (10:1-7)

Those who are interested in symbolism, metaphors, and analogy will enjoy this section of Revelation.

John has now moved from heaven (4:1) to earth (10:1). The angel descending from heaven to earth (10:1) and John later receiving the scroll from his hand (vv. 8-9) are the basis for this conclusion. As is his custom, the author pauses to share a vision designed to encourage and sustain the saints in their witness. This interlude is longer than the one between the sixth and seventh seals in chapter 7.[206]

The mighty angel is arrayed in a "cloud" which is probably associated with his mission of judgment. The description of the angel—"the rainbow over his head, and his face was like the sun, and his legs like pillars of fire"—suggests the appearance of heavenly glory. But we should not identify this angel with Christ (v. 1). The oath the angel takes in verse 6 precludes this identification.[207]

When the angel comes to earth, he has a "little scroll open in his hand" (v. 2a). This "little scroll" is to be distinguished from the one in God's hand which was sealed (5:1). The angel rests one foot upon the sea and the other upon the land. This symbolizes that the message of the little open scroll is for the entire world (v. 3). It contains a part of God's larger purpose for humanity.[208]

The angel then calls out with a loud voice, like a lion roaring. After this, "seven thunders sounded" (v. 3; compare Ps. 29). Each thunder speaks a definite message to John. However, when John starts to record them, he is forbidden to do so by a "voice from heaven" which tells him to "seal up what the seven thunders have said, and do not write it down" (v. 4). The voice from heaven was probably that of God or Christ (compare 1:11,19; John 12:28).[209]

The angel with the little scroll, with hands lifted toward heaven, then makes a fourfold vow in the name of the Eternal Creator. He affirms that after the seventh trumpet blast all of God's promises through His prophets would be fulfilled (vv. 5-7).[210]

Furthermore, there will be no more time intervening before the coming of the end. The consummation will be no longer delayed (v. 6). The prayers of the saints are about to be answered. The seventh trumpet will be sounded, and it will reveal the final judgments of the bowls and the final establishment of God's rule on the earth (v. 7).

This announcement in verse 7 contrasts sharply with the statement given to the souls under the altar who cried out for vindication and punishment for their oppressors. They were told "to rest a little longer" until the divine purpose has come to completion (6:10-11).[211]

The rendering of verses 6-7 in the King James Version, that there shall be "time no longer," is misleading. *The New English Bible* makes the meaning clear: "There shall be no more delay; but when the time comes for the seventh angel to sound his trumpet, the hidden purpose of God will have been fulfilled, as he promised to his servants the prophets."[212]

(2) John's commission as a prophet reaffirmed (10:8-11)

(a) The content of the little scroll (10:8)

God now addresses John, telling him to take the little scroll from the angel and eat it (vv. 8-9). The message of the scroll probably includes the substance of the seventh trumpet vision (which is the seven bowls) and the remainder of Revelation.[213]

(b) The bitterness and sweetness of the divine message (10:9-10)

Eating the scroll (vv. 9-10) symbolizes the reception of the Word of God into the innermost being as a necessary prerequisite to proclaiming it with confidence.[214]

The symbolism John uses is derived from Ezekiel 2 and 3, although there is some variation. After Ezekiel eats his scroll, he says, "It was in my mouth as sweet as honey" (Ezek. 3:3). After John eats his scroll, he says, "It was sweet as honey in my mouth, but when I had eaten it my stomach was made bitter" (v. 10). The bitterness was probably caused by the woes or the wrath of God which John had to proclaim in his seventh trumpet vision. The bitterness was also related to the woes resulting from the pouring out of the contents of the seven bowls. It was sweet to go before the heavenly council and to be commissioned to serve as God's prophet. However, a genuine prophet never "enjoys" preaching judgment and wrath.[215]

Martin Luther described the Christian message as "the message of Law and Gospel." Even the message of forgiveness is preceded by the realization of guilt and judgment. What is important to note is that John is commissioned to tell the whole world the twofold message, the whole truth—it is bitter and sweet. Only the false prophet proclaims the sweet and is silent about the bitter elements of the divine Word.[216]

(c) The importance and significance of the complete message of the prophet (v. 11).

In verse 11 the voice reiterates John's commission to prophesy. It is not a new commission, but a reaffirmation. John has already prophesied about the seven seals and six of the seven trumpets. Now with the coming of the period of the last trumpet, he must prophesy again. This prophecy will include the consummation itself and the coming of the final stages of God's kingdom.[217]

Many interpreters say that the implication of the message of the angel and the little book relates to the worldwide proclamation of God's Word throughout the entire gospel age by preachers and teachers of the Word. They have the responsibility of presenting both the law and the gospel. They must warn of God's hatred of sin and of the need for repentance. They must present the way of salvation so clearly that none will be in doubt about the way. Such preaching may cause some bitter reactions.[218]

Some people do not want to hear about sin and God's judgment on the impenitent. Thus the preacher may be tempted to soften his message to make it more acceptable to all. But if he has digested the whole Word of God, he has a divine compulsion to speak out fearlessly in love. Presenting the gospel of the love of Christ and seeing people respond to this gospel and grow in the grace and knowledge of Christ is, indeed, sweetness.[219]

In our personal experience in the Word, there is also the bitter and the sweet. When we digest the Word, it begins to show us our sin, weaknesses, failures, and disobediences. When we realize that we must die to self and let Christ be the absolute Lord of our lives, then we, too, may experience sorrow and bitterness. But if we acknowledge all that God shows us, accept His forgiveness, and grow in our surrender to His lordship, then we will experience the sweetness which the awareness of His presence brings us.[220]

c. THE MEASURING OF THE TEMPLE AND THE TWO WITNESSES (11:1-13)

Excursus on Major Interpretations of Chapter 11

In this chapter John is told to measure the Temple of God and its worshipers. However, he is to exclude from the measurement the outer court which is to be trampled down by the nations for forty-two months (vv. 1-2). God sends two witnesses to Jerusalem to testify against the nations, but the beast kills them (vv. 3-7). All the people rejoice at this martyrdom (v. 10). After three and a half days, the witnesses are revived and caught up to heaven (vv. 11-12). Then a great earthquake destroys a tenth of the city. Seven thousand people are killed, but the rest give glory to the God of heaven (v. 13).[221]

Most commentators agree that chapter 11 is especially difficult to interpret. Does John intend all this section to be understood literally? Or does he intend all or part of these as symbols? Furthermore, how does this section (vv. 1-13) relate to the total context (10:1 to 11:19)?[222]

The dispensational approach of Walvoord and Lindsey

The dispensational premillennial school of commentators understands the "temple" and the "city" to refer to a rebuilt Jewish Temple in Jerusalem. While in this view some elements in the description may be symbolic, the main import of the passage is seen as portraying a future protection of the nation of Israel before her spiritual regeneration. The Antichrist (beast) will permit the rebuilding of the Temple in Jerusalem, as well as the restoration of Jewish worship for three and a half years. But then the Antichrist will break his covenant and trample down a part of the Temple and the Holy City until Christ returns to deliver the Jewish people (compare Dan. 9:27)[223]

John Walvoord of Dallas Seminary represents the school of thought which approaches this material in a straight forward and literal manner. He contends that the Temple will actually exist during the tribulation and that the two witnesses are a resurrected Moses and Elijah and that the altar will be a place where ancient sacrifices are renewed.[224]

Hal Lindsey is in this same tradition. He states that in return for certain concessions from the Jews, the Roman Antichrist will guarantee protection for the Jews so that they can rebuild their Temple and reinstate animal sacrifices. The religious leaders of the Jews will push for this and accept the false prophet as the Messiah because he helps to secure the rebuilding of the Temple (13:11-18).

According to Lindsey, present-day believers in Christ will probably not be here when the Temple is rebuilt. It will most likely be started after the pretribulation rapture of the mystery church saints. However, Lindsey states that should a person begin to see work start on a new Jerusalem Temple on Mount Moriah, you had better finish up your business fast because things are winding down to a close.

Lindsey contends that, because a majority of the Jews living during the tribulation will not have accepted the truth about Jesus as the Messiah, this passage describes a precise period of judgment by the Gentile nations upon Jerusalem (11:2). During this period of forty-two months, Jerusalem will see nothing but war. One Gentile army after another will invade the city of Jerusalem and march up and down its streets. The time of the Gentiles ends with the return of Jesus the Messiah to the earth at the last battle of the tribulation, which is the battle of Armageddon.[225]

The Jewish emphasis of Ladd

George Ladd sees this passage as a prophecy of the preservation and ultimate salvation of the Jewish people. He believes that these verses teach that a literal Israel is yet to be included in spiritual Israel. Revelation 11 is John's way of predicting the preservation of the Jewish people and their final salvation.[226]

The Christian church emphasis of Mounce, Beasley-Murray, and Johnson

Robert Mounce understands this entire section to be symbolic of the fate of the witnessing church during its final period of opposition and persecution. The language of prophecy is highly figurative and, therefore, we should not take a literal approach to this chapter. Symbolism is not a denial of historicity. An authentic interpreter must take into account the type of language used in chapter 11. Apocalyptic language has as one of its basic characteristics the cryptic and symbolic use of words and phrases.[227]

G. Beasley-Murray agrees with Mounce and thinks that chapter 11 provides one of the clearest examples of the way in which John, the Christian prophet, utilizes the pictures and traditions of contemporary Jewish prophecy in order to convey his Christian message.[228]

Alan Johnson agrees with Mounce and Beasley-Murray. The Jewish view suffers from its inability to relate chapter 11 to the context of chapter 10, to the parallelism with the seal interlude (ch. 7), to the ministry and significance of the two witnesses, and to the further chapters in Revelation (esp. chs. 12—13). Therefore, it is better to understand chapter 11 as referring to the whole Christian community. I will follow this last interpretation.[229]

The opening two verses of chapter 11 convey a little prophecy complete in itself. The prophet is told to measure off the Temple at Jerusalem and its worshipers in order that both may be protected in the coming time of trial. The outer court of the Temple and the city itself are not to be measured, for they are given to the Gentiles for destruction.

If we interpret this as a Christian prophecy, then we see that Revelation is concerned primarily with the Christian church and the Jerusalem that comes down from heaven and not with the fortunes of the Jewish nation and its earthly capital city of Jerusalem. Whatever this prophecy may have meant to a non-Christian Jewish prophet, it is certain that John wishes us to interpret chapter 11 symbolically.[230]

History has shown that the belief, frequently expressed by the Jews, that Jerusalem and its Temple could not be taken by Gentile oppressors was false. At the very time when John wrote this book, the city of Jerusalem and the Temple lay in ruins.

In contrast to this view, John was certain—and he repeats it in many ways—that the church of Christ is indestructible. God Himself will preserve it in face of the violent onslaughts of people who would blot it out from existence. This is surely what this little prophecy in chapter 11 is intended by John to convey. It is not a promise that the Christian church will be preserved from suffering. But it is an assurance that the Lord's people can never perish. In face of this overwhelming pressure from adversaries, this is an important assurance for Christians to receive. [231]

(1) The measuring of the Temple (11:1-2)—the security of the church

In verse 1 John the prophet becomes actively involved in the vision. He is commanded to measure the Temple proper, including the various adjacent courts, the altar, and "those who worship there."[232]

(a) The Christian community preserved against spiritual danger (v. 1)

The biblical prophets commonly employed symbolic actions to dramatize their message. The measuring of the Temple in this context refers to preserving or protecting in time of peril (2 Sam. 8:2). With this in mind, John is told to measure, or seal, the Temple off for protection. The Temple, altar (of burnt offering), and those who worship are to be understood as referring to the faithful people of God, the new Israel (compare 1 Cor. 3:16).[233]

For John, the preservation symbolized by the measuring of the Temple is not security against physical suffering and death but against spiritual danger. This corresponds to the sealing of 7:1-8 which did not protect the Christians from physical death but ensured their entrance into the heavenly kingdom. This interpretation understands the Temple to stand for the church, the people of God, as in 1 Corinthians 3:16-17; 2 Corinthians 6:16; and Ephesians 2:19-22.[234]

In particular, the Temple represents the church in the Great Tribulation. It stands for the messianic community of both Jews and Gentiles, comparable to the symbol of the woman in chapter 12.[235]

The "altar," in a literal sense refers to the huge stone altar of sacrifice in the court of the priests. "Those who worship there" would indicate the priests and others in the three inner courts (the court of the priests, the court of Israel, the court of women). In a symbolic sense the worshipers represent the true servants of God. The measuring symbolizes their recognition, protection, and acceptance by God.[236]

(b) The limitation of pagan persecution of the Christians (11:2)

According to verse 2, the Gentiles (pagans) are permitted to touch the "outer court" (NIV) and to trample on the "holy city" for a limited time ("forty-two months"). However, they are not able to destroy the church because the inner sanctuary is measured or protected.[237]

From another perspective, the distinction between the inner sanctuary and the outer court is a way of pointing out the limitations placed upon pagan hostility. The pagans may physically kill off the witnessing church because in verse 7 the two witnesses are killed. But the pagans cannot touch the real source of the life of the church because the two witnesses are raised and ascend to heaven (vv. 11-12).[238]

Likewise, the church is to be oppressed and profaned by the beast out of the abyss (v. 7), but it will not be destroyed. To what extent its victory will be a triumph in death or victory during its continued existence on earth is not clear. In either case, the promise of Jesus in Matthew 16:18, "the powers of the underworld shall never overthrow it" (Williams) is carried through.[239]

Verse 2 states that the nations will "trample on the holy city for 42 months" (NIV). Opinion varies as to the literal or the symbolic significance of the term "the holy city." The more literal viewpoint sees "the holy city" as the earthly city of Jerusalem.[240]

(c) The holy city as the church (11:2)

Since Jerusalem was destroyed in AD 70, and since Revelation was written about AD 95, the more literalistic interpreters hold two views about the meaning of this reference to the city. Some believe that it refers to the rebuilt city and Temple during the future tribulation period. Others see the city as a representative or symbolic reference to the Jewish people, without any special implication of a literal city or Temple.

For Alan Johnson, it is far more in keeping with the emphasis of the whole book and of these chapters in particular to state that in the mind of John "the holy city," like the Temple, refers to the church. In fact, the expression "holy city" consistently means the community of those faithful to Jesus Christ. It is composed of believing Jews and Gentiles (21:2,10; 22:19; compare 3:12; 20:9). The vision of the future holy city (chs. 21—22) describes the condition of the city when she has completed her great ordeal and is finally delivered from the great deceiver. The reference in verse 2 is to the people as they must first endure the trampling of the pagan nations for "42 months."[241]

The trampling could metaphorically indicate defilement and apostasy. The evidence indicates that it probably means persecution in this context.[242]

(d) The two periods within the forty-two months (11:2)

The time designation of forty-two months (three-and-a-half years) in verse 2 became a conventional symbol for a limited period of time during which evil would be allowed free reign (compare Dan. 7:25; 12:7). For example, Daniel 9:27 speaks of a "week." The context makes it clear that this is a week of years (seven years). This "week" is divided in half (three-and-a-half years for each division). Daniel 7:25 refers to these half weeks of years as "a time, times, and half a time." Early interpretation, followed by early Protestant commentators, referred to this as the period of the reign of the Antichrist.[243]

In Daniel 12:7 the identical expression refers to the period "when the power of the holy people has been finally broken" (NIV). In Daniel 12:11 the same period refers to the time of the "abomination" and defilement of the Temple. Some scholars see these references as related to the activities of Antiochus Epiphanes in the second century BC. We do know that the Jews and later the Christians believed that these events at least foreshadow, if not predict, the last years of world history under the Antichrist. Thus John had available a rich background in this imagery to use in setting forth his revelation of the last days.[244]

Some commentators follow certain early church fathers who see in 11:2-13 two periods. The first three-and-a-half years is the period of the preaching of the two witnesses (vv. 3-6). The second half of the

week is the time of bitter trial when antichrist reigns supreme
(vv. 7-10). This twofold division seems also to be supported by
Jesus' Olivet discourse. In Matthew 24 Jesus speaks of the "beginning of birth pains" (v. 8, NIV) and then of the period of "great
distress" shortly before His second coming (v. 21, NIV).[245]

Following this approach, these two periods of three-and-a-half
years are to be seen as symbolic. A symbolic approach involves a
real period, yet understands the numbers to describe the *kind* of period rather than its length. This approach is in keeping with John's
use of numbers elsewhere (compare 2:10; 4:4; 7:4). Following the
twofold division of Daniel's seventieth week of seven years, the
preaching of the two witnesses occupies the first half (vv. 3-6). The
second half (vv. 7-10) would be the time of bitter trial when the beast
reigns supreme and the fearful events of chapters 13—19 take
place.[246]

(2) *The preaching, death, resurrection, and ascension of God's two faithful witnesses (11:3-12)*

This section is quite complicated. It is stated in verse 3 that for a
period of 1,260 days (or 42 months or 3 ½ years), two witnesses are
appointed to prophesy, clothed in sackcloth. The message they are to
preach is one of repentance and coming judgment, as suggested by
the "sackcloth" (compare Jer. 4:8; 6:26; Jonah 3:5).[247]

(a) The identity of the two witnesses (vv. 3-4)

Who are the witnesses? For the background of these witnesses,
we go to several Old Testament passages. In verse 4 we are reminded of Zechariah's identification of the "two olive trees" (4:3).
There "the olive trees represent the channels through which God
supplies His power for work to be done." John also sees two lampstands. The lampstands "symbolize the channels through which the
might of God is to work" (compare 1:20; 2:1). Note that these two
witnesses stand in close proximity to the Almighty Creator, "the
Lord of the earth" (v. 4). These witnesses symbolize the Christian
witness in the intense period at the end of the age (v. 3).[248]

But there is more Old Testament background. The descriptions of
the witnesses' deeds in verse 5-6 are dramatic. The witnesses have
fire issuing from their mouths to consume their enemies. They have
power to shut up the sky so that no rain will fall. In addition, they
have power to turn water into blood and strike the earth with every
kind of plague. These statements show that Moses and Elijah are in

mind. The last paragraph of the Old Testament contains the prophecy that Elijah will return among men before the end comes (Mal. 4:5-6).

These two witnesses who are in touch with God have phenomenal power. Like Elijah, they have power to withhold rain (v. 6*a*; compare 1 Kings 17:1; Luke 4:25; Jas. 5:17). Like Moses they have power to bring plagues upon the earth (v. 6*b*; compare Ex. 7:20). John, of course, has adapted the Old Testament background to convey the new Christian meaning.[249]

It appears that the two witnesses represent those in the church who are specially called, like John, to bear prophetic witness to Christ especially during the last intense period of history. They also represent those Christian prophets who will be martyred by the beast.[250]

Johnson contends that these two witnesses are representative of *many* individuals. Note that they are never seen as individuals but do everything together. They prophesy together, suffer together, are killed together, are raised together, and ascend together. This stresses their collective aspect. In verse 7 the beast "makes war on them." This is strange if they are merely two individuals. Verse 9 states that people throughout the whole world gaze at their dead bodies. This would be unlikely if only two individuals are involved. In verse 4 they are described as two "lampstands." This is a figure applied in chapters 1 and 2 to local churches comprised of many individuals.[251]

Thus this Christian vision yields the meaning that the function of the prophecy expected of Moses and Elijah at the end times is given to special representatives and to the church at large. Christian prophecy is the task of the entire Christian community in the time of trial.

(b) The resources of the two witnesses (vv. 5-6)

In verse 5 God gives the witnesses immunity from destruction until they complete their proclamation of God's saving work in Christ. This assures the people of God that no matter how many of its chosen saints are oppressed and killed, God's witness to Christ will continue until His purposes are fulfilled.[252] The purpose of John's portrayal at this point may be to express in dramatic terms "the truth that God's servants in the Christian era have just as great resources as did Moses and Elijah in the Old Testament period."

(c) The identity of the beast (v. 7)

Because of the testimony borne by the church, the beast from the abyss wages war on the two witnesses (v. 7). No statement is given to explain who the beast is. He is mentioned without introduction in verse 7.

The idea of the beast goes back to Daniel 7 where a succession of great world empires is symbolized by the appearance of four fierce beasts. In the Olivet discourse, Jesus foretold the coming of an eschatological figure called the "desolating sacrilege" (Mark 13:14; Matt. 24:14).[253]

Paul also was familiar with a similar figure whom he called "the man of lawlessness" because he defied the laws of God and man and claimed absolute sovereignty for himself (2 Thess. 2:3-4). This eschatological figure will be satanically inspired and will have as his chief end the turning of people from Christ that they might perish (vv. 9-10).[254]

The beast or Antichrist is a central figure in Revelation. He is primarily an eschatological figure of the last days in whom will be concentrated the centuries-long hostility to God manifested in the history of godless nations. This hostility is foreshadowed in Rome and its emperor and also in Antiochus Epiphanes in the second century before Christ. In the present passage, the beast represents every hostile evil power that oppresses and persecutes God's people. However, its primary reference is to the evil eschatological figure at the end of the age. Since the witnesses represent the church, it is probably the final conflict, which is mentioned in greater detail later (13:1 *ff.*), that John has in mind in verse 7.[255]

(d) The identity of the great city (v. 8)

The war which the beast wages has fearful results. The witnesses will be killed (v .7). Their corpses will lie in the streets of the great city, and the people will gloat over them (vv. 8-10).

The description of the great city is that it is "allegorically called Sodom and Egypt [which is the place], where their Lord was crucified" (v. 8). From a more narrow perspective, this city is Jerusalem (compare Isa. 1:10; Deut. 32:32; Jer. 23:14; Ezek. 16:46,49). By a single phrase the ancient city of God, Jerusalem, is associated with two evil places. The first is that city of greatest moral degradation, Sodom. The second is that place of oppression, slavery, and divine resistance to God's will, which is Egypt. As Jerusalem crucified Christ, so the godless world murders Christ's followers.

George Ladd contends that the fact that the city is the place where the Lord was crucified seems to point to a literal city. This prophecy, according to Ladd, could have no relevance for John's own day because in the Jewish war of AD 66-70, the city had been utterly razed and the Temple destroyed. Jerusalem had ceased to be a Jewish center. Ladd contends that here Jerusalem is not merely mentioned as an empty theoretical metaphor. In some way or another the earthly, geohistorical Jerusalem will have its place in the history of the last days.[256]

From a broader perspective, most commentators believe that John also has Rome in mind when speaking of the great city. If this is true, then there are at least five places which John sees as one—Babylon, Sodom, Egypt, Jerusalem, and Rome. This one great city represents, to the spiritually discerning, all places opposed to God and to the witness of His servants—Sodom, Tyre, Egypt, Babylon, Nineveh, Rome, and so forth.[257]

Wherever God is opposed and His servants are harassed and killed, there is the great city. It is the transhistorical city of Satan, the great mother of prostitutes (compare 17:1 *ff.*). What can happen to God's witnesses in any place is what has already happened to their Lord in Jerusalem. Bunyan's city, called "Vanity Fair," approaches this idea. John, however, uses actual historical places where this great transhistorical city found its manifestation.[258]

(e) The hostility of the world (vv. 8-10).

According to verses 8-10, the "dead" witnesses were left exposed in the street of Jerusalem. They were refused burial, and pagan people (Jews and Gentiles) rejoiced for three and a half days and exchanged gifts. The pagans rejoiced because the witnesses who once brought conviction and a sense of guilt upon the non-Christian world were now dead (vv. 8-10).[259]

In fact, a holiday is declared with merrymaking and the exchange of gifts. Lindsey calls this a "Satanic Christmas" celebration.[260]

The world has always shown hostility to the message of God. This is a truth which ought to give some concern to the contemporary church existing for the most part rather comfortably in a world of increasing wickedness. When the church *is* the church, she always provokes decision, causing some to turn to Christ and others to turn against Christ and His people (compare Acts 9:4 *ff.*; 2 Cor. 2:15-16).[261]

(f) The meaning of the breath of life (vv. 11-12).

But the rejoicing of the enemies of God is premature! Just when they think they have triumphed over the witnesses (the church), "a breath of life from God entered them, and they stood up on their feet, and great fear fell on those who saw them" (v. 11).[262]

John thus prophesies that God will resurrect His witnesses in the sight of their enemies and call them up to heaven (v. 12). The end of the church's passion, like that of its Lord, is resurrection. The resurrection of the church is a sure indication that God possesses the ultimate authority over life and death.[263]

This language about the breath of God breathed into the saints enabling them to stand on their feet comes from Ezekiel 37:10. In Ezekiel it refers to the spiritual quickening of the nation of Israel. In this passage, therefore, the resurrection of the dead church could signify revival so tremendous as to awe the world which witnesses it.

This breath of God could also relate to the resurrection-transformation of Christ's people at His coming as described in 1 Thessalonians 4:16-17 and 1 Corinthians 15.

The vindication of God's saints and their triumph over the forces of the Antichrist is complete. They will enter with their Lord into His victorious kingdom.

(3) A devastating earthquake and the great revival (11:13)

In verse 13 we read that, as the two witnesses are taken up into heaven, a great earthquake levels a portion of the city. It kills 7,000 people and forces the rest to acknowledge the transcendent majesty of God. Ezekiel 38:19-20 also predicted a great earthquake which would precede the end. Zechariah said that the Mount of Olives would be split in two from east to west when God returns to crush His enemies (Zech. 14:15). The population of the city is thought to be about 100,000. This indicates that the earthquake is a limited catastrophe.

The result of the resurrection and ascension of the two martyrs and of the following earthquake was the conversion of those who were not killed. Those who survive the devastation of the earthquake turn and give "glory to the God of heaven" (v. 13). This expression is an idiomatic phrase denoting repentance. The meaning is to pay the honor due to God by changing one's attitude and confessing, speaking, or doing, the truth as the truth of God (compare 16:9; John 9:24; Josh. 7:19; Jer. 13:16).[264]

Verse 13 also shows that, even in the midst of judgment, God is active in the world to save those who repent. If there is such hope in the terrible time of final judgment, how much more now! God has not abandoned the human race, regardless of the recurring waves of unbelief. Neither should we![265]

According to Ladd, verse 13 should be seen as a symbolic way of describing the final conversion of the Jewish people as a whole.

3. The Seventh Trumpet, the Time of the End (11:14-19)—The Third Woe

John has concluded his interlude about the angel and the little book and the measuring of the Temple (10:1 to 11:13). He states that the third woe (seventh trumpet) is soon to come. When the voice says, "the third woe is soon to come" (11:14), he means that it will begin with the seventh trumpet.[266]

a. THE CONTENT OF THE SEVENTH TRUMPET (11:15)

But when the seventh angel sounds his trumpet, no woe immediately falls upon people (v. 15). The woe involved in the seventh trumpet really consists of the seven bowls of 16:1-21. We remember that the seventh seal of 8:1 had of itself no specific content. Instead, John describes the sounding of the seven trumpets (8:1 to 9:20). We are forced to conclude that the seven trumpets constitute the seventh seal. In the same way, the seventh trumpet, which is the third woe, contains no plague or woe. We must conclude that the content of the seven bowls (16:1-21) constitutes the woe of the seventh trumpet.

b. THE VISION OF THE ESTABLISHMENT OF THE KINGDOM OF GOD (11:15)

Instead of a woe or plague, John hears loud voices in heaven (v. 15). John is now back in heaven, where, after the blowing of the seventh trumpet, he hears "loud voices" saying, "the kingdom of the world has become the kingdom of our Lord and of his Christ, and he shall reign for ever and ever."[267]

The kingdom of the world has been under the Antichrist. But now the rule of God "has come" and is being exercised over the kingdoms of this world. John sees this as a reality in heaven which is soon to take place on earth. Note that in the fullness of the kingdom both the Lord God and His Christ, the Anointed, shall reign for all eternity (compare Dan.2:44; 7:27; 1 Cor. 15:24-28).

Verse 15 gives us the central theme of Revelation which is the establishment of the kingdom of God (1:6,9; 5:10; 11:17; 12:10; 19:6; 20:4; 22:5). This kingdom involves the millennial kingdom and its blending into the eternal kingdom (chs. 20-22). The image of the kingdom of God suggests the transference of the world empire that was once dominated by a usurping power. It has at last passed into the hands of its true Owner and King. The present rulers are Satan, the beast, and the false prophet. The announcement of the reign of the King is made here. However, the final breaking of the enemies' hold over the world does not occur until the return of Christ (19:11 *ff*.).[268]

John does not distinguish here between the millennial kingdom of Christ and the eternal kingdom of the Father as Paul did (1 Cor. 15:24-28). This should be viewed as a difference merely of detail and emphasis, not of basic theology. Furthermore, in John's view this world becomes the arena for the manifestation of God's kingdom. At this point the emphasis is on the future, visible establishment of God's kingdom. However, in John's mind, that same kingdom is in a real sense present now, and he is participating in it (1:9).[269]

c. THE HYMN OF THANKSGIVING (11:16-17)

The proclamation of the angelic chorus is then followed by a "hymn of thanksgiving" from the prostrated twenty-four elders (v. 16). Their hymn in verse 17 seems to be an elaboration of verse 15. Several attributes of God are singled out for praise. First they give thanks to God for His omnipotence—"God Almighty." Secondly, note that they give thanks for His present reign—not for His future reign. They also recognize that God's rule has always been "who art and who wast."[270]

d. THE VISITATION OF GOD'S WRATH (11:18)

In verse 18 we read that the nations raged. In the last days, the Gentiles will make one last assault against God's power. But God's wrath came and His power meant the overthrow of the pagans (compare Ps. 2:1 *ff*.; Rev. 16:13 *ff*.; 20:8-10). God's kingdom can never be

completely established so long as hostile nations are allowed to defy
His rule and to oppress His people. The visitation of God's wrath is
absolutely essential to the establishing of His gracious rule in the
world.[271]

e. THE VISION OF THE FINAL COMMUNION WITH GOD (11:19)

Finally John is given a glimpse into the inner shrine of the Temple
(v. 19). The ark of His covenant is seen within the Temple. Under the
old covenant, the way into the holiest was barred to all except the
high priest. Now full and immediate access for all, as well as a perfect redemption, has been secured by Christ's death (Heb. 9:11-12;
10:19-22).[272]

This present access to the inner temple, however, is only a spiritual fact, not yet a visible reality. Through Christ's death, all people
now have access in the Spirit to God through Christ. But we remain
in our mortal bodies on earth, while God's temple is located in
heaven. The point of the present passage is to present a symbolic
representation of the opening up of the presence of God in the last
day. This is an encouragement and grants assurance. The fullest
communion will take place in the final stage of heaven. The opening
up of the temple in this final sense does not occur until chapters
21—22. In heaven we shall "see his face" (22:4). The entire scene is a
gracious reminder that God will faithfully carry out His covenant
promises and destroy the enemies of his People.[273]

f. JOHN, CELEBRATION, AND HANDEL'S *MESSIAH*

The music and sounds of celebration are the major ingredients in
the Old Testament Book of Psalms. Indeed, many of the psalms con-
tain instructions to the instrumentalists. Revelation is the musical
book of the New Testament. Very large parts of chapters 4—22 are
pure celebration.[274]

Revelation 11:15-17,19 is a part of the music and sounds of this
celebration. In fact Handel has put an unforgettable melody with
these words in his *Messiah*. All of us remember: "The kingdom of
this world shall become. . . ." in the *Messiah*. John is caught up by the
vision of the ark, the very presence of Almighty God. Then he attempts to tell of the sights and sounds which are beyond imagination: "flashes of lightning, voices, peals of thunder, an earthquake,
and heavy hail" (v. 19). As with the seven seals (8:5) and the coming
bowls (16:18), so now, the seventh trumpet issues in "flashes of
lightning," and so forth. There is more to come.[275]

4. An Interlude (12:1 to 14:5)—Conflict Between the Church and the Powers of Evil

Chapter 12 marks a major division in Revelation. Before the seven last plagues of chapter 16, in which the wrath of God is finished (15:1), John turns aside to explain the underlying cause for the hostility about to break upon the church. During His earthly ministry, Jesus had warned, "If they persecuted me, they will persecute you" (John 15:20). It is the agelong conflict between God and Satan which accounts for the persecution the church is to experience.

Although the crucial battle was won when Christ arose victorious over death and the grave, the adversary continues his struggle. Cast down from heaven, and knowing that his time is short (v. 12), Satan turns in rage against the faithful Christians who "keep the commandments of God, and hold the testimony of Jesus" (v. 17, ASV). By laying bare the root cause of persecution, John encourages believers to hold fast in the coming tribulation. The death struggle of a defeated foe will bring severe tribulation, but the outcome is certain—God will come in judgment to destroy His enemies (chs. 15—19) and reward his own (chs. 20—22). The stage is set for the final confrontation. Chapters 12—14 introduce the actors who play the major roles.[276]

Much has been written about the sources thought to lie behind the visions of chapter 12. In the time of John, stories circulated about a child who was attacked by the evil one and yet was victorious. The basic plot states that a usurper who was doomed to be killed by a yet unborn prince plots to succeed to the throne by killing the royal seed at birth. The prince is miraculously snatched from the usurper's clutches and hidden away until he is old enough to kill the usurper and claim the kingdom which rightfully belongs to him.[277]

The Babylonian version told of the overthrow of the wicked sea monster Tiamat by the young god of heaven Marduk, the child of Damkina, the earth mother. The Persian version spoke of the conflict between the good god Ahura Mazda and the evil Ahriman to secure the "kingly glory." The Egyptians told of the birth of the sun god Horus, whose mother was pursued by the red dragon Typon or Set and how Horus finally slew the dragon.[278]

On a visit to the Greek island of Delos, I heard a dramatic presentation of the Greek version of this story. The Greek account tells of the birth of Apollo. When Apollo's mother, the goddess Leto, reached the time of her delivery, she was pursued by the dragon Python who sought to kill both her and her unborn child. Only the tiny island of Delos welcomed the mother, where she gave birth to the god Apollo. Four days after his birth, Apollo found Python at Parnassus and killed him in his Delphic cave.[279]

Obviously this tradition had become international, and it embodied the universal longing for a deliverer who would redeem humanity from the powers that threaten it.

The Old Testament has reference to the birth of the Messiah through a messianic community (Isa. 9:6-7; Mic. 5:2). In the Old Testament, the image of a woman is frequently associated with Israel, Zion, or Jerusalem.

Even though John perhaps obtained some of his imagery from the thought world of his day, he is a literary artist. Under divine inspiration, John constructs a Christian scenario which is distinctly his own. John Court states that John's work is a deliberate and highly skillful achievement and not simply the unconscious product of the influences in a particular environment. Here we have that rare situation of a creative artist with the ability to communicate effectively. He can translate his Christian experience and the revelation from God into vivid and unforgettable words and images.[280]

John declares that the hope of the world expressed in these universal stories is fulfilled in Jesus. All other names under heaven in which people have trusted are eliminated as the true source of salvation and deliverance. Regardless of the sources or allusions, John reinterprets the older stories and presents a distinctively Christian view of history in the imagery of the woman and her child.[281]

John thoroughly baptizes any material he draws upon into the Christian faith for his specific purpose. Under the Spirit's guidance, he uses his intellectual resources to the glory of God.[282]

a. The Dragon, the Woman, and the Male Child (12:1-6)

The first vision of this interlude is pictured in dramatic colors. John sees a pregnant woman, "clothed with the sun, with the moon under her feet" (v. 1) wearing a victor's crown. John calls the sight a "great sign" (v. 1, ASV). This shows that the woman is more than a mere woman. Rather, she signifies something. John generally uses "sign" to refer to a miraculous event or object (John 2:11,18; Rev. 12:1,3; 13:13-14; 15:1).[283]

The vision completely transcends the usual categories of time and space. It is not meant to be a foretelling of the details of history but a representation of the struggle in the spiritual world which lies behind history.[284]

The most obvious interpretation of this sign of the woman in childbirth is that this is a flashback vision of the event of the birth of Christ. John shows in a dramatic fashion that the birth of Jesus in Bethlehem was a moment of cosmic significance. Herod's attempt to destroy the infant Jesus was a historical event that is overshadowed by a greater search and the intention of a more ominous foe than Herod the Great. The birth of the Messiah is represented in verses 2 and 5, but there is no room in the story for His life and ministry. He is suddenly caught up to heaven (v. 5).[285]

(1) The woman as a symbol of the covenant community giving birth to Christ (12:1-2)

Some state that the woman is an actual person (for example, Mary). The evidence, however, clearly shows that she, like the woman in chapter 17, has symbolic significance.[286]

The context indicates that the woman under attack represents a continuous entity from the birth of Christ until at least John's day or later. This shows that the identity in the author's mind must be the believing covenant-messianic community. This group would include the early messianic community. Under John the Baptist's ministry, this group was separated from the larger Jewish community to be the people prepared for the Lord (Mark 1:2-3). Later this group merged into the new community of Christ's disciples called the church, or the new Israel, composed of both Jews and Gentiles. Thus we can understand the woman, in a broad sense, as the ideal Zion, the heavenly representative of the people of God (v. 1). It should be noted that the church viewed as a woman is found elsewhere in the New Testament (2 Cor. 11:2; Eph. 5:25-27,32).[287]

(2) The red dragon or Satan (12:3-4)

In the vision of verse 3, John is apparently standing on earth and beholds the struggle in heaven against the backdrop of the sky. Here we have a description of the great red dragon. In verse 9 this dragon is further identified as "that ancient serpent, who is called the Devil and Satan." This is obviously a picture which represents a spiritual being as though he were a fierce sea monster. The dragon is portrayed in majestic scale with his seven heads. He is something like one of the hydra monsters of Greek mythology and therefore diffi-cult to destroy.[288]

The idea of a dragon as the embodiment of evil is found in the Old Testament references to leviathan, Rahab, behemoth, and to a fear-ful sea monster (compare Job 7:12; Pss. 74:14; 89:10; Isa. 27:1; 51:9; Ezek. 32:2). The seven heads crowned with seven diadems or crowns suggest the great degree of power which the dragon was allowed to exercise. The ten horns go back to Daniel 7 and are sym-bolic of Satan's great might.[289]

All of these symbols portray Satan's great power as the god of this age. In verse 4 the dragon is described as such a colossal creature that with one sweep of his tail he can brush a third of the stars out of their natural position. John is describing spiritual realities in vivid dramatic terms.[290]

Satan is shown in verse 4 as placing himself before the woman, expecting certain victory over the messianic child. Through this im-age, the church shows her awareness that Satan is always threaten-ing the purposes of God within history. The greatest attempt to devour the child must certainly be the crucifixion.[291]

(3) The frustration of Satan's attack on Christ and the church (12:5-6)

In verse 5 John says that the child is caught up to God and to His throne. This is John's vivid way of asserting the victory of God's anointed Messiah over every satanic effort to destroy Him. The mes-sianic child comes, finishes His mission, is delivered from the dragon, and is enthroned in heaven.[292]

In verse 6 we see the dragon, frustrated in his efforts to destroy the Messiah, turning on the Messiah's mother—the heavenly woman. But the dragon's efforts again were in vain. God protected and preserved the woman even as He had saved His Messiah, the Anointed One. In the wilderness, the woman was protected for 1,260 days.[293]

Most scholars understand the wilderness symbolically as the place of safety, discipline, and testing. This view is preferable be-cause of the highly symbolic nature of the whole chapter, the sym-bolic use of "desert" in 17:3 (Williams), and the parallelism with the Exodus.[294]

Here again we meet the symbolic number of three and a half years which represents the period of evil during which Satan tries to frustrate the purposes of God. This particularly refers to the last days of history. This verse asserts that even in the time of most severe trouble, God will preserve the heavenly woman. This in turn includes the idea that He will preserve His church on earth.[295]

b. WAR IN HEAVEN (12:7-12)

(1) The defeat of Satan in heaven (12:7-9)

In verse 7 John reports a war in heaven between Michael and his angels and the dragon with his angels. It is an all-out attempt on the part of Satan to regain his position in the presence of God. The archangel Michael, not the Messiah, wars against Satan in this final struggle. Michael is noted elsewhere in the Old and New Testament. In Jude 9 he is identified as the archangel who contends with the devil.[296]

Verse 8 reports that Satan and his forces are defeated in battle and must forfeit their place in heaven. Until this time, Satan in some sense had a place in heaven. Satan was thought to dwell in the lower sphere of heaven (compare Eph. 2:2; Luke 10:18). He had access to God's presence and is described as the chief foe of the saints, "the accuser of our brethren," verse 10 (compare Job 1:6 *ff.*; Zech. 3:1 *ff.*).[297]

In this passage, Michael is represented as the defender of God's people as a whole against the evil power of Satan. The single intent of this passage is to assure the people who will meet satanic evil on earth that it is really a defeated power, however contrary this defeat might seem to human experience.[298]

Verse 9 points out that Satan is thrown down to earth and his angels are thrown down with him. The ancient serpent who tempted Eve with lies about God (Gen. 3:1 *ff.*) is in John's mind the same individual as "the Devil and Satan."[299]

Paul in Ephesians 2:2 called Satan "the prince of the power of the air" and his angels were described as "spiritual hosts of wickedness in the heavenly places" (Eph. 6:12). This passage describes a victory over Satan by virtue of which his accusations against God's people lose their force (v. 10). A parallel saying is found on the lips of Jesus: "I saw Satan fall like lightning from heaven" (Luke 10:18).[300]

Revelation 12:11 clearly shows that the victory over Satan which John has described in dramatic terms actually was accomplished in history at the cross. The shed blood of Christ is the real means of victory over Satan.[301]

(2) The significance of the defeat of Satan at the cross and in the martyrs' testimony (12:10-11)

The song (vv. 10-12) is another dramatic flashback. This chorale ponders the meaning of the cross of Christ. We now know that in the death and resurrection of Jesus Christ more is involved than the fulfillment of the righteousness of the law or the expression of holy love. Both are true, but now we know of a great battle that has been waged at the cross. Now we see that Christ is the triumphant Lamb who has won the cosmic battle over the devil at the cross. A terrific battle, of which humanity was unaware, was under way at the cross.[302]

The secondary means of victory in verse 11 is the word of the martyrs' testimony. This testimony refers to their witness to the saving power of the blood of Christ. The background of martyrdom stands behind these words. The martyrs love their Lord more than life itself and willingly suffer death rather than deny Christ. Jesus said, "He who endures to the end [that is to the point of death] will be saved" (Matt. 24:13).[303]

(3) Satan's last convulsive attacks (12:12)

In verse 12 the defeat of Satan is described as meaning woe to people who inhabit the earth and who sail on the sea. While Satan has been overthrown, he has not yet been destroyed. He knows that his final doom is sealed, but he is still allowed to exercise great power. Satan is still able to attack the saints on earth and bring them to martyrdom. By this he hopes to conquer them and compel them to deny their faith. This is the background for the last convulsive effort of Satan to crush the church and destroy the saints. Even though he knows his power is broken and his doom sure and soon, he attacks the church with great wrath.[304]

Lindsey makes the point that the greatest weapon a believer ultimately has against Satan is that he is prepared for death. The word *martyr* actually means in the original Greek language "a witness." To see how martyrs went to their deaths with songs of praise to God on their lips has strengthened many Christian people.[305]

c. WAR ON EARTH (12:13-17)

(1) Satan's attack on the church (12:13)

In verse 13 John resumes the story of Satan's effort to destroy the heavenly woman—the ideal people of God. In verse 6 we saw that the woman had fled from the dragon into the wilderness where she was preserved for three and a half years. Now, Satan pursues her into the wilderness and renews his efforts to destroy her.[306]

(2) God's care for the church (12:14)

The wings of the great eagle (v. 14) given to the woman is John's way of assuring the church members of their ultimate safety, even in the face of martyrdom. The reference to the wings of the eagle introduces imagery borrowed from the Exodus account. There Israel was pursued by the dragon in the person of Pharaoh: "You have seen what I did to the Egyptians, and how I bore you on eagles' wings and brought you to myself" (Ex. 19:4). As God's people were delivered from the enemy by their journey into the Sinai desert, so God's present people will be preserved miraculously from destruction (compare Deut. 32:10-12; Isa. 40:31).[307]

The same forty-two months or three and a half years is used in verse 14 to indicate the last terrible time of unparalleled persecution and martyrdom.

(3) Satan's second attack on the church and God's rescue (12:15-16)

Next, in verses 15-16, the serpent spews a floodlike river of water out of his mouth to engulf and drown the woman. The water imagery symbolizes destruction by an enemy (Pss. 32:6; 69:1-2; 124:2-5; Nah.1:8) or calamity (Ps. 18:4). As the desert soil absorbs the flash torrent, so the covenant people will be helped by God and preserved from utter destruction (Isa. 26:20; 42:15; 43:2; 50:2). The dragon-inspired Egyptians of old were swallowed by the earth: "Thou didst stretch out thy right hand, the earth swallowed them" (Ex. 15:12). In similar fashion, the messianic community will be delivered by God's power. Whatever specific events were happening to Christians in Asia in John's day would not exhaust the continuing significance of the passage.[308]

(4) Satan's third attack on the Christians (12:17)

In verse 17 the dragon is angry with the woman and the rest of her offspring. The woman has already given birth to the Messiah whom Satan was unable to destroy. The woman has other children against whom Satan now directs his wrath. These are actual Christians who constitute the empirical church on earth. John turns from the ideal to the actual. The spiritual conflict in the heavens is the backdrop for the actual struggle on earth between the church and the Antichrist.[309]

The close identification of the seed of the woman as, first of all,

Jesus and then also those who have become His brethren through faith agrees with other New Testament teaching (Matt. 25:20; Heb. 2:11-12). While Satan cannot prevail against the Christian community itself, he can wage war on certain of its members who are called on to witness to their Lord by obedience even unto death. The church, then, is paradoxically both invulnerable (the woman) and vulnerable (her children) (compare Luke 21:16-18).[310]

In order to fulfill this purpose of directing wrath against the church on earth, the dragon now takes his stand on the seashore so that he may call forth from the deep the beast who will be his primary instrument in the last persecution (v. 17).[311]

(5) Lindsey's view of the rescue

Lindsey sees the two wings of the great eagle (v. 14) as indicating a plane which will fly the group of Jewish believers to a protective place in the wilderness. He thinks this wilderness refers to the natural fortress of Petra, the ancient "City of Rock" in the Jordanian wilderness south of the Dead Sea.

Since the eagle is the national symbol of the United States, Lindsey thinks that it is possible that this refers to an airlift from the U.S. Sixth Fleet in the Mediterranean.

Lindsey further suggests that since the Antichrist is not going to stand for these Jewish believers getting out from under his dominion, he will send a flood of pursuers after them. These will probably be soldiers from the armies controlled by the Antichrist. As this great army seeks to trap and annihilate the believers, God will cause the earth to open up and swallow them (v. 16). The Jewish believers will not be hurt by the second death, but will live forever with God.[312]

Excursus on the Great Tribulation

At this point a look at the biblical idea of tribulation in broad perspective should be helpful. Tribulation is part of the lot of God's people in a world whose values are shaped by Satan. The tribulation may vary in intensity from era to era, but it has almost always been present to beset the Christian church somewhere in the world, just as Jesus promised.[313]

The biblical emphasis is on the fact that the intensity of Satan's effort to turn people against God will increase just before Christ comes again. In fact, that period of tribulation, usually called the Great Tribulation, is a vitally important part of the context of the second coming (7:14).[314]

We cannot put a date on the Great Tribulation. Its timing, like the hour of

Christ's coming, is hidden in the mysteries of God. The Bible does, however, tell us two things about its timing.[315]

First, the Great Tribulation will come just before Christ returns (Matt. 24:29-31). It is the last significant period of human history immediately prior to the second coming of Jesus Christ. The length of that period is not fully clear from Scripture, although there is some indication that it may last seven years. Part of the uncertainty has to do with the interpretation of the number *seven*. It often symbolizes fullness or completeness. Hence its meaning in relationship to the tribulation could be a period of time long enough for the turmoil and testing of Satan's hosts to do their full work.[316]

The seven years is sometimes divided into two periods of three and a half years. In general, it can be said that Daniel's number, "time, and times, and half a time" (12:14), "forty-two months" (11:2; 13:5), and "1260 days" (11:3; 12:6, NIV), or three-and-a-half years, can be equated chronologically with the Great Tribulation (7:14; compare 3:10). For Ladd, three and a half refers to the final outbreak of Antichrist, but the "entire course of the age" may be so described as a preview.

According to Beasley-Murray, identifying three and a half with the interim of the church era can be done (compare 12:6,13 *ff*.), but it violates John's intention. Three and a half is the period of Antichrist's "raging" and does not characterize the period from the ascension to the second coming.

Johnson, as noted in our discussion of 11:2, sees two periods of three and a half years in 11:2-3. The first three and a half years refers to the time of the two witnesses which could include the age of the church. The second three and a half years implies that, at the end of the activity of the two witnesses, there is a second three and a half years which refers to the final murderous reign of the beast (13:5,7,15).

The second thing to be understood about the timing is that we will know the Great Tribulation has arrived when the final Antichrist appears (2 Thess. 2:1-12). Persecution in biblical history is virtually always connected with an evil, influential leader.[317]

At the end of history, a vicious and powerful ruler, called "a beast" will arise (13:1). Satan will give him authority and power. For a period of three and a half years, he will ravage the people of God, exercise dictatorial powers over the earth, and demand to be worshiped in the place of the true and living God (13:1-10).

The appearance of this beast who will be a political-economic-religious dictator is the clearest mark of the Great Tribulation. No wonder John concluded his description of the beast's savagery with these words: "Here is a call for the endurance and faith of the saints" (13:10)![318]

Why would God allow such a brutal experience to batter the world He has made and the people He loves? God's first purpose in the Great Tribulation is to display His wrath. God's second purpose is to test His people.[319]

The conflict between the lordship of Jesus and the authority of Antichrist reminds us that one feature of the Great Tribulation will be its totalitarian structure. The totalitarian structure will promote a blasphemous religious system.

In order to get ready, we should be aware of three things. First, we should be aware of the way evil works. We must always have an eye on what governments are doing to throttle human rights or to resist the authority of God.

Second, we should be alert to the meaning of Christ's lordship. In the small choices of life, we must learn to put Him first. This will prepare us in case the big choice comes—the choice between the command of a beastly government and the demand that we be loyal to Jesus.

Finally, we should be assured of the powerful love of God which has seen and will see his people through.[320]

d. THE BEAST FROM THE SEA (13:1-10)

Chapter 13 continues the interlude between the sounding of the seven trumpets and the outpouring of the seven bowls. It describes the appearance of the Antichrist and his persecution of the church.

(1) The power and intelligence of the beast (13:1-2)

Although Satan is defeated, he will be allowed at the end time to wage one final convulsive warfare against the saints through the agency of the beast. This first beast comes out of the sea. He is a grotesque, ten-horned, seven-headed monster with one head mutilated by the slash of a sword. He combines characteristics of leopards, bears, and lions.(vv. 1-2).[321]

The last verse of chapter 12 pictures Satan standing by the sea as if to summon his henchmen from the troubled waters. Unable to reach the woman, he calls upon his wicked cohorts to destroy the woman's offspring. Although the vision employs references to the first century, its complete fulfillment is reserved for the final eschatological conflict.[322]

In verse 1 we see the beast rising out of the sea. Remember that he has already appeared in 11:7 as one who ascends from the bottomless pit or abyss to make war upon the two witnesses. The kinship between the beast and the dragon (Satan) is seen in the fact that both have ten horns and seven heads.[323]

In terms of dramatic imagery, the sea symbolizes the abyss which is the source of demonic powers that are opposed to God (compare 9:1; 20:1-3). This view agrees with the Old Testament images of the sea as the origin of the satanic sea monsters—the dragon, Leviathan, and Rahab (Job 26:12-13; Ps. 74:13-14; 87:4; 89:10; Isa. 27:1; 51:9). The ancient Hebrews used the sea monster images to picture the victory of the Lord of Israel over the demonic forces of evil that in various manifestations had sought to destroy the people of God. And John later foresees the final day of Christ's victory when there will "no longer [be] any sea"(NIV) or source of demonic opposition to God and his people (21:1).[324]

John describes the beast in verse 1 in words similar to those he used in 12:3 of the dragon: "He had ten horns and seven heads, with ten crowns on his horns" (NIV). Any attempt to identify the heads or horns as separate kings or kingdoms should be resisted. The image of the seven-headed monster is often used in ancient Sumerian, Babylonian, and Egyptian texts.[325]

(2) Lindsey, the ten-horned beast, and the Common Market

Lindsey contends that the beast's ten horns picture ten nations that will form a confederacy which the beast will rule during the tribulation period. When God is about to climax world history on this planet, ten nations will emerge from the ancient people and culture of the fourth empire, Rome. They will form a tight confederation that will become a sovereign political entity.

At this point, a scintillating personality will rise to world prominence and be proclaimed the head of this new confederacy. Of the ten nations that confederate, seven will come into the Common Market willingly, but three will have to be brought into the union unwillingly. This will be accomplished by the Roman leader who thereafter becomes a virtual dictator.

Lindsey affirms that one of the reasons he is convinced that we are living in the closing days of the world's history is because of the emergence of the European Common Market. He says that there is no doubt in his mind that the Common Market is the forerunner of the revived Roman Empire which the prophet Daniel spoke about with such certainty. Daniel predicted that the number of nations in the confederacy would be limited to ten. This is the very number which the Common Market has set as its goal for its "inner" membership.

According to Lindsey, Daniel also said that this confederacy would be the greatest Gentile power to ever gain control of the whole world and that it would acquire this worldwide control through its economic strength and its great leader. As of now, Europe has become the largest trading block in the world, and this is beginning to cause some alarm in the United States.

In order for there to be an emergence of this superpower in Europe which the apostle John and Daniel the prophet predicted, according to Lindsey, there must be a decline in American economic status in the world. Many world economists believe this is already happening.[326]

(3) The beast as an archetypal symbol of all types of evil (13:3-6)

Avoiding such attempts at pinpointing this passage, we should note that the beast is the eschatological Antichrist who was fore-shadowed in certain aspects of Rome and in other totalitarian states as well. John's vision grows out of the details of his own historical situation, but its complete fulfillment awaits the final unfolding of human history.[327]

In verse 1 the beast wears the name of deity upon his heads, de-manding the worship of people. This is also mentioned in verse 4. This self-deification of Antichrist has its forerunners in history. We remember Julius Caesar, Augustus, Vespasian, and Titus. In the time of John, an open claim to deity was made by government offi-cials for Domitian. They demanded that Domitian be addressed by the title, *Dominus et Deus*—Lord and God.

Johnson contends, however, that the beast is not to be identified with any one historical form of its expression or with any one institu-tional aspect of its manifestation. In other words, the beast may manifest itself as a political power, an economic power, a religious power, or a heresy (1 John 2:18,22; 4:3).[328]

The description of the beast by John has theological overtones, not just political ones. This does not exclude the possibility that there will be a final climactic appearance of the beast in history. This mani-festation may be in a person, in a political, religious, or economic system, or in a final totalitarian culture combining all of these sug-gestions. The point is that the beast cannot be limited to either the past or the future.[329]

Of crucial importance is the fact that the beast receives his power, dominion, and authority from the dragon (v. 2). This means that the beast could be a person or a system. He could be of a political, so-cial, economic, or religious nature. The beast is the person or system which cooperates with Satan. This can be done by an exaltation of itself against God's sovereignty and by setting itself up to destroy the followers of Jesus. There could also be an enticement of the fol-lowers of Jesus to become followers of Satan through deception, idolatry, blasphemy, and spiritual adultery.[330]

The description John gives of the beast from the sea in verse 2 does not describe a mere political entity, such as Rome. Rather, it describes in archetypal language the hideous, Satan-backed system of deception and idolatry that may, at any time, express itself in human systems of various kinds. At the same time, John also seems to be saying that this blasphemous reality will have a final, intense, and, for the saints, utterly devastating manifestation.[331]

Note that the beast itself, in the person of one of its heads, was slain but later revived (v. 3). This may refer to the tremendous vitality of the beast. Though wounded, he returns with increased might. This is a mixed sign of the vulnerability of this evil beast and yet also of its tenacity.[332]

This wound can also be seen as the symbol of God's wrath, which has struck a death blow to the authority of the beast (and the dragon). This death blow has been deceptively covered up. We can also see this as referring to the fact that the beast has been dealt a fatal blow by the cross of Christ and yet still has time and the ability to wage war against the saints. He appears to be alive and in full command of the scene; his blasphemies increase. What the sea beast cannot accomplish, he commissions the earth beast to do (vv. 11 *ff.*). All three—the dragon, the sea beast, and the earth beast—are in collusion to effect the deception that leads the world to worship the dragon and the sea beast and destroy all who oppose them.[333]

In one sense, we can say that the beast described here is the great theological counterpart to all that Christ represents. Johnson contends that we should see John as referring to a transhistorical reality with many human manifestations. This view would prevent us from limiting the imagery merely to the Roman Empire, one of its emperors, or to any other single future political entity.[334]

In verse 4 the emphasis is on worship. We are so made to worship some absolute power. And in the last analysis, we will give our allegiance either to the beast or to the Lamb.[335]

The beast does not want merely to exercise political power. Rather he has the objective of capturing the loyalties of people and diverting them from the worship of God. The time of the Antichrist is a struggle for the souls of people. He will manifest such mighty power that he will convince the world of the futility of resisting him (v. 4). The motivation for worship is thus not his moral greatness but the awesome power of his might. The authority he wields is the authority of Satan himself.[336]

This section is the narrative of the terrible reality of the temptation of evil, of perverse distortion, and of blasphemy. It is a tragic section in that it tells of people who are willing and even enthusiastic to follow the twisted goals of evil. These people will even worship the dragon.

(4) The intimidating power of the beast (13:4-9)

The haunting question of verse 4, "Who is able to make war with him?"(KJV), is like the cry of the intimidated person who is at the breaking point. The power of evil seems so complete and sure; how can there possibly be any other way of life? The feeling described in verse 4 of both dread and fascination in relation to the heart is conveyed in certain novels and films. We especially sense this feeling in the *Heart of Darkness* (Joseph Conrad) and in the film *Apocalypse Now*. Evil is without match, apparently, and therefore, in the face of such odds, why not give way to its demands?[337]

We know from the study of first- and twentieth-century history that John's vision is socially and psychologically accurate. We human beings are often manipulated by the show or the promise of power. The power of the demonic often looks more fierce than it really is. At this point in the narrative, we must be assured by mysterious signs, such as the wound, and the fact that the dragon was not able to conquer the woman and her son.[338]

Verse 7 points out that the beast is allowed by the sovereignty of the divine purpose to exercise a worldwide authority. It is impossible to find a fulfillment of these words in any historical situation in the Roman Empire of the first century. John looks far beyond his own horizon to a time when an antichristian power will be allowed to exercise worldwide sovereignty.[339]

(5) The call for Christian endurance (13:10)

In verse 10 John seems to be indicating that, if one is destined for captivity, he must be willing to go meekly as a Christian. Yet this resistance, which may result in captivity and even martyrdom, seems to contribute to the eventual defeat of evil. Persecution is not the last word. There is divine retribution, and the final punishment of those who kill with the sword will fit the crime. The last word is not with the persecutor.[340]

e. THE BEAST FROM THE EARTH (13:11-18)

In verse 11 John sees another ("one of a similar kind") beast rising from the earth. This second beast completes the triumvirate of evil—the dragon, the sea beast, and the land beast. The land beast is subservient to the beast from the sea and seems utterly dedicated to promoting not himself but the wounded beast from the sea. Elsewhere the land beast is called the "false prophet" (16:13; 19:20; 20:10).[341]

(1) The religious approach of the land beast

Calvin and Luther, as well as other Reformers, drawing on earlier traditions, identified this beast with the papal rule of specific popes. They had a helpful insight in seeing the beast as a present threat and not just as some entity awaiting a future manifestation. Most modern commentators identify this beast as the priesthood of the imperial cultus of Rome. In the Roman Empire, there was an imperial priesthood, particularly in Asia, whose purpose it was to promote the worship of the city of Rome and its emperor.[342]

On the other hand, Johnson proposes that the land beast can also be seen as John's way of describing the false prophets mentioned by Jesus in the Olivet discourse (Matt. 24:24; Mark 13:22). This identification is consistent with the view of the sea beast as describing not just specific political reality but the worldwide anti-God system of Satan and its manifestation in periodic, historical human Antichrists. In this view, the land beast is the antithesis to the true prophets of Christ symbolized by the two witnesses in chapter 11.[343]

(2) Lindsey and religious apostasy

Lindsey contends that the second beast will amalgamate all religious systems into one counterfeit religious system. His two horns are like a lamb (v. 11), showing that he will be a personage who will try to imitate the real Lamb, Jesus Christ.

Millions of people will fall for his deception and honestly believe that this false prophet is the long-awaited Jewish Messiah. Already, says Lindsey, the World Council of Churches is hard at work merging various religions together. By the time the beast tackles the project, liberal Judaism will probably be ready to join the World Council merger since any true doctrine about Jesus Christ will have disappeared.[344]

(3) The religious and satanic counterfeits of the land beast (13:11-14)

Apart from such conjectures, we note that if the land beast represents satanic false teaching and false prophets, their evil is intensified because of its deceptive similarity to the truth. Even though the beast is like the Lamb, in reality he is evil because "he [speaks] like a dragon" (for example, he teaches heresy, v. 11, NIV). Jesus gave a similar twofold description of false prophets in the Sermon on the Mount: "Watch out for false prophets. They come to you in sheep's clothing, but inwardly they are ferocious wolves" (Matt. 7:15, NIV).[345]

Verse 12 indicates that the single objective of the second or land beast is to capture the religious loyalties of people for the first beast or sea beast.

The second beast imitates the miracles of the true prophets in order to deceive the people into worshiping the beast (vv. 13-14). The apostle Paul spoke of the lawless one "whose coming is according to the working of Satan with all power and signs and lying wonders" (2 Thess. 2:9, ASV). Bruce calls the false prophet the Antichrist's minister of propaganda. The ability of the Satan-inspired prophets to perform deceiving miracles is attested to in numerous parts of the Bible (16:14; 19:20; Deut. 13:1-5; Matt. 7:22; 24:24; Mark 13:22; 2 Thess. 2:9). Distinguishing between the true and false prophets has always been difficult. This means that the followers of Jesus must be constantly alert to discern the spirits (1 John 4:1-3).[346]

The main point is that the false prophet, or the second beast, does not represent merely formal religion but actual satanic power. Magic played an important role in early pagan religion and was often used to deceive the gullible (Acts 16:6,16; 19:13 *ff*.). The false prophet will not only engage in pseudo-miracles but will also have power to make fire come down from heaven (vv. 13-14).[347] The reference to fire from heaven indicates that no mighty deed is too hard for these false prophets because they derive their power from the Antichrist and the dragon. Christ's true servants are not to be deceived even by any spectacular miracles the false prophets may perform. Such miracles in themselves are no evidence of the Holy Spirit. The fire in verse 13 is apparently not destructive fire but only a sign by the second beast to deceive people by his supposedly divine powers so they will worship Satan.[348]

Lindsey contends that the increase in demonic miracles in our time is just another sign of the approaching pretribulation rapture and tribulation. He further contends that the image of the beast mentioned in verses 14-15 which believers will have to worship will be erected right in the middle of the constructed Temple.[349]

(4) The beast and the occult (13:15)

Most interpreters identify the image of the beast with the statue of Caesar. They further attribute the "breath" and speaking of the image (v. 15) to the magic and ventriloquism of the imperial priests. But

John's language is much more theologically descriptive than this imperial priesthood view allows. This is not to deny that the imperial cult could be one form the worship of the second beast might take. However, the reality described here goes beyond the mere worship of a bust of Caesar.[350]

In every age the beast kills those who will not worship his image. In terms reminding us of the great golden image which Nebuchadnezzar made (Dan. 3:1-11), John describes the worldwide system of idolatry represented by the first beast and the false prophet who promotes it (vv. 16-17). John describes this reality as a blasphemous and idolatrous system that produces a violation of the first two commandments (Ex. 20:3-5).[351]

The contemporary phenomenon of the Korean religious leader Sun Myung Moon and his official interpreter and prophetess, Young Oon Kim, promote the Unification Church or the "Moonies." They embody what is interpreted by some to be an example of John's teaching about Antichrists and false prophets. Moon is being proclaimed as the "Lord of the Second Advent" by Kim and others. Many are being deceived into following him and his teaching.[352]

(5) The significance of the mark of the beast (13:16-17)

In verse 16 we see that the beast has a counter mark, which is similar to the sealing of God's people (7:3; 14:1). This mark is to be branded on the hand or forehead of all those who worship the beast. Thus we have two bands of people—those sealed for God and those marked for the beast. The mark of the beast is obviously intended to be a parody of the mark of God on the Christians.[353]

The mark is not a literal impress seal, certificate, or similar mark of identification. Rather it is John's way of symbolically describing authentic ownership and loyalty. Those who worship the beast have his mark or brand of ownership on them, as the followers of Jesus have the brand of God's possession on them. John may also have in mind here a counterpart of the Jewish practice of wearing phylacteries or black leather boxes containing Scripture passages. They are bound on the left hand and forehead with leather straps. This practice is based on Exodus 13:9,16.[354]

Lindsey contends that each person's Social Security number may be used as the mark of the beast. He indicates that there is some discussion of a plan to tattoo our Social Security number on us so it will not be lost.[355]

In verse 17 we note that the mark of the beast will serve both a religious and an economic purpose. John expects the beast, aided by the false prophet, to achieve a totalitarian rule in which he has complete control over politics, religion, and economics with the purpose of compelling the worship of all people. Other New Testament writers also apparently refer to socio-economic sanctions practiced against Christians (Rom. 15:26; Heb. 10:34).[356]

(6) The significance and meaning of the symbolic number (666) of the beast (13:18)

In verse 17 John indicates that the "mark" is "the name of the beast or number of his name." In verse 18 he reveals the number of the beast: "His number is 666" (NIV). The list of views concerning the meaning of the number is large. Taking their cue from the words "let him calculate the number of the beast," most of these interpreters have tried to play the ancient Hebrew game of gematria or its Greek equivalent. Ancient languages, including Hebrew and Greek, used standard letters from their alphabets as numerical signs. A series of letters could form a word and at the same time indicate a number. Thus a name could be converted into its corresponding number. A wall scribbling has been found in Pompeii which reads, "I love her whose number is 545."[357]

In such a context, it is not difficult to understand why most commentators have understood John's words "Let him calculate the number. . . . His number is 666" (NIV) to be an invitation to the reader to play gematria and discover the identity of the beast. This approach is not new. Irenaeus (second century) mentioned that many names of contemporary persons and entities were being offered in his day as solutions to this number mystery. Yet he cautioned against the practice and believed that the name of the Antichrist was deliberately concealed because he did not exist in John's day. Irenaeus expressly refuted the attempt of many to identify the name with any of the Roman emperors. He felt however, that the gematria approach is John's intended meaning but warns the church against endless speculations. Irenaeus's fear was not misplaced. Endless speculation has happened in the history of the interpretation of verse 18.[358]

In our time this mysterious number is interpreted as a reference to a personal Antichrist or false messiah. Mussolini, Hitler, Henry Kissinger, and Anwar Sadat have been so identified in this century. At other times the number is taken as a real numerical code that is being subtly pushed on the people of the world to prepare them for the appearance of the Antichrist. In a kind of eschatological panic, it has been claimed that products from the People's Republic of China, the United States, and other countries have been marked with 666 as their product code. It is also supposed to be a common prefix in computer programs of large department stores and international institutions. Eschatological excitement and a certain fearfulness is thus aroused in relation to computerization, identification numbers of all sorts, and even cable television.[359]

The sheer disagreement and confusion created through the years by the gematria method should have long ago warned the church that it was on the wrong track. Nowhere does John use gematria as a method. Everywhere, however, he gives symbolic significance to numbers (7 churches, seals, trumpets, bowls; 24 elders; 144,000 sealed). It is important to note that in 15:2 the victors have triumphed over three enemies: the beast, his image, and the number of his name. This suggests a symbolic significance connected with idolatry and blasphemy rather than victory over a mere puzzle of correctly identifying someone's name.[360]

John seeks to give "wisdom" and "insight" to believers as to the true identity of their enemy (v. 18, NIV). A similar use of "insight" and "wisdom" occurs in 17:9 where John calls attention to the identity of the beast ridden by the harlot. What John seems to be asking for in both cases is divine wisdom and not mathematical ingenuity! Believers need to penetrate the deception of the beast and John's reference to his number will help them to recognize his true character and identity.[361]

The number is a symbol rather than a cryptogram; 666 is the number which falls short of perfection in each of its digits. For Hendriksen it represents "failure upon failure." It is symbolic of the beast's continuing failure to accomplish his purpose. It is the trinity of imperfection. Torrance writes, "This evil trinity 666 apes the Holy Trinity 777, but always falls short and fails."[362]

The significance of the name of the beast is abundantly clear in Revelation (12:3; 13:1-6; 14:11; 17:3 ff.). Wherever there is blasphemy, there the beast's name is found. The interpretation of 666 as a symbolic number referring to the unholy trinity of evil or to the human, imperfect imitation of God rather than a cipher of a particular name has been held by a long line of conservative commentators.[363]

f. THE REDEEMED AND THE LAMB ON MOUNT ZION (14:1-5)

Chapter 14 continues the interlude between the seven trumpets and the seven bowls. In order to keep before his readers the ultimate reward of their endurance, the author of Revelation intersperses glimpses of final blessedness among his presentations of judgment. The detailed descriptions of the beast and the false prophet in chapter 13 were somber reminders of what lay in the immediate future. A note of encouragement is in order. John moves quickly beyond the storm about to break to the bright morning of eternity. There the Lamb and His followers will stand on the heavenly Zion with the anthem of redemption everywhere resounding like the roar of a mighty waterfall and the echo of thunder (14:1 *ff.*).[364]

After the awful threatening picture of the church being persecuted by the two agents of the dragon, John reveals a vision which portrays the glory which awaits the suffering saints at the second coming of Christ.[365]

(1) The meaning of Mount Zion (14:1)

John sees the Lamb standing on Mount Zion with 144,000 who have the name of the Lamb of God upon their foreheads (v. 1). Mount Zion is one of the hills upon which Jerusalem is built, and it is a term that is associated with King David and the triumph of his kingdom: "Mount Zion, in the far north, the city of the great King./Within her citadels God has shown himself a sure defense" (Ps. 48:2-3). The prophecy from Joel which Peter quoted in his sermon on the day of Pentecost concludes with a triumphant reference to Mount Zion: "It shall come to pass that all who call upon the name of the Lord shall be delivered; for in Mount Zion and in Jerusalem there shall be those who escape" (Joel 2:32).[366] Mount Zion thus symbolizes the strength and security which belong to the people of God.

The number is 144,000, about which we first heard in 7:4. The number is symbolic of the vast and complete number of God's people. It refers to all of the redeemed of God—those who have been faithful to Christ through their trials and testings. The 144,000 have on their foreheads the names of the Father and the Lamb, showing that they belong to God, not the beast.[367]

(2) The character and dedication of the people of God who learn the new song (14:2-5)

Verses 2-3 indicate that the singers about the throne are not the 144,000 but some angelic chorus. While the angels sing, only the 144,000 can "learn" the new song. This is true for they alone of earth's inhabitants have experienced God's mighty victory over the beast through their ordeal of suffering and death. The word "learn" in this context probably means to "hear deeply."[368]

John refers to the members of the redeemed host who are taught the new song as those who have not defiled themselves with women for they are chaste (v. 4). This does not refer to celibates, as some maintain, but probably to moral purity and fidelity to Christ (compare 2 Cor. 11:2). In prophetic literature, apostasy and rebellion are often expressed by the figure of adultery or unfaithfulness (compare Jer. 5:7; Hos. 2:1 ff.).[369]

It is better, then, to see the reference to purity as contrasting with the defilement of idolatry. In fact, John seems to use "defile" in this way elsewhere as referring to cult prostitution (3:4; compare 2:14,20,22).[370]

The 144,000 who follow the Lamb are also described as those who have been redeemed by Christ to be the firstfruits for God and the Lamb (v. 4b). The firstfruits are seen as the best of the crop and so John uses this term to symbolize the holiness and dedication which characterizes the redeemed (compare Deut. 26:1-11; Lev. 23:10-14; Rom. 16:15; 1 Cor. 15:20). The point is that by offering themselves to God they were set free from human entanglements and belonged solely to Him. Purchased from among men by the blood of the Lamb, they are an offering to God.[371]

In verse 5 the church, the bride of Christ, is seen as sinless and spotless by virtue of the finished work of Christ. The redeemed become like the Redeemer.[372]

5. *An Interlude (14:6-20)—Visions of Final Judgment*

Visions concerning the final judgment are given in the interlude of 14:6-20. This section contains three visions of final judgment. In Revelation, the idea that God is going to pour out His wrath upon the rebellious and unrepentant constitutes an important aspect of the character and nature of God. When the martyrs learn that God is going to express His wrath, they exult, they praise Him, and they glorify Him.

I was teaching Revelation in a large Protestant church. We came to the teaching on the holiness of God and the possibility of hell for some people. I was surprised at the reaction of some of the people. "Nobody believes in hell anymore." "We thought that this doctrine was for another day."

But Revelation states that the *holiness of God* is a very important part of His character. We live in a sentimental age. Some people would state that all people, regardless of their lives, are going on to a glorious future. But this is not biblical teaching. Universalism has other origins. Perhaps the teachings of Elizabeth Kübler-Ross about "life after life" developed out of her efforts to help older people with whom she was counseling who needed encouragement. Raymond Moody, M.D., who wrote about "life after life" experience and its pleasantness for all did admit that he primarily interviewed middle-class, churchgoing people.

In contrast, in Revelation the martyrs think that it is appropriate that there should be a time of punishment on evil people. This approval does not mean that they are expressing the kind of sadism which characterizes some ministers who seem to be happy that some people are going to hell. The people in Asia Minor had had a revelation of the cosmic Christ in nature and in conscience, and many of them had had an opportunity to hear the gospel. But they had not repented. In fact, in some cases God had disciplined them, seeking to lead them to repentance. But they were obstinate. They would not repent. Their judgment is in a final sense their own fault.

a. IMPENDING JUDGMENT ANNOUNCED (14:6-13)

(1) Call to repentance (14:6-7)—first angel (worldwide evangelism)

John turns again, in verses 6-7, to call all people to repentance in view of the coming judgment. In the midst of this judgment, another angel appears who proclaims the eternal gospel to every tribe, tongue, and people.

This is the only place in Revelation where the word *gospel* appears, and its use here is decisive. In the very middle of the scene of battle, the note of hope and good news is announced in a loud voice. It is a thrilling new possibility at the heart of darkness, at the place of broken dreams. John states that it is not too late—even now—for the world to hear and repent and turn to the Lamb. Jesus Christ the Lamb proves His power most wonderfully in His power to forgive and heal precisely at the times when the options seem closed and inopportune. This good-news interlude interrupts the darkness at the edge of the fearful judgment of God upon the earth.[373]

Jesus said that before the end, the gospel must be preached to all nations (Mark 13:10). Could this be John's way of showing the final fulfillment of Mark 13:10? Let us not fail to see how in the New Testament the announcement of divine judgment is never separated from the proclamation of God's mercy.[374]

(2) Fall of Babylon (14:8)—second angel

In verse 8, the second angel proclaims the idea of the future fall of Babylon. The Babylon of the Old Testament was the place of captivity following the fall of Jerusalem in 586 BC. But it is unlikely that John intends his readers to think here and now of the remote and distant territory of Babylon on the Euphrates River. The word "Babylon" is obviously used to refer to a more immediate danger that confronts the first-century Christians.[375]

John is not the only New Testament writer to make use of Babylon with a symbolic intention. The first letter of Peter contains a very interesting sentence in this regard (1 Pet. 5:12-13). It is clear that Peter intended a symbolic reference. In the light of his and Mark's ministry at Rome, we conclude that the name of Babylon is used as a cryptic reference to Rome.[376]

But Babylon also refers to any apostate civilization that develops in history. Many sensitive observers believe that our Western civilization could well be on its way to becoming an apostate civilization.

Such a civilization will drink the wine of God's wrath. Wine was used to intoxicate and to seduce to fornication. Now Babylon is going to know the fullness of God's wrath.

(3) Doom to worshipers of the beast (14:9-12)—third angel (eternal hell)

Not only does the angel announce the doom of the Babylonian state but also the wrath of God against all those who worship the beast and receive his mark (vv. 9-10). The angel says that those who refuse to repent "shall drink the wine of God's wrath, poured unmixed into the cup of his anger." The figure of the cup of God's wrath is frequently used to convey God's terrible judgment (compare Jer. 25:15; Job 21:20; Ps. 75:8; Isa. 51:17). "Unmixed" wine suggests the undiluted wrath of God.[377]

In verse 10 the punishment of the wicked is made almost unbearable because it will be experienced in the presence of "the holy angels" and "the Lamb" (v. 10; compare Luke 16:23). Jesus is holy as well as loving. We have already read in another passage about the wrath of the Lamb (6:16).

In verse 11 it is made clear that there is no second chance after death—those who worship the beast suffer forever and ever. Here is a description of judgment and torment forever. This wrath is the reaction of God's holiness to man's sinfulness and rebellion as described in Romans 1:18 and following verses and John 3:36.

The reference to "torment" (v. 10; compare 9:5; 11:10; 12:2; 20:10) has troubled some commentators since the torment takes place "in the presence of the Lamb." While the view that some unrepentant individuals will suffer eternal hell seems repugnant to Christian sensitivity, it is clear that it is not only John's understanding but that of Jesus and of other New Testament writers as well (Matt. 25:46; Rom. 2:3-9; 2 Thess. 1:6-9).[378]

The worshipers of the beast will be unable to rest day or night (v. 11). Notice the contrast with the saints who will "rest" from their labor (v. 13). The beast worshipers have their time of rest while the saints are persecuted and martyred. However, in the final time of judgment God will reverse their roles (7:15 *ff.*; compare 2 Thess. 1:6-7).[379]

C. S. Lewis (see *Problem of Pain*) acknowledges that hell is a detestable doctrine that he would be willing to remove from Christianity if it were in his power. But Lewis states that the question is not whether it is detestable but whether it is true. We must recognize that the reality of hell has the full support of Scripture and of Christ's teaching. Indeed, it has always been held by evangelical Christians and has the support of reason.[380]

In verse 12 John pauses to appeal to the saints ("those who keep the commandments of God") to hold fast and have faith *in* Jesus, not just keep the faith *of* Jesus, although the Revised Standard Version translators have retained the latter wording.[381]

(4) Beatitude on the martyrs (14:13)

A fourth voice comes from heaven and pronounces a beatitude. This is the second beatitude in Revelation (compare 1:3). Its general teaching is clear: John expects the imminent intensification of persecution associated with the beast. The beatitude indicates that those who remain loyal to Jesus when this occurs will be blessed, indeed.[382]

When we read these words, we hear echoes of the promise of Jesus Christ in the Sermon on the Mount: "Blessed are you when men revile you and persecute you and utter all kinds of evil against you falsely on my account. Rejoice and be glad, for your reward is great in heaven" (Matt. 5:11-12).[383]

Not only are they "blessed indeed" because they "rest from their labors," but because "their deeds follow them" (v. 13). Their deeds follow them in two ways: (1) their witness leaves a positive example for the saints on earth, and (2) their deeds will be a witness to their faithfulness to Christ at the last judgment (1 Cor. 15:58; 3:14; Rev. 20:13).[384]

   b. HARVEST JUDGMENT OF THE EARTH (14:14-16)—FOURTH ANGEL

After the brief pause in verse 13 to encourage the faithfulness of the saints, John returns to the theme of divine judgment on the world. He does this by first describing the judgment in terms of a harvest. This scene of world judgment is elaborated later in 19:11-21. In verse 15 notice the coming world judgment. Everything is fully ripe. The martyrs have been praying to God for judgment to come on evil people. God is watching. He knows when the world is ripe for judgment. In God's hour, the judgment is coming.

There can be no question as to the identity of the divine figure seated on the cloud. It refers to Jesus. Christ is pictured as having returned to execute the judgment of God, even as He will return to reward the saints (compare vv. 15-16; Matt.13:36-43; 25:31 *ff.*; 2 Thess. 1:7 *ff.*).[385]

   c. VINTAGE OF GOD'S WRATH (14:17-20)—FIFTH AND SIXTH ANGELS

The prayers of the saints are about to be answered. Judgment is falling on the wicked. It is a terrible day.

Another angel, a fifth, comes out of the temple of heaven with a sharp sickle (v. 17). Then a sixth angel comes forth "from the altar" to aid the Son of man in the harvest (v. 18; compare 6:9-11; 8:1-5; 9:13; 16:7). This angel has power over fire. He is perhaps Gabriel, whom Jewish tradition assigned this task. The symbol used in verses 18-20 to convey the wrath of God is the familiar figure of the treading of the winepress of God's wrath found in Isaiah 63:3 and Joel 3:13.[386]

Revelation 14:20 is gruesome in its description of blood flowing up to the horses' bridles for a distance of about two hundred miles.

This length may suggest the length of Palestine. The source of the imagery is Isaiah 63:1-6, heightened by John's hyperbole.[387]

The judgment is not the task of human vengeance but belongs exclusively to the Son of man and His angelic reapers (compare Rom. 12:19-21). The symbolism is that of a head-on battle, a great defeat of the enemy and a sea of spilled blood. To go beyond this and attempt to link the scene to some geographic location (compare 16: 4-6) is pure speculation. The city mentioned in verse 20 probably refers to the community of the saints.[388]

D. The Seven Bowls or Last Plagues (15:1 to 16:21)

Now we come to the last series of seven: the seven bowls or the last plagues in chapters 15 and 16. These plagues are very closely related to the Old Testament, especially Exodus. We cannot properly understand this section of Revelation until we have a grasp of the Book of Exodus.

Seen as a whole, chapter 15 is a kind of celestial interlude before the final judgment. It is preparatory to the execution of the bowl series described in chapter 16, while chapters 17 and 18 elaborate the fall of Babylon. The bowl judgments have already been anticipated under the preceding figures of the divine judgment—the cup of wine (v. 10), the harvest of the earth (vv. 14-16), and the grape harvest (vv. 17-20). Details are further described under the symbolism of the seven bowls.[389]

In this last series of woes, the seven bowls, a fuller revelation of the judgment of God is given, which builds upon the one given in the trumpets. The divine retribution revealed by the seals and announced by the trumpets is now executed by the bowls. From a literary standpoint, the bowls seem to be the expansion of the seventh trumpet, just as the trumpets were an expansion of the seventh seal.[390]

As has been noted, the first reference to the eschatological judgments is found in 6:17: "For the great day of their wrath has come, and who can stand before it?" After the interlude of the sealing of the saints from spiritual harm (ch. 7), the seven trumpets are sounded (8:1 ff.). The sixth one involves three plagues that kill a third of mankind (9:18). The third woe (11:14) includes the bowl judgments that are called the "last" plagues. From this we may conclude that the eschatological wrath of God begins with the trumpets and ends with the seven bowls.[391]

These last plagues take place "immediately after the distress of those days" referred to by Jesus in the Olivet discourse (Matt. 24). They may well be the fulfillment of His apocalyptic words: "The sun will be darkened, / and the moon will not give its light; / the stars will fall from the sky, / and the heavenly bodies will be shaken" (v. 29, NIV). Also note that the event that follows this judgment in Matthew, the coming of the Son of man in the clouds (v. 30), is the same event John describes following the bowl judgments (19:11).[392]

1. The Preparation (15:1-8)—Visions Introductory to the Bowls

a. THE FIRST VISION (15:1-4)

(1) The marvelous sign and the victors (15:1-2)

In verse 1 another sign or portent now appears to John: seven angels who are to bring the seven plagues of punishment as the conclusion of the wrath of God toward evil. But in verse 2 John focuses his attention on a scene that contrasts sharply with the coming judgment. This is an indication of his pastoral concern. He sees before the throne the likeness of a sea of glass intermingled with fire. It is a scene of worship. The imagery is suitable for picturing the majesty and brilliance of God. The sea of glass reflects God's glory in a virtual rainbow of color. The harps of God which the victors hold belong to the heavenly worship (compare 5:8; 14:2).[393]

Firmly planted on the sea are those who were victorious over the beast (v. 2). They are the same ones who are seen throughout Revelation as having won out over the idolatrous beasts through their faithful testimony to Christ, even to the extent of martyrdom. They are the 144,000 elect of God (7:4; 14:1), the completed company of martyrs (6:11).[394]

(2) The song of Moses and the Lamb (15:3-4)

In verses 3-4 we are told that these troops of the Lord now sing the song of Moses and the Lamb. The Old Testament's song of Moses is the great psalm of Exodus 15. There are similarities in theme between that song of Exodus 15 and this song of Revelation 15: "I will sing to the Lord, / for he has triumphed gloriously; / the horse and his rider he has thrown into the sea" (Ex. 15:1-2).[395]

The deliverance from Egypt, with its divine plagues of judgment on Israel's enemies, became for the Jews a signpost of God's just rule over the world. In a similar manner, God's eschatological judgment and the deliverance of the followers of the Lamb bring forth from the victors over the beast exuberant songs of praise to God for His righteous acts in history (15:3-4).[396] Revelation 15:3-4 refers to God's judgment and not to the redeeming acts of God. It is the judgment of God they are singing about.

The last stanza of the song reiterates the prophecy of the Old Testament prophets that in the end all nations shall acknowledge Jehovah as sovereign "because of the manifestations of God's righteous acts of judgment" (v. 4; compare Phil. 2:11; 1 Cor. 15:24 *ff.*; Isa. 2: 2-4; 66:23).[397]

There is a strong wrath motif in Revelation. The glory of God is manifested as the angels get out their bowls of wrath.

b. THE SECOND VISION: THE SEVEN ANGELS OF THE LAST PLAGUES (15:5-8)

In verses 5-8 a second and still more impressive scene follows. The door to the temple in heaven is again opened (compare 11:19), and the seven angels dressed in white and gold come out of the temple. The fact that the seven angels came out of the temple suggest that the judgments they are to deliver are expressions of God's righteous and holy will.

God sends to these seven angels one of the four living creatures "with seven bowls full of the wrath of God" (v. 7). The bowls are shallow bowl-shaped vessels that were often used for banquet drinking (Amos 6:6). They could also refer to ritual bowls used for collecting the blood of sacrifices (Ex. 27:3). These are open bowls, pouring out their burning contents upon the earth.[398]

The manifestation of God's glory, power, and special presence are symbolized by the smoke which fills the temple (v. 8). Smoke is a familiar symbol in the Old Testament (Ex. 24:16; 40:34-38; 1 Kings 8:10-11). The smoke continues and the angels cannot enter until the plagues are finished and the voice in the temple cries, "It is done!" (16:17)[399]

2. *The Nature of the Seven Bowls (16:1)*

In verse 1 the seven angels are given the seven bowls, and they go forth in obedience to the voice from the temple which commands them to "Go and pour out on the earth the seven bowls of the wrath of God."[400]

This verse introduces a chapter which contains the most tragic part of the whole vision. We now read of the final judgment and conflict between God's just and holy wrath and those who are marked by the authority of the devil's beast. As the seven bowls of wrath are poured out, the restraint that was present in all of the previous visions is now gone. There is in this vision no apparent restraint on the punishment. It is not now only a third of the sea that experiences destruction (8:9) but "every living thing died that was in the sea" (16:3).[401]

The seven bowl judgments occur in rapid succession with only a brief pause for a dialogue between the third angel and the altar. This rapidity accentuates the justice of God's punishments (vv. 5-7). This rapid succession is also probably due to John's desire to give a telescopic view of the first six bowls and then hasten on to the seventh bowl, where the far more dramatic judgment on Babylon occurs. This seventh bowl calls for a detailed account.[402]

Although the trumpets and bowls are separate judgments, they both are described in language drawn from the pattern of God's judgment on Egypt under Moses. The final three bowl plagues are social and spiritual in their effect and shift from nature to humanity.[403]

These descriptions should probably not be taken in a strictly literal sense. The important point is that they picture God's sure and righteous judgment that will one day be literally and actually executed in this world.[404]

3. The First Bowl (16:2)—Like the Sixth Plague of Egypt

The first bowl in verse 2 is ulcers or malignant sores. This is very similar to the sixth plague which was visited on Egypt by God (Ex. 9:10-11).

4. The Second Bowl (16:3)—Like the First Plague of Egypt

The second bowl is the sea turned to polluted blood. This was also one of the plagues of Egypt (Ex. 7:17-21).

5. *The Third Bowl (16:4-7)—Like the First Plague of Egypt*

The third bowl is that rivers are to be turned into blood. This is also like the first plague of Egypt. The third bowl affects the fresh waters of the earth, which are essential to human life.

In 16:5-7 the reference to blood calls forth the dialogue between the angel of water and the altar concerning the logic of the plagues. The blood that sinners now drink is just punishment for their shedding of the blood of the saints (15:1-4) and prophets (11:3-13; compare 17:6; 18:20). With blood, God vindicates the blood of the martyrs of Jesus. God's wrath is exercised in recognition of their love.[405]

The "altar" in verse 7 is a personification of the saints who abide under the altar. The saints utter words of approval (compare 6:10; 14:18; 19:1-2). People must choose whether to drink the blood of saints or to wear robes dipped in the blood of the Lamb.

6. *The Fourth Bowl (16:8-9)*

The fourth bowl is the scourging heat of the sun. They did not repent of their deeds and acknowledge the Creator. Repentance is held out to the sinners as an act that could even now turn away God's wrath. Instead, the earth's inhabitants curse God for sending them agonizing pain (vv. 11,21). Yet their problem goes beyond the awful physical pain and is moral and spiritual (compare Isa. 52:5; Rom. 1:25; 2:24).[406]

7. *The Fifth Bowl (16:10-11)—Like the Eighth Plague of Egypt*

The fifth bowl is darkness on the face of the beast's kingdom. That is like the eighth plague in Egypt.

The "throne of the beast" (v. 10) symbolizes the seat of the world-wide dominion of the great satanic system of idolatry. This system is plunged into spiritual darkness or disruption, bringing chaos on all who sought life and meaning in it.[407]

This plague strikes at the very seat of satanic authority over the world. The darkness is probably moral and spiritual rather than physical (compare 21:25; 22:5; John 8:12; 12:35-36,46; 1 John 1:5-7; 2:8-10). Again the terrible refrain is repeated: "But they refused to repent of what they had done" (v. 11, NIV).[408]

8. The Sixth Bowl (16:12-16)—Kings of Earth Assemble for the Battle of Armageddon

The sixth bowl brings together all the kings of the nations of the earth for the battle of Armageddon (v. 12).

a. THE SIGNIFICANCE OF THE EUPHRATES RIVER (16:12)

Verse 12 has a great deal of symbolism. The Euphrates River was the barrier that kept the pagan kingdoms of the East from coming over to conquer the Holy Land. Now the river is dried up so that these kings from the East can cross over and join with the evil powers of the West and prepare the way for the battle of Armageddon where God Himself will enter into battle with them. This is different from the sixth trumpet which released demonic hordes to inflict death on the earth's inhabitants.

Many see here the fear that the Parthians, led by Nero, whom many believed would be restored to life, might attack Rome. But there is certainly more to be found here in this sixth bowl than a contemporary reference to Rome and the Parthians. This may have been the short-range reference, but the long-range application is to the final conflict which will precede the coming of the millennium.[409]

Thus John does not describe an invasion of the Parthian hordes advancing on Rome or any future military invasion of Israel. How could such political groups be involved in the battle of the great day of God Almighty? Instead, in terms which remind us of the ancient battles of Israel, John describes the eschatological defeat of the forces of evil, the "kings from the East."[410]

b. THE SIGNIFICANCE OF THE THREE FROG-LIKE SPIRITS (16:13-14)

In verses 13-14 we see further confirmation that these kings of the East represent the combined forces of evil in the world. Note John's reference to the three frog-like evil ("unclean") spirits that proceed out of the mouths of the dragon, the beast, and the false prophet. Frogs were considered unclean animals by the Jews (Lev. 11:10,41).

The background for the frog figure probably relates to pagan metaphors for evil. To the Persian, the frog was the double of Ahriman, god of evil and agent of plagues. To the Egyptian, the frog was the symbol of Heqt, a goddess of resurrection and fertility. For the Jewish mind, however, such gods were demons (v. 14), Satan's emissaries, and inseparable from idolatry (9:20; 18:2; 1 Cor. 10:20-21)[411]

These demons produce miraculous signs like the false prophet (13:13-14). This connects their activity with the deception of the earth's kings. Since these demons come from the "mouths" of the figures, lying and deceptive words are implied.[412]

These kings are summoned by the demon spirits to the battle of the great day of God Almighty (v. 14). Not until the seventh bowl do we see their defeat actually occur (19:19-21). These kings of the whole world (vv. 13-14) are identical with those in 17:12-14. Thus we see that, deceived by the black magic of the satanic trinity (the dragon, beast, and false prophet), the rulers of this world prepare for a last great battle with God. The deception of humanity from the beginning by the serpent, leading to man's rebellion against God, reaches a climactic proportion at the end of history. It is symbolically set forth as a great battle against God on the battlefield of Armageddon.

c. THE CALL FOR VIGILANCE (16:15)

Verse 15 is a parenthetical ejaculatory word of warning and encouragement which was to stimulate the believers to hold fast. This verse is an elaboration of 3:3 and reflects the words of Christ (Matt. 24:43), of Paul (1 Thess. 5:2,4), and of Peter (2 Pet. 3:10).[413]

We need to be awake. To be asleep is to lose sight of the ultimate issues of life and to find security falsely on a human level.

In some ways this is similar to the exhortation given to those in the churches at Sardis (3:2-4) and Laodicea (v. 18). The warning about Jesus' coming "like a thief" implies a need for alertness to the deception of idolatry and disloyalty to Jesus (compare Matt. 24:43 *ff.*; 1 Thess. 5:2,4). Like a guard who watches by night, the true Christian will remain steadfast and prepared. It is not necessary to relate this warning only to the end time as in the context since the appeal for the steadfast loyalty of Christians is relevant at any time. Such appeals, however, are associated in the Gospels with the return of Christ (Mark 13:32-37).[414]

d. THE MEANING OF ARMAGEDDON (16:16)

In verse 16 we read that the final scene of John's judgment vision will happen at a place which is called in Hebrew *Armageddon*. This word literally translated would be "Hill of Megiddo."[415]

The reference to Megiddo would remind those who know Old Testament history of the defeat of Judah under King Josiah by Egypt under Pharaoh Neco at Megiddo. This was the defeat that paved the way for the downward destruction of Judah. In less than thirty years after the battle of Megiddo, Judah fell to Nebuchadnezzar II of Babylon.

There is a subtle portrayal of the balancing of the scales by means of this place name. The new Babylon—the Roman Empire—is to bear the judgment of God at the place where previously the old Babylon had been, in effect, the conqueror. But, as we shall see, there is a larger context in the final judgment scene which goes beyond the judgment of the Roman tyranny.[416]

Beyond Josiah's battle, the region of Megiddo was the classic battleground of Old Testament Scripture—the scene of many crucial battles (Judg. 5; 2 Kings 6:17,23; Zech. 12:11). In addition to Hebrew battles, the valley has known conflicts involving Napoleon and the contending powers of World War I.[417]

The valley surrounding Megiddo is near Nazareth and Haifa in the Valley of Esdraelon. Jesus could have looked down on this valley from His home in Nazareth. The valley is approximately fourteen by twenty miles in size.

Excursus on Interpretations of Armageddon

a. *New Scofield Bible* view

The *New Scofield Bible* states that Armageddon and the Megiddo Valley is the appointed place where the armies of the beast and false prophet will be destroyed by Christ's descending to earth in glory (19:11,15,19,21). Christ will also destroy any other forces which will come against the beast in their attack on Palestine (that is, the remainder of the Far Eastern army of 200 million men) and others. The battle is a fulfillment of the striking-stone prophecy of Daniel 2:35.[418]

b. The view of John Walvoord

According to Walvoord, Revelation 16 describes Oriental rulers who will descend upon the Middle East in connection with the final world conflict. The rising power of countries of the Orient in our day, such as Japan, China, India, as well as lesser nations, makes such an invasion a reasonable prediction. The armies of the world will combine their efforts against Christ and His army from heaven when the glory of the second coming appears in the heavens. It will be the final challenge to divine sovereignty and power. In fact, the military might of the world of that day will be engaged in fighting on the very day that Christ returns (compare Zech. 14:1-3).[419]

For Walvoord, the conclusion of the combined action of the sixth bowl and the enticement of the demons is that the armies of the earth are gathered in the Middle East in a place described as Armageddon. The area, though it is a large one, is not sufficient for the armies of all the world. What the Scripture seems to indicate is that this area is the central point for the military conflict which ensues. Actually the armies are deployed over a 200-mile area up and down from this central location. Zechariah 14:1-3 indicates that some of the armies will be in Jerusalem.[420]

In the sixth trumpet, an army of 200 million men is loosed to slay a third part of mankind (9:15). This army is related to the Euphrates River even as is the army of the kings of the East. According to Walvoord, the best explanation is that the seven bowls follow very rapidly after the trumpets. The events, such as a great invasion, are pictured in their early stages in the sixth trumpet with a statement of their ultimate purpose that is actually realized in the sixth bowl.[421]

c. The view of J. Dwight Pentecost

Pentecost is even more explicit in his description of the complexities of Armageddon. In 16:14 this conflict is referred to as the battle of that great day of God Almighty. The word translated "battle" does not refer to an isolated skirmish or meeting of two armies. Rather it refers, according to Pentecost, to a number of battles that we call a campaign. What John refers to here is the consummation of a group of battles.

For Pentecost, during the tribulation period (the last seven years of history), there will be no less than four invasions of the land of Israel. In Daniel 11 and Ezekiel 38, there is a reference to an invasion of Israel by the king of the south and a second invasion by the king of the north. The king of the south seems to be a reference to those nations allied to the nation to the south of Israel that was Israel's ancient enemy, that is Egypt. Pentecost refers to the king of the south as the Arab states. The king of the north in Ezekiel 38 is a reference to that coalition of peoples who come from the land to the north of Israel. Pentecost believes this to be the Soviet Union and her allies.

At approximately the middle of the tribulation period, Israel will find her peace broken. The peace had been guaranteed by the covenant (Dan. 9:24-26) made with the Western confederacy. Israel will be simultaneously invaded by Arab and Soviet armies. Jerusalem will be destroyed and the land will be overrun and occupied by the invaders.

At this time, according to Daniel 11, the little horn in Daniel 7 (the Antichrist) will move his armies from the west, evidently across Egypt into the land of Israel. While he is approaching Israel with his armies, the kings of the north and the south are destroyed by a divine judgment comparable to the judgment upon Sodom and Gomorrah. Ezekiel 38 describes this.

Israel is then occupied, in the vacuum left by the destruction of Arab and Soviet armies, by the armies of the fourth beast who occupies Jerusalem. Jerusalem becomes the world headquarters of the beast. This would be the third invasion. The land of Israel is occupied by this dictator for the last half of the tribulation period. Next, according to Revelation 16:12, the kings of the East, which seem to be Oriental people coming from beyond the Euphrates, move into the land. They come to contest the beast's right to rule.

At that time the sign of the Son of man appears in heaven and those armies assembled against Christ are smitten by the sword/word that proceeds from the lips of Christ at His second coming. This is described in Revelation 19. Armageddon, then, is that campaign that sees Israel invaded and occupied by the Arabs and the Soviets who are consequently destroyed by the beast and the kings of the earth who are together destroyed at Christ's coming.[422]

d. The view of Hal Lindsey

For Hal Lindsey, Revelation describes a series of military maneuvers of the four great political empires who will be involved in the last military conflict of the world, of which the battle of Armageddon is the very last battle. The fifth stage of the war is when the 200-million-man army from the Orient reaches the Euphrates and prepares to attack the Antichrist, who will be in Israel at that time (Rev. 16:12).[423]

The sixth stage is the mobilization of all the rest of the world's armies to fight under the command of the Antichrist against the "kings of the East" (v. 12). At this point, all the armies move into the Middle East and spread out along the entire length and breadth of Israel, with the greatest concentration poised for the fiercest and final battle on the plains of Armageddon (vv. 13-14).

It is almost impossible for us to imagine the magnitude of what is predicted here. Just imagine—at least 300 million soldiers strung out across the entire Middle East and poised for the final mad act in man's most finely developed art—war! The human waves of the East are pitted against the superior weaponry of the West.

Then it happens—the final battle begins! There is the horrible carnage of the Valley of Armageddon (v. 16). There are also indescribable clashes around Jerusalem and Judea (Zech.14:1-15). It is no wonder that John predicts that blood will stand to the horses' bridles for 200 miles in the Jordan Valley (Rev. 14:20)![424]

e. The view of Alan Johnson

Johnson contends that while the literal emphasis on the final battle in the valley of Armageddon is not impossible, it is better to take the name as being symbolic. In Hebrew *har* means hill or mountain, while *megiddon* could mean Megiddo, a Canaanite stronghold in the Jezreel Plain later captured by the Israelites (Josh. 12:21; Judg. 5:19). Megiddo, however, is a tell (artificial mound—only seventy feet high in John's day) and not a hill or a mountain and is never so designated. It is true, however, that the fact that over two hundred battles have been fought in this vicinity makes the site an appropriate symbol for the eschatological battle. Therefore, it is better to understand the term symbolically.[425]

It probably does not refer to any geographical location we can now identify, whether in Palestine or elsewhere. Rather, it describes the actual eschatological confrontation where God will meet the forces of evil in their final defeat.[426]

f. The view of R. H. Mounce

Geography should not be our major concern. For Mounce, wherever it takes place, Har-Megedon is symbolic of the final overthrow of all the forces of evil by the might and power of God. There is a great conflict between God and Satan, Christ and Antichrist, good and evil which lies behind the perplexing course of history. In the end, this conflict will issue in a final struggle in which God will emerge victorious and take with Him all who have placed their faith in Him. This is Har-Magedon.[427]

g. Conclusion

Armageddon has become a term of widespread interest and sharply varying interpretations. In the midst of this variety of views we must remember that it refers to a real point in history and to real persons who will encounter God's just sentence.

9. *The Seventh Bowl (16:17-21)—Great Cosmic Disturbances*

In verse 17 the fact that the bowl is poured into the air suggests that that which is vital to all of life is affected. It is God's final attack upon the diabolical forces which oppose him, both human and spiritual (compare Eph. 2:2).[428]

When the bowl is poured out, a voice cries out from the temple, proclaiming the end of the diabolical kingdom of evil—"It is done!" Earlier our Lord Jesus said from the cross, "It is finished" (John 19:30). Christ had paid the price of redemption which made the final triumph over evil certain. Now John proclaims in an anticipatory statement the complete victory over evil.[429]

With this seventh bowl, the eschatological wrath of God is completed. In verse 18 flashes of lightning, peals of thunder, and a severe earthquake occur. These eschatological nature signs symbolize the destruction of the anti-God forces throughout the world.

In verse 19 the great earthquake of God's judgment reaches the strongholds of organized evil represented by the cities of the pagans ("nations"). Even the great city Babylon, which seduced all the earth's kings and inhabitants (17:2), now comes under final sentence.[430]

Revelation 16:20 refers not to the dissolution of the earth, but to the sinking of islands and mountains because of the earthquake. In verse 21 the tremendous hailstones are also a sign of the end. Instead of God's judgment producing repentance, people turn from God and curse Him.[431]

While catastrophe continues to be described in geophysical terms (islands and mountains disappearing, huge hailstones accompanying a gigantic storm), John probably does not intend this destruction to be merely of natural or even politico-historical entities. In fact, John, by means of his dramatic pictures of last things, pictures the unspeakable "awe-fullness" of God's judgments and deliverances at the end of history.

In any event, like the Egyptian plague of hail that further hardened Pharaoh's heart, this plague of hail falls on the unrepentant to no avail. Instead of repenting, they curse God for sending His judgment on them (compare Ex. 9:24; Josh. 10; 11; Ezek. 38:22).

Thus John describes the rising pitch of God's wrath on the rebellious powers of the earth. His words should not be politicized as if he spoke merely of Rome or of some impending historical crisis for the church. He is speaking of the great realities of the end, when God has put down all His enemies.[432]

IV. The Third Vision—Fall of Babylon, Final Victory

17:1 to 21:8

A. The Mystery of Babylon (17:1-18)

Chapters 17—18 form one continuous unit dealing with the judgment on Babylon. The woman is identified as the great city (17:18) whose fall is described in chapter 18. From internal evidence, Babylon the woman (ch. 17) and Babylon the great city (ch. 18) refer to the same entity. These two chapters form an extended appendix to the seventh bowl, where the judgment on Babylon was mentioned (16:19).

In this section John uses a suspenseful literary approach. He first describes the nature of the harlot and the beast she rides (ch. 17). Then John describes her momentous fall in terms drawn from the Old Testament descriptions of the fall of great cities (ch. 18).[1]

Excursus on the Meaning of Babylon

The interpretation of Babylon in chapter 17 is of crucial importance to our understanding of Revelation. For a majority of modern exegetes, Babylon represents the city of Rome. The beast stands for the Roman Empire as a whole, including its subject provinces and people. The seven hills (v. 9) are seen as the seven dynasties of Roman emperors from Augustus to Domitian. The ten kings are heads of lesser and restless states, eager to escape their enslavement to the colonizing power. John's prediction of the fall of Babylon is then the announcement of the impending fall of the Roman Empire in all its aspects.

There is considerable evidence for this view. Babylon was a term used by both Jews and Christians for Rome. Rome was a great city (v. 18), set on seven hills (v. 9). By the time of Domitian (AD 85), Rome was notorious for persecuting and killing the saints (v. 6). Many outstanding scholars have been fully convinced that Babylon represents Rome.

Johnson contends, however, that there is evidence that calls for a more comprehensive understanding of John's intention. It is simply not sufficient to limit the identification of Babylon to Rome. Babylon should not be confined to any one historical manifestation, past or future. It should be seen as having multiple equivalents (compare 11:8).[2]

The details of John's description do not neatly fit any past city, whether literal

Babylon, Sodom, Egypt, Rome, or even Jerusalem. Babylon is found wherever there is satanic deception. It is defined more by dominant idolatries than geographic or temporal boundaries.

Babylon is better understood in Revelation as the archetype of all entrenched worldly resistance to God. Babylon is a reality that includes idolatrous kingdoms as diverse as Sodom, Egypt, Babylon, Tyre, Nineveh, and Rome. Babylon is a dramatic end-time symbol of satanic deception and power. This means that Babylon is a symbol which can never be completely identified with a certain earthly city or nation or institution. It can be said that Babylon represents the total culture of the world apart from God. In contrast, the divine system is portrayed by the New Jerusalem. Rome is simply one manifestation of the total Babylonian system. The two realities are related but they are not identical.[3]

1. Vision of Babylon in Her Glory (17:1-6)—The Harlot and The Scarlet Beast

a. THE JUDGMENT OF BABYLON—AN EXTENSION OF THE SEVENTH BOWL (17:1)

The reference to "one of the seven angels" in verse 1 connects this vision with the preceding bowl judgments. In other words, the judgment of Babylon is a further expansion of the final bowl and not an additional event.[4]

John is invited to view the judgment which is to come upon the harlot, the great city, Babylon (v. 1). In verse 15 we are told that the waters represent the people and nations over whom Babylon has dominion. Thus the "great harlot" is identified with Babylon and her great empire—in the ancient world, today, and in the end time.[5]

b. THE HARLOT AND HER LOVERS (17:2)

In verse 2 the earth's kings and inhabitants are said to have committed fornication with the prostitute. This language goes back to references to the harlot cities of the past (for example, Jer. 51:7). It means that the people of the world have become drunk with abundance, power, pride, violence, and especially false worship.[6]

The literary image of the harlot is familiar to those who know the Old Testament. Lindsey traces the place of the harlot in a section called "A Short History of Hookers." The harlot is often used as a representation of rebellious Israel and as a symbol of foreign, idolatrous peoples. Jeremiah said of Judah: "Judah did not fear, but she too went and played the harlot . . . committing adultery with stone and tree" (Jer. 3:8-9). Note that Judah's harlotry is a description of her idolatry. She abandoned God's love and chose idols for pay. Ezekiel accused Jerusalem, "How lovesick is your heart, says the Lord

God, seeing you did all these things, the deeds of a brazen harlot" (Ezek. 16:30). Isaiah accused Tyre of being a harlot (Isa. 23:15-17). The imagery of harlotry is not new to readers of the Bible.[7]

The best background for understanding the language of chapter 17 is not the history of the Roman Empire or parallels with a pagan god. Rather, it is the description of Jerusalem the harlot in Ezekiel 16 and 23 and Babylon the harlot in Jeremiah 51.[8]

c. THE HARLOT AND THE SCARLET BEAST (17:3-4)

In verse 3 John is carried in the Spirit into a "desert" (NIV). In the desert, he sees the prostitute seated on "a scarlet beast." Scarlet symbolizes the beast's blasphemy in contrast to the white horse rider and those dressed in white, who are faithful and true (19:8,11,14). This beast is a seven-headed monster and so is to be identified with the first beast in chapter 13. This beast in chapter 13 is inseparable from the seven-headed dragon of chapter 12.[9]

Verse 4 describes the woman as beautifully dressed, wealthy, and impure. The beauty of gold and pearls, jewels, and purple gowns is turned luxurious and crude by its drunken chaos.

She is swinging in her hand a golden cup full of her idolatrous abomination and wickedness. Note the contrast and mixture of descriptions—beauty and gross wickedness. Her costly and attractive attire suggests the prostitute's outward beauty and attraction (Jer. 4:30). The golden cup filled with wine alludes to Jeremiah's description of Babylon's worldwide influence in idolatry (51:7).[10]

d. THE IDENTIFICATION OF THE HARLOT (17:5)

The harlot's forehead described in verse 5 reveals the name which symbolizes her true nature. Moffatt suggests that "a name of mystery" should be translated "a name . . . by way of symbol." The title on her forehead was in keeping with the custom of that day which called for the display of the harlot's name on her brow.[11]

This prostitute, Babylon the great, is the mother of all the earth's idolatrous prostitutes. She is the fountainhead, the reservoir, the womb that bears all the individual cases of historical resistance to God's will on earth. Furthermore, she is the unholy antithesis to the woman who weds the Lamb (19:7-8) and to the New Jerusalem (21:2-3). Therefore, she cannot be merely ancient Babylon, Rome, or Jerusalem because these are only her children—she is the mother of them all.[12]

Babylon could equally well be seen in any of these classic manifestations from the past or in modern times. These could include Nazi Germany, Idi Amin's Ugandan regime, the Soviet Union, or Mao's China. William Stringfellow in *An Ethic for Christians and Other Aliens in a Strange Land* contends that Babylon also represents many aspects of American life.[13]

All the harlot-city societies mentioned in Scripture have certain common characteristics that are also reflected in John's description of the great Babylon. In this grand composite, we find royal dignity and splendor combined with prosperity, overabundance, and luxury. There is also self-trust or boastfulness, power, and violence, especially against God's people. There is oppression, injustice, and idolatry. Wherever and whenever these characteristics have been manifested historically, there is the appearance of Babylon.[14]

e. THE HARLOT—THE KILLER OF CHRISTIANS (17:6)

Verse 6 states that this mother prostitute is also the source of the shed blood of the followers of Jesus. This same mother harlot who killed the saints throughout salvation history is now also responsible for the deaths of the Christians (compare 2:13). Early Christian readers would understand that whenever they were threatened with death by any temporal power—whether political, religious, or both—they were in reality facing the bloodthirsty mother prostitute whom God was about to judge and destroy once for all.[15]

2. *The Vision Explained (17:7-18)—Babylon's Doom*

a. THE ANGEL'S PROMISE TO DISCLOSE THE MYSTERY OF THE HARLOT AND THE BEAST (17:7)

In 17:6b and 17:7, John is astonished over the arresting figure of the woman on the beast. But this astonishment is quickly subdued by the interpreting angel's announcement that John will be shown the explanation of the divine mystery of the symbolic imagery of woman and beast.

There has been much difficulty in interpreting verses 7-18. Johnson contends that this difficulty has resulted from incorrectly applying John's words either to the Roman emperors (the seven heads) or to the Nero revival myth ("once was, now is not, and will come up out of the Abyss" v. 8, NIV). Johnson suggests that John's description of Babylon is theological, not political. John describes a reality behind the earth's sovereigns, rather than Babylon's successive manifestations in history.[16]

b. The theological meaning of the beast (17:8)

In verse 8 John is told that the beast "once was, now is not, and will come up out of the Abyss." This seems clearly to be a paraphrase of the image in chapter 13 of the wounded beast who was healed (vv. 3,14). The play here on the tenses "was, . . . is not, . . . will come" refers to a three-stage history of the beast that requires "a mind with wisdom" (v. 9) to understand its mystery.[17]

That John's beast "is not" refers to his defeat by the Lamb on Calvary. Satan once had unchallenged power over the earth ("was"; compare Luke 4:6; Heb. 2:14-15). Now he is a defeated sovereign ("is not"; compare John 12:31-32). However, he is given a "little time" to oppose God and His people (12:12c; 13:5; 20:3b) before his final sentencing to "destruction" (17:11; compare Matt. 7:13; John 17:12; Rom. 9:22; 2 Thess. 2:3). This apparent revival of Satan's power and authority over the world after his mortal wound (Gen. 3:15) causes the deceived of the earth to follow him.[18]

c. The relationship of the seven hills, seven heads, and the beast (17:9-10)

At first glance, verses 9-11 appears to favor the Roman emperor interpretation of this section. The woman not only sits on many waters (vv. 1,15) and on the beast (v. 3) but also on seven hills (v. 9). Most scholars believe that the seven hills refer to the seven hills of Rome and the seven kings to seven successive emperors of that nation.[19]

And so there have been many attempts to fit the date of Revelation (the then contemporary king would be he who "is") into the emperor lists of the first century. But immediately problems arise. Where do we begin—with Julius Caesar or Caesar Augustus? Are we to count all the emperors or just those who fostered emperor worship? A careful examination of the historical materials yields no satisfactory solution. If Revelation were written under Nero, there would be too few emperors; if under Domitian, too many. The original readers would have had no more information on these emperor successions than we do, and possibly even less.[20]

Recognizing the problems, others have sought different solutions to John's five-one-one succession of kings. Since the word "king" (v. 10) may also represent kingdoms, Seiss (followed by Ladd and Walvoord) has suggested that an interpretation that takes the five-one-one to refer to successive world kingdoms that have oppressed the people of God: Egypt, Assyria, Babylon, Persia, Greece (five fallen), Rome (one is), and a future world kingdom. While this solves some of the emperor succession problems and fits nicely, it too must admit arbitrary omissions, such as the devastating persecution of the people of God under the Seleucids of Syria, especially Antiochus IV, Epiphanes. This view also suffers in not respecting the symbolic significance of John's use of seven throughout the book.[21]

There is good reason to doubt that these interpretations constitute the meaning John intended. In the first place, the seven hills belong to the beast, not the woman. The woman (that is, the "city," v. 18) sits upon (that is, has mastery over) the seven heads (or seven hills) of the beast.

Verse 9 states that the interpretation calls for "a mind with wisdom." Whenever divine wisdom is called for, the description requires theological and symbolical discernment, not mere geographical or numerical insight. It seems better, therefore, to interpret the seven mountains as a reference to the seven heads or kings, which describe not the city but the beast.

We must remember how John uses numbers in Revelation. By his use of seven, he indicates completeness or wholeness. The seven heads of the beast symbolize fullness of blasphemy and evil.

If we can see that the seven heads show qualitatively the fullness of evil power residing in the beast, then the "falling" of five heads conveys the message of significant victory over the beast (v. 10).[22]

John's message is that five of the monster's seven heads are already defeated by the power of the Lamb's death and by the identification of the martyrs of Jesus in that death (12:11). One head is now active (17:10). This shows the reality of the beast's contemporary agents who afflict the saints. One head remains. This indicates that the battle will soon be over but not just the defeat of the contemporary evil agents. There will have to be a last manifestation of the beast's blasphemous power. This, however, will be short—"he must remain for a little while" (v. 10, NIV). This statement seems to go with the function of the ten horns (kings) who for "one hour" (v. 12) will rule with the beast.[23]

For Lindsey, John looks to the future when he says of the seventh head that "the other has not yet come, and when he comes, he must remain only a little while" (17:10c). This refers to the future revival of the Roman empire.

This seventh head is different from all the other six because it has ten horns on it. This indicates that this seventh kingdom will be made up of ten nations from the old Roman Empire (the sixth head) which will have confederated. For Lindsey, this unquestionably refers to the European Economic Community, which will bloom into the last great world empire represented by the seventh head with the ten horns. This revived Roman Empire will become dominated by the same Babylonish religious system that has dominated the past great world empires.[24]

d. THE EIGHTH BEAST AND THE RESURRECTION OF CHRIST (17:11)

If John has a theological rather than a historical or political identification in mind, verse 11 may yield further insight into the mystery of the beast.

First, we note the strange manner in which the sequence of seven kings gives way to the eighth, who is really the whole beast (v. 11). The eighth day was the day of the resurrection of Christ, Sunday. It was also the beginning of a new week. The seventh day, the Jewish sabbath, is held over to be replaced by the first of a new series, namely Sunday.

In order to recruit as many as possible for his side of the war, the beast will imitate the resurrection of Christ (he "is an eighth king" v. 11, NIV) and will give the appearance that he is alive and in control of the world (compare Luke 4:5-7). But John quickly adds, for the pastoral comfort of God's people, that the beast belongs to the seven (as if he were a former king revived). But the beast is in reality not a new beginning of life but a part of the seven-headed monster that has been slain by Christ and, therefore, he goes "to his destruction" (17:11, NIV). This imagery reveals the true mystery of the beast in a fashion that exposes the dynamics of satanic deception so that every Christian may be forearmed.[25]

e. THE MEANING AND DEFEAT OF THE TEN HORNS AND THE TEN KINGS (17:12-14)

Verse 12 refers to ten horns. The ten horns are usually understood as either native rulers of Roman provinces serving under the emperors or native rulers of satellite states. Others, as already indicated, see in them a ten-nation confederacy of the future revived

Roman Empire of which the European Common Market is a fore-runner.

Johnson contends that there are substantial reasons for abandon-ing these explanations. In the first place, the number ten should—like most of John's numbers—be understood symbolically. "Ten" symbolizes a repeated number of times or an indefinite number. It is another number like seven, indicating fullness (Neh. 4:12; Dan. 1:12; Rev. 2:10). Thus the number should not be understood as refer-ring specifically to ten kings (or kingdoms) but as indicating the multiplicity of sovereignties in confederacy that strengthen the power of the beast.

Second, note that these kings enter into a power conflict with the Lamb and His followers (v. 14). The kind of power which they exer-cise must be the true antithesis to the kind of power the Lamb and His followers exercise. These rulers, as well as the beast with which they will be allied, should thus be seen as the principalities and powers. They are the rulers of the darkness of this world, the spiri-tual forces of evil in the heavenly realms that Paul described as the true enemies of Jesus' followers (Eph. 6:12). They do use earthly instruments, but their reality is far greater than any specific histori-cal manifestations. These "kings" embody the fullness of Satan's attack against the Lamb in the great eschatological confrontation. They are the "kings from the east" (16:12-14,16), and they are also the "kings of the earth" who ally themselves with the beast in the final confrontation with the Lamb (19:19-21).

These kings have "one purpose" (NIV): They agree to oppose the Lamb (v. 13). But the Lamb will overcome them (v. 14) because He is Lord of lords and King of kings (compare 19:16). He conquers by His death, and those who are with Him also aid in the defeat of the beast by their loyalty to the Lamb even to death (compare 5:5,9; 12:11).[26]

f. THE SELF-DEFEATING NATURE OF EVIL (17:15-17)

Verse 15 teaches that the influence of the idolatrous satanic system of Babylon is universal and embraces all people, from the humblest to the kings of the earth.

In verses 16-17 the beast and his allied kings ironically turn upon the harlot, the diabolical empire, and destroy her as God had prede-termined. The references to the prostitute being hated by her former lovers, stripped naked, and burned with fire (v. 16) remind us of the Old Testament prophets' descriptions of the divine judgment falling on the harlot cities of Jerusalem and Tyre (for example, Ezek. 16:39-40; 23:25-27; 28:18). According to Caird, "The ravaging of the whore by the monster and its horns is John's most vivid symbol for the self-destroying power of evil."[27]

That is a basic theological and historical principle which is taught in the law and gospel. Because of the long-term, bedrock reality of God's righteousness, the human systems which depend upon injustice shall not endure. They are badly infected from within by their own fatal illness (v. 17). The greed that gave them power, in time, shall destroy their power. The weapons by which they conquered will, in the end, conquer them. What they sowed they will reap.[28]

In the declaration that "God has put it into their hearts to accomplish his purpose" (v. 17, NIV) lies another indication of God's use of the forces of evil as instruments of his own purposes of judgment (Jer. 25:9-14; compare Luke 20:18).[29]

g. The identification and meaning of the harlot (17:18)

In verse 18 John states that the "woman" and "the great city" are one. According to Johnson, this city is not just a historical entity. It is the *great* city, the *mother* city and the archetype of every evil system opposed to God in history. Her kingdom holds sway over the powers of the earth. As we have seen, John's concept of the city of Babylon in Revelation involves much more than a historical city even in its political and sociological aspects. The two cities in Revelation are communities. We have the city of God, the New Jerusalem, and the city of Satan, Babylon the Great. The meaning cannot be confined to Sodom or Egypt or Jerusalem or Rome or any future city. Instead, John describes the real transhistorical system of satanic evil that infuses them all.[30]

Hal Lindsey, in contrast, states that the "harlot" in chapter 17 is *not* a city. It is an occult religious system and influence which exists in a spiritually adulterous relationship with the city of Rome and the kingdom of the Antichrist for the first half of the tribulation. It then moves to its new headquarters in a rebuilt city of Babylon on its ancient site. After a brief reign from there, it is destroyed by the Antichrist. At the end of the tribulation, Babylon the great, the capital of the revived Roman Empire (Rome) and the subject of chapter 18, is destroyed by God Himself.[31]

Mounce agrees with Johnson that Babylon the great is more than first-century Rome. Every great center of power which has prostituted its wealth and influence revives the spirit of ancient Babylon. John's words go beyond his immediate setting in history and sketch the portrait of an eschatological Babylon, which will provide the social, religious, and political base for the last attempt of Antichrist to establish his kingdom.[32]

B. The Judgment of Babylon (18:1 to 19:5)

In 17:1 an angel told of a coming judgment of the great harlot. This harlot, according to 17:18, is the great city of Babylon. And so, in chapter 18, under the imagery of the destruction of a great commercial city, John describes the final overthrow of the great prostitute, Babylon.

In describing the destruction of Babylon, John describes God's judgment on the great satanic system of evil that has corrupted the earth's history. This vivid description draws especially from the Old Testament accounts of the destruction of the ancient harlot cities of Babylon (Isa. 13:21; 47:7-9; Jer. 50—51) and Tyre (Ezek. 26:17-21). It is so dramatic that it might well be the basis of a mighty oratorio. In chapter 18 is some of the most beautifully expressive language in the whole book. John combines the song of triumph and the wailing strains of lamentation into an unforgettable funeral dirge.[33]

1. Angelic Announcement of Babylon's Fall (18:1-3)

In verse 1 an angel with great authority, which includes power to speak so that all might hear, comes down from heaven to announce the downfall of Babylon. When the angel appears, the earth is "made bright with his splendor." This reminds us of the shekinah glory of God which returned to the Temple of Jerusalem after it was rebuilt (compare Ezek. 43:2).[34]

The words in verse 2 remind us of those of the prophets who encouraged the people of God as they faced ancient Babylon. The angel announces that Babylon the great, mother of all the earthly prostitute cities, has fallen (compare Isa. 21:9; Jer. 51:8).

John hears that the city will experience judgment similar to that against ancient Babylon. This means that she will be inhabited only by detestable creatures and evil spirits (Isa. 13:19-22; 34:11; Jer. 50:39).[35]

The "haunt" in verse 2 is a watchtower. Here the evil spirits, watching over fallen Babylon like night birds waiting for their prey, build their nests in the broken towers that rise from the ashes of the city. She who was a great city has become a wilderness.[36]

In verse 3 the reason given for Babylon's destruction is the corrupting influence she has had upon nations, kings, and merchants. She has led them astray by causing them to drink "the wine of her impure passion." Part of the way in which the nations have been corrupted was through unscrupulous merchants who used Babylon's craving for luxuriousness or wantonness to their own advantage.[37]

The close relationship of fornication to luxury in verse 3 suggests that there is a fornication with Babylon that involves more than idolatry (cult prostitution). Fornication also involves pride in excessive wealth.[38]

2. Warning to God's People (18:4-5)

In verse 4 God (or Christ) calls for Christians to separate themselves ideologically and, if necessary, physically from all the forms of Babylon. John has already warned the churches of her deceit and snares (chs. 2—3). If they refuse to separate themselves, they will "share in her sins" and also in the divine judgments.

If professing Christians succumb to the wiles of the queen prostitute and abandon their loyalty to Jesus, Christ will be forced by their own decision to pour out judgment upon them. They will, therefore, be included in the plagues designed for Babylon when she is judged (compare 3:5).[39]

We are reminded of Paul's admonition to the Corinthian Christians to separate themselves from the world which is hostile to God and His children (2 Cor. 6:17; compare 1 John 2:15-17; Jas. 4:4).

In verse 5 John describes the sins of Babylon as "heaped as high as heaven" (compare Jer. 51:9; Ezra 9:6). Although it looks as though the wicked go unpunished, John reminds his readers that "God remembers" (author's translation) and in His own time he will come with judgment.[40]

3. Cry of Vengeance (18:6-8)

The Lord calls for those who are to execute vengeance to come and punish Babylon (v. 6). Babylon has been ruthless and oppressive and now God will mete out to her double for all her wickedness (vv. 6-7a; compare Isa. 40:2; Jer. 50:15,29).[41]

Her punishment will fit her crimes. This Old Testament principle of "an eye for an eye" is never taught to God's people in the New Testament but, as here, is reserved for God alone (Matt. 5:38-42; Rom. 12:17-21). "Mix her a double portion from her own cup" (v. 6, NIV) reflects both the severity of God's judgment on those who persistently refuse to repent and the truth that God's wrath is related to the outworking of sin (compare Rom. 1:24-32).[42]

The boasting of Babylon in verse 7 reminds us of the arrogant pride of Tyre and Babylon in the Old Testament. In Isaiah 47:8b Babylon said: "I am, and there is no one besides me; I shall not sit as a widow or know loss of children." But the Lord prophesied doom upon her and it came to pass. In verse 8 God promises again that Babylon, because of her arrogant pride, shall be destroyed suddenly. This shall be done "in a single day" by the invading hosts led by the Antichrist (v. 8; compare 17:16; Jer. 50:34). God uses the Antichrist as the "rod of his anger."[43]

4. The Lament of the Kings, Merchants, and Seamen (18:9-19)

In this section, those who participated in Babylon's sins lament her passing. The background here seems to be Ezekiel's description of the judgment of the city of Tyre (Ezek. 26—28).[44]

Even a quick reading of Ezekiel 27 shows that in these verses Ezekiel's lamentation over the fall of ancient Tyre was in the back of John's mind. In terms drawn from the fall of harlot cities in the past, John describes the end of the great reality of evil, Babylon the great. While allusions to Rome may seem to be present, it is only because Rome, like Tyre, Babylon, or Jerusalem, is herself a prostitute city. The characteristics of all these cities are found in the queen mother of prostitutes.[45]

a. THE LAMENT OF THE KINGS OF THE EARTH (18:9-10)

First, the kings cry out their dirge. In verse 9 we are told that the kings have committed adultery with Babylon and shared her luxury. Luxury appears to be part of their adultery (compare Ezek. 26:16; 27:30-35).[46] Verse 10 reflects their pain at the suddenness of Babylon's downfall ("in one hour") and the emptiness of their own existence without her.

b. THE LAMENT OF THE MERCHANTS (18:11-17*a*)

The merchants have the most to lose because Babylon the great was built on luxury. When Babylon falls, so does her empire, bringing industry and trade to a virtual standstill. Therefore, the merchants of the earth weep and lament because there is no one to buy her wares (v. 11). Compare Ezekiel 27:12-24 for a similar list of commodities that the nations traded with Tyre (vv. 12-13).[47]

The lists which follow are inventories of exotic items which remind us of the Oriental marketplaces (vv. 12-13). In verse 13 "slaves, that is, human souls" are bought and sold. Perhaps John uses two terms for slaves to express his abhorrence at so brutal a system that crushed men's bodies and souls alike.[48]

Verse 14 is addressed directly to Babylon by the prophet John. The once affluent city is now utterly stripped of her material splendor. Just as the kings stood at a distance and lamented the fall of Babylon, so do the merchants grieve the fact that the harlot city no longer is decked out with all the finery she once knew (vv. 15-16).[49]

c. THE SHIPMASTERS AND SAILORS LAMENT (18:17*b*-19)

Finally, in verses 17*b*-18 the shipmasters and sailors add their lament because they too suffer irreparable loss because of the city's burning (compare Ezek. 27:28). Quite naturally, the shipmasters cast ashes upon their heads, for their source of wealth has gone up in smoke. This language is more suited to Tyre, a great port city, than Rome, which was inland and had the not-too-distant Ostia as its port. In any case, it is not John's intent to describe any one city but the great harlot city, the archetype of the earth's evil cities.[50]

5. A Call for Rejoicing (18:20)

The kings, merchants, and seamen wept at Babylon's fall. In contrast, there is heavenly jubilation. Babylon has persecuted the church of Jesus (saints, apostles, prophets). John attributes the deaths of the martyrs to Babylon the great. She killed Jesus (11:7-8) and Stephen by the hands of unbelieving Jews (Acts 7:57-60) and the martyr Antipas by the hands of pagan cultists (2:13).[51]

The prayer of the martyred saints beneath the altar (6:9) and others for vindication is here answered. They are to rejoice because God has heard their cry and answered with judgment.[52]

6. The Final Lament over Babylon (18:21-24)

In verse 21 John sees a vision in which a mighty angel picks up a huge stone, like a giant millstone, and flings it into the sea. The angel then interprets his actions to John. This vision of the millstone illustrates how Babylon shall be destroyed, never to rise again (compare Jer. 51:63-64).[53]

Verses 9-19 describe the ruin of Babylon in relation to the world outside. In verses 22-23a, the angel tells of the terrible effect within the actual city. All semblance of pleasure (music), business and industry (craftsman and millstone), or family life (voice of the bridegroom) are gone (compare Jer. 25:10; 7:34; Isa. 24:8; Ezek. 26:13). The melancholy recollection of the pulsing life that once filled this great city with the joy of life sounds through these verses.[54]

In verses 23b-24 the angel gives the reason why Babylon has been cast down. First, her merchants exalted themselves. Second, through her sorceries she has deceived all nations. Third, she has spilled "the blood of prophets and of saints."[55]

In John's mind, Babylon the great (v. 2) is much more comprehensive than ancient Babylon, Nineveh, Jerusalem, or Rome. She encompasses all the persecution against the servants of God until the words of God are fulfilled (compare 17:17).[56]

Revelation 18 is seen by some to support the theory of D. H. Lawrence that Revelation was written by and for "have-nots" out of spite and envy of the "haves." According to Collins, this theory results from a superficial reading of the text.[57]

In this passage, Babylon is condemned primarily for pride and murder. The theme of wealth or luxury is also present, but in a secondary way. The call, "Come out of her, my people" (v. 4) implies that at least some of the earliest readers had a share in Roman prosperity. The lists of fine wares are so detailed that they imply a certain admiration for the quality and quantity of Roman trade.

The impression one receives from these scenes of mourning is not one of envy. Revelation 18 does not condemn civilization as such. Rather, it shows an awareness of the way in which wealth and power can be misused. It shows the fleeting character of wealth and power—in one hour all of this wealth has been laid waste. The scenes of mourning remind the readers of the limits which God has set to human accomplishments and enjoyments.[58]

Excursus on God's Judgment

The stern justice by which Babylon is destroyed was inevitable because the God who judges is the God of truth and love. Rome as a representative of the transhistorical Babylon had done real harm upon the face of the earth. Revelation 18 calls out the song of doom so that humanity shall never forget that real harm and shall never forget that God judges all those who do harm. But in a deeper sense, people must never forget God's justice and love that made the fall of tyranny a necessity. The character of God stands behind the judgment.[59]

How then are we to interpret these portrayals of the judgment of Babylon? This is also a problem for the interpretation of Old Testament prophetic/apocalyptic books. In the Old Testament, nations and kings are also destroyed and the judgment of God is pronounced upon them. There are numerous examples in the Old Testament. We think of the accounts in Genesis and Exodus concerning Egypt in the time of the Exodus. Certainly among Christians and Jews of the first century the judgments upon Egypt were well known because of the feasts that celebrated the memory of the Exodus.[60]

There are many other examples in the Old Testament. There is the judgment of God upon Sodom and Gomorrah, as told in Genesis 18 and 19. Jeremiah 50—51 contains prophetic lamentations of doom that tell of God's judgment of Babylon. The Book of Amos begins with a statement of the judgment of God against the nations that surround Judah. And the final judgment in Amos is against Judah itself. Therefore, the question we must ask about the meaning for us today of these apocalyptic visions of judgment against Babylon is the same question we must ask with regard to all the biblical pronouncements of judgment against nations.[61]

What does it mean for us to read Revelation 18 in our century? Sodom and Gomorrah are destroyed cities that lie in ruin beneath the Dead Sea. Babylon was destroyed at the time of Alexander the Great. Ancient Rome and its caesars are gone.

According to Palmer, an adequate answer has two aspects. First, the Bible is a historical record as much as it is a theological affirmation. The Bible is a narrative about real people and real places. God reveals His character within the framework of history. The Exodus was a real event in the life of an enslaved people who were led out of Egypt by Yahweh.[62]

The whole of the Bible has an event perspective. Therefore, we must learn the law and the gospel from judgment accounts in Revelation in the same way that we learn the law and the gospel from reading the accounts of Amos and Jeremiah as they spoke God's judgment and forgiveness in Israel's earlier history. We are watching God's justice and grace as an event.

The difference in vision literature is that the event of God's judgment is expressed in symbolic language. When Jeremiah first spoke for God the news about the impending Assyrian attack of Samaria, he stated: "I see a boiling pot, facing away from the north" (Jer. 1:13). That hidden and symbolic language described a real historical event. Likewise, Revelation 18 portrays the event of judgment. The judgment probably refers initially to a nation in first-century history, but the code words and the time frame are expressed in symbolic language. The historical fact is that judgment has happened against Roman tyranny.[63]

In the second place, we should note that there is a timeless relevance to everything that God has revealed about Himself. That timeless relevance stretches beyond the historical context of the first century.

In Revelation 18, we discover more than simply the narratives of Rome and its lusts and its fall. These texts of judgment and hope teach us about the theology of power, of accountability, of the eternal measuring of human institutions, and of the hope that is rooted in God's character.

One sees the picture in Revelation 18 of a grieving John walking among the now silent wasteland of human arrogance. Everything has collapsed in the crashing sounds of chapter 18. The lamps are out, voices are silent, and the flutes and minstrels are no longer playing. The scene is stark and hopeless. The city was powerful, rich, and cruel; and now it has all come to this.[64]

Excursus on the Relation of the United States and Babylon

In his book, *An Ethic for Christians and Other Aliens in a Strange Land,* William Stringfellow argues that Revelation's portrayal of Babylon provides us with a parable which reveals the condition of "death" that prevails in all "fallen societies." We must see Babylon as a symbol of any city or nation that defies God and His revealed way. Babylon is an archetype of all rebellious nations.[65]

For Stringfellow, however, the United States is the current successor to Nazi Germany as a special and obvious manifestation of Babylonian patterns. American life is almost completely given over to the way of "death." This is a "moral reality" of corruption and destruction which can come to permeate the life of a nation.[66]

Some fundamentalist writers have also attempted to identify contemporary America with the biblical picture of Babylon. It is interesting to compare these attempts with Stringfellow's account. In his book, *Is the U.S.A. in Prophecy?,* S. Franklin Logsdon combines the references in Revelation 18 with those in Jeremiah 50—52 and produces a list of sixteen similarities between the United States and "prophetic Babylon." These similarities include a deteriorating position of world leadership, a populace made up of a "mingled people," spiritual decadence, and others.[67]

Stringfellow sees America's Babylonian patterns as revealed in its militarism, racial discrimination, and unjust legal structures. Logsdon worries about the United States' vulnerability to foreign "subversion," "the uprisings" of its minorities, and general patterns of "lawlessness." Both accounts agree in condemning consumerism and technolatry.[68]

Stringfellow's unbending commitment to a certain position leaves him open to the criticism that he fails to note some positive tendencies in American life. If these tendencies are taken into account, doubt is cast on his too simplistic identification of the United States with Babylon. For example, even granting the idolatrous and oppressive patterns he points to in American life, the United States has also provided in recent decades an arena for what appears to be an unprecedented and unparalleled discussion and critique of those very patterns.

In all fairness, it should be noted that when Stringfellow makes the straightforward claim that "America *is* Babylon," he does not mean to imply thereby (as Logsdon does) that Revelation 18 refers to a single historical entity, namely the United States. Rather, the picture of Babylon denotes a political/cultural condition toward which all nations tend, and which the United States presently approximates in a very special way. During Hitler's day, according to Stringfellow, it would also have been correct to say, "Germany *is* Babylon."[69]

According to Mouw, it would be more appropriate if Stringfellow would say—not that America *is* Babylon—but that America, like all nations in the fallen condition, exhibits Babylonian tendencies.[70]

What we can say with certainty on the basis of Revelation's portrayal of Babylon's fate is that all which is truly Babylonian—in contemporary America or in any other dimension of God's creation—will ultimately be destroyed. Babylon is doomed, and Jerusalem will triumph.

A biblical approach would not accept Stringfellow's attitude of hopelessness about nations as such—and perhaps even about institutions as such.[71]

However, as we contemplate John's descriptions of Babylon, we are struck by the many similarities to our world today. What are some marks of contemporary Babylon?[72]

1. Between the nations of the world: the arms race, distrust among nations, lust for power, war, planning and seeking peace without God, and depending on technology for security rather than on God.

2. Within society: lust for things, pleasure madness, crime, corruption, permissiveness, and hard-core pornography. Historian and columnist Max Lerner says, "We are living in a Babylonian society, perhaps more Babylonian than Babylon itself."

3. In religion and the church: the growing interest in the occult and Eastern religions which are attracting thousands of young people; false religions which deny the deity and vicarious atonement of Jesus Christ. There is also the tendency in some Christian groups to emphasize social action and community outreach to the exclusion of the preaching of the gospel. In other groups, there is the tendency to become so ingrown and concerned with their own survival that they are blinded to the needs of others. There is also the temptation of the church to imitate and adopt the methods of the world to achieve success rather than to rely on the power of the Holy Spirit.

4. On the personal level: becoming too enamored with the world, permitting "things" to play too important a role in our lives. There is also a compromising with truth and ethical behavior in order to succeed, planning without God, pride, and self-sufficiency.

All are marks of Babylon![73]

7. Thanksgiving for the Judgment of Babylon (19:1-5)

The cry, "Rejoice over her, O heaven" (18:20), is answered in 19:1-5. John tells of the jubilant hallelujahs that the angelic multitude in heaven raises to God (compare 11:15 *ff*.).

The multitude sings "Hallelujah!" because the "salvation and glory and power" which people have looked for is about to come from God (v. 1). They praise God because these things belong to Him and can only come from Him. The word *hallelujah* is used only in verses 1,3, and 6 in the New Testament. In Hebrew, it means "praise the Lord"; and we get the English word from the Greek, which is the transliteration of the Hebrew. It is found in the closing verses of Psalms 104—106. Our Christians hymns get their hallelujahs from this passage (vv. 1-10).[74]

The first shout of praise in verse 2 is the sound of a great multitude praising God for His condemnation of the prostitute. We are reminded once again of the song of Moses in Exodus 15 and its closing lines in Deuteronomy 32, "Praise his people, O you nations; for he avenges the blood of his servants, and takes vengeance on his adversaries" (v. 43).

This is a song of salvation, and the principal theological content is the praise of God for the triumph of His justice and the judgment that must go with justice. These visions in Revelation show that God is not indifferent to human suffering, to tyranny, to idolatry. Everything in the life of humanity is grappled with by God. This grappling is the judgment of the God who cares.[75]

Next, in verse 3, they shout out in celebration of Babylon's eternal destruction. The smoke arising to the accompaniment of the song is proof that Babylon has come to a permanent end (v. 3; compare 18:9; 14:11; Isa. 34:10).

The third shout in verse 4 is the antiphonal response of the voices of the twenty-four elders and the four living creatures.

The last shout in verse 5 is a single voice from the throne which calls on all the servants of God to praise Him. Note that the call is not limited to the martyrs. Instead the call is for all of God's servants, both the "small and great," to praise Him (compare Pss. 113:1; 134:1).[76]

When this section of Revelation is read, the "Hallelujah Chorus" in Handel's *Messiah* is recalled.

C. The Final Triumph and Consummation (19:6 to 21:8)

1. Marriage of the Lamb Announced (19:6-10)

a. THE JOY ACCOMPANYING THE MARRIAGE OF THE LAMB (19:6-9)
God grants John a vision of the impending, blessed, messianic

age, which appears under the figure of "the marriage supper of the Lamb" (v. 6). Just as the fall of Babylon, the Antichrist, and his empire are spoken of as already fallen, so this prophetic vision hails the kingdom as if already realized. Actually this event does not take place until the return of Christ (vv. 11 *ff.*)[77]

The singers are in heaven, as suggested by the similes of the "many waters" and "mighty thunder" (compare 1:15; 6:1; 14:2). The angels cry hallelujah because they see the Lord God Almighty as already reigning. God's supreme lordship over the universe is everywhere assumed in biblical thought. However, in a special eschatological sense, He is said to become king when His perfected kingdom shall have been established and all opposing powers of evil destroyed (for example, 11:15,17; 12:10; Matt. 6:10; 1 Cor. 15:24).

The cause for rejoicing is the marriage of the Lamb to His bride (v. 7). In the Old Testament, God is described as married to His people (compare Hos. 2:19; Isa. 54:1-8; Ezek. 16:7). In the New Testament, Jesus used the figure of a marriage feast to illustrate the kingdom of heaven (Matt. 22:2-3; 25:1 *ff.*). But the apostle Paul explicitly referred to the church as the bride of Christ (2 Cor. 11:2; Eph. 5:23 *ff.*). John presents the consummation of their marriage as if it were already accomplished (compare 21:9-10 where the New Jerusalem is identified as the bride of Christ).[78]

The time of engagement or betrothal has ended. Now it is the time for the church, prepared by loyalty and suffering, to enter into her full experience of salvation and glory with her beloved husband, Christ. The fuller revelation of the realization of this union is described in chapters 21 and 22.[79]

This passage is one of the sources for the parallel image of the soul as the bride of Christ. This image was very powerfully employed by J. S. Bach in his cantata, *Wachet Auf* ("Awake"). Here the tenderness, intimacy, and companionship of marriage illuminates the spiritual fulfillment which is experienced in union with Christ.[80]

In verse 8 we note that the church's garments are white linen—in marked contrast to the purple and scarlet clothing of the great mother of prostitutes (17:44; 18:16). John tells us that the fine linen represents the righteous deeds of the saints (3:5; 6:11; compare Phil. 2:12-13).[81]

The speaker addresses John and commands him to write the

benediction (v. 9). Those invited are identical with the bride. Unlike those invited in the parable of the wedding feast in Matthew 22:1-14, the guests invited to this feast all come.[82]

The banquet or feast as an image for the kingdom of God occurs frequently in the New Testament. In all of these cases, the well-known joy of a feast is used to illuminate the less-known delight of God's rule.[83]

b. THE DANGER OF IDOLATRY (19:10)

In verse 10, John, who is himself a prophet and who has received a clear revelation about idolatry, now falls prey to its temptation. After the final vision, he again slips into idolatry (22:8). Perhaps John included these references to his own failure because he knew of the tendency toward angel worship in the churches of Asia (compare Col. 2:18; Heb. 2:5). In any case, we need to recognize how easy it is to fall into idolatry. Whenever a Christian gives anyone or anything other than God control of his life, he has broken the first commandment. Only God deserves human worship. We are to worship nothing in heaven or earth—only the eternal Lord.[84]

John concludes this vision with the important statement that "the testimony of Jesus is the spirit of prophecy" (v. 10). Here John joins hands with all of the prophets to state that Jesus' testimony to God—His complete revelation of God—is the very spirit and heart of the entire message of God's Word.[85]

2. *The Warrior-Messiah Appears (19:11-16)*

a. THE SECOND COMING OF CHRIST AS THE CLIMAX OF THE BIBLICAL VIEW OF HISTORY (19:11)

We now come to the climax of the struggle to which the preceding chapters have looked forward with great anticipation—the defeat of the Antichrist and his forces. John's faith follows the biblical view which teaches a plan of divine action grounded in the unity and goal of history. God's plan in Revelation is a goal-directed sequence of intrusions by God into human history.[86]

The tension of the end time is resolved by the second coming or parousia of Christ which is the final revelation and accomplishment of salvation. Revelation sees in the second coming of Christ the beginning of a new "history," which, by means of the millennial kingdom and the judgment of the world, leads the new Jerusalem to the new Paradise.[87]

Again the veil of the heavens is pulled back, and John sees Christ seated upon a "white horse" (v. 11). Christ has come to do battle with the beast and the false prophet who are at Armageddon (compare 16:13-16 and 19:19). The "white horse" of Christ symbolizes the victory anticipated (compare 6:2). The title of Christ is "Faithful and True." These are titles which testify to the ideal character of the Messiah (compare 1:5; 3:7,14). He has come to execute righteous judgment and to make war against the Antichrist and his allies (compare Isa. 11:3-5).[88]

b. THE DESCRIPTION OF THE CHARACTER OF CHRIST (19:12-13)

In verses 12-13 the character of Christ is described. The "many diadems" are appropriate for one who is King of kings and Lord of lords (v. 16). Some have suggested that the name which no one knows and its meaning will be shared with the saints in the new age.[89]

There are good reasons for believing that Christ's blood-dipped robe in verse 13 is red with His own blood. If the blood is that of His enemies, how is it that Christ comes from heaven with His robe already dipped in blood before any battle is mentioned? Furthermore, the blood that is always mentioned in connection with Christ in Revelation is His own lifeblood (1:5; 5:6,9; 7:14; 12:11). Moreover, the word "dipped" does not fit the imagery of Isaiah 63:2, but it does fit the imagery used in Revelation of believers' garments being washed thoroughly in Christ's blood (7:14; 22:14). Finally, the sword with which Christ strikes down the nations comes from His mouth and is not in His hand (v. 15). This fact is incompatible with battle imagery.[90]

Another name by which Christ is called is "the Word of God" (v. 13). This title definitely links the thought of Revelation with the prologue of the fourth Gospel (compare John 1:1-18).[91]

c. THE MEANING OF THE ARMIES OF HEAVEN (19:14)

In verse 14 the armies which were in heaven and which were following Christ could mean either angelic companies or risen saints.

It could mean angelic hosts since some passages in the Old Testament and New Testament speak of the armies or soldiers of heaven as angels (Pss. 103:21; 148:2; Luke 2:13; Acts 7:42). Moreover, elsewhere in the New Testament the coming of Christ is associated with angels (for example, Matt. 13:41; 16:27; 24:30-31).

On the other hand, it could mean the risen saints. Their clothing of bright and clean linen is identical to the bride's attire (compare 19:8). Thus it could be the victors who accompany Christ, either all of them (see 1 Thess. 4:16-17) or the company of the martyrs. Revelation 17:14 seems to indicate this: "They [the beast and the ten kings] will make war on the Lamb, and the Lamb will conquer them, for he is Lord of lords and King of kings, and those with him are called and chosen and faithful" (compare 15:1-2).[92]

In any case, the conquest is achieved primarily not by the following hosts but by the Lamb.

d. THE MEANING OF THE SHARP SWORD AND CHRIST'S NAME (19:15-16)

Note that the enemy is defeated by the "sharp sword" which issues from Christ's mouth (v. 15). This points to the symbolic nature of the picture presented. These are numerous references to the conquest of the forces of evil by the "word of his mouth" (see especially 1:16; 2:12; Isa. 11:4; Heb. 4:12).[93]

It is hardly possible to equate this sword from Christ's mouth with the weapons used by Charlemagne and Rome. This military figure of speech is a metaphor for the glorious power which the King shall exercise. Paul could thus describe the destruction of the Antichrist by the "breath" of Jesus' mouth and the "brightness" (KJV) of His coming (2 Thess. 2:8). We may be sure that His glorious rule will be consistent with Himself. This does not empty His coming and reign of their literalness. This does not relegate His coming and return to the world of spiritual, nonspatial reality. He shall reign over the nations on the earth by an exercise of power and of force. But the weapons of His warfare may not be those of the earth.[94]

God's kingdom, whose mediatorial King is Christ, always operates by heavenly supernatural power. By such power was the kingdom revealed in the person and earthly ministry of our Lord. By such power is it now proclaimed. And by the same power, although manifested in a different realm, shall the kingdom be revealed in the time of His return. It is the same supernatural power of God, whether it be demonstrated in the quiet inner work of the Spirit, or in the outward rule of the iron rod. His Word shall speak and His will shall be done![95]

The nations which are smitten are those which are hostile to Christ, and He (emphatic) shall rule them with a "rod of iron" (vv. 15,19-21; Isa. 14:4; Ps.2:9). The messianic prophecy long foretold by the psalmist (2:9) is now to be fulfilled. John says that Christ will tread the "wine press of the fury of the wrath of God the Almighty" and thereby press out the "wine" for the cup of God's wrath which the wicked must drink (compare Isa. 63:3; 19:19-20; Rev. 14:10; 16:19).

Not only is Christ called the Faithful and True, the Word of God but also, in verse 16, He is designated as the "King of kings and Lord of lords." The titles ascribed to God the Father are here applied to the Son (compare 1 Tim. 6:15).[96]

3. The Battle of Christ and Antichrist (19:17-21)

a. THE DESCRIPTION OF THE SUPPER OF GOD (19:17-18)

John sees an angel standing in the sun (in mid heaven), and the angel calls to all the birds to come to the great feast which God is preparing for them (v. 17). The background for the great feast is Ezekiel 39:17-20. There the feast comes after the messianic age and after the battle of Gog of the land of Magog. Here it precedes the messianic age. (It is helpful to read Isa. 25:6; Luke 14:15 *ff.*; 22:27-30 where the idea of the banquet is associated with the coming of the messianic kingdom.)[97]

Note the dramatic contrast between the marriage supper of the Lamb and this "great supper" (vv. 6-10, 17-18). In verse 18 it is the supper of God in the sense that God will provide it. The ranks of the enemy are composed not only of kings and captains but of all kinds of people, free and bond, small and great. The bodies of the enemy will lie on the field of battle to be devoured by birds of prey. To remain unburied for the pleasure of the predators was considered by the ancients to be an ignominious fate. The scene is one of universal dishonor and destruction.[98]

b. THE DESCRIPTION AND MEANING OF THE BATTLE OF ARMAGEDDON (19:19-21)

John sees the beast and his armies arrayed against the Messiah and his army (v. 19). The battle of Armageddon has arrived. In 16:13-14 we learned that demonic spirits went forth from the mouth of the beast and the false prophet to assemble the kings of the whole world for battle on the great day of God the Almighty. According to 16:16, they gathered them together into the place which is called in Hebrew *Har-Magedon*.[99]

(1) The dramatic end of the Antichrist and his forces

The scene in verses 19-21 is eschatological or final in an absolute sense. John is not describing the gradual conquest of evil in the spiritual struggles of the faithful. Rather, he tells of a great historical event which brings to an end the Antichrist and his forces and ushers in the long-awaited era of righteousness. History may offer examples of the triumph of right over wrong, but they do not exhaust the truth of Revelation. These historical examples rather prefigure the actual consummation with its end to wickedness and the beginning of the final stages of God's kingdom (compare 17:13-14).[100]

(2) The stages of Satan's undoing

Verse 20 points out the contrast between the assembling of the beast's might with his kings and their soldiers and the ease with which he is overthrown and captured. This highlights the beast's powerlessness before his mighty conqueror. No battle is actually fought. Only the assembling of the foes and the defeat of the beast are described. This is not accidental. John indicates that the battle has already been fought and that this is simply the final realization of that previous victory. In chapter 5 the Lamb had overcome (won the victory) by His death (vv. 5,9). Furthermore, in 12:7-9,11, we are told that there was a battle in heaven, and Satan was cast out and defeated by the blood of the Lamb and the word of His followers' testimony. Thus there is only one fundamental or basic battle described in Revelation.[101]

This means that the rest of the scenes in verses 20-21 may be understood as more judicial in character than as literal battlefield descriptions. Because of John's christological reinterpretations, no great eschatological military battle, such as that described in the Qumran War Scroll, will actually be fought. The decisive battle has already been won at the cross. These armies and the beast are the destroyers of the earth (11:18). Ultimately they are the satanic principalities of the world who ally themselves with the human puppets for their idolatrous ends. These have been triumphed over at the cross (Col. 2:15); they are finally stripped of all power at Christ's return.[102]

Although Satan has been dealt a death blow at the cross (compare John 12:31; 16:11), he nevertheless continues to promote evil and deception during this present age (compare Eph. 2:2; 1 Thess. 3:5; 1 Pet. 5:8-9; Rev. 2:10). He even uses historical persons, such as a Nero or a Hitler, to oppose and harass Christians. Yet he is a deposed ruler who is now under the sovereign authority of Christ. For a "little time" he is allowed to continue his evil until God's purposes are finished. In this scene in verses 19-21 of the overthrow of the beast and his kings and their armies, John shows us the ultimate and swift destruction of these evil powers by the King of kings and Lord of lords. They have met their Master in this final and real confrontation.[103]

(3) The final state of the beast and false prophet (19:20)

The beast and false prophet are seized and cast alive into the lake of fire (v. 20). The beast is the personification of secular power in its opposition to the church. The false prophet represents the role of false religion in persuading man to worship the antichristian power (compare 13:1,11). The false prophet is again described in terms which make it clear that he is the same as the second beast of 13:11-17. He deceives people by working great signs (compare 13:13-15). He also brands with the mark of the beast all but those who are willing to die for their faith (compare 13:16-17)

The designation of the lake of fire for the place of final torment occurs only in Revelation, although the idea of punishment by fire is described in other places in the Bible. The Antichrist and the false prophet are the first inhabitants of the lake of fire. Later the devil (20:10), death and Hades (20:14), and all evil people (21:8) will join them in this place of ceaseless torment.[104]

(4) The meaning of the sword from Christ's mouth (19:21)

In verse 21 we are told that the armies of Antichrist are killed by the sword which proceeds from the mouth of Messiah. While this is obviously not to be understood as a literal sword, neither is it to be taken as a metaphor for the gospel message. The scene is one of judgment. The sword is the proclamation of divine retribution that slays all who have in the final alignment of loyalties arrayed themselves against God and the forces of righteousness. The supper of God is ready, and the vultures gorge themselves on the flesh of the wicked.[105]

Beasley-Murray comments that Revelation is full of Christ and speaks often of the coming of the kingdom of God and yet gives little space to the actual event of the appearing of Christ. When it does describe the event, it deliberately uses dramatic and impressionist effects.

There is no battle when Christ appears. Rather, there is a revelation of His glory and an act of judgment. The sole weapon He possesses is the sword of His mouth, by which the will of God is declared and thereby performed. At the end, as at the beginning, the Word of God speaks, and it is done.

The chief point of John's picture, therefore, is that Christ, whose power is limitless and whose sovereignty is universal, reveals that sovereignty at the God-ordained time and makes it effective in the universe. The revelation is action—a declaration of "thus far and no further" to the destructive powers in God's world.[106]

4. The Binding of Satan, the Resurrection, and the Millennial Kingdom (20:1-6)

a. THE BINDING OF SATAN (20:1-3)

In verses 1-3 we come to the complete conquest of Satan to which everything in Revelation has been pointing. Although Satan's two agents have already been cast into "the lake of fire," Satan was still free to work his wiles. As long as he was free, neither the millennial kingdom nor the new heaven or earth could become a reality. It was with profound gratitude and rejoicing, therefore, that John received the vision of the binding of Satan.[107]

(1) The angel and the binding of Satan (20:1)

In verse 1 note that an angel has the key to the bottomless pit and the great chain, and not Christ. The angel is probably the one who in chapter 9 released the demonic locusts by opening the shaft leading to the abyss. The "bottomless pit" or "abyss" is not the lake of fire or the place of the final judgment (20:1; compare 9:1; 17:8).[108]

We would expect Satan to be thrown at once into the lake of fire, but this doom is delayed. Only at the end of the one thousand years, when he is released and is again able to entice people to rebel against Christ and the saints, is he finally destroyed. Then the dragon, who is the devil, is cast into the lake of fire along with the beast and the false prophet.

(2) Satan and the serpent (20:2)

In verse 2 John identifies the dragon with the serpent and clearly states that he is none other than the devil and Satan. The "serpent" title reminds us of him who tempted Adam and Eve in Paradise, and all "the sons of Adam" since. The "devil" is the New Testament name for the "evil one" (Matt. 4:1 and elsewhere). Satan, "the accuser," is the title used in prophetic literature and elsewhere (Zech. 3:1-2; Job 1:6; Ps. 109:6; compare 1 Tim. 3:11 with 3:6).[109]

(3) The meaning of the binding of Satan (20:2)

The idea of Satan being bound is a familiar one in the early Jewish literature (Tobit 8:3; 1 Enoch 10:4,11-12; 88:1-3; Jubilees 23:29; Testament of Levi 18:21).[110]

From at least the time of Victorinus (died about 303), some have interpreted the binding of Satan as the work of Christ in the lives of believers. Thus Satan is "bound" for believers since he no longer deceives them, but he is still "loose" for unbelievers who are deceived. This explanation, however, does not take seriously the language of the abyss and the prison in which Satan is confined, nor does it account for the releasing of Satan after the one thousand years.[111] In fact, Ostella argues that discontinuance of deception in Revelation 20:3 is a critically decisive exegetical point and ultimately demands the conclusion that the millennium involves an extension of redemptive history subsequent to the second coming of Christ.[112]

There is, of course, one sense in which, according to the gospel account, Satan is in the process of being bound by the activity of Christ and the kingdom of God. However, this sense is clearly an event different from the total consigning of Satan to the abyss as taught in verses 1-3.[113]

(4) The limitation of the deception of Satan (20:3)

Satan is "sealed" in the pit so that he will not be able to deceive the nations as he had in the past or will do when released after the one-thousand year period (v. 3). "He must be loosed" refers to the fact that the release of Satan after the millennial reign of Christ is all in the plan of God.[114]

Note that John does not say in verse 3 that Satan could not deceive at all but that he could not deceive the nations. Evidently he did deceive some people because when the complete period of one thousand years is up, there will be enough who respond to Satan that he has a large group ready to wage another battle against Christ.[115]

(5) The relationship of the binding of Satan to the millennium (20:4-6)

Johnson also points out that the one-thousand year binding of Satan is concurrent with and inseparable from the one-thousand year reign of the resurrected saints and martyrs in verses 4-6. For one thousand years on this earth, within history, the activity of Satan leading humanity into false worship and active rebellion against God and His people will be curbed under the authority of Christ in His kingdom. If that reign is yet future, the binding is future. If the binding refers to an earthly situation, which it clearly does, the one-thousand year reign most naturally also refers to an earthly situation. This undergirds the historical premillennial approach used in this study.[116]

Excursus on the Millennium

In chapter 2, representative views about the millennium were discussed. In preparation for the exegesis of 20:4-6, more detailed arguments for the historical premillennial or covenant premillennial model or approach will be presented.

As indicated in chapter 2, the straightforward exegesis of 20:4-6 and other biblical material has led many evangelical scholars to advocate the historical premillennial view. It should be recognized, however, that there are problems with this view of 20:4-6, just as there are problems with other views of this difficult portion of Revelation. Responsible Christian scholars vary in its interpretation according to their study, convictions, and presuppositions.[117]

The optional millennial interpretations

The main problem is related to the question of the meaning of the millennium (from the Latin *mille,* one thousand; *annus* or *ennus,* year). Does the millennium indicate an earthly historical reign of righteousness that will manifest itself at the close of the present age, or is 20:4-6 symbolic of some present experience of Christians or some future nonhistorical reality?[118]

The early church view—historical premillennialism

As we saw in chapter 2, the ancient church down to the time of Augustine (354-430), with minor exceptions, held to the teaching of an earthly, historical reign of righteousness that was to follow the defeat of the Antichrist and the physical resurrection of the saints. The early Christians taught that this reign would precede both the judgment and the new creation.[119]

The early church view is advocated in this study. This approach teaches that the millennium will be in history and on the earth as an end-time reality. This view is in keeping with the way in which the kingdom of God was present in the life and ministry of Jesus—present, but yet still future.[120]

One of the unifying centers in the diversity of New Testament theology is the tension between experienced and futuristic theology. In the present age, there is a real overlapping of the two ages. While we live in the old age, we experience the powers of the age to come. This means that there should be no objection in principle to the idea that God in His redemptive purpose may yet have an age in which there is an even further interaction between the powers of the new age and the present evil age. The millennium is a further demonstration of Christ's power in this age before Christ turns over the kingdom to the Father's all-encompassing dominion in the age to come.[121]

The historical premillinnial view is also called the "end-historical" view. It follows the same chronological sequence as the early church's premillennial position. There is the parousia (return of Christ), the defeat of Antichrist, the binding of Satan, the resurrection, the millennium, the release of Satan, the final judgment and then the new heaven and the new earth.[122]

The millennium in Jewish thought

The strongest objection to historical premillennialism is that this truth is found in an explicit form in only one passage of Scripture—Revelation 20. Nonmillenarians appeal to the argument of analogy of faith. This method of interpretation states that difficult passages must be interpreted by clear passages. It is a fact that most of the New Testament writings say little about a millennium.[123]

It should be emphasized, however, that although Revelation is the only New Testament book which clearly refers to the millennial reign of Christ, it is by no means a new idea in Hebrew-Christian thought. The prophets of the Old Testament looked forward with great anticipation to a messianic age here on earth and John knew this well (compare Isa. 2:1-4; 11:6-9; and so forth). Later, Jewish thought was broadened to include not only a messianic age on earth but a new heaven and new earth. John reflects this two-phased hope of a messianic age on earth and an eternal age in glory (compare especially Ezek. 36—39 where a similar sequence is suggested; there is a messianic era of peace, battle of Gog of the land of Magog, followed by a new age). The pattern of Ezekiel's prophecy appears to have determined the presentation of John's vision of the kingdom in chapters 20—22, above all in chapter 20.[124]

There are also references to the millennial age of a fixed duration in other Jewish and early Christian writings. Ezra 7:28-32 anticipates a messianic age of 400 years. Second Enoch 33:2 and the Epistle of Barnabas 15:2-8 support Revelation in anticipating a messianic reign of one thousand years. The idea of a one-thousand year messianic age may also be related to Genesis 1 and Psalm 90:4 (that is, six millenniums of work followed by one of rest).[125]

The indirect millennial emphasis in the New Testament

The emphasis of Jesus

There are indications in the Gospels that the teachings of Jesus coincide with the implications of this prayer for the earthly kingdom, not least the Beatitudes with which the Sermon on the Mount begins. We think of Matthew 5:5, "Blessed are the meek, for they shall inherit the earth." Matthew 5:5 speaks quite definitely of a hope for the earth and not only a hope for something invisible, which stands beyond all earthly realities.

It is also quite certain that John would have known and used the prayer which Jesus taught His disciples to pray. The burden of that prayer is: "Thy kingdom come,/Thy will be done,/on earth as in heaven" (Matt. 6:10).

Jesus did not teach a doctrine of the millennium, but He did teach the coming of the kingdom of God among people through His own redemptive ministry. There are indications in Jesus' teaching that He looked for the triumph of that kingdom in this world—as the prayer He taught suggests.

The hope of the Bible carries throughout a double aspect. It embraces a hope for the earth and then beyond that a hope for the final consummation. This does not mean that Jesus taught a doctrine of the millennium, but it does suggest that the millennium is harmonious with His teaching.[126]

The emphasis of Paul

Another passage which is often associated with the concept of a millennial reign of Christ, although it is not explicit, is 1 Corinthians 15:23-24. With this passage is usually associated Philippians 3:21; 1 Thessalonians 4:14-17; Luke 14:14, and others.[127]

In 1 Corinthians 15:23-26, Paul pictured the triumph of Christ's kingdom as being accomplished in several stages. The resurrection of Christ is the first stage. The second stage will occur at the second coming when those who are Christ's will share His resurrection. "Then comes the end, when he delivers the kingdom to God the Father after destroying every rule and every authority and power. For he must reign until he has put all his enemies under his feet. The last enemy to be destroyed is death" (1 Cor. 15:24-26). The adverbs translated "then" denote a sequence: "after that." There are three distinct stages: Jesus' resurrection; after that the resurrection of believers at the great resurrection; after that the end. An unidentified interval falls between Christ's resurrection and His second coming. We are now in that interval. Then a second undefined interval falls between the second coming and the end, when Christ completes the subjugation of His enemies. This interval is the millennium.[128]

This exegesis is defended by Oscar Cullmann in *The Early Church*.[129] K. L. Schmidt likewise states that the idea of the millennium clearly developed in Revelation 20 lies concealed by Paul in 1 Corinthians 15:23-28.[130] Thus it appears to be thoroughly possible that Paul, in 1 Corinthians 15:23-26, was thinking of the same period which the Revelation describes as the millennium.

The emphasis of Christian scholars

Many serious Christian scholars agree that there is a clear straightforward statement of an earthly millennium in Revelation 20. Eric Rust contends that the presence of the millennium in Revelation is beyond dispute. John places a messianic kingdom on earth between the parousia and the end.[131] K. L. Schmidt states that the person who refuses to find an intermediary stage between the two ages in Revelation 20 approaches the text with preconceived ideas, and thus gains from it neither the exact sense nor the value.[132]

The purpose of the millennium

A number of theologians have also suggested reasons for the purpose of the millennium in God's redemptive plan. For Hubbard, Johnson, Bruce, and Ladd, the doctrine of the millennium is important for two reasons.

First, the millennium provides an opportunity for Christ to openly manifest his kingdom in world history. The millennium will provide an actual demonstration of the truthfulness of the divine witness borne by Christ and His followers during their life on earth. It will be a time of the fulfillment of all God's covenant promises to His people.[133]

Christ is now reigning as Lord and King, but His reign is veiled, unseen, and unrecognized by the world. The glory that is now His is known only by people of faith. So as far as the world is concerned, Christ's reign is only potential and unrealized. The age to come will not be the time of Christ's reign but the age of the Father's glory. The millennial kingdom will be the age of the manifestation of Christ's glory. It will be the time when the sovereignty—which He now possesses but does not openly manifest and which He will turn over to the Father in the age to come—will be displayed in the world.[134] F. F. Bruce adds that Scripture encourages us to believe that on this earth, where He was rejected and crucified, Jesus will ultimately receive universal and joyful recognition as Lord and King.[135]

The hiddenness and apparent unreality of the church's existence as the community of messianic salvation cry out for its revelation to the world. The millennium as an obvious messianic kingdom is hence the proof of the divine truthfulness of the word given to the believer and of the testimony of the "true witness," which is "The Word of God" in person (19:13).[136]

The millennium will be a display of personal righteousness. Christ's people, who have overcome the temptations of the Antichrist and who have been transformed by resurrection, will be present in wholeness and perfection (Rev. 20:4). The millennium will also demonstrate political righteousness.[137]

Mouw suggests that it is not enough for Christ to rule in the hearts of the saints. Christ's rule must also be manifested in the transformation of political processes as we now know them.[138]

Beasley-Murray contends that the inspiration of Marxism is the biblical hope drained of God. Marxism is the secular hope that dominates the largest segment of Europe. It has taken over the largest nation in the world (China), and it has the prospect of taking over multitudes more. What has the church to say to it?

The answer is surely clear: If the church has dropped its hope, it must pick it up again. That will mean that it must take Revelation with its doctrine of the millennium seriously once more and recognize that it is a Christian book with authentic Christian doctrine. The belief that there will be a preliminary manifestation of the triumphant kingdom of God on earth is to be found in various forms in certain Old Testament books and in Jewish apocalyptic writings outside the Bible. John builds on this teaching. He shows its fulfillment in the kingdom of the crucified and risen Lord which will have a powerful manifestation in history before the age to come. Such a view can help meet the Marxist challenge.[139]

Second, the millennium will reveal that man's rebellion against God lies deep in man's own heart and not just in the devil's deception. Even when Satan is bound and righteousness prevails in the world, some people will still rebel against God. The final release of Satan will draw this hidden evil out into the open.[140]

The millennium is to be seen as a time of social and political and economic justice when people dwell together under the government of Christ in peace and prosperity. Before the final judgment God grants to people a time when their social environment is as nearly perfect as possible. And yet after such a period of righteousness, the hearts of unregenerate people prove still to be rebellious against God. In the final judgment every mouth will indeed be stopped and every excuse voided. Can there by any clearer picture of human perversity? What can God do but judge such rebellion?[141]

The very idea of eternal punishment is utterly repugnant to the modern mind. There is indeed a need to vindicate the judgment of God as well as to display His unlimited love. The millennial reign of righteousness is the backdrop for the last judgment. When the final terrible doom of the wicked is pronounced, God is justified in his acts and His righteousness is vindicated in His judgments.[142]

b. THE MILLENNIUM (20:4-6)
(1) The identity of those who reign in the millennium (20:4a-b)
(a) The reign of all the saints of God

John saw thrones and seated on them were those to whom judgment was committed (v. 4*a*). Some commentators teach that this resurrection is limited to the martyrs of the tribulation. They are, indeed, given special mention. However, the rather rough language of the Greek is well rendered in the Revised Standard Version: "Then I saw thrones, and seated on them were those to whom judgment was committed." This group is all the saints of God, who are now raised up and share Christ's reign. The promise that the saints will share Christ's rule and judgment is one that occurs frequently in Scripture (Dan. 7:9,22; Matt. 19:28; 1 Cor. 4:8; 6:2-3; 2 Tim. 2:12; Rev. 2:26,28; 3:12,21; 5:9-10).[143]

It will be helpful to examine in detail some of these verses relating to the fact that Christ's power to reign will be shared with all believers. Here are Jesus' words on the matter; "Truly, I say to you, in the new world, when the Son of man shall sit on his glorious throne, you who have followed me will also sit on twelve thrones, judging the twelve tribes of Israel" (Matt. 19:28). Paul expanded that idea to include the world: "Do you not know that the saints will judge the world?" (1 Cor. 6:2). Revelation echoes this promise of ruling power by promising a share in Jesus' throne to all who are overcomers (Rev. 2:26; 3:21).[144]

(b) The special role of the martyrs

John also saw the souls of those who had been beheaded for their testimony to Jesus (v. 4*b*). To the whole church is given authority to rule. The resurrected, believing Christians sit on the thrones. But John focuses sharply on part of that vast company, the Christians martyred by the powers of the Antichrist, called here by his suitable title, "the beast." This group was especially equipped to help Jesus rule for the millennium of power and righteousness which was part of His program.[145]

(c) The reign of the survivors

Others see a third group in verse 4*b* singled out for special attention. This group consists of those "who had not worshiped the beast or its image and had not received its mark on their foreheads or their hands." That this is, indeed, a third group does not appear in most English translations; but the syntax of the Greek sentence changes at this point. This third group designates those who survive the persecution of the tribulation and who are living when Christ returns.[146]

(d) The possible relationship of the martyrs and the overcomers

Johnson suggests that the martyrs may represent the whole church that is faithful to Jesus, whether or not they have actually been killed. They constitute a group that can in truth be described as those who "did not love their lives so much as to shrink from death" (12:11, NIV). "Martyr" is a synonym for "overcomers" (chs. 2—3). Thus John could count himself in this group, although he may never have suffered death by the ax of the beast.[147]

(2) The meaning of the first resurrection (20:4c-5)

Verse 4c says that all mentioned in verse 4a-b "came to life" and reigned with Christ during the millennium. If the third group designates the living saints, the words "came to life" includes both the resurrection of dead saints and the rapture of the living, as in 1 Thessalonians 4:16-17 and 1 Corinthians 15:51 *ff.*[148]

(a) The spiritual resurrection view

Since Augustine, some interpreters have taken the words "came to life" to refer to a spiritual resurrection, or new birth, or to the triumph of the church. Other scholars take more seriously the exegesis of 20:4-6. They agree that the language teaches bodily resurrection. However, they contend that the whole section (vv. 1-10) is apocalyptic language. It is figurative of the consolation and reward promised to the martys and should not be taken as predicting events within history. For Berkouwer, this vision should not be seen as a narrative account of a future earthly reign. Rather, it is the apocalyptic unveiling of the reality of salvation in Christ as a backdrop to the reality of the suffering and martyrdom that still continue as long as the dominion of Christ remains hidden. This view fails to take seriously the language of the one-thousand-year reign, which is everywhere in Revelation a reign on the earth within history.[149]

(b) The physical resurrection view

In answer to those who spiritualize the first resurrection, it should be said that in this context there is no justification for interpreting this "first resurrection" in a spiritual sense as referring to the "new birth." Surely John would have made this point clear if this is what he had in mind![150]

John plainly says that "This is the first resurrection" (v. 5). The word "resurrection," which occurs over forty times in the New Testament, is used almost exclusively of physical resurrection (Luke 2:34 is the only exception). There is no indication that John has departed from this usage in these verses.[151]

Why does John call this the "first" resurrection? The term "first" clearly implies the first in a series of two or more. John does not refer directly to a second resurrection. However, it is correctly inferred both from the use of "first" and from the expression "the rest of the dead did not come to life until the thousand years were ended" (v. 5). It is exegetically weak to make the first resurrection spiritual and the second one physical, unless the text itself clearly indicates this change, which it does not. Therefore, we may understand the first resurrection to be the raising to physical life of all the dead in Christ (compare 1 Cor. 15:12 *ff.*; 1 Thess. 4:13 *ff.*).[152]

(3) The participants in the first resurrection (20:6)

John states that for those who participate in this first resurrection "the second death has no power over them" (v. 6, NIV). Therefore, they are "blessed and holy" and shall be priests of God and Christ for the one thousand years. On the other hand, those over whom the second death will have power must be "the rest of the dead" (v. 5). They will be participants in the second resurrection, the "rise to be condemned" (NIV) of John 5:29 (compare Acts 24:15).

This first resurrection in verses 4-5 thus refers only to those who will share in the millennium kingdom. The evil people are not raised up. They stay in the intermediate state or Hades.[153]

(4) The duration of the thousand years (20:6)

A thousand years is probably symbolic of a perfect period of time of whatever length. But the number symbolisms of John in Revelation should not be used to argue against the reality of an earthly kingdom. The essence of historical premillennialism lies in its insistence that the reign will be on earth, not in heaven, for a period of time before the final judgment and the new heaven and earth and *after* Christ's return. In any case, it is not of primary importance whether the 1,000 years are actual 365-day years or symbolic of a shorter or longer period of bliss enjoyed by believers as they reign with Christ on earth (compare 5:10; 11:15; 22:5).[154]

5. *The Final Destruction of Satan and Death (20:7-15)*

a. THE LAST INSURRECTION OF EVIL AND THE DESTRUCTION OF SATAN (20:7-10)

(1) The last insurrection and the depth of evil (20:7-8)

John states that at God's bidding Satan will be loosed and will go forth to deceive the nations (v. 7). These nations are identified with Gog and Magog, whom Ezekiel reckoned as the diabolical leaders of the forces of evil.[155]

In Revelation, however, both Gog and Magog are symbolic figures representing the nations of the world which band together for a final assault upon God and His people. No specific geographical designations are intended. They are simply hostile nations from all across the world. The war for which they are gathered in 20:8 should be distinguished from that in 17:14 and 19:19 (Armageddon) in that it follows the one-thousand-year reign.[156]

But why would God allow this insurrection? If man alone were prophetically writing the history of the world, he would not bring the archdeceiver back after the glorious reign of Christ (vv. 4-6). But God's thoughts and ways are not man's (Isa. 55:8). Ezekiel's vision of Gog brought out of the land of Magog seems to be clearly in John's mind (Ezek. 38—39). Ezekiel also saw an attack on God's people, who had been restored for some time.[157]

The beast and his armies were destroyed (19:19-21). The rebellious groups in verse 8 are other people who during the millennial reign defected in their hearts from the Messiah. This section shows something of the deep, complex nature of evil. The source of rebellion against God does not lie just in man's environment, or fundamentally with the devil, but deep within man himself.[158]

The repeated rebellions of Satan reveal the irrepressible character of the forces of evil and chaos. The implication is that creation and order, peace and justice, are quite fragile and partial states and that they are in constant tension with their opposites. The definitive defeat of Satan implies that even though chaos is irrepressible, it is less powerful, less real, than creative order.[159]

(2) The protection of God's people and the destruction of the evil nations (20:9)

Verse 9 states that the innumerable hosts will surround "the camp of the saints and the beloved city." God, however, intervenes on behalf of His people and He sends fire down from heaven to consume the enemies (compare Ezek. 38:22; 39:6; Gen. 19:24).[160]

The word *camp* in the New Testament refers to either a military camp or the camp of Israel (Acts 21:34,37; 22:24; Heb. 11:34; 13:11,

13). It is a word that reminds us of the pilgrim character of the people of God even at the end of the millennium, as long as evil is active in God's creation.[161]

"The beloved city" is an expression parallel to Zion (after Pss. 78:68; 87:2). Zion, however, is completely divorced from its geographical significance in Revelation and has become a designation of the Christian church's meaning in salvation history. Thus John refers to the community of the redeemed without any specific geographical location in mind. This would be in harmony with his previous references to the city elsewhere in the book (compare 11:2,8). Following this understanding of the beloved city in no way weakens the validity of an earthly reign of Christ and the saints.[162]

(3) The destiny and function of the devil (20:10)

The devil or Satan is not consumed by the fire described in verse 9 (v. 10). Rather he is seized and thrown into "the lake of fire" where the beast and the false prophet have already been cast. There this trinity of evil is "tormented day and night for ever and ever" (v. 10; compare 19:20). Thus the devil, having accomplished his work of manifesting the hidden rebelliousness of humanity, is no longer tolerated to work further mischief.[163]

According to Beasley-Murray, this passage (vv. 7-10) is significant because it suggests that the function of the devil is not to originate sin but to reveal it and develop its latent possibilities in people. Since sin is directed against the will of God, it is primarily to be seen as rebellion against God. This rebellion seeks to destroy the works of God and even Christ and God Himself.

But we should also remember that the devil is not God, nor is he in any real sense a rival to God. He cannot go beyond the permission of God for his action and at the appointed time it will cease. The mystery of the devil, like the mystery of evil itself, lies hidden in the depths of the mystery of God's purpose for His creation. In the last analysis, the devil has to contribute to that purpose. It is beyond his power to frustrate it. For the early readers of Revelation that was a source of much comfort. It should provide such comfort for Christians in all ages.[164]

b. THE FINAL JUDGMENT (20:11-15)

(1) The white throne of judgment (20:11)

In verse 11 John begins his vivid description of the final judgment of humanity. Heaven and earth flee from the God who sits on the majestic white throne. The language of poetic imagery captures the fading character of everything that is of the world (1 John 2:17). Now the only reality is God seated on the throne of judgment before whom all must appear (Heb. 9:27). His verdict alone is holy and righteous. This is expressed symbolically by the "white" throne.[165]

In its flight from the presence of God, no place is found for the terrified universe. One is reminded of the psalmist's query, "Whither shall I go from thy Spirit?/Or whither shall I flee from thy presence?" (Ps. 139:7). There is no place, for God is everywhere.[166]

(2) The judgment and the books of judgment (20:12-13)

John states, in verse 12, that before the great white throne stand the dead, both great and small. Reference to the book of life as part of the final testimony suggests a general judgment of all humanity. The point is that no one is so important as to be immune from judgment and no one is so unimportant as to make judgment inappropriate.[167]

The basis of judgment is twofold, namely the books in which humanity's deeds are recorded and the "book of life." The idea of "books of judgment" is a familiar one in the Old Testament and in Jewish literature (compare Dan. 7:10; Mal. 3:16). It is most important to grasp the significance of this double check. It means that the great white throne judgment is not arbitrary but based upon the evidence written by the life of every person. Literature often treats the motif of character becoming destiny. In Dante's *Divine Comedy* "men are seen permanently fastened to the central meaning which they have given to their lives." Books are opened, and the dead are judged on the basis of their works as recorded therein. Jesus Himself said, "Not every one that says to me, 'Lord, Lord,' shall enter the kingdom of heaven, but he who does the will of my Father who is in heaven" (Matt. 7:21; compare 7:24 *ff.*; 25:31-46; 2 Cor. 5:10).[168]

Works are unmistakable evidence of the loyalty of the heart. They express either belief or unbelief, faithfulness or unfaithfulness. The judgment will reveal through the records whether the loyalties were with God and the Lamb or with God's enemies. John's theology of faith and its inseparable relation to works is the same as Jesus' and Paul's (John 5:29; Rom. 2:6 *ff.*). This judgment is not a "balancing of the books," a weighing of good works and bad works. Those who have their names in the Lamb's book of life will also have records of righteous deeds. The opposite will be true as well. The imagery reflects the delicate balance between grace and obedience.[169]

Verse 13 makes it clear that all people are to be judged on that day. Not only will those who died on earth be resurrected but also those who so tragically died at sea. "Hades" refers to the abode of the wicked.[170]

This view of one general judgment is in contrast to Hal Lindsey who teaches that there are three judgments: the judgment of the nations in Matthew 25, the judgment of the believers in 2 Corinthians 5:10, and unbelievers here.[171] Verse 13 indicates that there will be one universal judgment (compare Rom. 14:10).

(3) The lake of fire (20:14-15)

After the judgment, verses 14-15 state that those whose names were not found in the book of life are thrown into the "lake of fire," which is the second death (compare 20:6; 2:11; 21:8; Matt. 25:41). But even more important to the believer is the good news that God will cast both "Death and Hades," which seem to be personified here as two demons, into the lake of fire (compare 1 Cor. 15:26,54).[172]

This final scene in verse 15 is dark and fearful. When taken seriously, this final note evaporates all theories of universalism. God's mercy is vast beyond comprehension, but His mercy is not limitless. He will never reject any who come to Him for mercy, nor will He force Himself on any who choose to live without Him.[173]

Excursus on the Importance of Resurrection of the Dead and the Final Judgment

Why disturb the bodies long buried at sea? Why empty the graves of their dusty remains?

Human life—more than physical

Because human life is more than physical. The final resurrection of the dead declares that. It tells us that we are more than animals whose destiny is to lie forever in the dust, at one with the material world. Because we are made in God's image, we have to live eternally with the implications of who we are and what we have done.

It is true that death takes us all. However, death is not the great leveler. It is the great divider. It separates those who have trusted Christ from those who have not. It makes permanent the loyalty we have pledged to God or the rebellion we have mounted against Him.[174]

Sin has eternal consequences

Although death itself is a form of punishment, it is not thorough enough, just enough, nor final enough to accomplish what human rebellion merits. Sin is not just physical. We are spiritual creatures, and our sin has spiritual expressions. Most important, our sin has eternal consequences because it is rejection of the eternal God. If the punishment is to fit the crime, then death is not enough. Beyond death must come resurrection and judgment.[175]

A part of being human is to be accountable to God. He made us for His purposes. He will call us to account for those purposes and how we have fulfilled them. No person from any age or continent can escape the sweeping accountability of that judgment.

When we come to verses 11-15, the millennium with all its glory has ended. During the one thousand years of Christ's rule, many will come to trust Him, especially many from Israel. Their names will be in the book of life. They are welcomed into full fellowship with all of God's people. The others, including those who joined Satan's final burst of revolution, are not named in that book of grace and life (vv. 7-9).[176]

Destruction of "Death and Hades"

God's final judgment is awesome, sweeping, accurate, and final. It is so final that even "Death and Hades" are no longer needed. Death and Hades speak of the grave. The grave is that temporary means of judgment which God has used throughout human history. Death and Hades remind us of our frailty, our dependence on him and our accountability to him. Death and Hades have done their work and are destroyed along with everything else not needed in the new age.[177]

6. The New Creation (21:1-8)

Excursus on New Jerusalem

The new Jerusalem as an ideal

John brings to a dramatic climax his visions in chapters 21 and 22. He has a magnificent sight of the final state of things. Some scholars see this section as, in some ways, the most important in the whole book. It is only in comparison with the "new Jerusalem" that the queenly splendors of Babylon can be seen for what they are. This section has inspired countless works of art and music. It has inspired Christian efforts for the betterment of humanity. As we will see, John does not mean that human effort alone can realize God's ideal on earth. But the heavenly city is certainly the ideal set before Christians, and it is their inspiration to work for God and for good on earth.

Dale Moody reminds us that in the midst of gathering gloom, when people tire and civilization begins to crumble, God has a way of stirring people's hope by a vision of an invisible city that will not pass away. Augustine, for example, drew insight from the Bible as well as from Plato in constructing his vision of two cities. These cities were made by two loves: the earthly city by the love of self and the heavenly city by the love of God. God takes Israel and the church through the stages of the earthly Jerusalem, the heavenly Jerusalem, and the new Jerusalem in order to teach them that humanity's dream of a holy city is not a delusion. Rather, the holy city is the goal toward which redeemed people, salvation history, and the whole creation move.[178]

The earthly city and the heavenly city

Unfortunately, the earthly Temple in Jerusalem became such a symbol of security that few in Israel were able to see the great reality of God beyond the earthly symbol. Jeremiah renounced such false security and called on the people to find security in the inward reality of transformed heart and life (Jer. 7:1-13). The earthly symbol of the Temple had given the people an edifice complex that only tragedy could transform.[179]

The tension between the earthly symbol of Jerusalem and the heavenly reality became intense after the death of Jesus in Jerusalem. Even before the fall of the city in AD 70, Paul put the two in strong contrast in Galatians. For Paul, the "Jerusalem above" is the mother of the liberated community of God's people (Gal. 4:26).[180]

The heavenly Jerusalem in the New Testament is described as a reality now present only in a promissory way. The kingdom reality of the age to come has already appeared in history in the life of Jesus and also in the presence of the Holy Spirit in the church. While the Jerusalem that is from above has present implications for believers (Gal. 4:25-31), they are nevertheless, like Abraham, "looking forward to the city with foundations" (Heb. 11:10, NIV; compare 13:14). The hope related to the new Jerusalem does not make the church on earth and God's kingdom synonymous as in the medieval emphasis.[181]

The new Jerusalem as a dominant biblical theme

A careful student is amazed at John's knowledge of and multiple allusions to the Old Testament. John weaves Isaiah's vision of the new Jerusalem (Isa. 60, 65) together with Ezekiel's vision of the new temple (Ezek. 40—48) into a new tapestry. The multiple Old Testament promises converging in John's mind indicate that he viewed the new Jerusalem as the fulfillment of all these strands of prophecy. There are also allusions to Genesis 1—3, including the absence of death and suffering, the dwelling of God with people as in Eden, the tree of life, and the removal of the curse. Creation is restored to its pristine character.[182]

We should also note the close relationship of the vision of John in chapters 21 and 22 with the promises to those who overcome in the letters to the seven churches (chs. 2—3). For example, to the overcomers at Ephesus is granted the right to the tree of life (2:7; compare 22:2). In fact, there is a strand in almost every major section in Revelation related to chapters 21—22.[183]

Far beyond the Old Testament writings, there is a totality and uniqueness in John's vision. Especially noticeable is the centrality of Christ in the city and the absence of a temple in the new Jerusalem.[184]

Excursus on the New Heaven and the New Earth

The meaning of the new heaven and new earth

Correlative with John's vision of the new Jerusalem is his vision of the new heaven and the new earth. The expression "new heaven and a new earth" in 21:1 should be understood as a biblical way of designating the entire universe. This does not mean that the present universe will be totally annihilated, so that the new universe will be completely other than the present cosmos. Rather it means that the present cosmos will be renewed and purified.[185]

This teaching by John on the renewed cosmos is in keeping with Paul's argumentation in Romans 8. Paul said that creation waits with eager longing for the revealing of the sons of God so that it may be set free from its bondage to decay (Rom. 8:20-21). This means that the present creation will be liberated from corruption in the end time, not some totally different creation.[186]

The continuity between this life and the new heaven and new earth

On the basis of Paul's teaching in 1 Corinthians 15, there will be continuity between the present body and the resurrection body. There must be continuity, for otherwise there would be little point in speaking about a resurrection at all. The very language of 1 Corinthians 15:53 implies and even demands continuity: "For this perishable nature must put on the imperishable, and this mortal nature must put on immortality."[187]

Hoekema states that if the resurrection body were nonmaterial or nonphysical, the devil would have won a great victory. This is true because God would then have been compelled to change human beings with physical bodies, such as He had created, into creatures of a different sort, without physical bodies (like the angels). This would indicate that matter had become intrinsically evil so that it had to be banished. And then, in a sense, the Greek philosophers would have been proven right. But matter is not evil; it is part of God's good creation. Thus the goal of God's redemption is the resurrection of the physical body. Likewise, God will create a new earth on which His redeemed people can live and serve God forever with glorified bodies. Thus the universe will not be destroyed but renewed, and God will win the victory.[188]

The differences between our present bodies and our resurrection bodies, wonderful though they are, do not take away the continuity. Those raised with Christ will not be a totally new set of human beings but the people of God who have lived on this earth. By way of analogy, we would expect that the new earth will not be totally different from the present earth but will be the present earth wondrously renewed. In other words, the future will not be so ethereal or spiritualized that it will fail to do justice to the biblical promise of a new earth.[189]

For Rust, Christ's redemption involves the cosmos and humanity's historical existence in its totality. History must be consummated in its totality. It is not just a case of pilgrim souls traversing their course to their home in the spiritual order. Nature and history in their totality have a part in God's purpose that centers in the incarnate and risen Lord. The redeemed community will be consummated in a redeemed universe. Not entropy, but restoration is creation's destiny.[190]

Moody suggests that cosmic redemption presupposes the possibility that creation may be transformed by the same activity from which it finds its source and sustenance. The Redeemer is the Creator and Preserver of "all things." To rule out this possibility is to rule out miracle, and to rule out miracle is to rule out God. Belief in "God the Father Almighty, Maker of heaven and earth," is the solid rock on which the doctrine of cosmic redemption rests. Since God brought His creation into being He can bring it to its consummation.[191]

Cosmic redemption and science

A comprehensive theology of cosmic redemption, related in detail to modern scientific knowledge, has seldom been attempted on a satisfactory scale. Among

ancient Christian writers, the daring system of Origen in the third century suggests how revolutionary this type of eschatology can become. It is unfortunate
that presuppositions influenced by the Stoic ideas of immanent and impersonal
reason, together with Platonic dualism and universalism, limited the thrust of
Origen's cosmic eschatology.[192]

Among modern philosophical theologians, Hegel has revived the comprehen-
siveness that belongs to cosmic redemption. But the idealistic principle of identity,
removing the personal distinction between God and humanity and the ontologi-
cal distinction between God and the world, weakened Hegel's conclusions as
much as Stoic immanence created difficulties for Origen.[193]

Moody contends that the tension between John's vision and modern science
should be seen as a creative tension. John and the biblical writers presuppose that
at one point in space-time the energy that has become concrete matter came into
being by an act of God. At a second point life appeared, first plant and then animal, and this too was the creative act of God, who never withdraws His presence
from His creation. A third unique point in the creative process saw the appearance of mind and the transcendence of the human spirit over the process of nature. The greatest point in the historical movements which followed was that
unique point in which "the Word became flesh and dwelt among us" (John 1:14),
when "God sent forth his Son, born of woman" (Gal. 4:4).[194]

All of these points were unique and never to be repeated. On the basis of these
events, John tells of a yet higher dimension of the Spirit, which transforms all
matter, life, and mind in an event that can only be described as the new heaven
and the new earth. This is the event toward which the process of the whole creation and human history, especially salvation history, points. It is at this point that
the contradictions of creation and the ambiguities of history will be clarified and
consummated.[195]

The implications of cosmic redemption for this present life

And so John's vision is future in its realization and totally dependent on God's
power to create it. However, it has important present implications for the life of the
church in this age. It is an ideal and hope. It is also our inspiration and guide for
the Christian life on earth.

There is a continuity as well as a discontinuity between our present culture and
the culture, if so it will be called, of the world to come. As citizens of God's kingdom, we should not just write off the present earth as a total loss, or rejoice in its
deterioration. We must, indeed, be working for a better world now. Our efforts to
bring the kingdom of Christ into fuller manifestation are of eternal significance.
Our Christian life today, our struggles against sin—both individual and
institutional—our mission work, our attempt to develop and promote a distinctively Christian culture, have value not only for this world but even for the world
to come.[196]

At the beginning of history, God created the heavens and the earth. At the end
of history, we see the new heavens and the new earth, which will far surpass in
splendor all that we have seen before. At the center of history is the Lion who
became the Lamb. He was slain, He became the firstborn from the dead, and the
Ruler of the kings of the earth. Some day we shall cast all our crowns before Him,
"lost in wonder, love, and praise."[197]

Cosmic redemption and the millennium

All of John's vision in 21:1 to 22:5 is after the millennium. If the millennium is a true eschatological historical event like the person, ministry, and resurrection of Jesus, then John's vision should be viewed as the full manifestation of the kingdom of God. Of course, a partial manifestation of this vision will be realized in the one-thousand-year reign of Christ and the saints, during which Christ will defeat all His enemies, including death (1 Cor. 15:23-28). Some of the same conditions described in 21:1 to 22:5 would then, at least in part, characterize the millennium.[198]

a. THE NEW HEAVEN AND THE NEW EARTH (21:1)

John pictures the final age in verse 1. God originally created the earth to be man's permanent home. But sin and death entered the world and transformed the earth into a place of rebellion and alienation. Thus it became enemy-occupied territory. But God has been working in salvation history to effect a total reversal of this consequence of evil and to liberate earth and heaven from bondage to sin and corruption (Rom. 8:21). In the future, this reversal will be complete. John sees the completion of this work of God in the vision.[199]

John goes on to say that there will be "no more sea" (KJV). The sea is seen as the source of the satanic beast (13:1) and the place of the dead (20:13). The emphasis is not geological but moral and spiritual. The sea serves as an archetype with connotations of evil (compare 13:1). Therefore no trace of evil in any form will be present in the new creation.[200]

We should also remember that in antiquity people did not have the means of coping successfully with the sea's dangers, and they regarded it as an unnatural element, a place of storms and danger. In the end this seething cauldron, fraught with unlimited possibilities of evil, will disappear.[201]

To the people of the Bible, the sea was an enemy. God had to cleave it in two at the Exodus when He led Israel through the Red Sea. Jesus, demonstrating in His miracles the power of the new age, both calmed the sea and walked on the waters. He thoroughly tamed the ancient enemy.

John, who had been cut off from his loved ones during his captivity on the island of Patmos, must have hated the sea that formed such a barrier. The vision of no more sea must have been especially comforting to him.[202]

The absence of the sea from the new earth, therefore, means the absence of whatever would interfere with the God-desired harmony.

b. THE HOLY CITY, THE NEW JERUSALEM (21:2-4)

(1) The holy city as a community (21:2)

In verse 2 the new Jerusalem is described as a city. A city has life, activity, interest, and people. It is a community. It is social. It is no flight of the alone to the Alone. It is to be contrasted with the Hindu ideal of heaven as a sea into which human life returns like a raindrop to the ocean.[203]

(2) The holy city as a gift of God (21:2a)

John sees the city "coming down out of heaven from God" (v. 2). This expression stresses the idea that the city is a gift of God, forever bearing the marks of His creative activity. The direction is significant. The direction is downward. It is not an old Jerusalem rebuilt on earth by human hands. Rather it is a new Jerusalem coming down from heaven. Salvation from beginning to end is God's doing. It is heavenly work. It does not spring from earth to heaven as the builders of the Tower of Babel tried to do. It descends from God to humanity. The people of God are not to be seen as a voluntary organization created by man but a fellowship initiated and given by God (compare Matt. 16:18).[204]

The destination of the new Jerusalem is earth. God has come to make His eternal dwelling with us. The earth that God called good in the beginning He has now restored and called good again, so good that He is willing to dwell with us here. Our biblical faith is not an escape from the material world. Its final destiny is not an ethereal existence where floating spirits circle a heavenly throne. The Bible's last pictures show God on earth entering into fellowship with a resurrected people who live a bodily, human existence.[205]

(3) The holy city as a bride (21:2b)

John also calls the city a "bride" (v. 2). A bride-city captures something of God's personal relationship to His people (the bride), as well as their life in communion with Him. The purity and devotedness of the bride are reflected in her attire. A bride adorned for her husband is thoroughly prepared and looking her best on the day of her wedding. So with those who constitute "the bride" of Christ.[206]

Nothing is more characteristic of an eager, hopeful bride than a glorious glow that flames from within to light and warm all who see her. The contrast between the earthly city as harlot and the heavenly city as bride is obvious.[207]

The bride metaphor is the most intimate relationship language

possible, as much so in the first century as today. There is a tenderness and joyousness in the marriage image. That symbol is to become
our very first impression of God's new order. It is not the splendor of
the wealth of God that first confronts John in his vision of the new
heaven and new earth. Rather, first he sees God's beloved bride. We
are shown first of all that of which the Lamb is proudest. For Palmer,
it would be like visiting the estate of a great man who, as you first
enter his estate, proudly introduces you to his family, his bride, and
his children. Everything else is secondary in his mind. So it is in
God's eternal new order.[208]

We are so conditioned to think of ourselves in deprecatory terms
that we have a hard time really believing this vision. The seven
struggling churches of the province of Asia, made up of ordinary
Christians, together with ordinary men and women like them
throughout all time, constitute the beloved bride. This is John's experience as he looks in upon this great vision of his own future destiny! He sees in God's new heaven and new earth the people that he
knows.[209]

We who believe in the Lamb are the bride. No one has been forced
to come to the marriage. The grace of the Lamb is triumphant, but
that grace has not compelled men and women to believe. His grace
woos us but does not cancel us out (C. S. Lewis). The freedom to
believe or not believe has been preserved throughout Revelation.
That freedom is now fulfilled in the image of the bride. It is not a
slave brought to the king as the spoils of war, but the bride who will
dwell with her husband in love.[210]

(4) The holy city as God's dwelling place (21:3)

John states that in the new era God will dwell with His people
(v. 3). Of course, God is with us in Christ now. But here John tells of
finality, completeness, and permanence.

God's first dwelling with Israel was in a tent that could be moved
from place to place. On at least one occasion, the ark of His dwelling
was stolen by the Philistines and carted off to their cities, outside
Judah's boundaries. The Temple, where God dwelt after Solomon's
time, was destroyed by the Babylonians. But even before its destruction, Ezekiel saw its glory departing as part of God's judgment on
His wayward people (Ezek. 10—11).[211]

When in Jesus "the Word became flesh and dwelt [or tented]
among us," we, indeed, experienced the very presence of God (John

1:14). But even that was temporary—about thirty-three short years. Then Jesus ascended to the Father's side. We now experience the presence of God in Christ in the Spirit, as a partial realization of that which is to come.

John's vision marked the coming of a new day. A city coming down, God with His people on earth, a covenant of full fellowship inaugurated. This is a picture of completion and permanence. We can rejoice in the partial fellowship now and long for the fulfillment.

The material world may now be captured in the grips of entropy, energy, and matter wearing out in the whirl of prolonged activity. But God's people and His creation are headed for the renewal that permanent fellowship with Him will produce.[212]

As a backdrop for the scene, consider Genesis 3, where man lost his fellowship with God (compare Ex. 25:8; Ezek. 37:26-27). But the quality of life in the new eternal order described in verse 3 reveals that the complete fellowship broken by the fall will be restored.[213]

(5) The holy city as a place of care (21:4)

The language of relationship continues in verse 4 with the promise that God cares about the deep concerns that are on the hearts of His people. Once again in these verses, the Old Testament prophetic hopes for God's care are quoted (Isa. 25:8; 35:10). These deep yearnings of the prophets are now fulfilled.[214]

In a touching metaphor of motherly love, John says that God "will wipe away every tear from their eyes." These tears have come from sin's distortion of God's purposes for people. They are produced by death or mourning for the dead and by crying or pain. An enemy had done this to the old order. Now God has defeated the enemy and liberated His people and His creation.[215]

Rather than list all possible blessings, God's voice from the throne focused on the one indispensable blessing. This one great gift which truly captures the newness of the new Jerusalem is the absence of death and its tragic effects.[216]

c. GOD'S OWN WORD OF ASSURANCE AND INVITATION (21:5-6)

(1) God's promise of renewal (21:5)

God speaks to John in words that closely parallel those of the apostle Paul, "Behold, I make all things new" (v. 5; compare 2 Cor. 5:17; Isa. 43:19; Jer. 31:22). The "new Jerusalem" is only for those who have already experienced the "new life" in Christ. It is for those who have already "tasted the goodness of the word of God and the powers of the age to come" (Heb. 6:5).[217]

This renewal is not just modification or readjustment. It will have a freshness as startling as God's first defeat of chaos at the beginning. It is new *creation* to the last detail. All the limiting, compromising, threatening aspects of the old creation are put aside. The truly new has come as God alone can make it come.

The verdict of science is undoubtedly right: The vast universe of matter and energy is running down. But God's Word is even more right. Creation is headed for restoration. Fellowship with God will be renewed in permanence and blessings will be bestowed in abundance. As God's people we lead full lives now but it will be even more glorious then.[218]

Since these words are in truth God's words (compare 19:9; 22:6), it is of great importance that this vision of the new heaven and the new Jerusalem be proclaimed to the churches. So God said in verse 5, "Write this!"[219]

(2) God's promise of completion and sustenance (21:6)

With the words in verse 6, "It is done," God confirms the fact that His redemptive task is complete. The "It is done" of judgment has given way to the "It is done" of redemption (compare 16:17). This is accomplished by none other than Almighty God, "The Alpha and Omega, the beginning and the end" (v. 6; 1:8).[220]

In verse 6 John beautifully pictures salvation with the image of drinking at the spring of life. Twice in the last two chapters of Revelation God offers an invitation to those who sense their need and are drawn toward him. This promise, partially realized in Christ while on earth, is fully realized in His eternal kingdom (compare Isa. 55:1; John 4:13; 7:37; Rev. 22:17; with v. 6; 7:17).

d. LIFE'S BASIC CHOICE AND ITS CONSEQUENCES (21:7-8)

As a prophet, John once more wants to confront us with a choice. This choice must be made because there are two cities: the city of God and the city of Babylon.[221]

In verse 7 John states that those who resist the temptation to deny the Christ and remain true to the end will be rewarded with the heritage of the perfect sonship with God (compare Gal. 4:7; 1 John 3:2).

In contrast, in verse 8 John gives a description of those who have a list of sinful attributes which go against the will of God for life and

thus cannot endure the fellowship of God. This list shows by negative contrast what in the positive sense is the will of God. There
should not be fearfulness, but faith. There should not be distortion,
but truth. The first part of the list refers primarily to those who corrupt themselves by worshiping the beast rather than enduring persecution.

The second part of the list states that there should not be murder
but life; not sexual chaos, but wholeness; not mysticism, but relationship; not idols, but encounter with the living God; not deception, but the open face of trust.[222]

These people are called "murderers" because they are guilty of
the death of the saints (17:6; 18:24). The "sexually immoral" (NIV)
("fornicators"), practitioners of "magic arts, the idolaters and all liars" (NIV) are those associated with idolatrous practices (compare
9:21; 18:23; 21:27; 22:15; contrast 14:5). By their own choice, Babylon, not the new Jerusalem, is their eternal home.[223]

The torment of the second death is symbolized in verse 8 by the
familiar imagery of the "lake that burneth with fire and brimstone"
(KJV).

V. The Fourth Vision: The Heavenly Jerusalem

21:9 to 22:5

A. The City of God Described and Measured (21:9-27)

1. The Measuring of the City (21:9-17)

a. THE CITY DESCRIBED AS A BRIDE (21:9)

In verse 9 the bride of the Lamb contrasts with the great prostitute (17:1). As the prostitute is John's archetypal image for the great system of satanic evil, so the bride is the true counterpart. She is pure and faithful to God and the Lamb, whereas the prostitute is a mockery.

But in verse 10, John drops the bridal metaphor. He then proceeds to use magnificent imagery to describe the church in glory as a city with a lofty wall, splendid gates, and jeweled foundations.[1]

b. THE SIGNIFICANCE OF THE MOUNTAIN (21:10)

In verse 10, John is carried by the Spirit to a "high mountain" from which he is shown "the holy city Jerusalem coming down out of heaven from God." In Jewish thought, mountains played a significant role. Moses' historical encounter with God on Mount Sinai marked the origin of the Jewish nation (Ex. 19 *ff.*). Ezekiel's great vision of the restored temple and land was given to him "upon a very high mountain" (Ezek. 40:1-2). The descent is an announcement in visionary terms of a future event which will usher in the eternal state.[2]

c. LINDSEY'S LITERAL VIEW OF THE CITY

Lindsey describes the city in literal terms. It is to be fifteen hundred miles in each direction, from side to side, as well as straight up. He suggests that the holy city will be suspended above the earth during the millennium. It is temporarily withdrawn when the earth is destroyed at the end of the millennium. After the re-creation of the earth, the city will descend to the new earth and actually rest on it. This is true, says Lindsey, since the new Jerusalem is said to have foundations. (v. 19).[3]

Because of the emphasis of Lindsey and others, the question of the literalness of the city has received considerable attention. But if the city is the bride and the bride the glorified community of God's people in their eternal life, there is little question that John's descriptions are primarily symbolic of that glorified life. This in no way diminishes the reality behind the imagery. In the most suitable language available to John, much of it drawn from the Old Testament, he shows us something of the reality of the final aspect of the kingdom of God in its glorified existence. This means that there should be no warrant for thinking of the city as descending like a space platform to the mountain or hovering over the earth, as Lindsey and others suggest.[4]

d. THE GLORIOUS NATURE OF THE CITY (21:11-12a)

In verse 11 John describes the appearance of the city as all-glorious, "with the glory of God" (compare Ezek. 43:4). The city has a "brilliance" (NIV) ("light-bearer") given it by God's presence, that appears as crystal-clear jasper (Isa. 60:1-2,19; Rev. 21:23). This portion of Revelation inspired the hymn "Jerusalem, the Golden" which is ascribed to Bernard of Cluny, twelfth century. John Bunyan was also inspired by chapter 21 to write about the heavenly city in *The Pilgrim's Progress*

In verse 12 the wall is simply part of the description of an ideal city as conceived by ancient peoples accustomed to the security of strong outer walls.[5]

e. THE CONTINUITY OF GOD'S REDEEMED PEOPLE (21:12b-14)

John sees the radically new. As he comes to the pastoral task of putting it into words, he finds that nothing serves quite so well as the number twelve. Through the number twelve, we see the continuity and totality and perfection among God's redeemed people which alone can properly be called new.[6]

The twelve gates in verses 12-13 symbolize abundant entrance. Reference to twelve tribes emphasizes the continuity of the New Testament church with God's people of Old Testament times. The twelve angels are celestial gatekeepers and may reflect the picture of watchmen upon the walls of Jerusalem (Isa. 62:6). They belong to the concept of an ideal city.[7]

In verse 14 the repetition of the number twelve is deliberate. It features in every measurement of the city as the number of the people of God.

The inscription of the names of the twelve apostles on the foundations is related to the inscription of the gates with the names of Israel's twelve tribes. The unity of the people of the old and new covenants is thereby suggested. The twelve apostles stand at the beginning of the church's story, as Israel's patriarchs stand at the beginning of Israel's story. The apostles fittingly represent the church, even as the patriarchs serve as Israel's representatives. However, the twelve were the bearers of "the testimony of Jesus Christ" in a unique way, so that whoever builds on their testimony to Jesus and from Jesus rests on the Christ Himself. This conviction is embodied in the tradition which circulated in the church of John's day, represented in Matthew 16:17-19 and Ephesians 2:19-22. Here it finds its ultimate expression in his vision of the eternal city.[8]

f. The meaning of the city as a revelation of perfection (21:15-17)

In verses 15-17 the angel measures the city with a golden measuring rod. The act of measuring signifies securing something for blessing and to preserve it from spiritual harm or defilement. The measuring reveals the perfection, fulfillment, or completion of all God's purposes for His elect bride. Thus the city is revealed as a perfect cube of 12,000 stadia (12 x 1,000; about 1,400 miles). John is expressing by symbols the vastness, the perfect symmetry, and the splendor of the new Jerusalem.

These dimensions should not be interpreted as providing architectural information about the city. Rather, we should think of them as theologicaly symbolic of the fulfillment of all God's promises.[9]

2. *The Appearance and Character of the City (21:18-27)*

a. The meaning of the arrangement and description of the jewels in the holy city (21:18-21)

The main idea John seeks to convey in verses 18-27 is that the city is ideally perfect. The precious stones which adorn the "foundations of the wall" are almost all found in the breastplate of the high priest (compare Ex. 28:17 *ff.*; 39:10 *ff.*).[10]

The list of jewels in this section has presented a fascinating puzzle for interpreters of this vision. John has given a list in basically the reverse order of the instructions in Exodus 28:17-21 for the arrangement of jewels on the high priestly breastplate. His order of jewels is also the reverse order of the stones associated, according to Josephus and Philo, with the signs of the zodiac by which the ancient world traced the times and seasons of the year.

Palmer believes that this reversal is significant. It shows that all of the jewels are there, but they are placed in the new authoritative order of the Lamb. This indicates that nothing has been wasted in God's design, whether stars or jewels or colors or mountains. Everything is accounted for, and in this vision everything is fulfilled by the sovereign decision of God. Furthermore, this arrangement suggests that there are surprises even in the arrangement of that fulfillment.[11]

The overall picture in verses 18-20 is of a city of brilliant gold surrounded by a wall inlaid with jasper and resting upon twelve foundations adorned with precious gems of every color and hue. The city is magnificent beyond description. As the eternal dwelling place of God and His people, it is described in language which continually attempts to break free from its own limitations in order to do justice to the reality it so imperfectly describes.[12]

In verse 21 two descriptive touches remain. First, each of the twelve gates consists of a single pearl. The spectacle of a pearl large enough to serve as a city gate boggles the mind. Second, the street of the city was made of gold so pure that it seemed to be transparent as glass. Like the priests of the Old Testament (1 Kings 6:30) who ministered in the Temple, the servants of God walk upon gold. In the words of the hymn, "When We All Get to Heaven," we are told, "Soon the pearly gates will open;/We shall tread the streets of gold."[13]

Johnson suggests that the symbolism of precious jewels in verses 18-21 is not meant to give the impression of wealth and luxury but to point to the glory and holiness of God.[14]

b. THE MEANING AND SIGNIFICANCE OF THE LACK OF A TEMPLE IN THE HOLY CITY (21:22)

In verse 22 John says that in the heavenly city there is no temple. At this point John demonstrates how he has gone beyond the prophet Ezekiel whose imagery plays a prominent role in this vision. Ezekiel spent seven chapters describing the restored Temple and its ordinances (Ezek. 40—46). For John there is no temple because symbol has given way to reality. The Temple is replaced by "the Lord God Almighty and the Lamb."

Jesus told the woman at the well that the day would come when the worship of God would no longer be geographically limited (John

4:21). Paul later declared that the believing congregation was in fact the temple of the living God (2 Cor. 6:16). The final state toward which this points is eternity itself, where the presence of God the Father and the Lamb permeates and sanctifies all that the heavenly Jerusalem symbolizes. The purpose of the statement in verse 22 is not to describe the architecture of heaven but to speak meaningfully to a people for whom the Temple was supremely the place of God's presence.[15]

c. GOD AND JESUS AS THE TEMPLE IN THE HOLY CITY

Johnson points out, however, that paradoxically the holy city has a temple, for the Lord God Almighty and the Lamb are its temple. And in a sense the whole city is a temple since it is patterned after the most holy place (v. 16). Jewish expectation was centered on a rebuilt Temple and the restoration of the ark of the covenant. In his glorious vision, John sees the fulfillment of these hopes in the total presence of God with his purified people. The Lamb, the sign of the new covenant, is the fulfillment of the restoration of the ark of the covenant. As long as there is uncleanness in the world, there is need for a temple where God's presence and truth are in contrast to the uncleanness. But in the new city no such symbol is needed any longer.[16]

d. THE MEANING OF THE LACK OF THE SUN AND MOON IN THE HOLY CITY (21:23)

Hubbard presents a dramatic context for understanding verse 23. God used a star to guide the Wise Men to Bethlehem. From creation forward, He had used the sun, moon, and stars to light day and night and to mark days, months, seasons, years. But in the city of God, all this will be unnecessary.

Verse 23 is a dramatic description of the life-giving, light-shedding character of God. His presence renders the essential nonessential and His glory dispenses with what we call indispensable. It boggles the imagination to have life without the natural elements that have brightened and blessed human existence since the beginning. What more dramatic way could there be to show how glorious and vital the presence of God really is? When we live in the fullness of that presence, all other light becomes unnecessary. The elements themselves—the sun, moon, and stars—can be abandoned.[17]

For Beasley-Murray the statement, "the lamp is the Lamb" (v. 23), recalls the saying, "I am the Light of the world" (John 8:12), uttered

at the Feast of Tabernacles. This implies that what the shekinah was
to Israel in the desert, so Christ is for the whole world, the source of
salvation and the manifestation of the divine glory for all.[18]

e. THE SIGNIFICANCE OF THE NATIONS AND KINGS OF THE EARTH IN
THE HOLY CITY (21:24-26)

Verses 24-26 present a remarkable picture of "the nations" and
"the kings of the earth" entering the city and bringing their splendor
("glory," "honor," "magnificence") into it. John sees a vision of social life, bustling with activity. Elsewhere in Revelation, the "nations" are the pagan, rebellious people of the world who trample the
holy city (11:2,18). They have become drunk with the wine of Babylon, the mother of prostitutes (18:3,23). They are the ones who will
be destroyed by the second coming of Christ (19:15). The same applies to the "kings of the earth."

But there is another use of these terms, "nations" and "kings of
the earth," in verses 24-26. They stand for the people of the earth
who are the servants of Christ. They are the redeemed nations who
follow the Lamb and have resisted the beast and Babylon (1:5; 15:3;
19:16; 2:26; 5:9; 7:9; 12:5). This is the group John describes figuratively as having part in the activity in the holy city, the kingdom of
God.

Life in the age to come will certainly involve continuing activities
and relationships that will contribute to the glory of the holy city
throughout eternity. Instead of the nations bringing their precious
possessions to Babylon, the harlot city, the redeemed nations will
bring these offerings to the throne of God (compare Isa. 60:3 *ff.*).[19]

In this vision, we do not have the blurring of uniqueness or memory or relationships but rather the fulfillment of the ways in which
we have been originally created and the ways in which we have lived
out our created individuality. But the surprise is that the uniqueness
does not isolate us from each other. The nations of the world are
honored and set free from the old competitions and fears.

Palmer states that Teilhard was right in his letter to his atheist
friend, Julian Huxley, when he told him that the problem of human-
ism is its shortsightedness. He informs Huxley that his own intention as a Christian paleontologist is to continue his scientific
research on into eternity. The vision in Romans 8 and here in verses
24-26 is that of the fulfillment of what has been started in the order of
creation. There is not to be an obliteration as in the case of the Greek

hope of immortality. Greek spiritualization really amounted to the absorption of the human spirit into the vague tapioca pudding of eternity.

When Paul said, "The mortal puts on immortality" (1 Cor. 15:54), he did not have in mind a Greek vision of absorption but the Christian hope of resurrection. God who made us and redeemed us will raise us up again. He will fulfill us and the whole created order too (Rom. 8:18-25). This same emphasis is found in chapter 21.[20]

f. THE HOLY CITY AND THE SIGNIFICANCE OF CULTURE AND INSTITUTIONAL LIFE (21:24)

For Hoekema, these words in verses 24-26 indicate that the inhabitants of the new earth will include people who attained great prominence and exercised great power on the present earth—kings, princes, leaders, and the like. One could also say that whatever people have done on this earth which glorified God will be remembered in the life to come (compare Rev. 14:13). Furthermore, the unique contributions of each nation to the life of the present earth will enrich the life of the new earth. We will inherit the best products of culture and art which this earth has produced. Hendrikus Berkhof contends that whatever has been of value in this present life and whatever has contributed to "the liberation of human existence" will be retained and added to on the new earth.[21]

In commenting on verse 26, Mouw states that the bringing of "the glory and the honor of the nations" into the city emphasizes two factors. First, they bring their cultural splendor into a *city*. It has been observed by many writers that the biblical drama begins with a garden and ends with a city. Herein lies the Bible's recognition of the fact of cultural development. When the end time comes there will be an acknowledgment that the historical process has occurred, with all that this means in terms of cultural and institutional life. This is an important consideration to keep in mind, especially because of the subtle varieties of antiinstitutionalism which regularly tempt the Christian community. In some sense, historically-developed institutions will be "received" into the kingdom of God. They will not be merely forgotten or destroyed.

Second, in light of 22:2-3 where it is said that "there shall no more be anything accursed," it is at least possible that political institutions as we now know them—along with various other structures and activities associated with the culture-building life of a people—will not be destroyed in the last day. Rather, they will be purified and transformed into fitting dimensions of the kingdom of God. If this is the proper way to view matters, it is not enough to say, as we observe the institutions and practices of our political/cultural life, "Created, but *fallen*." We must also say, "Fallen, but *created*."

Sometimes it seems difficult to apply this restoration promise to political life. Because we look for a city which is yet to come, we will not be able to place our ultimate trust in the systems of the present age. But because the tree may sprout leaves for the healing of the kinds of nations of which we are presently citizens, we cannot completely dissociate ourselves from that which God has promised to heal.[22]

In verse 25 John's parenthetical remark about the absence of night explains why only day is mentioned in the preceding clause. Day extends indefinitely without interruption because darkness never comes. Thus there is no need of closing gates. Through these open gates the kings of the earth bring the glory and honor of the nations (v. 26). The reference is to the choicest of earthly treasures.[23]

g. THE LIMITATION OF PARTICIPATION IN THE HOLY CITY (21:27)

Verse 27 states that those who enter the city are not the wicked and defiant but those whose names have been written in the Lamb's book of life. In the imagery of this paragraph, the people with free access to the city are one with those who dwell within it.[24]

This should not be taken as implying that there will still be uusaved roaming around outside the new Jerusalem who may now and then enter it by repenting. Instead, the exhortation warns that the only way to participate in the future city is to turn one's total loyalties to the Lamb now (compare v. 7).[25]

B. The New Garden of Eden (22:1-5)

In this section, Paradise is regained. John returns to his archetypal images from Genesis 1—3 and Ezekiel 40 and following verses. As in the Old Testament imagery of the age to come, metaphors of water and light abound (compare Isa. 12:3; Zech. 14:7-8).[26]

1. The Water of Salvation (22:1-2a)

In verse 1 the angel shows John a sparkling river which flows crystal clear from the heavenly throne. The idea of a river in the restored Paradise comes from the description of the garden of Eden (Gen. 2:10). Elsewhere in Scripture "waters" and "living waters" are used to symbolize the blessings which flow to people from the presence of God (compare Jer. 2:13; Ezek. 47:1-12; Ps. 46:4; John 4:10; Rev. 7:7; 21:6). Whereas in Ezekiel the streams flow from the restored Temple, in John's vision the stream issues from the throne of God.[27]

Some writers find in the imagery of flowing water a reference to the Holy Spirit. Others find the promise of immortality or a reference to the abundant life which God now gives to his people. Obviously, all this is true. However, the central affirmation of verse 1 is that in the eternal state the faithful will live at the source of the life-giving stream which proceeds from the very presence of God. In the hot and arid climate of Palestine, this figure would hold special appeal.

The source of this life-giving water is the throne of God and of the Lamb. In 7:15 and 12:5 we read only of the throne of God. This place of honor is now shared with the Lamb, whose sacrificial death has made Him worthy of heavenly praise (compare 5:9-15).[28]

When we read verse 1, we are reminded of the well-known hymn by Robert Lowry whose verses reflect the imagery of this passage. Some of us have sung since childhood the verse, "Shall we gather at the river,/Where bright angel feet have trod;/With its crystal tide forever,/Flowing by the throne of God?/Yes, we'll gather at the river,/The beautiful, the beautiful river;/Gather with the saints at the river/That flows by the throne of God."

2. The Tree of Life (22:2b)

In verse 2 the exact placement of river, street, and trees is not clear. The specific geographical layout is of no particular importance in understanding the symbolism of the verse.[29]

In Ezekiel's vision, multiple trees on each side of the river bear fruit monthly, whose leaves are for healing (Ezek. 47:12). This means that the tree John speaks of could be a collective word for Ezekiel's trees.

What was once lost by Adam and Eve in Eden and denied to their posterity is now fully restored (compare Gen. 3:22-24). So abundant is the vitality of the tree of life that it bears a crop of fruit each month. Both the abundance and variety of fruit are being emphasized.

God's provision is ever new and always more than adequate. In the words of the hymn, "O they tell me of a land far away,/Where the tree of life in eternal bloom,/Sheds its fragrance thro' the unclouded day."[30]

Not only does the tree provide fruit to be eaten but also leaves that are therapeutic and bring about healing. Although John speaks of "the healing of the nations," we are not to infer that nations will continue to exist outside the new Jerusalem. The glory of the age to come is necessarily portrayed by means of imagery belonging to the present age. The healing leaves indicate the complete absence of physical and spiritual want. The life to come will be a life of abundance and perfection.[31]

These descriptions can also be understood as symbolic of the far-reaching effects of the death of Christ in the redeemed community, the holy city. So powerful is the salvation of God that the effects of sin are completely overcome. The eternal life God gives the redeemed community will be perpetually available, will sustain, and will cure eternally every former sin.[32]

3. The Curse Removed and the Vision of God Realized (22:3-5)

a. THE HIGH CHRISTOLOGY OF JOHN (22:3)

In verse 3 note John's emphasis on God and the Lamb. They share the same glory and the same throne, and they are the temple. The high Christology of John's vision is everywhere evident even though stated in functional terms.[33]

b. THE GREATEST BLESSING OF ETERNITY (22:4)

In verse 4 the greatest of eternity's blessings is reflected in one phrase, "they shall see his face." Moses, the great lawgiver of the old dispensation, was not allowed to see the face of God because God had declared, "Man shall not see me and live" (Ex. 33:20; compare v. 23 where Moses is allowed to see only the back of God). In the ancient world, criminals were banished from the presence of the king and not allowed to look upon his face (Esther 7:8; compare 2 Sam. 14:24). Jesus taught that only the pure in heart shall see God (Matt. 5:8). The First Epistle of John speaks of the great transformation to take place at the return of Christ when "we shall be like him, for we shall see him as he is" (3:2).[34]

Verse 4 is the inspiration for the lines of a beloved hymn. Many Christians have sung, "Face to face with Christ, my Savior/. . . Only faintly now I see him, /With the darkling veil between, /But a blessed day is coming, /When his glory shall be seen . . . Face to face in all his glory, /I shall see him by and by!"

Since God and the Lamb are always viewed together, there is no point in saying that the redeemed will see Jesus but not the Father.

On the foreheads of God's servants will be stamped the name of God (22:4). His name stands for His character. The faces of those who have experienced the beatific vision will reflect the unmistakable likeness of God. The process of transformation now under way in the life of believers (2 Cor. 3:18) will be brought to completion when the church enters its ultimate and ideal state. As the followers of the beast bore his mark upon their foreheads (Rev. 13:16), so will the faithful bear the name of God upon theirs (compare Rev. 3:12). The metaphor stresses ownership and likeness.[35]

   c. GLORIOUS LIGHT AND RULERSHIP (22:5)

In verse 5 a final burst of light engulfs the whole scene. This vision is modeled on Isaiah's description of that time in Zion's future when the light of the sun and the moon is to be replaced by the everlasting light of the glory of God (Isa. 60:19-20; compare Rev. 21:23). In the new Jerusalem, God is ever present; His glory makes unnecessary all other sources of light.

An announcement is made in verse 5a that the saints will reign forever and ever. This fulfills the first promise of the book (1:6; compare 5:10; 20:4-6; and esp. 11:15). Surely it is fitting for such a book of prophecy as Revelation to close around the throne, with God's servants both worshiping and ruling.[36]

When Jesus returns, we will enter the final phase of history that culminates in the eternal kingdom. Hubbard points out that the fruit of that kingdom are worship of God without impurity, vision of God without concealment, relationship with God without conflict, and the rulership of God without ending. With eagerness, we anticipate these fruit. By faith in Jesus Christ and through the power of the Holy Spirit, we can begin to experience them now.[37]

VI. Epilogue

22:6-21

This important concluding section sums up and presses home some of the important practical lessons of Revelation. The two major themes are the authenticity of Revelation and the nearness of the fulfillment of its message.

A. The First Words of Confirmation (22:6a)

In verse 6a the angel confirms the genuineness of the entire revelation. The words which relate the visions of things to come are faithful and true. They are worthy of belief because they correspond to reality.

B. The First Announcement of the Imminent Return of Jesus (22:6b-7a)

As in 1:1, an angel is sent to show to God's servants "the things which must shortly come to pass" (KJV). Through the servant John, the message then goes out to the members of the churches—the servants of verse 6 (compare v. 16). The source of the revelation is the Lord, who is further described as "the God of the spirits of the prophets." All true prophecy originates with God and comes through men moved by the Holy Spirit (2 Pet. 1:21).

The nearness of the consummation, as reflected by the clause in verse 6, "which must soon take place," is not peculiar to Revelation. Paul, as well, wrote that the time was short and that people should adjust their manner of life accordingly (1 Cor. 7:29-31). The end and the beginning are but two perspectives on the same great adventure.[1]

The words, "Behold, I am coming soon" in verse 7 are those of the risen Lord. The coming of Christ is to be "without delay" or "in a short time." As in the prologue, this is the idea of a foreshortened

327

perspective on the time of the end. It is not to be reinterpreted in the sense that Jesus "comes" in the crises of life and especially at the death of every person. Matthew 24:42-44 counsels every generation to be on the alert for the return of the Son of man. An infallible timetable would do away with that attitude of urgent expectation which has been the hallmark of the church through the centuries.[2]

C. The Sixth Beatitude (22:7b)

The sixth beatitude in verse 7b is pronounced upon those who stand fast in the great persecution about to break upon the church. They are those who keep the prophetic injunctions of the book. Note that John insists that his visions of the end constitute genuine prophecy. Under the impulse of the Holy Spirit, he has faithfully recorded what God has revealed concerning the end of all things.[3]

D. An Additional Warning Against Idolatry (22:8-9)

Reiterating what he said in 1:10, John proclaims in 22:8 that he has actually heard and seen all the things which are recorded in the book. His literary product is not the result of any flight of imagination.[4]

But once again, as in 19:10, John falls down to worship the angel because of what the angel had shown him. Once again the angel rebukes John for worship misplaced (v. 9). The angel defines himself to John as a fellow servant. John's double experience of misplaced worship has the effect of strongly impressing upon us the pastoral and theological importance of worship as the rightful human expression toward God alone.

In verse 9 it is pointed out that John's worship of the angel is a form of temptation which the angel resists by remembering two things. First, he remembers his solidarity with John and John's companions in faith. The angel is under orders as they are under orders. Second, he reminds John of the great theological fact which the Ten Commandments had long ago stated: Only God deserves worship. Worship is as dangerous a human act as it is wondrous. When worship is given to any part of the human created order, it becomes both a temptation to evil for those who receive such adoration and an act of idolatry for those who offer such adoration. This double experience of John has doubly warned us of this possibility.[5]

E. The Urgency for Immediate Choices (22:10-11)

In verse 10 John is told not to seal the notes that he has written of his vision but to share them with the churches because of the critical moment that is at hand.

The major thrust of verse 11 is that, since the end time is now at hand, people are certain to reap the consequences of the kinds of lives they have led unless they repent. The time arrives when change is impossible because character has already been determined by a lifetime of habitual action. The arrival of the end forecloses any possibility of alteration. The deliberate choice of each person fixes his fate.[6]

Verse 11 at first glance appears to be fatalistic. However, on further reflection we see that it stresses the imminency of the return of Jesus and the necessity for immediate choices. There is no reason to take this passage as teaching the irreversibility of human choices. Repentance is always an option as long as a person is living.[7]

John is clearly not teaching that the times are so far gone that there is no hope for the filthy or the evildoer. In a very few sentences, John will call upon those who are thirsty to come to the waters.[8]

F. The Second Announcement of the Imminent Return of Jesus (22:12-13)

In verse 12 Christ announces a second time that He is coming without delay and bringing with Him a reward which each man is to receive according to his work. Paul taught that God "will render to every man according to his works" (Rom. 2:6), and Peter declared that God "judges each one impartially according to his deeds" (1 Pet. 1:17). It is the quality of a person's life which provides the ultimate indication of what one really believes.

The names which the risen Christ applies to Himself in verse 13 set Him apart from the entire created order. The attributes of God belong to Christ as well.[9]

G. The Invitation to Enter the City of God (22:14-15)

The seventh and last beatitude in verse 14 is evangelistic in its appeal. It refers to 7:14 where the great multitude around the heavenly throne clothed in white robes are "they who have come out of the great tribulation: they have washed their robes and made them white in the blood of the Lamb." The washing of the robes in 7:14 indicates willing identification with Jesus in His death. Thus the washing of robes in verse 14 and 7:14 symbolizes a salvation that involves obedience and discipleship, since it is related to the tree of life (compare 22:2) and the gates of the city (compare 21:25).[10]

In verse 15 John describes representative types of evildoers who are excluded from the city. The term "dog" is used in Scripture for various kinds of impure and malicious persons. In Deuteronomy 23:17-18, the term designates a male cult prostitute. In the Jewish culture of first-century Palestine, it was used in reference to the heathen (Matt. 15:22 *ff.*). In Philippians 3:2, Paul applied it to the Judaizers. Sorcerers, fornicators, murderers, idolaters, and all liars are to be excluded along with the dogs. These have become like their leader, Satan, "the deceiver of the whole world" (Rev. 12:9; compare 13:13-15; 16:14).

Verse 15 does not intend to teach that in the eternal state all manner of wicked men will be living just outside the heavenly city. The contrast is between the blessedness of the faithful and the fate of the wicked.[11]

H. The Second Words of Confirmation (22:16)

In verse 16 Jesus Himself authenticates the angel who has guided John through the various visions of Revelation. It is to the angel of Christ that the revelation has been delegated. It is also stressed that the revelation is not a private affair but for the entire church.

Jesus identifies Himself as "the root and the offspring of David." In the throne-room vision of 5:5 he was "the Lion of the tribe of Judah, the Root of David." The morning star is a promise that the long night of tribulation is all but over and that the new eschatological day is about to dawn (compare Rev. 2:28; 2 Pet. 1:19).[12]

I. The Return of Christ and the Final
Invitation to Salvation (22:17)

The first part of verse 17 can be seen as requests to Christ for His return. The entire invitation can also be seen as addressed to the world. The "Spirit" is probably the Spirit of Christ speaking through John. The "Bride" is the church who joins with Christ in calling men to repentance. The one who "hears" is probably not the one who hears Revelation read but the one who hears and is converted and then joins in inviting others to "come" to Christ. The one who is "thirsty" is invited to "take the water of life" freely, without price (compare Isa. 55:1). This is the testimony of the church empowered by the Holy Spirit which constitutes the great evangelizing force of this age.[13]

The threefold use of the present imperative ("come/let him come") serves to extend the invitation until that very moment when history will pass irrevocably into eternity and any further opportunity for decision will be past.[14]

J. The Final Warning Against False Prophets (22:18-19)

Revelation draws to a close with a severe warning in verses 18-19 against adding to or taking away from its prophetic message. The warning is against willful distortion of the message. It is not unlike Paul's stern words in Galatians 1:6-7 to those who would pervert the gospel.[15]

The force of these words has been likened to the curses pronounced on disobedience in the covenant law codes of the Old Testament (compare Deut. 4:2; 12:32).[16]

Palmer reminds us that the traditional Christian marriage service ends with a similar postscript just prior to the benediction. That postscript is also a warning. The warning does not destroy the joy and wonder of the wedding vows and prayers. However, it has the effect of reminding people of how meaningful and important to God is the event of that wedding. The warning is: "Whom God has joined together let no man put asunder." That warning just prior to the benediction and the kiss of the bride and groom is both good and necessary. It is a warning in our behalf. It is a woe pronounced by the prophet of the Lord against any who would tamper with the vows and promises, the love and commitment that have been sealed between man and woman in marriage.[17]

In verses 18-19, Revelation concludes with an even more severe warning. So severe is the danger John warns against that he says that those who teach contrary to the message of Revelation will not only forfeit any right to salvation in the holy city but also will have visited on them the divine judgments (plagues) inflicted on the beast worshipers (compare 1 Cor. 16:22)[18]

We are to stand reverently before and beneath God's Word. We do not look over the Bible's shoulder to correct its theology. Rather, it is the Bible that corrects our theology.[19]

K. The Final Announcement of the Imminent Return of Jesus (22:20)

In verse 20 we have the third affirmation in this chapter of the imminent return of Jesus. The verse opens with the testimony of Christ that His coming will be without delay. John responds to this declaration of Jesus by saying, "Amen. Come, Lord Jesus." These fervent words were part of the liturgy of the early church. They were a prayer used at the close of the Lord's Supper. As Jesus appeared to His disciples alive on the first day of the week, so He was expected to be present in the Spirit at every first-day worship service and to appear again at the end. "Come, Lord Jesus" is the equivalent of the transliterated Aramaic in 1 Corinthians 16:22, *maranatha*.[20]

1. Living with the Mystery of Time

A question that inevitably emerges in the study of the New Testament second-coming expectation is this: How soon is soon? We must be careful not to measure the time of the second coming of Christ by an earthly, chronological measuring rod. We have seen that in Revelation and other New Testament books there is the prophetic shortening of time. We also have been introduced to the prophetic/apocalyptic mystery of time.

Palmer affirms that there is really no way to develop a chronological time-measurement scale for the language of time in John's vision in Revelation. God's time is not captive to the measurement frame of the solar system. The zodiac jewels are reversed in John's vision.

Time is a much more complicated reality than an hourglass or a stopwatch would suggest. The mathematician-physicist Albert Einstein found a witness to this fact in his discovery that time, even as we know and experience it, is altered by the speeds and gravitational fields of the created order.

Time itself is a baffling mystery, and the vision of John has borne witness to that mystery, but not in a way that confuses or distorts reality. His vision has helped us to see history meaningfully. All of time, as all of creation, belongs to its Lord. "We live each day as if it were our last, and each day as if there were to be a great future."[21]

2. The Implications of John's View of the "Soon" Return of Jesus

For most people, the abandonment of planning for the future means that they are forced back into living just for the moment in an irresponsible, frivolous, or resigned manner. Some people, on the other hand, dream longingly of better times to come and try to forget the present. Both of these courses are equally impossible for the Christian. There remains for us the very narrow way, sometimes difficult to find, of living every day as if it were our last, and yet living in faith and responsibility as though there were to be a great future.

This is the New Testament conviction about time that we have found in Revelation. "Soon" is the best word, the most accurate word, to describe the return of Christ as Lord because we have already received the companionship here and now of the Lord of the beginning and the end. The Holy Spirit has already confirmed and granted that living presence to everyone who trusts Jesus Christ here and now. We have the down payment—the earnest money of what eternity will be.[22]

3. The Importance of the Second Coming of Jesus

The central importance of the doctrine of the second coming of Jesus Christ is that Jesus Christ also stands at the end of history. He holds in His hand the destiny of the whole. Jesus Christ also stands at the end of each person's life. History does not trail off into emptiness; nor does it endlessly repeat its themes, like a vast confined circle. History from the biblical perspective has a meaningful beginning through the decision of God. History has the decisive center which is the radical intervention of God—the eternal Word and event Jesus Christ. History moves toward the decisive fulfillment.

The same Jesus Christ who stands at its beginning and at its center also stands to greet us at its end.

Especially during times of suffering and persecution the desire for the soon return of Christ grows intense. Even Paul, who longed so earnestly for Christ's return (1 Cor. 16:22), warned the Thessalonians they were not to withdraw from their obligations to work and live daily as responsible disciples (2 Thess. 2:1-2).[23]

But redemptive history remains incomplete until Christ returns. For the final act in the great drama of redemption, the church awaits with longing. Christ's return is the only sure hope for the future of the world. In fact, one author has said that the promise of the return of Jesus Christ is the sum of all promises and the sum of all living hope.[24]

L. The Final Benediction and Congregational Amen (22:21)

For a book written in apocalyptic language to end with a benediction is unusual. But we have seen that Revelation is also a prophetic book and an epistle. Thus it would be appropriate to close with a benediction, as Paul did so often (1 Cor. 16:23; Eph. 6:24; and so forth).

In verse 21 the benediction is pronounced upon all who have listened to the book as it was read aloud in the churches of Asia. It is also pronounced on all Christians in all ages who will read this book. In this benediction, John is once again stating that nothing less than God's grace is required for us to be overcomers and triumphantly enter the Holy City of God, where we shall reign with Him for ever and ever. Amen![25]

M. Conclusion

In the Bible, we find the model prayer as taught by Jesus in Matthew 6:9-15. It teaches us to pray, "Thy kingdom come,/Thy will be done,/On earth as it is in heaven." We have noted that the last great prayer of the Bible in verse 20 is, "Come, Lord Jesus." An authentic Christian prays this twofold prayer. First, you ask God to use you and your church as an instrument of the coming of God to the hearts of men and women and to the life of humanity here and now. You are to live a life of suffering love, as did the Lamb of God. But those in the evangelical Christian tradition also pray, look forward to, and anticipate the day when, as the Lion of the tribe of Judah and in a way which is beyond our finite understanding, Christ will come again.

In the second coming, Christ will not come humbly as the Lamb as He did in His first coming. Rather, He will come as the Lion, in glory and power. We are told to pray for this glorious coming and look forward to it. The final or ultimate answers to the problems of life are found in this final act in the great drama of redemption. The Bible says that we are to be ready at any time for the consummation and fulfillment of the age. The end is always near in the sense that each successive generation may be the last.

As a result of this study of Revelation, there should be an even greater sense of urgency in praying with understanding these two great prayers of the Bible: "Thy kingdom come . . . On earth as it is in heaven" and "Come, Lord Jesus." We should also have an even greater devotion to the Lion who became the Lamb for our redemption.

Notes

INTRODUCTION

1. J. Christiaan Beker, *Paul's Apocalyptic Gospel*, pp. 21-24.

2. Ibid., pp. 20-21.

3. Joseph Bettis and S. K. Johannesen, eds., *The Return of the Millennium*, pp. 17-18.

4. Richard N. Ostling, "Armageddon and the End Times," *Time*, 5 November 1984, p. 73.

5. Donald Tinder, "Future Fact? Future Fiction?" *Christianity Today*, 15 April 1977, p. 40.

6. Stanley D. Walters, "Hal Lindsey: Recalculating the Second Coming," *Christian Century*, 12 September 1979, p. 839; see also, Hal Lindsey, "The Great Cosmic Countdown," *Eternity*, January 1977, p. 19.

7. Ostling, p. 73.

8. William Sanford LaSor, *The Truth about Armageddon*, pp. 1-2.

9. Ibid., p. 6.

10. Ibid., p. 5; see also, Hal Lindsey, *The Late Great Planet Earth* (Grand Rapids: Zondervan, 1970), p. 122.

11. Ibid.

12. William Martin, "Waiting for the End," *The Atlantic Monthly*, June 1982, p. 34.

13. Ibid.

14. John F. Walvoord with John E. Walvoord, *Armageddon: Oil and the Middle East Crisis*, pp. 20-21.

15. LaSor, pp. 3-5.

16. Martin, p. 34.

17. Walvoord with Walvoord, pp. 19-23.

18. Ostling, p. 73.

19. Bettis and Johannesen, pp. 23-24; see also, *Pat Robertson's Perspective*, March 1981, p. 2

20. Ibid., pp. 24-25; see also "Advertisement," *Sword of the Lord*, October 31, 1980, p. 15

21. Ibid., p. 25; see also David Wilkerson, *The Vision* (Old Tappan, NJ: Fleming H. Revell Co., 1974), p. 27.

22. Ibid; see also David Wilkerson, *Racing Toward Judgment* (Old Tappan, NJ: Fleming H. Revell Co., 1974), p. 48

23. Richard L. Jeske, *Revelation for Today: Images of Hope*, p. 1.

24. Jacques Ellul, *Apocalypse*, pp. 9-10.

25. Pheme Perkins, *The Book of Revelation, Collegeville Bible Commentary*, 11, p. 7.

26. Elisabeth Schüessler Fiorenza, *Invitation to the Book of Revelation*, p. 15.

27. Billy Graham, *Approaching Hoofbeats: The Four Horsemen of the Apocalypse*, pp. 23-26, 27.

28. Robert G. Clouse, ed., *The Meaning of the Millennium*, p. 93.

29. Bettis and Johannesen, pp. 14-15; see also *Kindred Spirit, Fall 1980*, p. 14; John R. Rice, *Christ's Literal Reign on Earth* (Murfreesboro, Tenn.: Sword of the Lord Foundation, n. d.), p. 5.

30. Ibid., p. 15.

31. Timothy P. Weber, "The Two-Edged Sword: The Fundamentalist Use of the Bible," *Bible in America*, eds. N. O. Hatch and M. A. Noll, pp. 112-113.

32. Ibid., pp. 113 *f.*

33. Ibid., p. 114.

34. Ibid.

35. Ibid., p. 116.

36. Anthony A. Hoekema, *The Bible and the Future*, p. 175.

37. Millard J. Erickson, *Contemporary Options in Eschatology: A Study of the Millennium*, p. 71.

38. Bettis and Johannesen, p. 207.

39. Ibid., pp. 219-220.

40. Ibid., p. 220.

41. Ibid., pp. 226-227.

42. Ibid., p. 228.

43. Ibid.

44. Ostling, p. 73.

45. Ibid.

46. Bettis and Johannesen, p. 19; see also Lindsey, *The Late Great Planet Earth*, p. 43; Lindsey, *The 1980's: Countdown to Armageddon* (New York: Bantam Books, 1981), pp. 53-63.

47. Ibid; see also *Pat Robertson's Perspective*, Fall 1980, pp. 4-5.

48. Ibid; see also Lindsey, *The Late Great Planet Earth*, p. 82; Lindsey, *The 1980's*, pp. 87-96.

49. Ibid., p. 22; see also Lindsey, *The 1980's*, pp. 5, 173, 7.

50. Ibid., p. 23; see also Fundamentalist Baptist Fellowship of America *News Bulletin*, May-June-July 1979, p.3.

51. Martin, pp. 35 *f.*; see also Lindsey, *The 1980's*, p. 139.

52. Bettis and Johannesen, p. 26; see also Rice, pp. 7 *f.* and *Pat Robertson*, Fall 1980, p. 6.

53. Ibid., p. 27; see also Jerry Falwell, ed., *The Fundamentalist Phenomenon* (Garden City, NY: Doubleday and Co., 1981), p. 215; *Baptist Bible Tribune*, May 2, 1980, p.1.

54. Richard J. Mouw, *Politics and the Biblical Drama*, p. 121.

55. Beker, p. 61.

56. Ibid., pp. 61 *f.*

57. Ibid., p. 50.

58. Ibid., p. 16.

59. Alan F. Johnson, "Revelation," *Expositor's Bible Commentary*, ed. Frank E. Gaebelein, p. 407.

60. Ibid.

61. J. P. M. Sweet, *Revelation, Westminster Pelican Commentaries,* p. 43 f.

62. Beker, p. 28.

63. Ibid., p. 118.

64. Gordon D. Fee and Douglas Stuart, *How to Read the Bible for All Its Worth,* pp. 205-206.

65. Ibid., pp. 205 f.

66. Adela Yarbro Collins, *Crisis and Catharsis: The Power of the Apocalypse,* p. 165.

67. Ibid., p. 25.

68. Leland Ryken, *How to Read the Bible as Literature,* pp. 11-12.

69. Ibid., pp. 12, 30 f.

70. Ibid., p. 25.

71. Ibid., p. 26.

72. Ibid., p. 30.

73. Elisabeth Schüessler Fiorenza, "Revelation," *Proclamation Commentaries,* ed. Gerhard Krodel, p. 101.

74. Sweet, p. 13.

75. Fiorenza, "Revelation," p. 101.

76. Leland Ryken, *The Literature of the Bible,* p. 335.

77. Ibid.

78. Ibid., pp. 335-337.

79. Charles De Santo, *The Book of Revelation: A Study Manual,* pp. 18 f.

80. Ryken, *Literature,* p. 337.

81. Fiorenza, *Invitation,* pp. 25 f.

82. Ryken, *Literature,* p. 338.

83. Ryken, *How to Read,* p. 187.

84. Ryken, *Literature,* p. 338.

85. Ryken, *How to Read,* p. 79.

86. Ibid.

87. Ibid.

88. Ryken, *Literature,* p. 343.

89. Ryken, *How to Read,* p. 81.

90. Ryken, *Literature,* p. 343.

91. Ibid.

92. Ibid., p. 339.; De Santo, p. 19.

93. Ryken, *Literature,* p. 339.

94. De Santo, p. 19.

95. Ryken, *Literature,* p. 339.

96. Ryken, *How to Read,* pp. 170-172; *Literature,* p. 339.

97. Ryken, *Literature,* p. 339 f.

98. Fiorenza, "Revelation," p. 111.

99. Sweet, p. 15.

100. Ryken, *Literature,* p. 340.

101. Ibid.

102. Ibid.

103. Ibid., p. 342.

104. Ibid.

105. Ryken, *How to Read*, p. 167.
106. George R. Beasley-Murray, "Demythologized Eschatology," *Theology Today*, p. 66.
107. Ryken, *How to Read*, p. 167-168.
108. Ibid., pp. 168-169.
109. Ibid., p. 169.
110. Ibid.
111. Ibid.
112. Joel B. Green, *How to Read Prophecy*, p. 71.
113. Ibid., pp. 71-72.
114. Ryken, *How to Read*, p. 170.
115. Green, pp. 77-78.
116. Ibid., p. 78.
117. Ryken, *How to Read*, p. 174.
118. Sweet, pp. 13-14.
119. Fee and Stuart, p. 211.
120. Ibid., p. 155.
121. Beker, pp. 116-117.
122. Robert H. Mounce, *The Book of Revelation, New International Commentary*, p. 18.
123. Ibid.
124. Ibid., p. 20.
125. Ibid.
126. Ibid.
127. Ibid., p. 21.
128. Fee and Stuart, p. 207.
129. Ibid.
130. Mounce, p. 23.
131. Johnson, p. 402.
132. Fee and Stuart, p. 207.
133. Val J. Sauer, *The Eschatology Handbook*, p. 11.
134. Johnson, p. 401.
135. Ibid.
136. Ibid., p. 402.
137. Ibid.
138. Ibid.
139. Fee and Stuart, p. 208.
140. Ibid.
141. Earl F. Palmer, *1, 2, 3 John, Revelation, The Communicator's Commentary*, 12, p. 102.
142. Fiorenza, "Revelation," p. 108.
143. Ibid.
144. George R. Beasley-Murray, *The Book of Revelation, New Century Bible*, pp. 19-20.
145. Ibid., p. 23.
146. Fee and Stuart, pp. 208-209.
147. Ibid., p. 45.
148. Ibid., p. 209.

149. Alan F. Johnson, *Revelation, Bible Study Commentary,* p. 14.
150. Collins. pp. 25-26.
151. Ibid., p. 25.
152. Ibid., p. 26.
153. Johnson, "Revelation," p. 404.
154. Ibid.
155. Ibid., pp. 404-405.
156. Collins, 47.
157. Ibid., p. 48.
158. Robert H. Gundry, *A Survey of the New Testament,* rev. ed., p. 345.
159. Ibid.
160. Collins, p. 31 *f.*
161. Ibid., p. 33.
162. Ibid., pp. 26.*f.*
163. Ibid., pp. 29 *f.*
164. Johnson, "Revelation," p. 405.
165. Ibid.
166. Ibid.
167. De Santo, p. 21.
168. Ibid.
169. Collins, pp. 31-32.
170. Palmer, p. 104.
171. Collins, pp. 46-47.
172. Ibid., p. 46.
173. Ibid., pp. 49 *f.*
174. Ibid., pp. 134 *f.*
175. Ibid., pp. 136 *f.*
176. Ibid.
177. Ibid., p. 54.
178. Ibid., pp 54 *f.*
179. Ibid.
180. Ibid., pp. 54 *f.,* 57.
181. Ibid., pp. 57 *f.*
182. Ibid., pp. 70 *f.*
183. Ibid., pp. 72 *f*; De Santo, p. 22.
184. Sweet, p. 47.
185. Ibid., pp. 47 *f.*
186. Ibid., p. 48.
187. Ibid., p. 51.
188. Fiorenza, "Revelation," p. 113.
189. Sweet, pp. 22-23.
190. See Collins, p. 101 for an example of this point.
191. Fiorenza, "Revelation," p. 113.
192. Ibid.
193. Sweet, p. 23.
194. Fiorenza, "Revelation,": p. 116.
195. Ibid., pp. 117-119.

196. Johnson, "Revelation," pp. 400, 407.
197. Ibid., p. 407.
198. Elisabeth Schüessler Fiorenza, *The Apocalypse, Herald Biblical Booklets,* pp. 16-17.
199. Ibid., pp. 16 f.
200. James L. Blevins, "The Genre of Revelation," *Review and Expositor,* pp. 393 f.
201. Ibid., pp. 394 f.
202. Ibid., pp. 396 ff.
203. Ibid., pp. 399 ff.
204. Fiorenza, *The Apocalypse,* p. 18.
205. Collins, pp. 85-86.
206. Ibid., pp. 87 f.
207. Ibid., pp. 88 f., 134.
208. Ibid., pp. 94, 97.
209. Ibid., pp. 105-107.
210. Ibid., pp. 106 f, 141-144.
211. Ibid., pp. 143 f.
212. Ibid., pp. 146 f.
213. Ibid., pp. 147-150.
214. Ibid., p. 153.
215. Ibid., pp. 153 f.
216. Ibid., pp. 154, 156.
217. Ibid., p. 158.
218. Ibid., p. 161.

HOW DO YOU INTERPRET REVELATION AND SEE IT IN BROAD PERSPECTIVE?

1. Cedric B. Johnson, *The Psychology of Biblical Interpretation,* p. 86.
2. Ibid., pp. 86 f.
3. Adela Yarbro Collins, *Crisis and Catharsis: The Power of the   Apocalypse,* p. 19.
4. Ibid., p. 20.
5. Ibid.
6. Robert H. Mounce, *The Book of Revelation, New International Commentary,* p. 41.
7. Ibid., pp. 41 f.
8. Anthony A. Hoekema, *The Bible and the Future,* p. 173.
9. Ibid., pp. 173 f.
10. Millard J. Erickson, *Contemporary Options in Eschatology: A Study of the Millennium,* p. 76. Robert G. Clouse, ed., *The Meaning of the Millennium,* p. 96.
11. Dale Moody, *The Word of Truth: A Summary of Christian Doctrine Based on Biblical Revelation,* p. 551.
12. Erickson, p. 76.
13. Ibid.
14. Moody, p. 552.
15. Ibid.
16. Ibid.
17. Ibid.
18. Hoekema, p. 223.
19. Erickson, p. 83.

20. Hoekema, p. 227.

21. Erickson, pp. 76-77.

22. Ray Summers, "Revelation," *Review and Expositor,* 1960, 17, pp. 176-180.

23. Hoekema, p. 238.

24. Erickson, p. 74.

25. Ibid., pp. 83-84.

26. Ibid., p. 74.

27. Ibid.

28. Hoekema, p. 174.

29. Erickson, p. 85.

30. Ibid., pp. 85 *f.*

31. Ibid., p. 86.

32. Alan F. Johnson, "Revelation," *Expositor's Bible Commentary,* ed. Frank E. Gaebelein, p. 409.

33. Richard L. Jeske, *Revelation for Today: Images of Hope,* p. 9.

34. Ibid., pp. 9-11; Johnson, "Revelation," p. 409.

35. Robert H. Gundry, *A Survey of the New Testament,* p. 346.

36. Mounce, p. 42.

37. Hoekema, p. 175.

38. Erickson, pp. 55-56.

39. Ibid., p. 57; Hoekema, p. 176.

40. Hoekema, p. 177.

41. Erickson, p. 67.

42. Ibid., p. 68.

43. Ibid., p. 69.

44. Ibid., p. 65.

45. Ibid., p. 61.

46. Moody, pp. 553-554.

47. Ibid., p. 554.

48. Erickson, pp. 70 *f.*

49. Hoekema, p. 180; Erickson, p. 71.

50. Erickson, p. 72.

51. Hoekema, p. 177.

52. Erickson, p. 72.

53. Johnson, "Revelation," p. 410.

54. Ibid.

55. Mounce, p. 43.

56. Johnson, "Revelation," p. 410.

57. Ibid., p. 408.

58. Ibid.

59. Erickson, p. 109.

60. Ibid.

61. Ibid., p. 110.

62. Hoekema, p. 188.

63. Erickson, pp. 115-116.

64. Ibid., p. 117; Hoekema, p. 189.

65. Hoekema, p. 189.

66. Ibid., pp. 188 *f;* Erickson, p. 122.

67. Hoekema, p. 190.
68. Ibid.
69. Ibid., p. 191.
70. Ibid., p. 192.
71. Ibid.
72. Erickson, p. 111.
73. Clouse, pp. 12-13.
74. Ibid.
75. William Martin, "Waiting for the End," *Atlantic Monthly,* June 1982, p. 31.
76. Clouse, pp. 12-13.
77. Erickson, p. 114.
78. Ibid., pp. 114 *f.*
79. Ibid., pp. 122 *f.*
80. Ibid., p. 123.
81. Bruce Corley, "'Something There Is That Doesn't Love a Wall': Southern Baptists and Dispensationalism," chapel address, 3 July 1984 (typewritten), p. 4.
82. Hoekema, p. 196.
83. Moody, p. 556.
84. Hoekema, p. 195.
85. Ibid., p. 220.
86. Mounce, pp. 42-43.
87. Joseph Bettis and S. K. Johannesen, eds. *The Return of the Millennium,* p. 158.
88. Erickson, p. 94.
89. Moody, p. 548.
90. J. Christian Beker, *Paul's Apocalyptic Gospel,* p. 61; Erickson, p. 151.
91. Erickson, p. 97.
92. Clouse, p. 92.
93. Erickson, pp. 151-152.
94. Elisabeth Schüessler Fiorenza, "Revelation," *Proclamation Commentaries,* ed. Gerhard Krodel, pp. 111 *f.*
95. Ibid., p. 108.
96. George E. Ladd, *A Theology of the New Testament,* pp. 623 *f.*
97. George R. Beasley-Murray, "Revelation," *New Bible Commentary,* eds. D. Guthrie, et al., pp. 1168 *f.*
98. Erickson, pp. 91, 102.
99. Ibid., p. 146.
100. Ibid., pp. 101 *f.*
101. Ibid., p. 103.
102. Ibid., p. 147.
103. Beker, pp. 116 *f.*
104. Ibid., p. 118.
105. Hoekema, p. 183; Erickson, p. 147.
106. Erickson, p. 151.
107. Ibid., pp. 146 *f.*
108. Johnson, "Revelation," p. 410.
109. Beasley-Murray, pp. 1168 *f.*
110. Ladd, p. 626.
111. George E. Ladd, *The Blessed Hope,* pp. 105-119.

112. Erickson, p.106.

113. George E. Ladd, "Revelation 20 and the Millennium," *Review and Expositor,* 1960, 57, p. 171.

114. George E. Ladd, "The Revelation of Christ's Glory," *Christianity Today,* 1 September 1958, p. 14.

115. Erickson, p. 161.

116. Ibid., p. 104.

117. Ibid., p. 159.

118. Ibid., pp. 104, 159 *f.*

119. Ibid., p. 160.

120. Ibid.

121. Hoekema, p. 183; Erickson, p. 148.

122. Erickson, p. 183.

123. Gordon Fee and Douglas Stuart, *How to Read the Bible for All Its Worth,* pp. 213.

124. Ibid., pp. 213 *f.*

125. Ibid., pp. 213-215.

126. George R. Beasley-Murray, *The Book of Revelation, New Century Bible,* p. 41.

127. Ibid., p. 31.

128. Ibid.

129. Ibid.

130. Ladd, *A Theology,* p. 624.

131. Beasley-Murray, *The Book of Revelation,* p. 31.

132. Ibid.

133. Fee and Stuart, pp. 214 *f.*

134. Ibid.

135. Beasley-Murray, *The Book of Revelation,* pp. 31 *f.*

136. Mounce, pp. 46 *f.*; Leon Morris, *The Revelation of St. John, The Tyndale New Testament Commentaries,* pp. 40 *f.*

137. Mounce, p. 41.

138. Johnson, *The Psychology,* pp. 88 *f.*

139. Collins, p. 173.

140. Ibid.

141. Ibid., p. 174.

142. Ibid.

143. Ibid., pp. 174 *f.*

144. Ibid., p. 175.

145. Johnson, *The Psychology,* p. 85.

146. Ibid.

147. Ibid.

148. Beasley-Murray, *The Book of Revelation* p. 43.

149. William Sanford LaSor, *The Truth About Armageddon,* pp. 116-117.

150. Beasley-Murray, *The Book of Revelation,* p. 44.

151. Ibid., p. 45.

152. Leland Ryken, *The Literature of the Bible,* p. 341.

153. Charles De Santo, *The Book of Revelation: A Study Manual,* p. 23.

154. Beker, pp. 16, 90.

155. Ibid., pp. 111 *f.*, 88 *f.*

156. Johnson, "Revelation," p. 407.

157. Collins, p. 171.

158. Ibid.

159. Ibid.

160. Ibid., pp. 171 *f.*

161. Ibid., p. 172.

162. Ibid., p. 173.

163. Beasley-Murray, *The Book of Revelation*, pp. 45 *f.*

164. Ibid., p. 47.

165. LaSor, pp. 160 *f.*

166. George R. Beasley-Murray, "Demythologized Eschatology," *Theology Today,* 14, p. 68.

167. George E. Ladd, *A Commentary on the Revelation of John*, pp. 81-94.

I. Prologue

1. George R. Beasley-Murray, *Highlights of the Book of Revelation*, p. 10.

2. Alan F. Johnson, *Revelation, Bible Study Commentary*, p. 22.

3. Ibid.

4. Ibid., p. 23.

5. Hal Lindsey, *There's a New World Coming*, pp. 23 *f.*

6. Charles De Santo, *The Book of Revelation: A Study Manual*, pp. 25 *f.*

7. J. Christiaan Beker, *Paul's Apocalyptic Gospel*, p. 48.

8. Ibid., p. 98.

9. Ibid., p. 49.

10. Ibid., p. 120.

11. Johnson, p. 24.

12. De Santo, p. 27.

13. Ibid.

14. Johnson, p. 24.

15. Beasley-Murray, p. 12.

16. Ibid., p. 25.

17. Ibid.

18. Ibid., p. 14.

19. Johnson, pp. 25 *f.*

20. De Santo, p. 28.

21. Johnson, p. 26.

22. Ibid., p. 27.

23. De Santo, p. 28.

II. The First Vision of John

1. Charles De Santo, *The Book of Revelation: A Study Manual*, p. 28.

2. Ibid., p. 29.

3. George E. Ladd, *A Commentary on the Revelation of John*, pp. 29 *f.*

4. Ibid., p. 30.

5. Alan F. Johnson, *Revelation, Bible Study Commentary*, p. 32.

6. De Santo, p. 29.

7. Johnson, p. 32.

8. De Santo, p. 30.

9. Ibid.

10. Ibid.

11. Johnson, pp. 33-34.

12. Ibid., p. 33; De Santo, p. 30.

13. Johnson., p. 34.

14. De Santo, p. 30.

15. Johnson, p. 34.

16. De Santo, p. 30.

17. Ibid., p. 31.

18. Ibid.

19. Ibid.

20. Ibid.

21. Johnson, p. 35.

22. Ibid., pp. 35 f.

23. De Santo, p. 31.

24. Johnson, p. 36.

25. Robert H. Mounce, *The Book of Revelation, New International Commentary,* p. 82.

26. Johnson, p. 36.

27. Ibid., p. 37.

28. Ibid.

29. Earl F. Palmer, *1, 2, 3 John, Revelation, The Communicator's Commentary,* 12 pp. 123-124.

30. Ibid., pp. 123 f.

31. Ibid., p. 124.

32. De Santo, p. 33.

33. Ibid.

34. J. Dwight Pentecost, *Things to Come,* p. 153.

35. Ibid.

36. John F. Walvoord, *The Revelation of Jesus Christ,* p. 52.

37. Johnson, p. 38.

38. Ibid.

39. Ibid.

40. Ibid., p. 39.

41. Mounce, p. 84.

42. Ibid.

43. De Santo, p. 33.

44. Ibid.

45. Ibid., p. 34.

46. Ibid.

47. Johnson, p. 43.

48. De Santo, p. 34.

49. Johnson, p. 42.

50. Ibid.

51. Palmer, 12, p. 128.

52. Ibid., p. 129.

53. Esther Onstad, *Courage for Today—Hope for Tomorrow,* p. 17.

54. Johnson, p. 43.

55. Ibid.

56. Ibid.

57. Ibid., p. 44
58. De Santo, p. 35.
59. Johnson, p. 44.
60. De Santo, p. 36.
61. Ibid.
62. Ibid.
63. Ibid.
64. Johnson, pp. 45 f.
65. Ibid., p. 46.
66. De Santo, p. 37.
67. Johnson, p. 46.
68. De Santo, p. 37.
69. Ibid.
70. Johnson, p. 46.
71. De Santo, p. 37.
72. Ibid., p. 38.
73. Ibid.
74. Ibid.
75. Johnson, p. 48.
76. De Santo, p. 38.
77. Johnson, p. 48.
78. De Santo, p. 38.
79. Johnson, p. 49.
80. Ibid.
81. De Santo, p. 38.
82. Onstad, p. 20.
83. Johnson, p. 49.
84. Palmer, pp. 137-138.
85. De Santo, p. 39.
86. Johnson, p. 49.
87. Ibid., pp. 49 f.; Palmer, p. 138.
88. Johnson, p. 50.
89. De Santo, p. 40.
90. Ibid.
91. Palmer, p. 143.
92. De Santo, p. 40.
93. Ibid.
94. Johnson, p. 51.
95. De Santo, p. 41.
96. Johnson, p. 51.
97. De Santo, p. 41.
98. Johnson, p. 51.
99. Ibid.
100. Ibid., p. 52.
101. De Santo, p. 41.
102. Johnson, p. 52.
103. De Santo, p. 41.
104. Onstad, p. 22.

105. De Santo, p. 42.
106. Johnson, p. 53.
107. Ibid.
108. De Santo, p. 42.
109. Ibid., pp. 42 f.
110. Ibid., p. 43.
111. Johnson, p. 56.
112. De Santo, p. 43.
113. Johnson, p. 55
114. De Santo, p. 44.
115. Ibid.
116. Johnson, p. 56.
117. Ibid.
118. Ibid.
119. Ibid., p. 57.
120. De Santo, p. 45.
121. Johnson, p. 58.
122. De Santo, p. 45.
123. Ibid.
124. Ibid.
125. Palmer, p. 149.
126. Ibid., p. 150.
127. Johnson, p. 59.
128. De Santo, p. 46.
129. John P. Milton, *Prophecy Interpreted* (Minneapolis: Augsburg Publishing House, 1960), pp. 19 f.
130. Johnson, p. 60.
131. Ibid.
132. Ibid.
133. Ibid.
134. De Santo, p. 46.
135. George E. Ladd, p. 62.
136. Ibid.
137. De Santo, p. 46.
138. Johnson, p. 61.
139. Ibid.
140. Ibid.
141. De Santo, p. 47.
142. Johnson, p. 62.
143. Palmer, p. 152.
144. De Santo, p. 47.
145. Ibid.
146. Palmer, p. 155.
147. Johnson, p. 63.
148. Ibid.
149. Ibid.
150. De Santo, p. 48.
151. Ibid.

152. Johnson, pp. 63-64.
153. De Santo, p. 48.
154. Johnson, p. 64.
155. De Santo, p. 48.
156. Johnson, p. 64.
157. De Santo, p. 48.
158. Johnson, p. 65.
159. Ladd, p. 67.
160. Johnson, p. 65.
161. Ladd, p. 67.
162. Ibid., pp. 67 f.
163. Johnson, p. 65.
164. Ladd, p. 69.
165. Ibid.

III. THE SECOND VISION

1. George E. Ladd, *A Commentary on the Revelation of John*, p. 70.
2. Ibid.
3. Robert H. Mounce, *The Book of Revelation*, New International Commentary, p. 131.
4. Earl F. Palmer, *1, 2, 3 John, Revelation*, The Communicator's Commentary, 12, p. 158.
5. Ladd, p. 71.
6. Hal Lindsey, *There's a New World Coming*, p. 77.
7. Alan F. Johnson, *Revelation, Bible Study Commentary*, p. 70.
8. Ibid.
9. Ladd, p. 71.
10. Charles De Santo, *The Book of Revelation: A Study Manual*, p. 50.
11. Palmer, p. 158.
12. De Santo, p. 51.
13. Ladd, p. 74.
14. Johnson, p. 71.
15. Ibid.
16. De Santo, p. 51.
17. Ibid.
18. Palmer p. 159.
19. De Santo, p. 51.
20. Johnson, p. 72.
21. Ibid.
22. De Santo, p. 52.
23. Palmer, pp. 160-161.
24. Ibid., p. 161.
25. Ibid.
26. Ibid., p. 162.
27. Ibid.
28. Ibid., p. 163.
29. Ladd, p. 81.
30. Palmer, p. 165.

31. Ladd, p. 82.

32. Ibid.

33. Palmer, p. 165.

34. Ibid.

35. Ibid.

36. Ibid., p. 166; Johnson, p. 75.

37. Ladd, pp. 83 *f*.

38. Johnson, pp. 75 *f*.

39. Ibid., p. 76.

40. Palmer, p. 166.

41. Johnson, p. 76.

42. Ibid.

43. Ibid.

44. Ibid.

45. Ibid.

46. Ibid., p. 77.

47. Palmer, p. 170; Johnson, p. 78.

48. Ibid.

49. Ladd, pp. 86-87.

50. Ibid., p. 87.

51. Palmer, p. 167.

52. Ibid., p. 171.

53. Ibid.

54. Glenn W. Barker, William L. Lane, and J. Ramsey Michaels, *The New Testament Speaks*, p. 371.

55. Ibid., p. 372.

56. George E. Ladd, *A Theology of the New Testament*, p. 823.

57. Johnson, pp. 78-79.

58. Ladd, p. 823.

59. Ibid., p. 824.

60. Barker, Lane, and Michaels, p. 372.

61. Ibid.

62. Ladd, *A Commentary,* p. 96.

63. Johnson, p. 79.

64. Ladd, A Commentary, p. 97.

65. Ibid., pp. 97 *f*.

66. Gordon Fee and Douglas Stuart, *How to Read the Bible for All Its Worth,* pp. 209-210.

67. Ladd, *A Commentary,* p. 98.

68. Ibid., pp. 98 *f*.

69. Ladd, *A Theology,* p. 824.

70. Ladd, *A Commentary,* p. 99.

71. Lindsey, p. 103.

72. Ladd, *A Commentary,* p. 99.

73. Eric C. Rust, *Salvation History: A Biblical Interpretation,* p. 305.

74. J. Christiaan Beker, *Paul's Apocalyptic Gospel,* p. 52.

75. Ibid., pp. 53, 58.

76. Ladd, *A Commentary,* p. 99.

77. Ibid., pp. 99 *f,*

78. Ladd, *A Theology,* p. 550 *f.*

79. Oscar Cullmann, *Christ and Time,* rev. ed., p. 164 *f.*; Johannes Munck, *Paul and the Salvation of Mankind* (London: SCM Press, 1959), pp. 31-39.

80. Johnson, p. 80.

81. Lindsey, p. 104.

82. Palmer, 12, p. 176.

83. Mounce, p. 155.

84. Lindsey, pp. 104-105.

85. Johnson, p. 81.

86. Mounce, p. 156.

87. Lindsey, pp. 106-107.

88. Johnson, p. 82.

89. Ibid.

90. Ibid.

91. Ibid.

92. Ibid.

93. Ibid., p. 83.

94. Ibid.

95. De Santo, p. 58.

96. Johnson, p. 83.

97. Ibid.

98. Ladd, *A Commentary,* p. 107.

99. Ibid., pp. 107 *f.*

100. Ibid., p. 108.

101. Lindsey, pp. 109 *f.*

102. Johnson, p. 83.

103. Ibid., p. 84.

104. Mounce, p. 163.

105. De Santo, p. 58.

106. Mounce, pp. 162-163.

107. Ibid., p. 162.

108. Ladd, *A Commentary,* p. 109.

109. Ibid.

110. Palmer, p. 180.

111. Johnson, p. 84.

112. Ibid.

113. Mounce, p. 164.

114. Ladd, *A Commentary,* p. 110.

115. Ibid., p. 112.

116. De Santo, pp. 58-59.

117. Johnson, p. 85.

118. Ibid.

119. Ibid.

120. Ibid.

121. Ibid.

122. Ibid.

123. Ladd, *A Commentary,* p. 112.

124. Ibid.

125. Johnson, p. 86.

126. Ibid., p. 90.

127. Lindsey, pp. 112 *f.*

128. Ibid., p. 125.

129. Ladd, *A Commentary,* p. 116.

130. Ibid.

131. Johnson, p. 87.

132. Ibid.

133. Ibid.

134. Palmer, p. 181.

135. Johnson, pp. 87 *f.*

136. Ibid., p. 88.

137. Ibid., p. 89.

138. Ibid.

139. Ibid.

140. Ibid., p. 90.

141. Ibid.

142. Ibid., p. 91 *f.*

143. Ibid., p. 92.

144. Ibid.

145. Mounce, pp. 175-176.

146. Ibid., p. 176.

147. Palmer, pp. 183-184.

148. Ibid., pp. 184 *f.*

149. Johnson, p. 90.

150. Ibid., pp. 90 *f.*

151. Ibid., p. 91.

152. Ibid.

153. Ibid.

154. Ladd, *A Commentary,* p. 118.

155. Ibid., p. 119.

156. Palmer, p. 185.

157. Ladd, *A Commentary,* pp. 122 *f.*

158. Ladd, *A Commentary,* p. 122.

159. Mounce, p. 178.

160. Ibid.

161. Johnson p. 97.

162. Glenn W. Barker, William L. Lane, and J. Ramsey Michaels, *The New Testament Speaks,* p. 375.

163. Ibid., p. 376.

164. De Santo, p. 62.

165. Johnson, p. 95.

166. Ibid.; De Santo, p. 62.

167. De Santo, p. 63.

168. Johnson, p. 97.

169. De Santo, p. 64.

170. Lindsey, p. 131.

171. Lindsey, p. 133.

172. Palmer, 12, p. 187.

173. Ibid., p. 188.

174. De Santo, p. 68.

175. Ladd, p. 130.

176. Ibid., pp. 131 f.

177. Ibid., p. 132.

178. De Santo, p. 66.

179. Johnson, p. 100.

180. De Santo, p. 66.

181. Lindsey, p. 139.

182. De Santo, p. 67.

183. Ibid.

184. Ibid.

185. Ladd, p. 136.

186. Johnson, pp. 100 f.; Palmer, p. 189.

187. Johnson, p. 101.

188. Ibid.

189. Lindsey, p. 140.

190. Ibid.

191. Ibid., p. 141.

192. C. I. Scofield, ed., *The New Scofield Reference Bible*, p. 1323.

193. Johnson, p. 101.

194. Ibid.

195. Ladd, pp. 138 f.

196. Johnson, p. 102.

197. Ladd, p. 139.

198. Johnson, pp. 101-102.

199. Ladd, p. 139.

200. Lindsey, pp. 144-148.

201. Mounce, p. 205.

202. Ladd, *A Commentary,* p. 140.

203. George R. Beasley-Murray, *The Book of Revelation, New Century Bible*, p. 168.

204. Mounce, p. 205.

205. Ibid.

206. De Santo, p. 68.

207. Ibid.

208. Ibid.

209. Ibid.

210. Ibid., p. 69.

211. Ladd, p. 144.

212. Quoted by George R. Beasley-Murray, *Highlights of the Book of Revelation,* pp. 29 f.

213. De Santo, p. 69.

214. Johnson, p. 102.

215. De Santo, p. 69.

216. Palmer, pp. 191 f.

217. Ladd, p. 148.

218. Esther Onstad, *Courage for Today—Hope for Tomorrow,* p. 44.
219. Ibid.
220. Ibid., pp. 44 f.
221. Ladd, p. 149.
222. Johnson, p. 104.
223. Ibid.
224. John F. Walvoord, *The Revelation of Jesus Christ,* pp. 176-180.
225. Lindsey, pp. 156-161.
226. Ladd, *A Commentary,* pp. 152 f.
227. Mounce, p. 218.
228. Beasley-Murray, *The Book of Revelation,* pp. 178 f.
229. Johnson, p. 104.
230. Beasley-Murray, *Highlights,* pp. 30 f.
231. Ibid., p. 31.
232. De Santo, p. 70.
233. Ibid.
234. Mounce, pp. 221 f.
235. Johnson, p. 106.
236. Ibid.
237. Ibid., pp. 106 f.
238. Mounce, p. 220.
239. Ibid., p. 221.
240. Johnson, p. 107.
241. Ibid., pp. 107 f.
242. Ibid., p. 108.
243. Ibid., p. 109.
244. Ibid.
245. Ibid.
246. Ibid.
247. De Santo, p. 70.
248. Ibid.
249. Ibid., p. 71.
250. Johnson, p. 110.
251. Ibid.
252. Ibid., p. 111.
253. Ladd, *A Commentary,* pp. 155 f.
254. Ibid., p. 156.
255. Ibid.; De Santo, p. 71.
256. Ladd, *A Commentary,* p. 157.
257. Johnson, p. 112.
258. Ibid.
259. De Santo, p. 71.
260. Lindsey, pp. 165 f.
261. De Santo, p. 71.
262. Ibid., pp. 71 f.
263. Ibid., p. 72.
264. Ibid.
265. Johnson , p. 114.

266. De Santo, p. 72.

267. Ibid.

268. Johnson, p. 115.

269. Ibid.

270. De Santo, p. 72.

271. Ladd, *A Commentary,* p. 162.

272. Johnson, p. 116.

273. Ladd, *A Commentary,* p. 163.

274. Palmer, p. 197.

275. Ibid.

276. Mounce, p. 234.

277. Johnson, p. 117.

278. Beasley-Murray, *Highlights,* pp. 34 f.

279. Johnson, p. 117.

280. John M. Court, *Myth and History in the Book of Revelation,* p. 164.

281. Johnson, p. 118.

282. De Santo, p. 74.

283. Johnson, p. 117.

284. Ladd, *A Commentary,* p. 166.

285. Palmer, 12, p. 200.

286. Johnson, p. 118.

287. Ibid., p. 119.

288. Ladd, *A Commentary,* p. 167 f.; Palmer p. 200.

289. Ladd, *A Commentary,* p. 168.

290. Ibid., p. 169.

291. Johnson, p. 120.

292. Ibid.

293. Ladd, *A Commentary,* p. 170.

294. Johnson, p. 121.

295. Ladd, *A Commentary,* p. 170.

296. Palmer, p. 202.

297. De Santo, pp. 75 f.

298. Ladd, *A Commentary,* p. 171.

299. Johnson, p. 122.

300. Ladd, *A Commentary,* p. 172.

301. Ibid.

302. Palmer, p. 202.

303. Ladd, *A Commentary,* p. 172.

304. Ibid., p. 173.

305. Lindsey, p. 177.

306. Ladd, *A Commentary,* p. 173.

307. Johnson, p. 124.

308. Ibid.

309. Ladd, *A Commentary,* p. 174.

310. Johnson, pp. 124-125.

311. Ladd, *A Commentary,* p. 175.

312. Lindsey, p. 179.

313. David Allan Hubbard, *The Second Coming,* p. 35.

314. Ibid.
315. Ibid., p. 36.
316. Ibid., p. 36 *f.*
317. Ibid., p. 37.
318. Ibid., pp. 37 *f.*
319. Ibid., p. 38.
320. Ibid., pp. 39-41.
321. Mounce, p. 248.
322. Ibid.
323. Ladd, *A Commentary,* p. 177.
324. Johnson, p. 127.
325. Ibid.
326. Lindsey, pp. 184-187.
327. Mounce, p. 51.
328. Johnson, p. 128.
329. Ibid.
330. Ibid.
331. Ibid.
332. Palmer, pp. 203-204.
333. Johnson, p. 129.
334. Ibid., pp. 129 *f.*
335. Mounce, p. 253.
336. Ladd, *A Commentary,* p. 179.
337. Palmer, pp. 203-204.
338. Ibid., p. 204.
339. Ladd, *A Commentary,* p. 181.
340. Ibid., p. 182; Johnson, p. 132.
341. Johnson, p. 132.
342. Ibid.
343. Ibid., pp. 132 *f.*
344. Lindsey, p. 192.
345. Johnson, p. 133.
346. Ibid., pp. 133 *f.*
347. Ladd, *A Commentary,* p. 184.
348. Johnson, p. 134.
349. Lindsey, pp. 193 *f.*
350. Johnson, p. 134.
351. Ibid.
352. Ibid., p. 135.
353. Ladd, *A Commentary,* p. 185.
354. Johnson, p. 135.
355. Lindsey, pp. 194 *f.*
356. Johnson, p. 136.
357. Ibid.
358. Ibid.
359. Adela Yarbro Collins, *Crisis and Catharsis: The Power of the Apocalypse,* pp. 13-14.
360. Johnson, pp. 136-137.

361. Ibid., p. 137.
362. Mounce, p. 265.
363. Johnson, p. 137.
364. Mounce, p. 266.
365. De Santo, p. 79.
366. Palmer, p. 210.
367. Johnson, p. 139.
368. Ibid.
369. De Santo, p. 80.
370. Johnson, p. 140.
371. De Santo, p. 80.
372. Ibid.
373. Palmer, p. 211.
374. Johnson, p. 141.
375. Palmer, p. 213.
376. Ibid.
377. De Santo, p. 81.
378. Johnson, pp. 141-142.
379. Ibid., p. 142.
380. Ibid.
381. De Santo, p. 81.
382. Johnson, p. 142.
383. Palmer, p. 213.
384. De Santo, p. 81.
385. Ibid., p. 82.
386. Ibid.
387. Johnson, pp. 143-144.
388. Ibid.
389. Ibid., p. 145.
390. Mounce, p. 284.
391. Johnson, p. 146.
392. Ibid.
393. Ibid., pp. 146-147.
394. Ibid., p. 147.
395. Palmer, p. 216.
396. Johnson, p. 147.
397. De Santo, p. 84.
398. Ibid.
399. Ibid.
400. Ibid.
401. Palmer, p. 218.
402. Johnson, p. 148.
403. Ibid.
404. Ibid.
405. Ibid., p. 149.
406. Ibid.
407. Ibid.

408. Ibid., pp. 149-150.
409. De Santo, p. 86.
410. Johnson, p. 150.
411. Ibid., pp. 150-151.
412. Ibid.
413. De Santo, p. 86.
414. Johnson, p. 151.
415. Palmer, p. 219.
416. Ibid., pp. 219-220.
417. De Santo, p. 87.
418. Scofield, p. 1334.
419. Walvoord, pp. 236-237.
420. Ibid., pp. 238-239.
421. Ibid., p. 239.
422. J. Dwight Pentecost, *Things to Come*, pp. 340-358.
423. Lindsey, pp. 222, 225.
424. Ibid., p. 225.
425. Alan F. Johnson, "Revelation," *Expositor's Bible Commentary*, p. 551.
426. Ibid., p. 552.
427. Mounce, p. 302.
428. De Santo, p. 87.
429. Ibid.
439. Johnson, *Revelation*, p. 152.
431. De Santo, p. 87.
432. Johnson, *Revelation*, p. 152.

IV. THE THIRD VISION

1. Alan F. Johnson, *Revelation, Bible Study Commentary*, p. 153.
2. Ibid., pp. 152-153.
3. Ibid.
4. Ibid., p. 153.
5. Charles De Santo, *The Book of Revelation: A Study Manual*, p. 88.
6. Johnson, p. 154.
7. Earl F. Palmer, *1, 2, 3 John, Revelation, The Communicator's Commentary*, 12, p. 224.
8. Johnson, pp. 153-154.
9. Ibid., p. 154.
10. Ibid., pp. 154-155.
11. De Santo, p. 88.
12. Johnson, p. 155.
13. Alan F. Johnson, "Revelation," *Expositor's Bible Commentary*, p. 555.
14. Johnson, *Revelation*, p. 154.
15. Ibid., pp. 155-156.
16. Ibid., p. 156.
17. Ibid.
18. Ibid., pp. 156-157.
19. Ibid., p. 157.

20. Johnson, "Revelation," p. 559.
21. Ibid.
22. Johnson, *Revelation*, pp. 157-159.
23. Ibid., pp. 159-160.
24. Hal Lindsey, *There's a New World Coming*, pp. 236-237.
25. Johnson, *Revelation*, pp. 160-161.
26. Ibid., p. 161.
27. Ibid., p. 162.
28. Palmer, p. 225.
29. Johnson, *Revelation*, p. 162.
30. Ibid.
31. Lindsey, p. 249.
32. Mounce, p. 320.
33. Johnson, *Revelation*, p. 163.
34. De Santo, p. 91.
35. Johnson, *Revelation*, pp. 163-164.
36. Ibid., p. 164.
37. De Santo, p. 91.
38. Johnson, p. 164.
39. Ibid.
40. De Santo, p. 91-92.
41. Ibid., p. 92.
42. Johnson, *Revelation*, pp. 164-165.
43. De Santo, p. 92.
44. Ibid.
45. Johnson, *Revelation*, p. 165.
46. Ibid.
47. De Santo, p. 92.
48. Ibid., p. 93.
49. Ibid.
50. Johnson, *Revelation*, p. 166.
51. Ibid.
52. De Santo, p. 93.
53. Johnson, *Revelation*, pp. 166-167.
54. De Santo, p. 94.
55. Ibid.
56. Johnson, *Revelation*, p. 167.
57. Adela Yarbro Collins, *The Apocalypse*, 22, p. 129.
58. Ibid.
59. Palmer, p. 228.
60. Ibid., pp. 228-229.
61. Ibid., p. 229.
62. Ibid.
63. Ibid., p. 230.
64. Ibid., pp. 230-231.
65. William Stringfellow, *An Ethic for Christians and Other Aliens in a Strange Land*, p. 6.

66. Ibid., p. 71.

67. Richard J. Mouw, *Politics and the Biblical Drama*, p. 125.

68. Ibid., p. 126.

69. Ibid., p. 127.

70. Ibid., p. 128.

71. Ibid., pp. 128-129.

72. Esther Onstad, *Courage for Today—Hope for Tomorrow*, p. 71.

73. Ibid.

74. De Santo, p. 94.

75. Palmer, p. 232.

76. De Santo, p. 95.

77. Ibid., p. 95.

78. Ibid.

79. Johnson, *Revelation*, p. 169.

80. Collins, p. 132.

81. Johnson, *Revelation*, p. 169.

82. De Santo, p. 96.

83. Collins, p. 132.

84. Johnson, *Revelation*, p. 170; Palmer, 12, p. 233.

85. De Santo, p. 96.

86. Mathias Rissi, *Time and History*, p.113.

87. Ibid., pp. 113-115.

88. De Santo, p. 97.

89. Ibid.

90. Johnson, *Revelation*, pp. 176-177.

91. De Santo, p. 97.

92. Johnson, *Revelation*, p. 177.

93. De Santo, pp. 97-98.

94. George E. Ladd, *Crucial Questions About the Kingdom of God*, p. 176.

95. Ibid.

96. De Santo, p. 98.

97. Ibid.

98. Robert H. Mounce, *The Book of Revelation, New International Commentary*, p. 349.

99. Ibid.

100. Ibid.

101. Johnson, *Revelation*, p. 178.

102. Ibid., p. 179.

103. Ibid.

104. Mounce, p. 349.

105. Ibid., p. 350.

106. George R. Beasley-Murray, *Highlights of the Book of Revelation*, pp. 64-65.

107. De Santo, p. 99.

108. Ibid.

109. Ibid.

110. Ibid.

111. Johnson, *Revelation*, p. 185.

112. Mounce, p. 353.

113. Johnson, *Revelation*, p. 186.

114. De Santo, p. 100.

115. George E. Ladd, *A Commentary on the Revelation of John*, pp. 263-264.

116. Johnson, p. 186.

117. Ibid., p. 180.

118. Ibid.

119. Ibid., pp. 180-181.

120. Ibid., p. 183.

121. George E. Ladd, *A Theology of the New Testament*, p. 630.

122. Johnson, *Revelation*, p. 183.

123. Robert G. Clouse, ed., *The Meaning of the Millennium*, p. 38.

124. De Santo, pp. 100-101; George R. Beasley-Murray, *The Book of Revelation, New Century Bible*, p. 289.

125. De Santo, p. 101.

126. Beasley-Murray, *The Book of Revelation*, pp. 290-291.

127. De Santo, p. 101.

128. Clouse, pp. 38-39.

129. Oscar Cullmann, *The Early Church: Studies in Early Christian History and Theology*, pp. 111-112.

130. Rissi, p. 121.

131. Eric C. Rust, *Salvation History: A Biblical Interpretation*, pp. 310-311.

132. Ladd, *Crucial Questions*, p. 150.

133. Johnson, *Revelation*, p. 184.

134. Ladd, *A Theology*, p. 630.

135. F. F. Bruce, *Answers to Questions* (Grand Rapids: Zondervan, 1973), p. 227.

136. Rissi, p. 118.

137. David Allan Hubbard, *The Second Coming*, p. 89.

138. Mouw, p. 135.

139. Beasley-Murray, *Highlights*, pp. 74, 76-77 *ff.*

140. Johnson, *Revelation*, pp. 184-185.

141. Ladd, *A Theology*, p. 631; Hubbard, p. 91.

142. Ladd, *A Theology*, p. 631.

143. Ibid., p. 628.

144. Hubbard, p. 67.

145. Ibid., p. 68-69.

146. Ladd, *A Theology*, p. 628.

147. Johnson, *Revelation*, pp. 187-188.

148. Ladd, *A Theology*, p. 629.

149. Johnson, *Revelation*, p. 188.

150. De Santo, p. 100.

151. Johnson, *Revelation*, p. 189.

152. Ibid.

153. Ibid.

154. Ibid., p. 190.

155. De Santo, p. 101.

156. Mounce, p. 362.
157. Johnson, *Revelation*, p. 191.
158. Ibid., p. 191-192.
159. Collins, p. 141.
160. De Santo, p. 102.
161. Johnson, *Revelation*, p. 192.
162. Ibid.
163. De Santo, p. 102.
164. Beasley-Murray, *The Book of Revelation*, p. 298.
165. Johnson, *Revelation*, p. 194.
166. Mounce, p. 364.
167. Ibid.
168. De Santo, pp. 102-103; Mounce, pp. 364-365.
169. Johnson, *Revelation*, p. 195.
170. De Santo, p. 103.
171. Lindsey, pp. 279-282.
172. De Santo, p. 103.
173. Johnson, *Revelation*, p. 195.
174. Hubbard, p. 96.
175. Ibid., p. 97.
176. Ibid., pp. 98-99.
177. Ibid., p. 100.
178. Dale Moody, *The Word of Truth: A Summary of Christian Doctrine Based on Biblical Revelation*, p. 576.
179. Ibid., p. 578.
180. Ibid., p. 581.
181. Johnson, p. 200.
182. Ibid., p. 199.
183. Ibid., pp. 199-200.
184. Ibid., p. 200.
185. Anthony A. Hoekema, *The Bible and the Future*, p. 279.
186. Ibid., p. 280.
187. Ibid., p. 252.
188. Ibid., p. 250.
189. Ibid., p. 280-281.
190. Rust, p. 312.
191. Moody, pp. 567-568.
192. Ibid., pp. 573-574.
193. Ibid., p. 574.
194. Ibid., p. 575.
195. Ibid.
196. Hoekema, p. 287.
197. Ibid.
198. Johnson, *Revelation*, p. 184.
199. Ibid., p. 200.
200. Ibid., p. 201.

201. Leon Morris, *The Revelation of St John, The Tyndale New Testament Commentaries*, p. 243.

202. Hubbard, p. 106.

203. Johnson, *Revelation*, p. 201.

204. Ibid.; Hubbard, p. 107; Mounce, p. 371.

205. Hubbard, p. 108.

206. Johnson, *Revelation*, p. 201.

207. Hubbard, p. 108.

208. Palmer, 12, p. 241.

209. Ibid.

210. Ibid., p. 242.

211. Hubbard, pp. 108-109.

212. Ibid., pp. 108-109.

213. Johnson, *Revelation*, p. 202.

214. Palmer, p. 242.

215. Johnson, *Revelation*, p. 202.

216. Hubbard, p. 110.

217. De Santo, p. 105.

218. Hubbard, pp. 110 f.

219. Johnson, p. 202.

220. De Santo, p. 105.

221. Johnson, p. 203.

222. Palmer, p. 243.

223. Johnson, p. 203.

V. THE FOURTH VISION

1. Alan F. Johnson, *Revelation, Bible Study Commentary*, p. 204.

2. Robert H. Mounce, *The Book of Revelation, New International Commentary*, p. 378.

3. Hal Lindsey, *There's a New World Coming*, pp. 289, 291.

4. Johnson, p. 204.

5. Mounce, p. 379.

6. Edwin A. Schick, *Revelation: The Last Book of the Bible*, p. 75.

7. Mounce, p. 379.

8. George R. Beasley-Murray, *The Book of Revelation, New Century Bible*, p. 321.

9. Johnson, pp. 205 f.

10. Charles De Santo, *The Book of Revelation: A Study Manual*, p. 107.

11. Earl F. Palmer, *1, 2, 3 John, Revelation, The Communicator's Commentary*, 12, p. 245.

12. Mounce, p. 383.

13. Ibid.

14. Johnson, p. 206.

15. Mounce, pp. 383-384.

16. Johnson, p. 207.

17. David Allan Hubbard, *The Second Coming*, p. 118.

18. Beasley-Murray, p. 328.

19. Johnson, p. 208.

20. Palmer, pp. 246 f.
21. Anthony A. Hoekema, *The Bible and the Future*, pp. 285-286.
22. Richard J. Mouw, *Politics and the Biblical Drama*, pp. 136 f.
23. Mounce, p. 385.
24. Ibid.
25. Johnson, p. 208.
26. Ibid., p. 208 f.
27. De Santo, p. 108.
28. Mounce, p. 386.
29. Ibid., pp. 386 f.
30. Johnson, p. 209.
31. Mounce, p. 387.
32. Johnson, p. 209.
33. Ibid.
34. Mounce, pp. 387, 384.
35. Ibid., p. 388.
36. Johnson, p. 210.
37. Hubbard, p. 121.

VI. Epilogue

1. Robert H. Mounce, *The Book of Revelation, New International Commentary*, p. 390.
2. Ibid., p. 391.
3. Ibid.
4. Ibid.
5. Earl F. Palmer, *1, 2, 3, John, Revelation, The Communicator's Commentary*, 12, p. 250.
6. Mounce, p. 393.
7. Alan F. Johnson, *Revelation, Bible Study Commentary*, p. 214.
8. Palmer, p. 250.
9. Mounce, p. 393.
10. Ibid., pp. 393-394.
11. Ibid., p. 394.
12. Ibid., pp. 394-395.
13. Charles De Santo, *The Book of Revelation: A Study Manual*, p. 111.
14. Mounce, p. 395.
15. Ibid.
16. Johnson, p. 216.
17. Palmer, p. 256.
18. Johnson, p. 216.
19. Palmer, p. 256.
20. Johnson, p. 216.
21. Palmer, p. 254.
22. Ibid., pp. 254-255.
23. Ibid.
24. Mounce, p. 396.
25. Johnson, p. 216.

Bibliography

Preterist or Historical Background View

Barclay, William. *The Revelation of John. The Daily Study Bible*, 2 vols. Philadelphia: Westminster Press, 1960.

Beckwith, Isbon T. *The Apocalypse of John*. New York: Macmillian Publishing Co., Inc., 1919. Reprinted by Grand Rapids: Baker Book House, 1967.

Boer, Harry R. *The Book of Revelation*. Grand Rapids: Wm. B. Eerdmans, 1979.

Charles, R. H. *A Critical and Exegetical Commentary on the Revelation of St. John*. Vols. 19-20: *The International Critical Commentary*. Edinburgh: T. and T. Clark, 1920.

Glasson, T. F. *The Revelation of John. The Cambridge Bible Commentary on the New English Bible*. New York: Cambridge University Press. 1965.

Hanson, Paul D. *The Dawn of Apocalyptic*. Philadelphia: Fortress Press, 1975.

_____, ed. *Visionaries and Their Apocalypses. Issues in Religion and Theology*, vol. 2. Philadelphia: Fortress Press, 1983.

Kallas, James. *Revelation: God and Satan in the Apocalypse*. Minneapolis: Augsburg Publishing House, 1973.

Love, J. P. *Revelation. The Layman's Bible Commentary*, vol. 25. Richmond: John Knox Press, 1960.

Meinardus, Otto F. A. *St. John of Patmos and the Seven Churches of the Apocalypse*. Athens, Greece: Lycabettus Press, 1974.

Rowley, H. H. *The Relevance of Apocalyptic*, rev. ed. London: Lutterworth Press, 1963.

Swete, Henry Barclay. *The Apocalypse of St. John*. New York: Macmillan Publishing Co., Inc., 1906.

Amillennial or Realized Millennium View

Allis, Oswald T. *Prophecy and the Church*. Philadelphia: Presbyterian and Reformed Publishing Co., 1945.

Ashcraft, Morris. "Revelation." *The Broadman Bible Commentary*, vol. 12, pp. 240-361. Edited by Clifton J. Allen. Nashville: Broadman Press, 1972.

Dana, H. E. *The Epistles and Apocalypse of John*. Dallas: Baptist Book Store, 1937.

Hamilton, Floyd E. *The Basis of Millennial Faith*. Grand Rapids: Wm. B. Eerdmans, 1942.

Hendriksen, William. *More Than Conquerors*. Grand Rapids: Baker Book House, 1944.

Hobbs, H. H. *The Cosmic Drama*. Waco: Word Books, 1971.

Jones, R. Bradley. *Things Which Shall Be Hereafter*. Nashville: Broadman Press, 1947.

_____. *What, Where, and When Is the Millennium?* Grand Rapids: Baker Book House, 1975.

McDowell, E. A. *The Meaning and Message of the Book of Revelation*. Nashville: Broadman Press, 1951.

367

Mickelsen, A. Berkeley. *Interpreting the Bible*. Grand Rapids: Wm. B. Eerdmans, 1963.
Robbins, Ray Frank. *The Revelation of Jesus Christ*. Nashville: Broadman Press, 1975.
Summers, Ray. *The Life Beyond*. Nashville: Broadman Press, 1959.
_____. *Worthy is the Lamb*. Nashville: Broadman Press, 1951.
Wilcock, Michael. *I Saw Heaven Opened*. Downers Grove, IL: Inter-Varsity Press, 1975.

Historicist or Continuous-Historical View
Alford, Henry. "The Revelation." In *The Greek Testament*. London: Rivington's, 1884.
Elliot, E. B. *Horae Apocalypticae*. English transl., 4 vols. London: Seeley, Burnside, and Seeley, 1828.

Postmillennial View
Boettner, Loraine. *The Millennium*. Philadelphia: Presbyterian and Reformed Publishing Co., 1957.
Carroll, B. H. *An Interpretation of the English Bible*. Grand Rapids: Baker Book House, 1948.
Clarke, Adam. *Commentary on the Holy Bible*. Abridged by Ralph Earle. Kansas City, Mo.: Beacon Hill Press, 1967.
Hodges, Jesse Wilson. *Christ's Kingdom and Coming: With an Analysis of Dispensationalism*. Grand Rapids: Wm. B. Eerdmans, 1957.
Toon, Peter, ed. *Puritans, the Millennium and the Future of Israel*. Cambridge: James Clarke & Co., 1970.
Warfield, Benjamin B. "The Millennium and the Apocalypse." *Biblical Doctrines*, pp. 643-64. New York: Oxford University Press, 1929.

Eternal Theological Principles or Symbolical View
Allen, Cady H. *The Message of the Book of Revelation*. Nashville: Cokesbury Press, 1939.
Caird, G. B. *The Revelation of St. John the Divine*. *Harper's New Testament Commentaries*. New York: Harper and Row Pubs., Inc., 1966.
Calkins, Raymond. *The Social Message of the Book of Revelation*. New York: Woman's, 1920.
Farrer, Austin M. *The Revelation of St. John the Divine*. Oxford: Clarendon, 1964.
Kepler, Thomas S. *The Book of Revelation: A Commentary for Laymen*. New York: Oxford University Press, 1957.
_____. *Dreams of the Future: Daniel and Revelation*. Bible Guides, no. 22. London: Lutterworth Press, 1963.
Kiddle, Martin. *The Revelation of St. John*. *Moffatt New Testament Commentary*. New York: Harper, 1940.
Milligan, William. *The Book of Revelation*. *The Expositor's Bible*. London: Hodder & Stoughton, 1909.
Minear, Paul S. *Christian Hope and the Second Coming*. Philadelphia: Westminster Press, 1954.
_____. *I Saw a New Earth: An Introduction to the Visions of the Apocalypse*. Cleveland: Corpus Books, 1968.
Moffatt, J. *The Revelation of St. John the Divine*. *The Expositor's Greek Testament*, 5. Grand Rapids: Wm. B. Eerdmans, 1951.

Preston, R. H. and Hanson, A. T. *The Revelation of Saint John the Divine. Torch Bible Commentaries.* London: SCM Press, 1949.

Richardson, Donald W. *The Revelation of Jesus Christ.* Richmond: John Knox Press, 1964.

Rist, M. *The Revelation of St. John the Divine. The Interpreter's Bible,* 12. New York: Abingdon Press, 1957.

Scott, C. Anderson. *Revelation. The New Century Bible.* London: Henry Frowde Publisher, n.d.

Wilcock, Michael. *I Saw Heaven Opened.* Downers Grove: Inter-Varsity, 1957.

Extreme Futurist or Dispensationalist View
Extreme:

Larkin, Clarence. *The Book of Revelation: A Study of the Last Prophetic Book of Holy Scripture.* Philadelphia: by author, 1919.

Lindsey, Hal. *There's a New World Coming.* Santa Ana, Calif. Vision House, 1973.

_____, with C. C. Carlson. *The Late Great Planet Earth.* Grand Rapids: Zondervan, 1970. Forty-second printing, 1974.

_____. *The Terminal Generation.* Old Tappan, NJ: Fleming H. Revell, 1976.

Moderate:

Hoyt, Herman A. *The End Times.* Chicago: Moody Press, 1969.

McClain, Alva J. *The Greatest of the Kingdom.* Grand Rapids: Zondervan Publishing House, 1959.

Pentecost, J. Dwight. *Prophecy for Today.* Grand Rapids: Zondervan Publishing House, 1961.

_____. *Things to Come.* Findlay, Oh.: Dunham, 1959.

Ryrie, Charles C. *Dispensationalism Today.* Chicago: Moody Press, 1965.

_____. *Revelation.* Chicago: Moody Press, 1968.

Scofield, C. I., ed. *The New Scofield Reference Bible.* Editorial committee, E. Schuyler English, et al. New York: Oxford University Press, 1967.

Walvoord, John F. *The Blessed Hope and the Tribulation.* Grand Rapids: Zondervan Publishing House, 1976.

_____. *The Millennial Kingdom.* Findlay, Oh.: Dunham, 1959.

_____. *The Revelation of Jesus Christ.* Chicago: Moody Press, 1966.

_____ with Walvoord, John E. *Armageddon: Oil and the Middle East Crisis.* Grand Rapids: Zondervan Publishing House, 1974.

Moderate Futurist, Historical
Premillennial or Covenant Premillennial View

Barker, Glenn W., Lane, William L., and Michaels, J. Ramsey. *The New Testament Speaks.* New York: Harper & Row, 1969.

Beasley-Murray, George R. *The Book of Revelation. New Century Bible.* London: Oliphants, 1974.

_____. "Demythologized Eschatology." *Theology Today* (April 1957): 14, 61-79.

_____. *Highlights of the Book of Revelation.* Nashville: Broadman Press, 1972.

_____. "Revelation," *New Bible Commentary,* F. Davidson, ed. Grand Rapids: Wm. B. Eerdmans, 1953.

_____. "The Revelation," *The New Bible Commentary,* rev. ed. D. Guthrie, et al. ed. Grand Rapids: Wm. B. Eerdmans. 1970.

Bell, William Everett, Jr. "A Critical Evaluation of the Pretribulation Rapture Doctrine in Christian Eschatology." Ph.D. dissertation, New York University, 1967.

Bruce, F. F. "The Revelation to John." In *A New Testament Commentary.* Edited by G. C. D. Howley, F. F. Bruce, and H. L. Ellison. Grand Rapids: Zondervan Publishing House, 1969.

Cullmann, Oscar. *Christ and Time,* rev. ed. Trans. by Floyd V. Filson. Philadelphia: Westminster Press, 1964.

_____. *The Early Church: Studies in Early Christian History and Theology.* Philadelphia: Westminster Press, 1956.

_____. *Salvation in History.* Trans. S. G. Sowers. New York: Harper & Row, 1967.

De Santo, Charles. *The Book of Revelation: A Study Manual.* Grand Rapids: Baker Book House, 1967.

Erdman, C. R. *The Revelation of John.* Philadelphia: Westminster Press, 1936.

Erickson, Millard J. *Contemporary Options in Eschatology: A Study of the Millennium.* Grand Rapids: Baker Book House, 1983.

Fuller, Daniel P. *Gospel and Law: Contrast or Continuum?* Grand Rapids: Wm. B. Eerdmans, 1980.

Gundry, Robert H. *The Church and the Tribulation.* Grand Rapids: Zondervan Publishing House, 1973.

_____. *A Survey of the New Testament,* rev. ed. Grand Rapids: Zondervan Publishing House, 1981.

Harrison, E. F. *Introduction to the New Testament.* Grand Rapids: Wm. B. Eerdmans, 1964.

Hubbard, David Allan. *The Second Coming.* Downers Grove, Ill.: Inter-Varsity Press, 1984.

Johnson, Alan F. *Revelation. Bible Study Commentary.* Grand Rapids: Zondervan Publishing House, 1983.

_____. "Revelation." In *The Expositor's Bible Commentary,* pp. 399-603. Edited by Frank E. Gaebelein. Grand Rapids: Zondervan Publishing House, 1981.

Ladd, George E. "Apocalyptic." In *Baker's Dictionary of Theology.* Grand Rapids: Wm. B. Eerdmans, 1960.

_____. *The Blessed Hope.* Grand Rapids: Wm. B. Eerdmans, 1956.

_____. *A Commentary of the Revelation of John.* Grand Rapids; Wm. B. Eerdmans, 1972.

_____. *Crucial Questions About the Kingdom of God.* Grand Rapids: Wm B. Eerdmans, 1952.

_____. *The Gospel of the Kingdom.* Grand Rapids: Wm. B. Eerdmans, 1959.

_____. *The Presence of the Future.* Grand Rapids: Wm. B. Eerdmans, 1974.

_____. *A Theology of the New Testament.* Grand Rapids: Wm. B. Eerdmans, 1974.

LaSor, William Sanford. *The Truth About Armageddon.* San Francisco: Harper & Row, 1982.

Moody, Dale. *The Hope of Glory.* Grand Rapids: Wm. B. Eerdmans, 1964.

_____. *The Word of Truth: A Summary of Christian Doctrine Based on Biblical Revelation*. Grand Rapids: Wm. B. Eerdmans, 1981.

Morris, Leon. *Apocalyptic*. Grand Rapids: Wm. B. Eerdmans, 1972.

_____. *The Revelation of St. John. The Tyndale New Testament Commentaries*. Grand Rapids: Wm. B. Eerdmans, 1969.

Mounce, Robert H. *The Book of Revelation. New International Commentary*. Grand Rapids: Wm. B. Eerdmans, 1977.

Rissi, Mathias. *Time and History*. Trans. by Gordon C. Winsor. Richmond: John Knox Press, 1966.

Rust, Eric C. *Salvation History: A Biblical Interpretation*. Richmond: John Knox Press, 1962.

Tenney, Merrill C. *Interpreting Revelation*. Grand Rapids: Wm. B. Eerdmans, 1957.

DEVOTIONAL OR PRACTICAL APPROACH

Franzmann, Martin H. *The Revelation to John*. St. Louis: Concordia Publishing House, 1976.

Graham, Billy. *Approaching Hoofbeats: The Four Horsemen of the Apocalypse*. Waco: Word Books, 1983.

Jeske, Richard L. *Revelation for Today: Images of Hope*. Philadelphia: Fortress Press, 1983.

Onstad, Esther. *Courage for Today—Hope for Tomorrow*. Minneapolis: Augsburg Publishing House, 1974.

Palmer, Earl F. *1,2,3 John, Revelation*. Vol. 12: *The Communicator's Commentary*. Waco: Word Books, 1982.

Perkins, Pheme. *The Book of Revelation*. Vol. 11: *Collegeville Bible Commentary*. Collegeville, Minn.: The Liturgical Press, 1983.

Schick, Edwin A. *Revelation: The Last Book of the Bible*. Philadelphia: Fortress Press, 1977.

DRAMATIC APPROACH

Blevins, James L. "The Genre of Revelation." *Review and Expositor* (Summer 1980): pp. 393-408.

_____. *Revelation. Knox Preaching Guides*. Atlanta: John Knox Press, 1984.

_____. *Revelation as Drama*. Nashville: Broadman Press, 1984.

Bowman, J. W. *The Drama of the Book of Revelation*. Philadelphia: Westminster Press, 1955.

GENERAL OVERVIEW

Clouse, Robert G., ed. *The Meaning of the Millennium*. Chapters by George E. Ladd, "Historic Premillennialism;" Herman A. Hoyt, "Dispensational Premillennialism"; Loraine Boettner, "Postmillennialism"; and Anthony A. Hoekema, "Amillennialism." Downers Grove: Inter-Varsity Press, 1977.

Pilch, John J. *What Are They Saying About the Book of Revelation?* New York: Paulist Press, 1978.

Sauer, Val J. *The Eschatology Handbook*. Atlanta: John Knox Press, 1981.

HERMENEUTICAL EMPHASIS

Fee, Gordon D., and Stuart, Douglas. *How to Read the Bible for All Its Worth*. Grand Rapids: Zondervan Publishing House, 1982.

Green, Joel B. *How to Read Prophecy*. Downers Grove, Ill.: Inter-Varsity Press, 1984.

Newport, John P. *What Is Christian Doctrine?* Nashville: Broadman Press, 1984.

—————— and Cannon, William. *Why Christians Fight Over the Bible*. Nashville: Thomas Nelson, 1974.

Schultz, Samuel J., and Inch, Morris A. *Interpreting the Word of God*. Chicago: Moody Press, 1976.

Sproul, R. C. *Knowing Scripture*. Downers Grove, Ill.: Inter-Varsity Press, 1977.

Weber, Timothy P. "The Two-Edged Sword: The Fundamentalist Use of the Bible." *Bible in America: Essays in Cultural History*, pp. 101-120. Edited by N. O. Hatch, M. A. Noll. New York: Oxford University Press, 1982.

HISTORICAL PERSPECTIVE

Bass, Clarence B. *Backgrounds to Dispensationalism*. Grand Rapids: Wm. B. Eerdmans, 1960.

Berkhof, Louis. *The Kingdom of God: The Development of the Idea of the Kingdom, Especially Since the Eighteenth Century*. Grand Rapids: Wm. B. Eerdmans, 1951.

Bryant, M. Darrol, and Dayton, Donald W., eds. *The Coming Kingdom: Essays in American Millennialism and Eschatology*. Barrytown, NY: International Religious Foundation, 1983.

Kraus, C. Norman. *Dispensationalism in America*. Richmond: John Knox Press, 1958.

LIBERATION APPROACH

Gonzalez, Catherine Gunsalus, and Gonzalez, Justo Luis. *Vision at Patmos*. Cincinnati: Women's Division, Board of Global Ministries, The United Methodist Church, 1978.

LITERARY NATURE

Caird, G. B. *The Language and Imagery of the Bible*. Philadelphia: Westminster Press, 1980.

Court, John M. *Myth and History in the Book of Revelation*. Atlanta: John Knox Press, 1979.

Farrer, Austin M. *A Rebirth of Images*. Boston: Beacon Press Inc., 1949.

——————. *The Revelation of St. John the Divine*. Oxford: Clarendon, 1964.

Ricoeur, Paul *Philosophical Hermeneutics and Theological Hermeneutics: Ideology, Utopia and Faith*. Berkeley: Center for Hermeneutical Studies in Hellenistic and Modern Culture, 1976.

Ryken, Leland. *How to Read the Bible as Literature*. Grand Rapids: Zondervan Publishing House, 1984.

——————. "Literary Criticism of the Bible: Some Fallacies." In *Literary Interpretations of Biblical Narratives*. Edited by K. R. R. G. Louis, et al. Nashville: Abingdon Press, 1974.

——————. *The Literature of the Bible*. Grand Rapids: Zondervan Publishing House, 1974.

Sweet, J.P.M. *Revelation (Westminster Pelican Commentaries)*. Philadelphia: Westminster Press, 1979.

Wilder, Amos N. *Jesus' Parables and the War of Myths*. Philadelphia: Fortress Press, 1982.

_____. "The Rhetoric of Ancient and Modern Apocalyptic." *Interpretation*, 25: 1971.

PSYCHOLOGICAL APPROACH

Johnson, Cedric B. *The Psychology of Biblical Interpretation*. Grand Rapids: Zondervan Publishing House, 1983.

RELATIONSHIP TO THE JEWS AND ISRAEL

LaRondelle, Hans K. *The Israel of God in Prophecy*. Berrien Springs, Minn.: Andrews University Press, 1983.

RELATIONSHIP TO THE OLD TESTAMENT

Ezell, Douglas. *Revelation on Revelation: New Sounds From Old Symbols*. Waco: Word Books, 1977.

Jenkins, Ferrell. *The Old Testament in the Book of Revelation*. Grand Rapids: Baker Book House, 1972.

McCurley, Foster R. *Ancient Myths and Biblical Faith: Scriptural Transformations*. Philadelphia: Fortress Press, 1983.

SOCIOLOGICAL APPROACH

Bettis, Joseph, and Johannesen, S. K., eds. *The Return of the Millennium*. Barrytown, NY: International Religious Foundation, Inc., 1984.

Collins, Adela Yarbro. *The Apocalypse. New Testament Message*, vol. 22. Wilmington, Del.: Michael Glazier, Inc., 1979.

_____. *The Combat Myth in the Book of Revelation*. Missoula, Mont.: Scholars Press, 1976.

_____. *Crisis and Catharsis: The Power of the Apocalypse*. Philadelphia: Westminster Press, 1984.

Ellul, Jacques. *Apocalypse*. New York: Seabury Press Inc., 1977.

Fiorenza, Elisabeth Schüessler. *The Apocalypse. Herald Biblical Booklets*. Chicago: Franciscan Herald Press, 1976.

_____. *The Book of Revelation: Justice and Judgment*. Philadelphia: Fortress Press, 1985.

_____. *Invitation to the Book of Revelation*. Garden City, NY: Image Books, 1981.

_____. "Revelation." *Proclamation Commentaries*, pp. 99-120. Edited by Gerhard Krodel. Philadelphia: Fortress Press, 1977.

Gager, John G. *Kingdom and Community: The Social World of Early Christianity*. Englewood Cliffs, NJ: Prentice-Hall, 1975.

Mouw, Richard J. *Politics and the Biblical Drama*. Grand Rapids: Baker Book House, 1976.

Stringfellow, William. *An Ethic for Christians and Other Aliens in a Strange Land*. Waco: Word Books. 1973.

THEOLOGICAL EMPHASIS

Beker, J. Christiaan. *Paul's Apocalyptic Gospel: The Coming Triumph of God*. Philadelphia: Fortress Press, 1982.

Berkhof, Louis. *The Second Coming of Christ*. Grand Rapids: Wm. B. Eerdmans, 1953.

Berkouwer, G. C. *The Return of Christ*. Grand Rapids: Wm. B. Eerdmans, 1972.

Braaten, Carl E. *Apocalyptic Themes in Theology and Culture: Christ and Counter-Christ*. Philadelphia: Fortress Press, 1972.

Brunner, Emil. *Eternal Hope*. Trans. by Harold Knight. London: Lutterworth Press 1954.

Eller, Vernard. *The Most Revealing Book of the Bible: Making Sense Out of Revelation*. Grand Rapids: Wm. B. Eerdmans, 1974.

Hoekema, Anthony A. *The Bible and the Future*. Grand Rapids: Wm. B. Eerdmans, 1979.

Hughes, Philip E. *Interpreting Prophecy: An Essay in Biblical Perspectives*. Grand Rapids: Wm. B. Eerdmans, 1976.

Kantonen, T.A. *The Christian Hope*. Philadelphia: Muhlenberg Press, 1954.

Lilje, Hanns. *The Last Book of the Bible*. Trans. by Olive Wyon. Philadelphia: Muhlenberg Press, 1957.

Moltmann, Jurgen. *Theology of Hope*. Trans. J. W. Leitch, New York: Harper & Row, 1967 (Orig. pub. 1964).

Niles, D. T. *As Seeing the Invisible*. New York: Harper & Brothers, 1961.

Peters, Ted. *Futures—Human and Divine*. Atlanta: John Knox Press, 1978.

Quistorp, Heinrich. *Calvin's Doctrine of the Last Things*. Trans. Harold Knight. London: Lutterworth Press, 1955.

Schwarz, Hans. *On the Way to the Future*. Minneapolis: Augsburg Publishing House, 1972.

Torrance, Thomas F. *The Apocalypse Today*. Grand Rapids: Wm. B. Eerdmans, 1959.

INDEX OF SUBJECTS

INDEX OF PEOPLE